This Is My Country

*T*his Is My Country
Land of my choice.
This is my country
Hear my proud voice.

*Don Raye
and Al Jacobs*

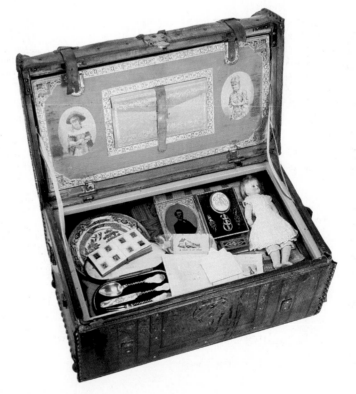

Beverly J. Armento
J. Jorge Klor de Alva
Gary B. Nash
Christopher L. Salter
Louis E. Wilson
Karen K. Wixson

This Is My Country

Houghton Mifflin Company • Boston

Atlanta • Dallas • Geneva, Illinois • Princeton, New Jersey • Palo Alto • Toronto

Consultants

Program Consultants

Edith M. Guyton
Associate Professor of Early
  Childhood Education
Georgia State University
Atlanta, Georgia

Gail Hobbs
Associate Professor of Geography
Pierce College
Woodland Hills, California

Charles Peters
Reading Consultant
Oakland Schools
Pontiac, Michigan

Cathy Riggs-Salter
Social Studies Consultant
Hartsburg, Missouri

Alfredo Schifini
Limited English Proficiency Consultant
Los Angeles, California

George Paul Schneider
Associate Director
  of General Programs
Department of Museum Education
Art Institute of Chicago
Chicago, Illinois

Twyla Stewart
Center for Academic Interinstitutional
  Programs
University of California—Los Angeles
Los Angeles, California

Scott Waugh
Associate Professor of History
University of California—Los Angeles
Los Angeles, California

Teacher Reviewers

David E. Beer (Grade 5)
Weisser Park Elementary
Fort Wayne, Indiana

Jan Coleman (Grades 6–7)
Thornton Junior High
Fremont, California

Shawn Edwards
  (Grades 1–3)
Jackson Park Elementary
University City, Missouri

Barbara J. Fech (Grade 6)
Martha Ruggles School
Chicago, Illinois

Deborah M. Finkel
  (Grade 4)
Los Angeles Unified
  School District,
  Region G
South Pasadena,
  California

Jim Fletcher (Grades 5, 8)
La Loma Junior High
Modesto, California

Susan M. Gilliam
  (Grade 1)
Roscoe Elementary
Los Angeles, California

Vicki Stroud Gonterman
  (Grade 2)
Gibbs International
  Studies Magnet School
Little Rock, Arkansas

Rosemarie Greene
  (Grade 4)
Hillside Elementary
Needham, Massachusetts

Lorraine Hood (Grade 2)
Fresno Unified School
  District
Fresno, California

Jean Jamgochian
  (Grade 5)
Haycock Gifted and
  Talented Center
Fairfax County, Virginia

Susan Kirk-Davalt
  (Grade 5)
Crowfoot Elementary
Lebanon, Oregon

Mary Molyneaux-Leahy
  (Grade 3)
Bridgeport Elementary
Bridgeport, Pennsylvania

Sharon Oviatt
  (Grades 1–3)
Keysor Elementary
Kirkwood, Missouri

Jayne B. Perala (Grade 1)
Cave Spring Elementary
Roanoke, Virginia

Carol Siefkin (K)
Garfield Elementary
Sacramento, California

Norman N. Tanaka
  (Grade 3)
Martin Luther King Jr.
  Elementary
Sacramento, California

John Tyler (Grades 5, 8)
Groton School
Groton, Massachusetts

Portia W. Vaughn
  (Grades 1–3)
School District 11
Colorado Springs,
  Colorado

Acknowledgments

Grateful acknowledgment is made
for the use of the material listed below.
    The material in the Minipedia is
reprinted from *The World Book* *Encyclopedia* with the expressed permission of the publisher. © 1993 by World
Book, Inc.

–Continued on page 429.

From Your Authors

Within seconds, a roar like a cannon blast stopped them in their tracks. The frightened men looked up to see a black gusher of oil shooting into the air. They didn't know it, but they had just struck what was the world's largest oil field.

So begins the exciting story of the discovery of oil at Spindletop, Texas, in 1901. In the next few years, thousands of people rushed to Texas, hoping to strike it rich. In Chapter 10 of this book, you will read more about those exciting days, which had such a big impact on the history of the United States.

Many of the people you will meet in this book lived long ago. Others lived in parts of the country that are very different from where you live. But they have all had feelings like yours and have faced the same challenges you will face. Whether they were great leaders or ordinary people, their decisions and actions helped shape the country you live in.

As you read about the people, places, and events, we hope you will ask many questions. Some questions may be about history: "What caused people to come to the United States?" or "How do we know about these events?" Other questions may be about geography: "What are the land and weather like in that place?" Still other questions may be about people and resources: "Why did people in different parts of the country live in such different ways?"

Most of all, we hope you catch the excitement of thinking, questioning, and discovering answers about your country, in the past and present.

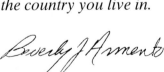

Beverly J. Armento
Professor of Social Studies
Director, Center for Business and
Economic Education
Georgia State University

Christopher L. Salter
Professor and Chair
Department of Geography
University of Missouri

Louis E. Wilson
Associate Professor
Department of Afro-American Studies
Smith College

J. Jorge Klor de Alva
Professor of Anthropology
Princeton University

Gary B. Nash
Professor of History
University of California—Los Angeles

Karen K. Wixson
Associate Professor of Education
University of Michigan

Contents

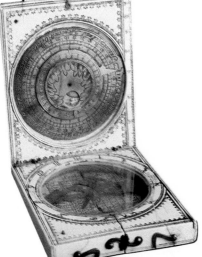

Understanding Skills

Each "Understanding Skills" feature gives you the opportunity to learn and practice a skill related to the topic you are studying.

Understanding Concepts

Each "Understanding Concepts" feature gives you more information about a concept that is important to the lesson you are reading.

Making Decisions

Much of history is made of people's decisions. These pages take you step-by-step through fascinating problems from history and today. What will you decide?

Exploring

As you visit each region, its story comes to life. "Exploring" pages also show you how to discover more about where you live.

Literature

Throughout history people have expressed their deepest feelings and beliefs through literature. Reading the stories, legends, poems, and short passages that appear in the chapters will help you experience what life was like for people of other times and places.

Primary Sources

Reading the exact words of the people who made and lived history is the best way to get a sense of how they saw themselves and the times in which they lived. You will find more than 50 primary sources throughout this book including the following:

Charts, Diagrams, and Timelines

These visual presentations of information help give you a clearer picture of the people, places, and events you are studying.

A Closer Look

Take a closer look at the objects and pictures spread out on these special pages. With the clues you see you'll become a historical detective.

A Moment in Time

A person from the past is frozen at an exciting moment. You'll get to know these people by reading about where they are, what they're wearing, and the objects around them.

Maps

The events of history have been shaped by the places in which they occurred. Each map in this book tells its own story about these events and places.

Starting Out

What makes this textbook so much more interesting than others you've used? In this book, the people of the United States speak to you, through their words and through the objects they use. You'll walk inside their houses and look inside their cooking pots. You'll follow them as they settle regions, irrigate deserts, build cities, and develop modern industries.

From unit to chapter to lesson—each step lets you see history in closer detail. The photos show you where events happened. The art introduces you to the people.

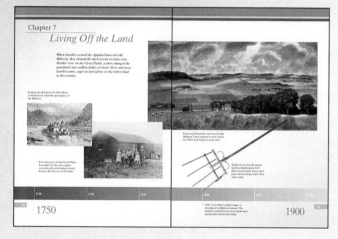

When and what? The timeline at the beginning of each lesson tells you when these events took place. The lesson title tells you what the lesson is about.

Right from the beginning the lesson opener pulls you into the sights, the sounds, the smells of what life was like at that time, in that place.

Like a road sign, the question that always appears here tells you what to think about while you read the lesson.

Look for these key terms. They are listed here so that you can watch for them. The first time they appear in the lesson they are shown in heavy black print and defined. Key terms are also defined in the Glossary.

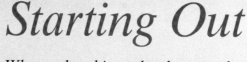

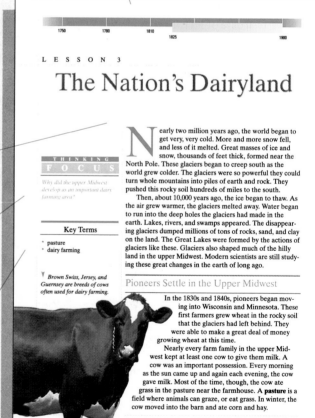

1750 1780 1810
1825 1900

THINKING FOCUS

Why did the upper Midwest develop as an important dairy farming area?

Key Terms

* pasture
* dairy farming

Brown Swiss, Jersey, and Guernsey are breeds of cows often used for dairy farming.

LESSON 3

The Nation's Dairyland

Nearly two million years ago, the world began to get very, very cold. More and more snow fell, and less of it melted. Great masses of ice and snow, thousands of feet thick, formed near the North Pole. These glaciers began to creep south as the world grew colder. The glaciers were so powerful they could turn whole mountains into piles of earth and rock. They pushed this rocky soil hundreds of miles to the south.

Then, about 10,000 years ago, the ice began to thaw. As the air grew warmer, the glaciers melted away. Water began to run into the deep holes the glaciers had made in the earth. Lakes, rivers, and swamps appeared. The disappearing glaciers dumped millions of tons of rocks, sand, and clay on the land. The Great Lakes were formed by the actions of glaciers like these. Glaciers also shaped much of the hilly land in the upper Midwest. Modern scientists are still studying these great changes in the earth of long ago.

Pioneers Settle in the Upper Midwest

In the 1830s and 1840s, pioneers began moving into Wisconsin and Minnesota. These first farmers grew wheat in the rocky soil that the glaciers had left behind. They were able to make a great deal of money growing wheat at this time.

Nearly every farm family in the upper Midwest kept at least one cow to give them milk. A cow was an important possession. Every morning as the sun came up and again each evening, the cow gave milk. Most of the time, though, the cow ate grass in the pasture near the farmhouse. A **pasture** is a field where animals can graze, or eat grass. In winter, the cow moved into the barn and ate corn and hay.

Frozen at a moment in time, this gold miner almost jumps off the page in his excitement. You learn all about him by reading about his clothes, the objects he has with him, and the place he's working.

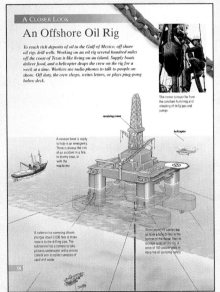

A picture is worth a thousand words. But just a few words in a caption can help you understand a picture or a photograph. In this case, the caption tells you the dairy products farm families depended on cows for.

Take a closer look, in this case at an offshore oil rig. Look at the small submarine the workers use to repair the drilling pipe. Find the pipeline that carries the oil from beneath the ocean floor to tanks on the rig.

A farm family's daughter often did the milking. When she finished she would let the milk stand in a pail for a few hours. Soon the cream rose and floated on top. The family would use the cream to make butter.

In *Little House in the Big Woods*, Laura Ingalls Wilder describes how a mother and her daughters make butter on a frontier farm. First they put some cream in a churn, a large wooden container with a hole in its top. Then Ma Ingalls uses pumping motions to stir the cream with a plunger-like tool called a dash:

> She churned for a long time. Mary could sometimes churn while Ma rested, but the dash was too heavy for Laura.
>
> At first the splashes of cream showed thick and smooth around the little hole. After a long time, they began to look grainy. Then Ma churned more slowly, and on the dash there began to appear tiny grains of yellow butter.

Families like the Ingalls would drink some of their cow's fresh milk right away and use the rest to make cheese. Cheese-making involved many steps and was done over a number of days right on the farm.

Not only would a cow provide a family with milk, butter, and cheese, it would also give birth to a calf each spring. The family would keep some of the calves to build a small herd and then sell the others. In years when crops were poor, farm families depended even more heavily on their milk cows for food.

▲ *Farm families depended on cows for such food as cheese, butter, cottage cheese, and cream.*

Across Time & Space

Margarine is a product that many people use instead of butter. When margarine first went on sale in the 1870s, dairy farmers feared they would sell less butter and make less money. They asked the government to put a tax on margarine so it would cost more and people might buy less of it. In Wisconsin, shoppers could not buy margarine at all until the 1960s.

■ *In what ways did frontier farmers depend on their milk cows?*

171

Living Off the Land

Giving you the inside story is the purpose of two special paragraphs. Across Time & Space connects what you're reading to things that happened centuries ago or continents away. Its companion, How Do We Know?, tells you where information about the past comes from. (See page 160 for an example.)

Every age has its great storytellers. Chapters include short examples of fine writing from or about the period. The literature is always printed on a tan background with a blue initial letter and a multicolored bar.

Continuing On

As you get to know the regions of the United States, you'll want ways of understanding and remembering them better. This book gives you some tools to use in learning about people and places and remembering what you've learned.

You're in charge of your reading. See the red square at the end of the text? Now find the red square over in the margin. If you can answer the question there, then you probably understood what you just read. If you can't, perhaps you'd better go back and read that part of the lesson again.

Every map tells a story. The large maps in this book each tell a story. This map, for instance, tells how corn and wheat became the major crops of the Midwest.

of this grain down the Ohio and Mississippi rivers to sell in New Orleans. To trace the routes of these rivers see the map on pages 404 – 405. The Midwest was on its way to becoming the country's corn-growing center. ■

Why did the Midwest become such a good place to grow corn?

Farmers Grow More Wheat

Some Midwestern farm families began to grow wheat as well as corn. European immigrant settlers especially enjoyed the taste of wheat bread, which they had eaten in their home countries. At first, farmers used hand-tools to harvest the wheat in their fields, but the work was hard and slow. One person could cut only two acres a day by hand. Then in the 1840s, a Virginian named Cyrus McCormick introduced a horse-drawn reaper for cutting grain. With this machine a farmer could cut 12 acres of wheat in a day. Now settlers could plant much larger fields of crops because they could harvest a lot of grain more quickly.

McCormick's reaper helped many farm families earn more money growing wheat. More and more farmers in the Midwest now turned to growing wheat instead of corn. Wheat growing became a booming business in northern Indiana and Illinois and southern Wisconsin and Michigan.

▲ *Wheat is a kind of grass that can be dried and ground into flour and used to make foods like whole-wheat bread. The reaper helped farmers harvest larger and larger fields of this valuable grain.*

Chapter 7

152

Corn and Wheat Spread West, 1830–1860

1830
CANADA
N. Dak. Minn.
S. Dak. Wisc. Mich.
Nebr. Iowa Ill. Ind. Ohio
Colo. Kans. Mo. Ky.
Okla. Ark. Tenn.
Ala.

Corn
Wheat
Present-day boundary
150   300 mi
150 300 km
Albers Equal-Area Projection

1860
CANADA
N. Dak. Minn.
S. Dak. Wisc. Mich.
Nebr. Iowa Ill. Ind. Ohio
Colo. Kans. Mo. Ky.
Okla. Ark. Tenn.
Ala.

Corn
Wheat
Present-day boundary
150 300 mi
150 300 km
Albers Equal-Area Projection

During the 1860s, settlers pushed farther west into the Great Plains of what are now Kansas, Nebraska, South Dakota, and North Dakota. This area has less rain and a shorter growing season than the rest of the Midwest. Frontier farmers found that under these conditions, wheat grew better than corn. Soon, wheat became the most important crop of the Great Plains.

Pioneer farm families faced many different challenges on the Plains and all over the Midwest. Storms, dry spells, and insects such as grasshoppers often ruined or damaged their crops. Despite these hardships, settlers made good use of the soil and the other natural resources in the area. Large, successful corn and wheat farms soon covered the rich land of the Midwest. ■

▲ *In the 1830s, settlers thought that the soil of the grasslands would be poor for farming because few trees grew in the region. Thirty years later, inventions such as the reaper and the steel plow helped farmers make good use of what proved to be rich farmland.*

Why did farmers on the prairies and Great Plains turn from growing corn to growing wheat?

R E V I E W

1. FOCUS What helped pioneer farmers turn the Midwestern frontier into an important corn- and wheat-growing area?

2. CONNECT In what ways was the culture of the early frontier farmers in the Ohio Valley like the culture of the Miami Indians?

3. GEOGRAPHY Compare the map on this page with the map on page 409. How might the differences in the climate of the Great Plains and the climate of the Central Plains have affected the development of corn- and wheat-

growing in these areas?

4. CRITICAL THINKING How might Midwestern farming have developed differently if John Deere and Cyrus McCormick had not introduced the steel plow and the modern reaper?

5. ACTIVITY Imagine you are a new pioneer farmer in the Ohio Valley in 1800. Write a letter to your sister in New York, describing your life. Urge your sister to move to the frontier to join you.

Living Off the Land

153

The titles outline the lesson. The red titles tell you the main topics discussed in the lesson on "Waves of Grain." (The McCormick reaper helped farmers to grow more wheat.)

After you read the lesson, stop and review what you've read. The first question is the same one you started out with. The second question connects the lesson to what you've studied earlier. Other questions and an activity help you think about the lesson you've read. Chapter Review questions help you tie the lessons together. (See pages 174 and 175 for an example.)

A special kind of Understanding page looks at concepts--the big ideas that help put all the pieces together. This section helps you understand ideas like Culture, Technology, and in this case, Conservation.

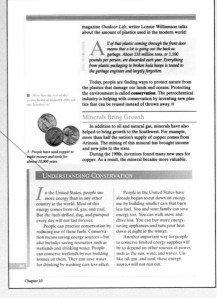

Some tools you'll always use. The Understanding pages walk you through skills that you will use again and again, as a student and later on in life. On this page you learn about the different time zones in the United States.

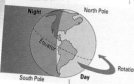

The things people make and use tell a great deal about them. In this book you'll find lots of photographs of the paintings, ships, and maps people made. You'll also see the tools, clothes and machines they used.

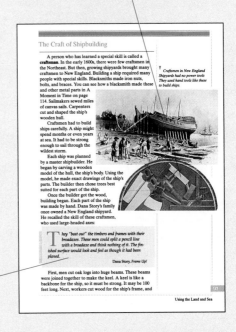

Diagrams make clear things that are hard to understand. Here the diagram shows how night follows daylight as the earth revolves around the sun. Other illustrations, charts, and graphs tell you how things work and how one bit of information relates to another.

Letters, diaries, books--short passages from these primary sources let people from the past speak to you. When you see a tan background, a red initial letter, and a gray bar, you know that the quotation is a primary source.

Also Featuring

Some special pages show up only once in every unit, not in every lesson in the book. These features continue the story by letting you explore an idea or activity, or read a story about another time and place. The Time/Space Databank in the back of the book brings together resources you will use again and again.

What would you do? The Making Decisions pages present you with a decision about an important issue. Then you practice the steps that will help you to make a good choice.

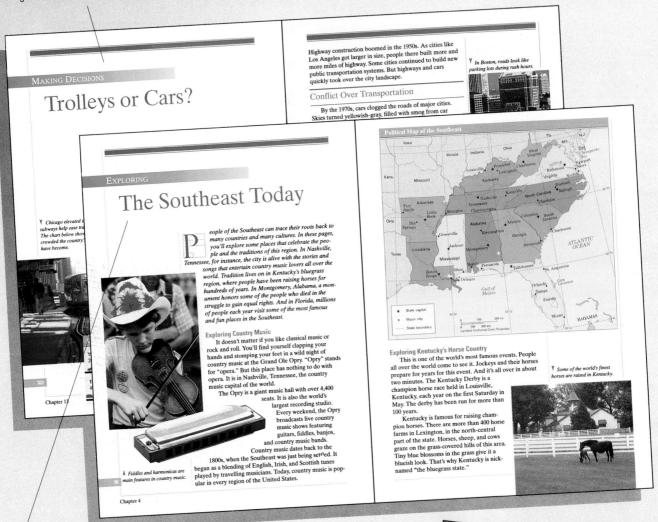

MAKING DECISIONS

Trolleys or Cars?

Highway construction boomed in the 1950s. As cities like Los Angeles got larger in size, people there built more and more miles of highway. Some cities continued to build new public transportation systems. But highways and cars quickly took over the city landscape.

▼ *In Boston, roads look like parking lots during rush hours.*

Conflict Over Transportation

By the 1970s, cars clogged the roads of major cities. Skies turned yellowish-gray, filled with smog from car

EXPLORING

The Southeast Today

People of the Southeast can trace their roots back to many countries and many cultures. In these pages, you'll explore some places that celebrate the people and the traditions of this region. In Nashville, Tennessee, for instance, the city is alive with the stories and songs that entertain country music lovers all over the world. Tradition lives on in Kentucky's bluegrass region, where people have been raising horses for hundreds of years. In Montgomery, Alabama, a monument honors some of the people who died in the struggle to gain equal rights. And in Florida, millions of people each year visit some of the most famous and fun places in the Southeast.

Exploring Country Music

It doesn't matter if you like classical music or rock and roll. You'll find yourself clapping your hands and stomping your feet in a wild night of country music at the Grand Ole Opry. "Opry" stands for "opera." But this place has nothing to do with opera. It is in Nashville, Tennessee, the country music capital of the world.

The Opry is a giant music hall with over 4,400 seats. It is also the world's largest recording studio. Every weekend, the Opry broadcasts live country music shows featuring guitars, fiddles, banjos, and country music bands.

Country music dates back to the 1800s, when the Southeast was just being settled. It began as a blending of English, Irish, and Scottish tunes played by travelling musicians. Today, country music is popular in every region of the United States.

▲ *Fiddles and harmonicas are main features in country music.*

Political Map of the Southeast

Exploring Kentucky's Horse Country

This is one of the world's most famous events. People all over the world come to see it. Jockeys and their horses prepare for years for this event. And it's all over in about two minutes. The Kentucky Derby is a champion horse race held in Louisville, Kentucky, each year on the first Saturday in May. The derby has been run for more than 100 years.

Kentucky is famous for raising champion horses. There are more than 400 horse farms in Lexington, in the north-central part of the state. Horses, sheep, and cows graze on the grass-covered hills of this area. Tiny blue blossoms in the grass give it a blueish look. That's why Kentucky is nicknamed "the bluegrass state."

▼ *Some of the world's finest horses are raised in Kentucky.*

School isn't the only place where you can learn social studies. This feature gives you a chance to explore history and geography outside the classroom—at home or in your own neighborhood.

Stories have always been important parts of people's lives. Each unit in the book has at least one story or group of poems about the time and place you're studying. In this case, it's a story about a famous Texas cowboy.

LITERATURE

George McJunkin Cowboy

Franklin Folsom

In the late 1800s and early 1900s, George McJunkin was one of the most colorful figures on the Western frontier. He was born a slave in Texas, but after the Civil War, he found freedom and an exciting life as a cowboy in northern New Mexico. As you read about McJunkin, ask yourself, "What was life like for a cowboy?"

After a meal of hot corn bread and bacon, George thanked the woman and rode on to a place where it was still daylight when he'd find plenty of grass for his mule. It was still daylight when he'd dismounted and tied of his lariat to the mule's halter.

George McJunkin was a legend among the cowboys you read about in Lesson 3. He was one of the best riders, ropers, shooters, fiddlers and storytellers of the Old West.

dismounted got off
lariat rope used by a cowboy
halter part of a saddle

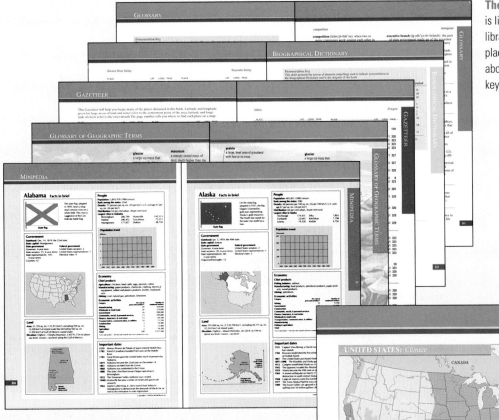

The Time/Space Databank is like a reference section of a library at your fingertips. It's the place to go for more information about the places, people, and key terms you meet in this book.

What's a minipedia? It's a small version of an encyclopedia, one that you don't have to go to your library to use. It's bound right into the back of your book so you can quickly look up its articles, charts, and graphs.

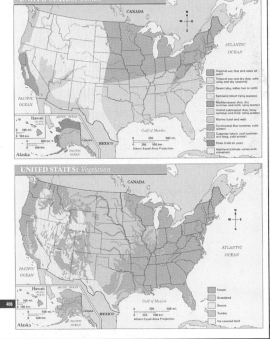

The Atlas maps out the world. Large maps show you the political divisions of your world, your country, and your state. Special maps tell you about the climate, vegetation, population, and time zones of the United States.

some white. All of them were hauling smelly loads of buf- falo hides, and two also had supplies of dried buffalo meat. Jerky, they called it. They were glad to give George strips of the tough stuff, which was hard to chew but tasted good, and it kept him from being hungry.

Finally George turned away from the Brazos and headed for the Leon. Here and there along the wagon tracks, a soli- tary man, or a man and his wife, had cut chunks of sod out of the prairie and piled them up, brick-fashion, to form the walls of a house. The people who lived in these soddies fed him, too. One of them even paid him to help dig a well. When the job was done, George wrapped a strip of cloth around a fistful of quarters that the man had given him. It was the first money he had ever earned, and he wanted to take good care of it.

A little cluster of houses made up the town of Comanche, the place that the freighter had told him about. "Anybody around here looking for cowboys?" George asked a man on the street. The man was white. There were no blacks anywhere.

"There's a trail b___ __t

Brazos a river in Texas
Leon a river in Texas
solitary single, alone

Map and Globe Handbook

*Y*ou are about to start on a great journey. This trip will take you across maps and globes. You will go around the world, visiting places you may never have heard of before. Your adventure will take you to such faraway regions as the Caribbean, Africa, and Australia. Your around-the-world adventure will also give you a new view of your own country.

You'll find your guide to the world inside this Map and Globe Handbook. The Handbook will help you discover the hidden information found in maps and globes. So get ready. Turn to page G1 and begin your journey.

Contents

Mapping Our World

A map is a special kind of drawing. It shows the land and water of the whole world or part of the world. Look at this photo taken from high above the earth. The picture shows the Great Lakes—a small part of the world. A mapmaker looked at a photo like this one to draw the map below. Both the map and the picture show this region as you would see it from above.

◄ *This view shows the Great Lakes from high above. Look at the map to name the five lakes in the picture. These lakes make up the largest group of fresh-water lakes in the world.*

Look at the shape of Lake Ontario in the picture. On the map, its shape is the same.

A map shows some things a picture does not. You don't see this line in the picture. Government leaders agreed upon this line, or border, to separate the United States and Canada. A map that shows the borders of countries and states is called a political map.

The Great Lakes

Minnesota
Lake Superior
CANADA
Wisconsin
Michigan
Lake Michigan
Lake Huron
Mississippi River
UNITED   STATES
St. Lawrence River
Lake Ontario
New York
Illinois
Lake Erie
Indiana
Ohio
Pennsylvania

N
W   E
S

0   100   200 mi.
0   100   200 km
Lambert Conformal Conic Projection

Understanding a Map

Quickly look through the pages of this Handbook. Each map has a different size and shape. Each map shows a different place. Each gives different kinds of

The **title** is the name of the map. The title often tells you the kind of map it is. The title also tells you the place the map shows.

An **inset** is a small map inside a larger one. The inset tells you more about the larger map.

World: Physical

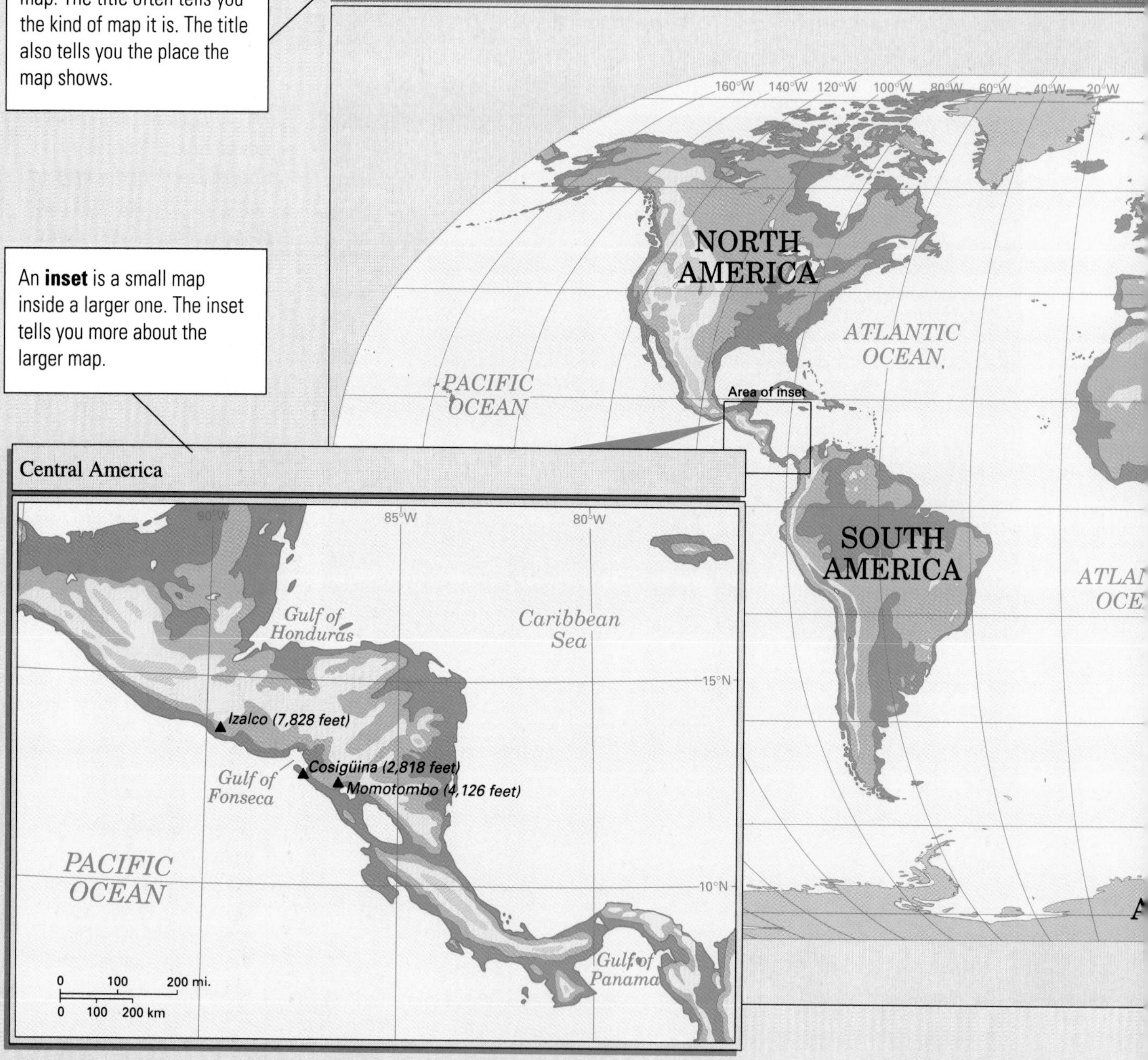

160°W 140°W 120°W 100°W 80°W 60°W 40°W 20°W

NORTH
AMERICA

ATLANTIC
OCEAN

PACIFIC
OCEAN

Area of inset

SOUTH
AMERICA

ATLAN
OCE

Central America

90°W 85°W 80°W

Gulf of
Honduras

Caribbean
Sea

15°N

Izalco (7,828 feet)

Gulf of
Fonseca

Cosigüina (2,818 feet)
Momotombo (4,126 feet)

PACIFIC
OCEAN

10°N

Gulf of
Panama

0   100   200 mi.

0   100   200 km

information. For example, the map on page G6 shows the continent of Africa. The map on G14 shows the path of a powerful hurricane over the southeastern United States.

While maps may differ, they all have many of the same parts. You can read a map more easily once you know how to use its main parts.

A **grid** is a set of lines that cross each other. The grid helps you find places on a map. On this map, and on many other maps, lines called **latitude** and **longitude** form the grid. Some maps mark grid lines with letters and numbers.

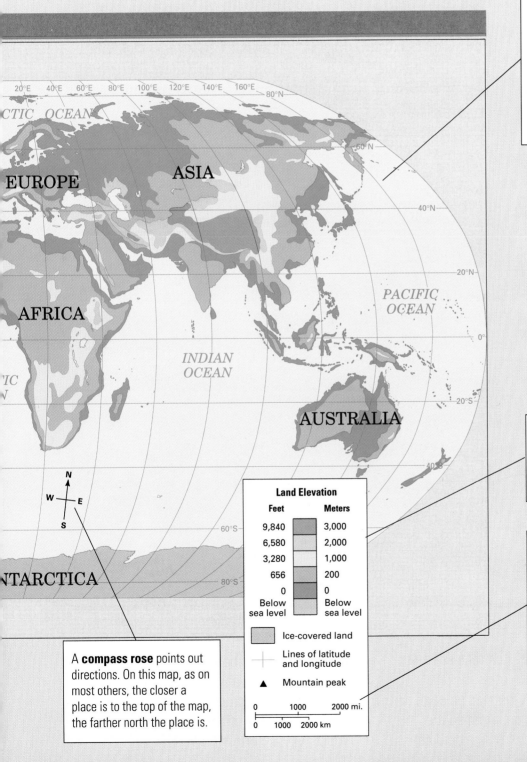

Land Elevation

Feet		Meters
9,840		3,000
6,580		2,000
3,280		1,000
656		200
0		0
Below sea level		Below sea level

Ice-covered land

Lines of latitude and longitude

▲ Mountain peak

0   1000   2000 mi.

0   1000   2000 km

A **legend,** or **key**, is a list that tells what the colors, pictures, shapes, and lines on a map show.

A **scale** is a line on a map. The scale helps you measure the size of a place or the distance between places. This map's scale shows that each inch on the map stands for 2,000 miles on the earth.

A **compass rose** points out directions. On this map, as on most others, the closer a place is to the top of the map, the farther north the place is.

Using a Compass Rose

▲ *This native artist creates works of art on bark. The art of barkpainting is handed down from one generation to another.*

Look at this political map of Australia. Do you notice something familiar about Australia? This country, like the United States, is divided into states. How can you tell which state is directly north of Victoria? You use the compass rose. The compass rose shows the main, or cardinal, directions: north **(N)**, south **(S)**, east **(E)**, and west **(W)**. On most maps, north is at the top of the map. South is at the bottom. East is to the right. West is to the left.

The city of Darwin is at the top of the map. That means Darwin is in the northern part of Australia.

Perth is south and west, or southwest of Darwin.

The compass rose also points out the in-between, or intermediate, directions. **NE** means northeast. **SE** means southeast. **SW** means southwest. **NW** means northwest.

Australia: Political

National capital
★ State capital
— State boundary

130°E   140°E   150°E   10°S

Darwin

INDIAN OCEAN

PACIFIC OCEAN

Northern Territory

20°S

Queensland

Tropic of Capricorn

Western Australia

South Australia

Brisbane

New South Wales

30°S

Perth

Adelaide

Sydney
Canberra

Victoria

Melbourne

0   500   1000 mi.
0   500   1000 km
Conic Projection

Tasmania
Hobart

40°S

N
NW   NE
W   E
SW   SE
S

N
NW   NE
W   E
SW   SE
S

MAP SKILLS

1. **REVIEW** In which part of Australia are most of its cities?

2. **THINK ABOUT IT** Look at the map on page 181. Why would using an intermediate direction be more helpful than a cardinal direction to describe how to go from Charleston to Savannah?

3. **TRY IT** Write directions from your classroom to the principal's office. Ask your teacher which way is north.

Using a Map Scale

Look at the United States on the map. It seems to be only a few inches wide. The real United States, of course, is almost 3,000 miles from coast to coast.

All maps are drawn "to scale." Scale is the way a map's size compares to the size of the same area on the earth. A map may have a scale that shows one inch is equal to 1,000 miles. That means, two places one inch apart on the map are 1,000 miles apart on the earth.

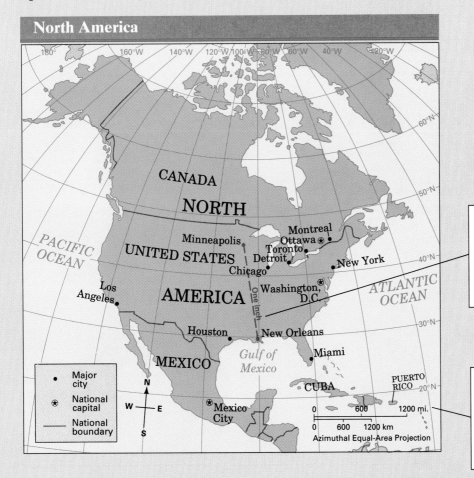

North America

The map distance between New Orleans and Minneapolis is about one inch. This means that the cities are about 1,200 miles apart.

The scale line on the map is one inch long. It says 1,200 mi. Now you know that one inch on the map equals 1,200 miles of real distance on the earth.

MAP SKILLS

1. **REVIEW** If two cities are three inches apart on this map, how far apart are they in real distance?

2. **THINK ABOUT IT** Why do you think the map on page 14 uses a different scale than this map?

3. **TRY IT** Draw a map to show where you walk from home to a place in your neighborhood, such as a friend's house. Put your scale line on the map to show what one inch equals in real distance.

Using an Inset Map

Suppose that your ancestors came from the western part of Africa. You want to find out what this area is like today. This map of Africa can help.

Notice the two small inset maps. The top inset shows details of the West African coast that the main map can't. Many African Americans have ancestors who came from here. The other inset is a locator inset to help you find Africa in the world.

You can see more West African cities here than on the large map because this inset makes a part of the map bigger.

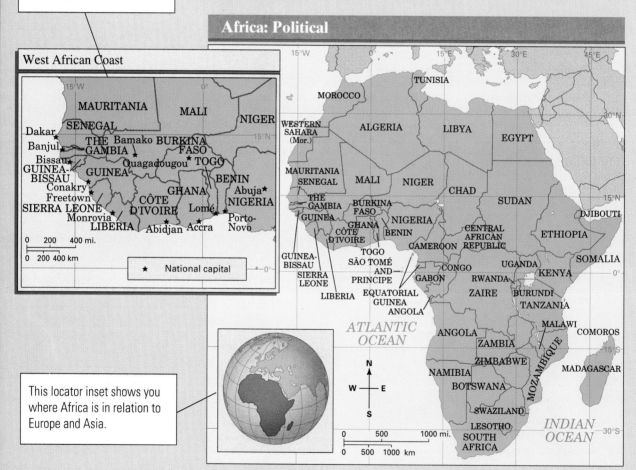

Africa: Political

West African Coast

MAURITANIA   MALI   NIGER

Dakar ★
SENEGAL   THE   Bamako   BURKINA
Banjul ★   GAMBIA ★   FASO
Bissau ★   Ouagadougou ★   TOGO
GUINEA-   GUINEA
BISSAU
Conakry ★   GHANA   Abuja ★
Freetown ★   CÔTE   NIGERIA
SIERRA LEONE   D'IVOIRE   Lomé ★   Porto-
Monrovia ★   Abidjan ★   Accra ★   Novo
LIBERIA

0   200   400 mi.
0   200 400 km

★   National capital

TUNISIA
MOROCCO
WESTERN
SAHARA   ALGERIA   LIBYA   EGYPT
(Mor.)
MAURITANIA
SENEGAL   MALI   NIGER   CHAD   SUDAN
THE   BURKINA   DJIBOUTI
GAMBIA   FASO
GUINEA   GHANA   NIGERIA   CENTRAL   ETHIOPIA
CÔTE   BENIN   AFRICAN
D'IVOIRE   REPUBLIC   SOMALIA
TOGO   CAMEROON   UGANDA
GUINEA-   SÃO TOMÉ   CONGO   KENYA
BISSAU   AND   GABON   RWANDA
SIERRA   PRINCIPE   ZAIRE   BURUNDI
LEONE   EQUATORIAL   TANZANIA
LIBERIA   GUINEA
ANGOLA   MALAWI
COMOROS
ATLANTIC   ANGOLA
OCEAN   ZAMBIA   MADAGASCAR
ZIMBABWE
N   NAMIBIA   MOZAMBIQUE
W   E   BOTSWANA
S   SWAZILAND   INDIAN
LESOTHO   OCEAN
0   500   1000 mi.   SOUTH
0   500   1000 km   AFRICA

This locator inset shows you where Africa is in relation to Europe and Asia.

MAP SKILLS

1. REVIEW Is Africa north or south of Europe? How does your locator inset help you answer this?

2. THINK ABOUT IT Name two countries that are shown in the top inset map.

3. TRY IT Trace a political map of one African country. Add its capital city. Then add a locator inset to help find that country in Africa (trace from the map on page 401). Draw the country's boundary on the inset.

Using a Map Legend

Maps give information by using symbols. Symbols are figures, shapes, lines, and colors that show where places and things are on a map. A map's legend tells you what the symbols mean. On this map, the color of an area tells the kind of vegetation, or plant life, that grows naturally in that part of China.

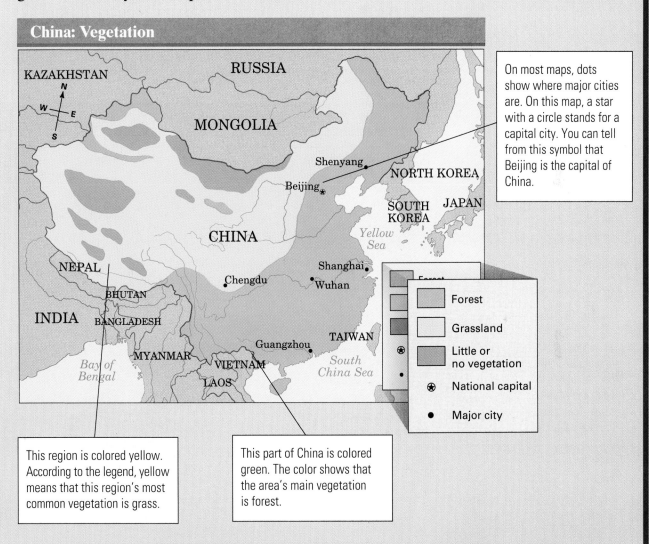

China: Vegetation

On most maps, dots show where major cities are. On this map, a star with a circle stands for a capital city. You can tell from this symbol that Beijing is the capital of China.

Legend:
- Forest
- Grassland
- Little or no vegetation
- ⊛ National capital
- • Major city

This region is colored yellow. According to the legend, yellow means that this region's most common vegetation is grass.

This part of China is colored green. The color shows that the area's main vegetation is forest.

MAP SKILLS

1. **REVIEW** What kind of vegetation grows in eastern China?

2. **THINK ABOUT IT** Why do you think there are no large cities in places where little or no vegetation grows?

3. **TRY IT** Imagine that you live in China. You want to work as a forest ranger. Use the map above to decide in which part of China you might look for a job. Why would you choose this area?

Using A Map Grid

Imagine you're in the city of Calcutta, India. You must meet a friend at Howrah Bridge. Your only clue to finding the bridge is **B4.** With this clue, the map grid can help you.

A grid is a set of lines drawn on a map. The lines cross and form squares. You can use the grid lines to find places on a map. On this map of Calcutta, letters run along each side. Numbers run across the top and bottom of the grid. A square on the grid is named by its letter and number, such as **B4.**

This box is **A1.** It lies across from **A** and below **1.** No other square has this name

The Jain Temple is in square **B4.** It lies across from the letter **B** and below **4.**

This index, or list, helps you find places on the map. To find the Indian Museum, look up Indian Museum on this index. The index tells you it is in square **C4.**

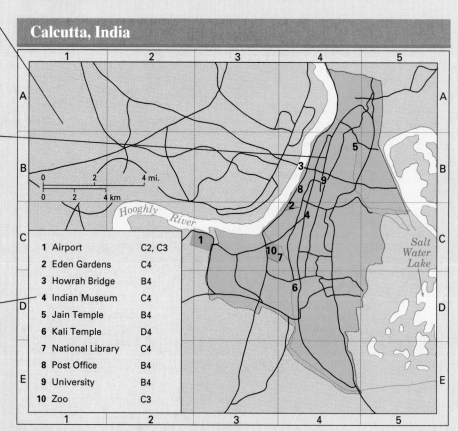

Calcutta, India

1	Airport	C2, C3
2	Eden Gardens	C4
3	Howrah Bridge	B4
4	Indian Museum	C4
5	Jain Temple	B4
6	Kali Temple	D4
7	National Library	C4
8	Post Office	B4
9	University	B4
10	Zoo	C3

MAP SKILLS

1. REVIEW Name two places in the grid square C4.

2. THINK ABOUT IT Where can you look to find the name of the square where the zoo lies? In which square will you find the zoo?

3. TRY IT Take out a map you have drawn, or draw a simple map. Draw a grid over it. Put letters and numbers on the map. Ask a friend to find a place on your map. Tell your friend the number and letter of the correct box.

Understanding the Globe: Hemispheres

A globe is a sphere, or ball, that is a model of the earth. A globe is also like a world map. Both show the land and water areas of the earth. Because there are so many places on the earth, geographers draw latitude and longitude lines on the globe. These lines help you find places. Certain lines divide the earth into half spheres, or hemispheres.

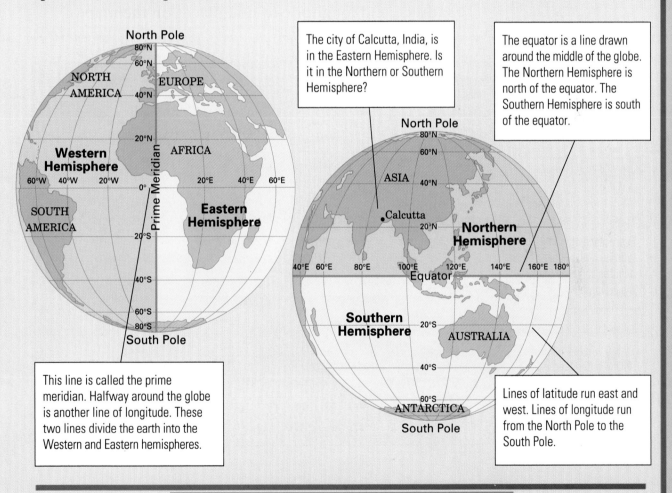

The city of Calcutta, India, is in the Eastern Hemisphere. Is it in the Northern or Southern Hemisphere?

The equator is a line drawn around the middle of the globe. The Northern Hemisphere is north of the equator. The Southern Hemisphere is south of the equator.

This line is called the prime meridian. Halfway around the globe is another line of longitude. These two lines divide the earth into the Western and Eastern hemispheres.

Lines of latitude run east and west. Lines of longitude run from the North Pole to the South Pole.

GLOBE SKILLS

1. REVIEW What line divides the globe into the Northern and Southern hemispheres?

2. THINK ABOUT IT On a globe, name three countries in the Eastern Hemisphere and three in the Western Hemisphere.

3. TRY IT Take turns looking at a globe. Find the island of Greenland. Is it located in the Eastern or Western Hemisphere? Is Greenland located in the Northern or Southern Hemisphere?

Using Latitude and Longitude on a Map

You know that lines of latitude and longitude divide the globe into hemispheres. These lines also can be used to find any place on the globe. Latitude and longitude are measured in degrees. Lines of latitude are numbered in degrees north and south of the equator. The equator is at 0° latitude. Lines of longitude are numbered in degrees east and west of the prime meridian. Use latitude and longitude to find places on the map of Southeast Asia below.

Southeast Asia

Every place along this longitude line is 120 degrees east (120°E) of the prime meridian.

Every place along this latitude line is 5 degrees south (5°S) of the equator.

To tell where the city of Ujung Pandang is, you can say it is about 5 degrees south (5°S) latitude and about 120 degrees east (120°E) longitude.

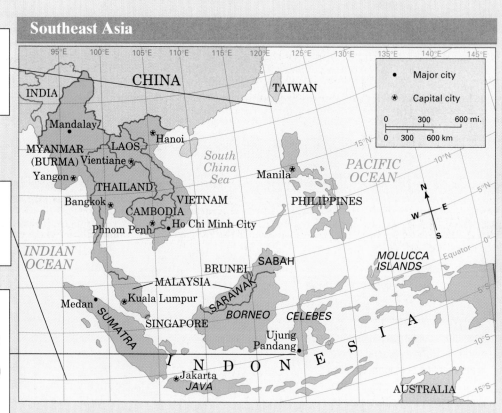

MAP SKILLS

1. REVIEW Use the closest lines of latitude and longitude to tell where Manila is.

2. THINK ABOUT IT How would this place be labeled on a map: 10 degrees north, 120 degrees east?

3. TRY IT Pick a place on the map. Use lines of latitude and longitude to name where it is. Write down where the place is. Give the paper to a classmate. Ask him or her to find the place on a map or globe.

Reading Different Kinds of Maps

In this part of the Map and Globe Handbook, you'll learn how to read four different maps. You'll find out that maps can show more than the shape of the earth. They can also tell you about certain subjects. Do you want to know what a country produces? Do you need to know where most people in a country live? Maps can help you answer questions like these.

A Regions Map

Before Europeans came, many groups of Native Americans were already living in North America. The groups were different from each other. However, many shared similar ways of life. A regions map can show you where similar groups lived. A region is an area of land that shares one or many of the same features. For example, these features might be climate or ways of life.

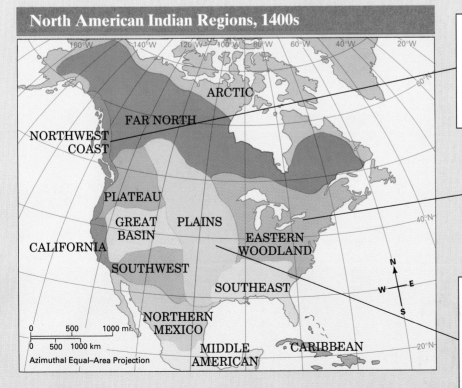

North American Indian Regions, 1400s

ARCTIC
FAR NORTH
NORTHWEST COAST
PLATEAU
GREAT BASIN
PLAINS
CALIFORNIA
SOUTHWEST
EASTERN WOODLAND
SOUTHEAST
NORTHERN MEXICO
MIDDLE AMERICAN
CARIBBEAN

0   500   1000 mi.
0   500   1000 km
Azimuthal Equal–Area Projection

The Nootka lived in the Northwest Coast region, shown in dark green. The Nootka and others in this region fished from canoes in the Pacific Ocean.

Light green shows the Eastern Woodlands region. Native Americans here used wood from this region's forests to build houses.

The Plains region, shown in gold, was once the home of many buffalo. The Comanche and others got from the buffalo meat for food, hides for clothing, and bones for tools and weapons.

A Product Map

Imagine that you have to give a report on the useful goods made in your state. You can begin by looking at a product map. One type of product map shows the crops farmers grow and animals they raise in an area. This product map shows three important crops grown in the Caribbean region.

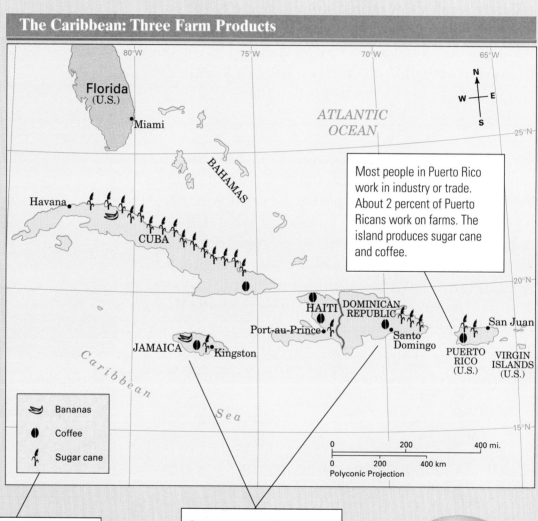

The Caribbean: Three Farm Products

Most people in Puerto Rico work in industry or trade. About 2 percent of Puerto Ricans work on farms. The island produces sugar cane and coffee.

The map uses symbols to show the country where each crop is grown. The legend tells what each symbol means. Farmers grow sugar cane, coffee, and bananas in the Caribbean.

Sugar cane and coffee are important crops in the Dominican Republic. In Jamaica, farmers grow coffee, bananas, and sugar cane.

Legend:
- Bananas
- Coffee
- Sugar cane

0   200   400 mi.
0   200   400 km
Polyconic Projection

A Population Density Map

Many people live in each square mile of a city. A square mile is an area that is one mile wide by one mile long. Fewer people live in each square mile of small towns and farmlands. A population density map can compare the number of people living in one place with the number of people living in another. The map below shows population density in the South American nation of Brazil.

Brazil: Population Density

The purple color of cities shows they have a high population density. Many people live in a small area.

This part of the map is orange. This part of Brazil has a very low population density of less than 25 people per square mile.

Legend

People per square km	People per square mi.
More than 78	More than 125
31-78	50-125
16-31	25-50
Less than 16	Less than 25

• Major city
★ National capital

The legend tells what the colors on the map mean. The four colors on this map show four different population densities. The most crowded places have more than 125 people per square mile.

Brazil's cities (left) are crowded. Few people, however, live in Brazil's rain forests (right).

A Route Map

A route map shows the path or movement of people or goods across an area. It can show the path you traveled on a vacation. It can show the direction birds migrate, or travel. This map shows the direction a hurricane moved. In late August 1992, a hurricane from the Atlantic Ocean blew across the Bahamas, southern Florida, and onto the coast of Louisiana. Hurricane Andrew caused thirty billion dollars worth of damage.

Route of Hurricane Andrew, 1992

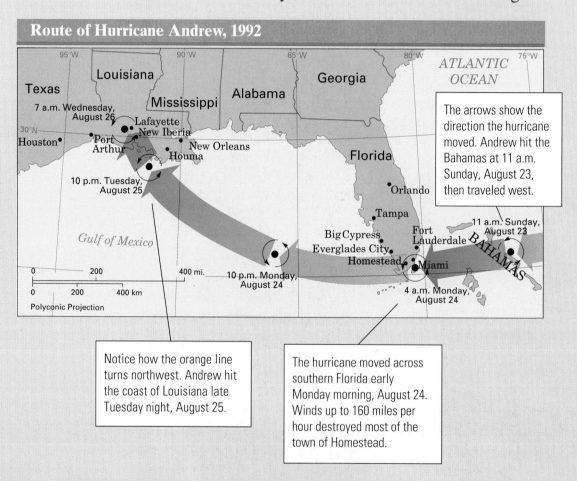

The arrows show the direction the hurricane moved. Andrew hit the Bahamas at 11 a.m. Sunday, August 23, then traveled west.

Notice how the orange line turns northwest. Andrew hit the coast of Louisiana late Tuesday night, August 25.

The hurricane moved across southern Florida early Monday morning, August 24. Winds up to 160 miles per hour destroyed most of the town of Homestead.

MAP SKILLS

1. **REVIEW** Look at the animal regions map on page 33. Find your state on the map. In which animal regions is your state?

2. **THINK ABOUT IT** Imagine you move to Brazil. You want to live in a city located in an area that is not crowded. Which city will you choose?

3. **THINK ABOUT IT** Look at the route map on page 213. Use the legend to find the route of Juan de Oñate. Did he travel from Santa Fe to Mexico City, or from Mexico City to Santa Fe? How can you tell?

4. **TRY IT** Make a product map of your state. Explain your symbols in your map legend.

Using Geographic References

What does a strait look like? Where is Albany, New York? What is the capital of Mississippi? Turn to the Time/Space Databank at the back of your book. You can find the answers to these questions there.

The Atlas on pages 400–410 has a map of the world and maps of the United States. This map section from the Atlas shows the state of Mississippi and its capital city, Jackson.

PLACE	LAT.	LONG.	PAGE
A			
Africa (continent)			**G6**
Alabama (state)	32°N	87°W	**403**
Alaska (state)	64°N	150°W	**402**
Albany (capital of New York)	43°N	74°W	**145**
Annapolis (capital of Maryland)	39°N	76°W	**145**
Appalachian Mountains (range in Eastern U.S.)	37°N	82°W	**14**
Arizona (state)	34°N	113°W	**403**

The Gazetteer on pages 411–413 gives the locations of many places in the United States. This section from the Gazetteer tells you that Albany is the capital of New York. It also tells you that Albany is at 43°N latitude and 74°W longitude and can be found on a map on page 145.

The Glossary of Geographic Terms on pages 414–415 shows some of the earth's natural features. This example tells you what a strait is and also shows what a strait looks like.

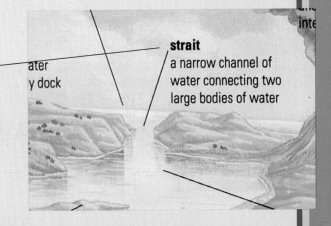

strait
a narrow channel of water connecting two large bodies of water

---

REFERENCE SKILLS

1. **REVIEW** The climate map on page 408 is a regions map. Which region of the United States has the coldest climate? How can you tell?

2. **THINK ABOUT IT** Which part of the Time/Space Databank tells where you can find a map of the state of Mississippi?

3. **THINK ABOUT IT** In which part of the Databank would you find a definition and a picture of a peninsula?

4. **TRY IT** Your teacher tells you to look for information about the Ohio River in the Atlas, Gazetteer, and Glossary of Geographic Terms. What will you learn in each section?

Our Land and People

O beautiful for spacious skies,
For amber waves of grain,
For purple mountains' majesty
Above the fruited plain!

The opening words of "America the Beautiful"
paint a picture of our country. This land stretches
"from sea to shining sea," as the song says. And
between our two coasts are a wonderful variety of
people, places, plants, and animals.

Iowa
Photograph Copyright David Muench.

Chapter 1

The United States Today

Question: Where is it rainy and dry, hilly and flat, noisy and quiet, hot and cold? Answer: the United States. You live in a nation with many types of land, people, wildlife, and weather. That's why the United States has so much to see and do. So pack your snow boots and your bathing suit. You're about to take a trip across the country.

Red, white, and blue flags celebrate our country's birthday. On July 4, families gather for picnics, fireworks displays, and parades, like the one pictured here.

A trip across the country treats visitors to the many historic sites, natural wonders, and interesting people that each state has to offer.

Many people enjoy the natural beauty of the United States by hiking and camping in parks and forests such as this one in the state of Washington. Here Mount Baker towers in the distance.

Millions of people live in or around America's busy cities. Workers shown here are building one of the thousands of skyscrapers where many people work and live.

Our Nation's People

Key Terms

- ethnic group
- population

► *The Statue of Liberty, in New York Harbor, is a symbol of the freedom and the opportunities that the United States offers to all people.*

Every rooftop in New York City was jammed with people, all waiting for the big moment. Thousands of boats floated side by side in New York Harbor. They surrounded a graceful copper statue that stood in the middle of the harbor. It was a statue of a woman wearing a crown and holding a burning torch toward the sky.

Suddenly, the sky seemed to rip apart. From every part of the city, fireworks shot into the air. Colored light and thick smoke blanketed the city in one of the biggest fireworks shows in history. The noise of explosions, music, cheers, and honking boat horns was deafening.

This was July 4, 1986, and New York City was throwing a party for the newly restored Statue of Liberty. Why so much fuss for a statue? For 100 years the lady in the long robes had stood watch over the harbor, welcoming the ships that enter it. Many of the ships carried people coming from other countries to start a new life here. When New York City celebrated the statue, it also celebrated all the people who have made the United States their home.

People from Different Places

Today, many in the United States can trace their families back to people who came across the Atlantic Ocean from the continents of Europe and Africa. During the 1600s and 1700s, people from the European countries of England, Ireland, France, Sweden, Spain, and the Netherlands settled much of the East Coast. The Spanish came from Mexico to settle areas to the south and west. Though some Africans came to North America as free people, most were forced to come to serve as slaves in the South.

The groups who came to the United States are called ethnic groups. **Ethnic groups** are people who are from the same country, like Italian people, or who share the same religion, such as Jewish people. An ethnic group also includes people of the same race, such as black people.

Names of Places

The word *new* in a place name may be a clue that the place was founded by ethnic groups from Europe. Look at the map on pages 404–405 for places that start with *new*. New Hampshire was named after Hampshire, England. The first settlement in Delaware

For some families, apple picking in the fall has become a new American tradition.

People from different ethnic groups have brought their traditions and celebrations to this country. This girl breaks open a Mexican piñata full of surprises.

5

The United States Today

■ *How have different ethnic groups affected the growth of the country?*

➤ *Many classrooms have students from different parts of the world.*

was called New Sweden. The Europeans also named some places after the Native American tribes that lived here, such as the Massachusetts. Native Americans were the first people who lived in this country.

European ethnic groups brought to this country the ways of life of their home countries—their businesses, holidays and celebrations, types of houses, foods, and games. The Spanish, for example, brought the first horses to the United States. Horses were used for hundreds of years to farm, hunt, travel, and carry supplies.

The contributions of these ethnic groups, with all of their ways, ideas, and languages, are a big part of our history. They help explain why people in the United States are different from one another.

More People Arrive

In the 1800s and 1900s, people from Asia, Africa, and South America came to the United States. Like the Europeans, these people brought their own ways of life. This has made the country even more varied and rich.

Look again at the names of some places in the United States today. In San Francisco, California, there is a section called Chinatown. Thousands of Chinese families live there. Miami, Florida, has many people who come from the island country of Cuba to the south. One Miami neighborhood is called "Little Havana." It is named after the capital of Cuba. ■

A United Country

During its 200-year history, the country grew. People moved west and formed new states. The people who live in a place are called its **population**. Over the years, the population of the United States grew to have many things in common. For example, one idea that took hold throughout the nation during the 1800s was that education is very important. So children all over the country go to school, whether they live in Vermont or Wyoming or Hawaii.

As a nation, we have other things in common. Most families eat three meals a day. Many adults go to work for five days, then have the weekends off.

Different People, One Government

There is something else that people in the United States share—their government. In fact, the word *united* means "joined together." The 50 states are joined under one government. This government not only joins people together, it also protects people's right to be different. For example, citizens have the right to have different ideas and religions. People have the opportunity to choose the type of work they want to do or to start their own businesses. The government of the United States has helped shape the way cities and states have developed.

In this book you will find many examples of how different parts of the country developed differently. But, at the same time, you will also discover how much the different areas have in common. ■

▼ *Children all over the country go to school, no matter who they are or where they live.*

■ *What kinds of things unite the population of this country?*

REVIEW

1. **FOCUS** How are people in the United States different from each other and how are they alike?

2. **CULTURE** How are ethnic groups different from each other?

3. **GEOGRAPHY** What can place names tell you about a city's or state's beginnings?

4. **CRITICAL THINKING** What three things do you and one of your classmates have in common?

5. **ACTIVITY** Use the Minipedia to find out the size of your state's population. Look up its "Rank Among the States." Is the population of your state large or small, compared to the other states?

This Land is Your Land

Woody Guthrie

As you learned in Lesson 1, the United States is one land, just as our Earth is one world. This song and poem both show how many different types of land and water can join together to create a perfect whole.

Woody Guthrie was a folksinger who loved the United States and the people in it. He traveled from coast to coast on freight trains in the 1930s and came to know most of the country. This song expresses Guthrie's love of the United States and its people. As you read, ask yourself, "What different parts of America are described in this song?'

Redwood a very tall hardwood tree that grows on the northern Pacific Coast

Gulf Stream a warm current that flows from the Gulf of Mexico up the Atlantic Coast of the United States

This land is your land,
This land is my land
From California to the New York Island;
From the redwood forests to the Gulf
    Stream waters;
This land was made for you and me.

As I was walking that ribbon of highway,
I saw above me that endless skyway;
I saw below me that golden valley;
This land was made for you and me.

I've roamed and rambled and I followed my
    footsteps
To the sparkling sands of her diamond deserts;
And all around me a voice was sounding:
This land was made for you and me.

Reading Further

Born to Win. Woody Guthrie. A collection of poems, stories, songs, and essays by this well-known writer of folk songs.

In 1967, Orbiter 5 *took the first photograph of Earth from the moon. This photograph gave May Swenson the idea for this poem. As you read, try to find in the photograph the figures she describes.*

ORBITER 5 SHOWS
HOW EARTH LOOKS FROM THE MOON

There's a woman in the earth, sitting on
her heels. You see her from the back, in three-
quarter profile. She has a flowing pigtail. She's
holding something
in her right hand—some holy jug. Her left arm is thinner
in a gesture like a dancer. She's the Indian Ocean. Asia is
light swirling up out of her vessel. Her pigtail points to Europe
and her dancer's arm is the Suez Canal. She is a woman
in a square kimono,
bare feet tucked beneath the tip of Africa. Her tail of long hair is
the Arabian Peninsula.   A woman in the earth.

                                    A man in the moon.

*three quarter
profile* turned so that
three-quarters of the
body faces the viewer

vessel bottle or jar

kimono a robe tradi-
tionally worn in
Japan

Reading Further

New & Selected Things Taking Place. May Swenson. A collection of poems
by May Swenson.

9

Our Nation's Land

T H I N K I N G
F O C U S

What are the major landforms of the United States?

Key Terms

- continent
- climate

➤ *On a trip from Los Angeles to Boston, a plane cruises at an altitude of 35,000 to 40,000 feet, giving passengers a wide view of the country below.*

F asten your seat belts, please," the voice of the captain comes loudly through the airplane's speaker. The jet engines rumble as you buckle your belt. You smile with excitement as you begin your journey across the country, from Los Angeles, California, to Boston, Massachusetts.

The plane speeds down the runway and takes off into the sky. From your window you can see the cars, the roads, and the buildings below get smaller and smaller. The enormous city of Los Angeles goes for miles and miles. The pattern of houses, swimming pools, yards, and roads looks like the patchwork quilt on your bed at home. In the distance, the blue waters of the Pacific Ocean sparkle in the sunlight. When the airplane turns, you see the curving rows of mountains that surround the city. You look in wonder as the wide land of the United States spreads out beneath you.

Across the Western Sky

During this flight, you will get an excellent view of the many landforms that cover the continent of North America. A **continent** is one of the seven very large areas of land on

the earth. Woody Guthrie's song, "This Land Is Your Land," on page 8 describes many of the landforms that cover the United States.

▲ *High mountains rise from the dry land of the Death Valley National Park, which lies in southeastern California.*

The Desert

As your plane heads east, the California coast disappears behind you. Now from the window you see a dry, dusty stretch of land covered with only a few bushes and trees. There are no lakes, streams, or ponds here. The land seems to be empty of cities and people. The land that you are flying over is called a desert. In the poem *Mojave*, the poet Diane Siebert has the desert tell about its rugged and dry land.

Great mountain ranges stretch for miles
To crease my face with frowns and smiles.
My lakes are dry and marked by tracks
Of zigging, zagging, long-eared jacks [rabbits].
Dust devils swirl and slowly rise;
They whistle, whirling to the skies,
While tossed and blown in great stampedes
Are stumbling, bumbling tumbleweeds.

11

The United States Today

The desert is a place with a dry and often very hot **climate**. The climate is the type of weather, including temperature, rainfall, and wind, that is most common for an area. The climate of the desert is so dry that sometimes months go by without a single drop of rain falling. Few plants or animals can live in the desert. Deserts cover much of the southwestern United States.

Death Valley in the California desert is one of the hottest places on earth. There the temperature can rise as high as 125 degrees and as little as two inches of rain falls a year. The Native Americans who live there call the valley Tomesha (*toh MEE shuh*), which means "ground on fire."

The Mountains

As your plane continues flying east, the brown and yellow colors of the dry desert give way to the green, forested peaks and valleys of an enormous range of mountains. You are flying over the Rocky Mountains, the tallest and longest range of mountains in the United States. The Rockies stretch from the state of New Mexico into Canada. These mountains have a much cooler climate than the desert. Throughout the year, the tallest peaks in the Rockies are covered with snow. ■

The Rocky Mountains, pictured above, are over 3,000 miles long. The illustration below shows that this mountain range is just one of many landforms in the United States.

■ *How are the desert and the mountains alike and how are they different?*

Flying Toward the East

Now as you look down at the ground below, you see the tall mountains fade behind you and low hills spread before you. As your plane flies farther east, the land becomes almost totally flat. Green and gold farms and fields stretch

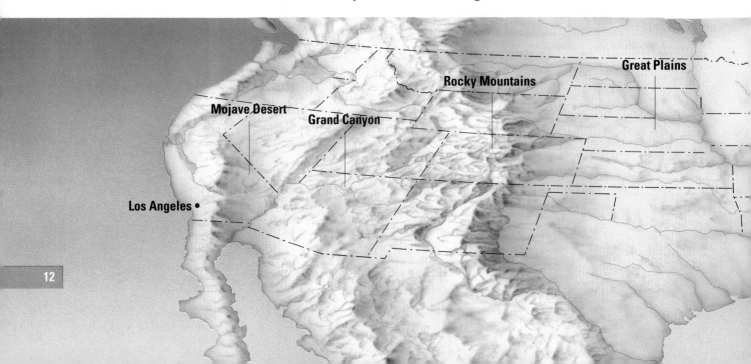

Los Angeles •

Mojave Desert

Grand Canyon

Rocky Mountains

Great Plains

as far as your eye can see. The area that you are flying over is called the Central Plains.

The Plains

A plain is a wide, flat area of land with very few trees on it. From the air, you see that the towns of the Plains are separated by wide distances. The climate of the open Plains is hot in the summer and very cold in the winter. The wind blows hard most of the time. The plentiful rain that falls on the Plains helps farmers grow much of the country's grain. One writer described the flat farmland like this:

> **B**road fields, deep skies, wind, and sunlight . . . herds of cattle grazing on the sandhills; red barns and white farmhouses surrounded by fields of . . . corn and ripening wheat; windmills and wire fences; and men and women who take their living from the soil.
>
> Bernard A. Weisberger, *WPA Guide to America*, 1985

The River

Your plane flies on and more trees and towns appear as the Plains pass behind you. Now you are surprised to see a very broad river splitting the land in two. Towns stretch out along both of this river's banks. Boats travel up and down its busy waters. This is the Mississippi River—one of North America's longest rivers. The Mississippi flows more than 2,000 miles from Minnesota in the north to Louisiana in the south, where it empties into the Gulf of Mexico. Trace the route of the Mississippi River on the map on pages 406–407.

In the Plains, crops like corn, wheat, and soybeans spread for miles on the flat, treeless land.

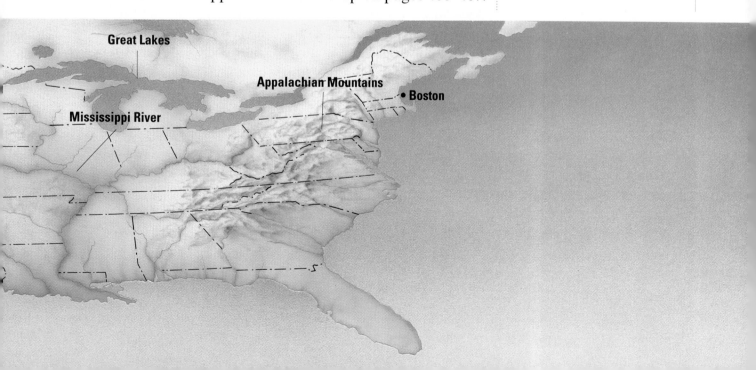

Great Lakes

Appalachian Mountains

• Boston

Mississippi River

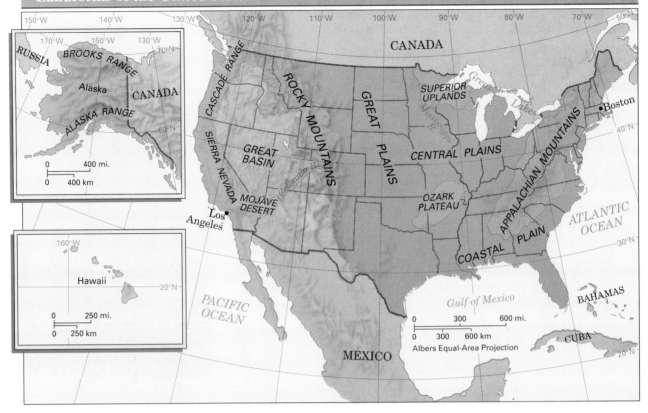

▲ *Name two mountain ranges and one plains region, besides the Rocky Mountains and the Central Plains.*

East of the Mississippi River, the towns and fields slowly give way to dark green forests, and another range of mountains, the Appalachians. These mountains spread across much of the eastern part of the United States. After passing over more fields and forests, you begin to see many homes, towns, and large cities dotting the land. Finally, you catch sight of the blue waters of the Atlantic Ocean.

"Fasten your seatbelts," the captain again commands. The plane dips its wing and begins a downward curving path. From your window you can see the cluster of skyscrapers in downtown Boston. You get one last bird's-eye view of the land. The coastline is rocky and ragged, unlike the wide, flat beaches of southern California that you left behind just a few hours ago. ■

■ *How is the land west of the Mississippi River different from the land east of the river?*

R E V I E W

1. **FOCUS** What are the major landforms of the United States?

2. **GEOGRAPHY** Describe the climate of the deserts of the Southwest.

3. **CONNECT** Look at the landforms on the illustration on pages 12–13. Which areas might have been easier for early European ethnic groups to settle?

4. **CRITICAL THINKING** Do you think it would be more fun to live in the mountains or near a river? Why?

5. **CRITICAL THINKING** Write a paragraph describing the landforms and the climate where you live. If you live in a city, write about the land nearby.

Using Latitude and Longitude

Here's Why

Suppose you want to locate some of the places described in the Lesson 2 airplane flight. You would use a globe or a map. The globes and maps that you use today are marked with imaginary lines called lines of latitude and longitude. Learning how to use these lines will help you locate specific places more easily.

Here's How

You know that Earth looks like a round ball from a space shuttle. Since globes are models of the Earth, they are also shaped like balls, or spheres. The most northern point on the Earth is the North Pole. It is found at the top of the globe. The South Pole is found at the bottom. Find the North and South Poles on the two maps below. Where would the North and South Poles be found on any flat world map?

Now find the red line on Map A below. It is called the equator. The equator is an imaginary line that circles the Earth from east to west. It divides the sphere-shaped Earth into two half spheres, or hemispheres. All the land and water north of the equator is called the Northern Hemisphere. All the land and water south of the equator is called the Southern Hemisphere.

Another imaginary line called the prime meridian runs halfway around the Earth from the North Pole to the South Pole. Find the prime meridian on Map B below. On the opposite side of a globe from the prime meridian is the International Date Line. Together, the International Date Line and the prime meridian make a circle around the Earth that divides the Earth into Eastern and Western hemispheres. All the land and water that stretches west from the prime meridian to the International Date Line is known as the Western Hemisphere. What do you think the land and water east of the prime meridian is called?

The equator is a line of latitude, or a parallel. However, it is not the only

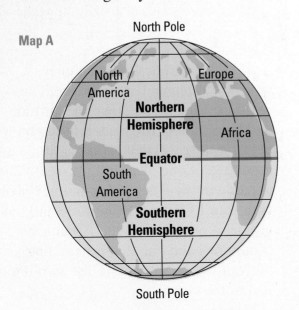

Map A

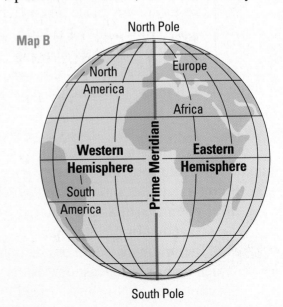

Map B

Map C

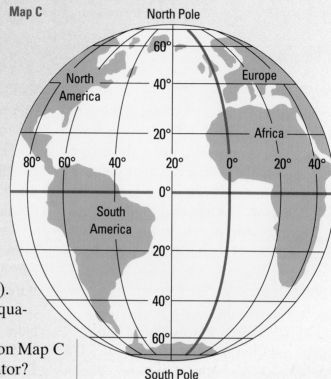

North Pole

North America

Europe

Africa

South America

South Pole

parallel. Others run north and south of the equator. Parallels on globes and maps are numbered. The equator is labeled 0° (zero degrees latitude). The numbers of the other parallels show how far north or south of the equator they are. On Map C to the right, the first parallel north of the equator is 20°N (20 degrees north latitude). The first parallel south of the equator is 20°S (20 degrees south latitude). What other parallels on Map C are north and south of the equator?

The prime meridian is a line of longitude, or a meridian. Find the other meridians on the map above. They are numbered, too. The prime meridian is labeled 0° (zero degrees longitude). On Map C, the first meridian east of the prime meridian is 20°E (20 degrees east longitude). How is the first meridian west of the prime meridian labeled on Map C?

You can locate any place on earth by identifying its latitude and longitude. On Map C, find the place where 20° north latitude meets 20° east longitude. You should find it in the continent of Africa.

Try It

Use the world map on page 400 to answer the following questions.

1. Find the equator on the map. Which three countries in South America does the equator pass through?
2. Find the prime meridian on the map. Which hemisphere, east or west, is the continent of North America in?

3. What three continents does the prime meridian go through?
   Use the physical map on pages 406–407 to answer the next questions.
4. Between what lines of longitude does the Mississippi River flow? Are these lines the same as meridians?
5. Between what lines of latitude do you find California's Central Valley? Are these lines also called parallels?

Apply It

Use the physical map on pages 406–407 to plan a trip to different land features. First, write down the latitude and longitude of the place where you will begin your trip. Then list the latitude and longitude of one place in the Great Plains and one in the Rocky Mountains. Finish your tour by listing the latitude and longitude of one place in the Appalachian Mountains and one that is near a large body of water. Share your list with the rest of the class.

Working on the Land

Each year on the Fourth of July, hundreds of loggers gather in Albany, Oregon, for the world's largest log-cutting contest. After spending all year working at cutting down trees, these loggers gather to spend a day having fun at what they do best. Some have traveled hundreds of miles to get to this town in the northwestern part of the country.

Today the loggers and their families enjoy a picnic lunch on the grass under the tall green trees. Then someone announces that the contest will begin. Some of the strongest loggers step forward with their giant hand saws.

"On your mark . . . Get set . . . Go!" Several teams of two loggers begin pulling sharp saws across a thick log. Their faces turn red as they push and pull their saws faster and faster. Sawdust and wood chips fly everywhere as the saw cuts through the wood.

Finally, one team's log falls to the ground with a heavy thud. The other teams let go of their saws and wipe their brows as the crowd cheers for the winners.

THINKING FOCUS

What are natural resources and why are they important?

Key Terms

- natural resources
- vegetation
- mineral

◀ *Loggers push and pull their long saws at a Fourth of July timber carnival in Albany, Oregon.*

17

The United States Today

People who dig minerals such as coal from the ground are called miners.

Kinds of Resources

Loggers cut down trees in the forests of the United States every day. At factories, the trees are cut into wood that is used for building or for making paper. Trees are one of many natural resources found in the United States.

Natural resources are useful materials found in nature that help people live their lives. Natural resources include the foods people eat, the gasoline people use to run their cars, and the materials people use to build houses, trains, and airplanes. Natural resources can come from either living or nonliving sources.

Living and Nonliving Natural Resources

One kind of living natural resource is vegetation. Anything that grows in the ground, such as plants, trees, and grass, is **vegetation**. People use many kinds of vegetation as food, such as corn, wheat, and apples. They use other kinds of vegetation to make materials such as cotton clothing.

Animals are also an example of a living natural resource. Farmers raise chickens, cows, sheep, and pigs to provide food for people. The fish, lobster, and clams that fishermen catch are also important sources of food.

Nonliving natural resources, such as minerals, also help people live their lives. A **mineral** is a natural resource usually found by digging in the ground. The United States is rich in minerals. Gold, copper, iron, clay, silver, and many other minerals lie among layers of rock and earth.

Fishermen in Nantucket, Massachusetts, catch living resources.

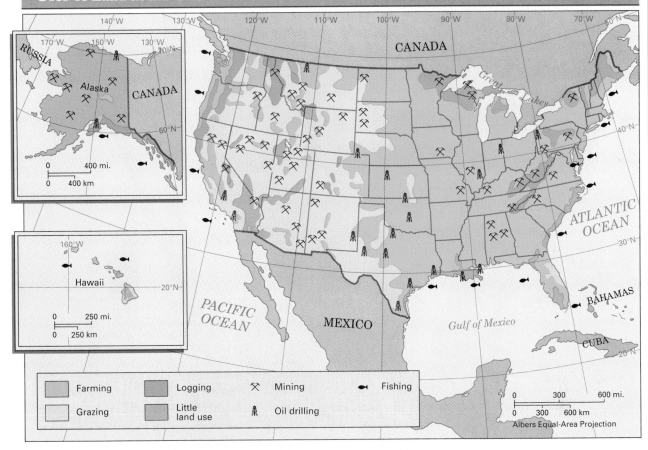

The natural resources found in an area are closely connected to the types of landforms there. For example, tall and strong trees grow best on cold mountaintops. Vegetables usually grow best on land that is flat and treeless, in places where there is plenty of sunshine. Gold is found in rivers near mountains or in the earth nearby. Because of this, different parts of the country are rich with different kinds of natural resources, depending on what types of landforms the area has. ■

▲ *What kinds of resources are found in your state or in states near you?*

■ *What types of natural resources are found in the United States?*

People and Resources

Many people in the United States do work related to natural resources. Loggers chop down trees, farmers grow fruits and vegetables and other crops, and miners dig for minerals like gold and silver. Often this kind of work is done outdoors. Because of this, workers depend on good weather to help them do their jobs. Rain makes a logger's job slippery and dangerous. Dry or cold weather can ruin a farmer's crops, and rough and windy storms put fishermen in danger.

People who do work related to natural resources have some of the most important jobs in the United States.

19

The United States Today

A Smokejumper

4:13 P.M., July 5, 1997
150 feet up in the air over
Oregon's Ochoco National Forest

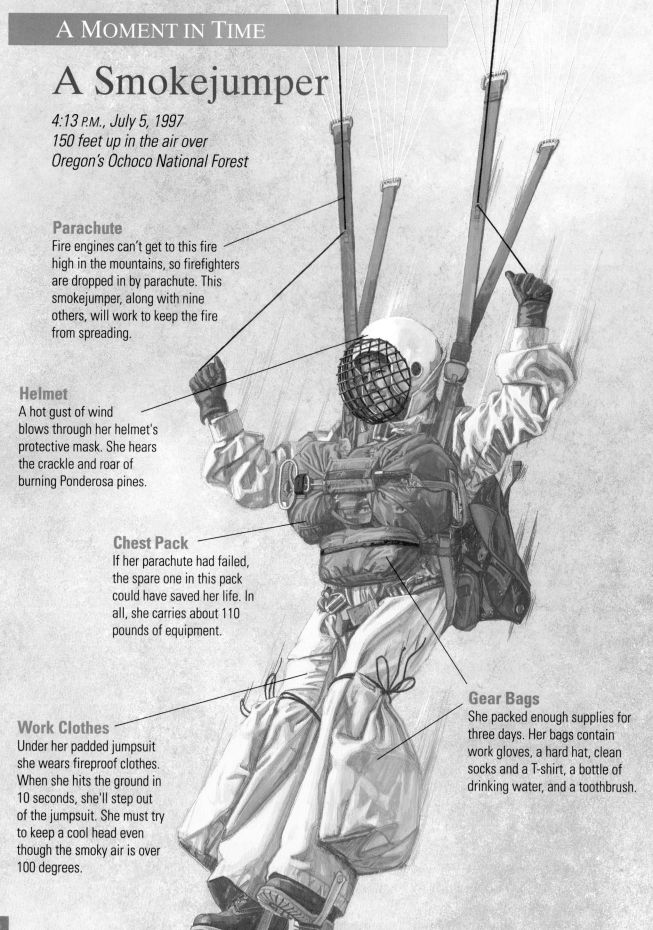

Parachute
Fire engines can't get to this fire high in the mountains, so firefighters are dropped in by parachute. This smokejumper, along with nine others, will work to keep the fire from spreading.

Helmet
A hot gust of wind blows through her helmet's protective mask. She hears the crackle and roar of burning Ponderosa pines.

Chest Pack
If her parachute had failed, the spare one in this pack could have saved her life. In all, she carries about 110 pounds of equipment.

Work Clothes
Under her padded jumpsuit she wears fireproof clothes. When she hits the ground in 10 seconds, she'll step out of the jumpsuit. She must try to keep a cool head even though the smoky air is over 100 degrees.

Gear Bags
She packed enough supplies for three days. Her bags contain work gloves, a hard hat, clean socks and a T-shirt, a bottle of drinking water, and a toothbrush.

Without the workers who drill for oil, people would not have enough fuel to run the cars or machinery that is necessary to their daily lives. Many people would go hungry without the farmers and the fishermen of the country.

Caring for Resources

Since people depend so heavily on natural resources to live their lives, it is important to take care of them. No one wants the country's rich supply of natural resources to run out. The trees in the forests are protected by laws that say logging companies may not cut down too many trees in one place. Trees are also protected from fires by smokejumpers, the firefighters of the forest described in A Moment in Time on page 20. To learn more about caring for forests and other resources, see Making Decisions on pages 22-23.

Farmers also must take care of their natural resources, such as the soil in the fields. Crops must have plenty of good soil if they are to grow. However, strong winds can blow fine soil off the land and heavy rains can wash it away into a river. Farmers can help the soil stay where it belongs by planting trees and crops in certain ways. Farmers, loggers, smokejumpers, and people like you must work hard to protect the nation's natural resources. ■

▲ Water is an important natural resource that helps crops to grow.

■ Why is taking care of natural resources important to the people of the United States?

R E V I E W

1. **FOCUS** What are natural resources and why are they important?
2. **CONNECT** What natural resources might you have seen on your airplane ride across the United States in Lesson 2?
3. **GEOGRAPHY** Compare the maps on pages 14 and 19. What landforms are most of the mineral resources in the country near?
4. **CRITICAL THINKING** Why do you think there are few farmers and loggers in the desert?
5. **WRITING ACTIVITY** Make a list of five things that you have touched or eaten today. Then write whether each item came from a living or nonliving natural resource.

A Valley or a Dam?

> We do not believe that the vital interests of the nation at large should be sacrificed and so important a part of its National Park destroyed to save a few dollars for local interests.
>
> Sierra Club, 1907

> The city would have a cheap and bountiful supply of electric energy for pumping its water supply and lighting the City and its municipal buildings . . . .
>
> Secretary of the Interior Garfield, 1908

▼ *Below, John Muir (on right) stands with President Theodore Roosevelt. Muir took many important leaders on tours of the Yosemite Valley. He wrote letters to newspapers to tell people about the need to save the nation's natural resources.*

Background

John Muir was the chairman of the Sierra Club committee that drafted the 1907 statement. Muir, a nature lover, had founded the Sierra Club in 1892 to help preserve California's environment.

Muir is best known for his work in California's Yosemite Valley. His studies showed that all living things depend upon each other to live. He believed that harming one form of life could someday harm all living things. Muir saw that the Yosemite Valley was in danger. Lumber companies, for example, were cutting down trees like redwoods and sequoias that had stood for hundreds of years.

Muir started a project to set aside Yosemite as a protected area. As a result, in 1890 Yosemite became a national park.

Conflict Over the Land

Not everyone shared Muir's views about the best use of land and resources. In 1900, the city of San Francisco asked the United States government to build a dam in the Hetch Hetchy Valley of Yosemite. The big concrete dam would trap the waters of the Tuolumne River. That would cause water to build up behind the dam, creating a reservoir. San Francisco wanted the water that the reservoir would hold. The growing city feared it could not survive without the new water supply from the Hetch Hetchy Valley.

Muir, of course, was strongly against the plan. The dammed-up water would flood the valley, destroying the land and trees that provide homes for millions of animals and birds. He suggested that the city find some other source of water. In 1908 the citizens of San Francisco voted in favor of the dam. The national government also said yes to the plan. San Francisco got the water it needed to grow. But a beautiful natural resource disappeared forever.

▲ *Today the Hetch Hetchy Valley is flooded with the waters of the Tuolumne River, above.*

Decision Point

1. What was the argument in favor of building the dam?
2. What was the argument against building the dam?
3. If you had been a San Francisco citizen in 1908, what information would you have wanted to vote wisely on the issue?
4. Imagine that your community today is running out of water. It needs to destroy a nearby natural resource to find a new water supply. What action would you want to take as a citizen?

```
           Should the Hetch
          Hetchy dam be built?
              ↙        ↘
  New water supply      Dam floods valley,
  for San Francisco     destroying major area
  allows city to grow.   of natural beauty.
         ↓                    ↓
                      Look for a different water
   Build the dam.      source for San Francisco.
```

▲ *The O'Shaughnessy Dam was finished in 1923.*

L E S S O N 4

Working with Others

THINKING FOCUS

How are human resources important to the United States?

Key Term

- human resources

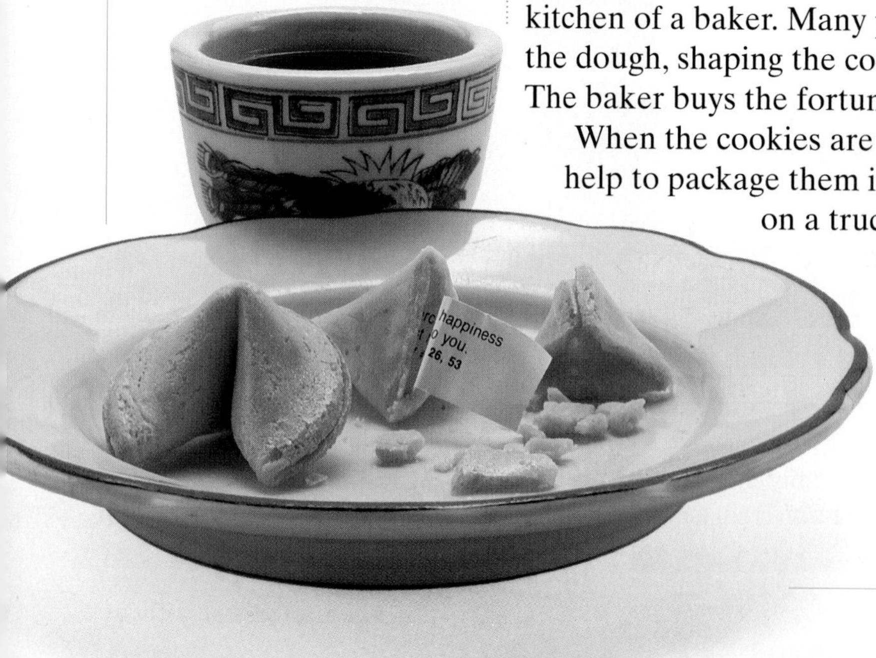

The last part of dinner is the most fun when you're at a Chinese restaurant. After eggrolls, hot and sour soup, and pineapple chicken on steamed rice, Amy Chin delivers a plate of fortune cookies to your table.

You crack open your cookie and read the crumpled piece of paper inside. "Everyone will notice you tomorrow," it says. What does that mean? Will you do something special—or something embarrassing? You ponder this mystery as you munch on the crunchy cookie.

Did you ever wonder how they get the little pieces of paper in those funny, folded cookies? Amy won't tell. That's part of the mystery.

People Are a Resource

There is actually a long story behind the simple fortune cookie in your hand. The story involves a lot more people than you would think. For instance, the cookie started out as flour, water, sweeteners, and other ingredients in the kitchen of a baker. Many people may have helped in mixing the dough, shaping the cookie, and tucking in the fortune. The baker buys the fortunes from a nearby printing shop.

When the cookies are baked and cooled, other people help to package them in bags. Then a driver loads them on a truck and delivers them to Amy Chin's restaurant. Amy started this busy, successful restaurant after she moved here to Seattle, Washington, from China 10 years ago.

Amy serves Chinese tea and fortune cookies to her customers.

◄ *Carpenters are human resources. They use their tools, such as this hammer and tape measure, to build houses.*

Amy Chin and everyone else who brought the fortune cookie to you are human resources. **Human resources** are people who use their ideas, skills, and energy in different ways. Amy's knowledge of Chinese cooking and the energy she puts into her work make her a valuable human resource.

Human and Natural Resources

In Lesson 3 you learned that the country is rich in natural resources. But many of these resources, like oil, coal, or wood, need human resources to develop them.

John Taylor is an example of a human resource who uses natural resources in his work. John is a carpenter in Santa Fe, a small city in the dry mountains of New Mexico. Carpenters do everything from building the frames of houses, to putting in kitchen cabinets and stair rails, to making beautifully carved furniture. They do just about anything that involves working with wood.

Wood from trees is the natural resource that John uses. In fact, he uses many different types of wood—hard or soft, light or dark—depending on what he's making. Few trees grow in the hot, dry climate of the Santa Fe area, so John must use wood that comes from other areas of the country.

John's skills make him a valuable human resource. One of his skills is knowledge—like the knowledge needed to choose the right type of wood for the job. His imagination, his sense of beauty, and his experience are skills too. They help him to come up with handsome designs for his furniture. Finally, John uses another skill, physical strength, to cut, shape, and join pieces of wood into useful objects. ■

■ *How do Amy's and John's jobs combine natural and human resources?*

The Human Mind as a Resource

Anita Sampson is another example of a human resource. Unlike John, she needs no natural resources to do her job. All she needs is a computer.

Anita is a computer programmer in Raleigh, North Carolina. Programs are the instructions that tell computers what do to. Computers do all kinds of jobs, from solving complicated math problems, to playing chess, to helping composers write music.

UNDERSTANDING HUMAN RESOURCES

Did you know that you are a resource? So is Amy Chin, who runs a restaurant. So are John Taylor, the carpenter, and Anita Sampson, the computer programmer.

In Lesson 3, you read about some of the natural resources of the United States. But people are also resources. They are human resources.

People Are Valuable

The term *human resources* has to do with the value, or importance, of people. Every person is valuable in some way and is a part of the nation's resources. These resources include scientists, ballet dancers, children, basketball players, and teachers.

Some of the United States' human resources help to develop its natural resources. For example, loggers cut down the trees used for wood and paper, and miners dig coal and iron out of the earth. By growing crops and raising animals, farmers help develop living natural resources.

The skills, ideas, and energy that all of these people bring to their jobs make them valuable resources. But you don't have to have a job to be a good resource. You are also important for how you help your friends, family, and neighbors. You can read to your younger brothers and sisters or help with charity drives or help clean up a park. In these ways, you yourself help make the United States a country that is rich in human resources.

◄ *Computer programmers need a good education to do their jobs.*

But before a computer can do anything, it needs people to tell it how to do its work. Anita Sampson makes computer programs that teach fourth-graders to speak Spanish. Students anywhere can use the programs in their own computers. Before long, they'll be able to speak *Español*.

Computer programmers like Anita need a lot of knowledge to do their jobs. First of all, Anita needs to know how to speak Spanish. She needs to know how to teach fourth-graders. Finally, she needs to understand how computers work. This is a skill that takes years of study and practice. All of these skills make people like Anita very valuable human resources.

Each part of the country has different kinds of human resources, like Amy Chin, John Taylor, and Anita Sampson. Each has its own natural resources, as you will learn in later chapters. These differences have made cities and states grow in different and special ways. ■

■ *What makes Anita Sampson a valuable human resource?*

R E V I E W

1. **FOCUS** How are human resources important to the United States?
2. **CONNECT** What natural resources might Amy Chin use in her restaurant work?
3. **ECONOMICS** Describe the human resources needed in running a school, a grocery store, and a library.
4. **CRITICAL THINKING** If a worker goes on vacation, or if she is ill and can't work, is she still a human resource? Why or why not?
5. **WRITING ACTIVITY** Interview a family member about his or her job. Then write a paragraph describing the skills that make that person a valuable human resource.

27

Chapter Review

Reviewing Key Terms

climate (p. 12)
continent (p. 10)
ethnic group (p. 5)
human resources (p. 25)
mineral (p. 18)
natural resources (p. 18)
population (p. 7)
vegetation (p. 18)

A. Write the key term that best completes each of the following sentences.
1. Different kinds of _____ grow in the deserts and in the mountains.
2. Miners dig _____, such as coal and iron ore, from the ground.
3. _____ include workers who program computers or serve food at restaurants.
4. The _____ of the United States is about 250 million.
5. We live on the _____ of North America.
6. Each _____ has its own traditions.

B. Write the key term for each definition below.
1. the total number of people who live in an area
2. the kind of weather common to a certain place
3. those things found in nature that help people live their lives
4. one of the seven very large land areas on Earth
5. a group of people who share the same background, which may include language, religion, or other features
6. plants, trees, and grass
7. people who use their ideas, skills, or energy in different ways

Exploring Concepts

A. Copy the chart to the right on a separate piece of paper. Write at least one more example for each category listed on the left.

B. Support each of the following statements with details from this chapter.
1. Millions of people from other countries have settled in the United States.
2. Each ethnic group has its own customs and way of life.
3. All United States citizens have the right to be different.
4. The desert and the plains have different climates.
5. People depend on the natural resources of the land.

What Makes America?	Examples
Ethnic groups	Italians
Landforms	mountains
Natural resources	forests
Human resources	carpenters

6. People are an important human resource for our country because of the work they do.
7. The U.S. Census provides information about the population.
8. People in the United States are both alike and different in many ways.

Reviewing Skills

1. Look at the map on pages 400–401 of the Atlas. Name two countries that are located in the Northern Hemisphere and two countries that are located in the Eastern Hemisphere.
2. Using this same map again, name the two hemispheres that the continent of Australia is located in.
3. Imagine that you were traveling on a road that followed the same path as a meridian. Which direction might you be traveling in?
4. Using the map on pages 404–405 of the Atlas, find which city is further north of the equator: Minneapolis, Minnesota or Augusta, Maine.
5. Is it possible for a country to be in both the Northern and Southern hemispheres? In both the Eastern and Western hemispheres?

Using Critical Thinking

1. "Variety is the spice of life." What does this saying mean to you? How might the saying describe the United States and its people?
2. At the base of the Statue of Liberty is a poem by Emma Lazarus, welcoming people to this country. The poem begins with these words: "Give me your tired, your poor, your huddled masses yearning to breathe free." What do you think these words mean? How do they apply to the United States?

Preparing for Citizenship

1. **GROUP ACTIVITY** Create a "tree of people" that shows the different countries represented by people in your class. First, each student in the class should interview family members or friends to find out what country his or her family came from. Write the names of the people you interviewed and the countries they came from on small strips of paper. Three or four students can then draw a large tree with several branches and place it on the bulletin board. The rest of the class can attach their strips of paper to the tree's branches. Finally, students should work in small groups to locate each of the countries from the strips of paper on the map on pages 400–401 of the Atlas.
2. **ART ACTIVITY** Make a poster that shows your state, its landforms, its population, and other important information about the state. Use the Minipedia on pages 350–399, the maps on pages 406–410 of the Atlas, and an encyclopedia for information. Then create a scene that would help a stranger understand what life in your state is like. Add a slogan that tells why you think your state is a great place to live.
3. **COLLABORATIVE LEARNING** The United States is made up of different landforms, natural resources, and ethnic groups. As a class project, design a large patchwork quilt that shows some of these differences. Work in three groups to draw pictures of the land, people, and resources of the country on large squares of paper of the same size. Then put the pictures together to make the patchwork quilt. Add to the quilt throughout the school year as you read about new places and people.

29

Chapter 2

Regions and Borders

*Imagine what the country would be like if every state were
completely covered with mountains or if flat, treeless land
stretched like a tabletop from coast to coast. Fortunately, the
United States is far more unusual and interesting than that.
Each part of the country has land, people, and activities that
make it special.*

The steep mountains
of the West challenge
brave climbers.

This hawk soars over the
deserts and canyons of
the Southwest.

Many people in the Northeast make a living catching lobster and other seafood in the Atlantic Ocean.

The Midwest is home to many farmers, like the ones shown here harvesting their corn crop.

A scuba diver swims among the brightly colored plants and animals in the waters off the Southeast.

What Is a Region?

Key Terms

- region
- border

➤ *Alligators swim by moving their tails from side to side. They eat fish, snakes, frogs, and turtles.*

It's a hot, humid summer day. You are drifting slowly through the dark and murky water of Florida's Okefenokee *(OH kuh fuh NOH kee)* Swamp. Spanish moss droops like thick, long hair from the cypress trees that grow in the swamp. The only noise is the soft lapping of water against your canoe. Just ahead, you see something that looks like a log covered with dark green moss. You paddle in for a look.

As you get closer, you notice that this "log" is wider in the middle than at the ends. You lean over to get a closer look. You could just about touch two green bumps on the log. . . but suddenly they blink at you! Your heart drops as you realize that you have just come within two feet of an alligator. Terrified, you paddle away as fast as you can.

Paddling wildly, you throw a look over your shoulder to see the green reptile staring at you with its cold eyes. It looks like it might attack any second. Luckily, you manage to paddle the canoe to shore. Breathlessly, you crawl out of the canoe and run to safety.

Where Animals Live

Alligators live on both land and water in places where the climate is warm. With its hot climate, warm waters, and many swamps, lakes, and rivers, Florida is one of the few states where alligators can live. Louisiana and Georgia also have the right conditions for alligators. Most other areas in the United States are too cold for alligators.

The map on this page shows where alligators live in the United States. This area has warm weather, lots of rain, and many swamps and rivers. Because it has so many of the same features, this area can be called a region. A **region** is an area having one or more features in common that set it apart from other areas.

Any feature can define a region. Rainfall, temperature, plant and animal life, and types of land are some features that can set different regions apart. The part of the southeastern United States shown on the map below could be called the alligator region.

How Do We Know?

GEOGRAPHY *To find out where borders of animal regions are, people study the movements of animals. They also find out what types of food, weather, and land an animal needs to live. The animal can make its home in any region that has this food, weather, and land.*

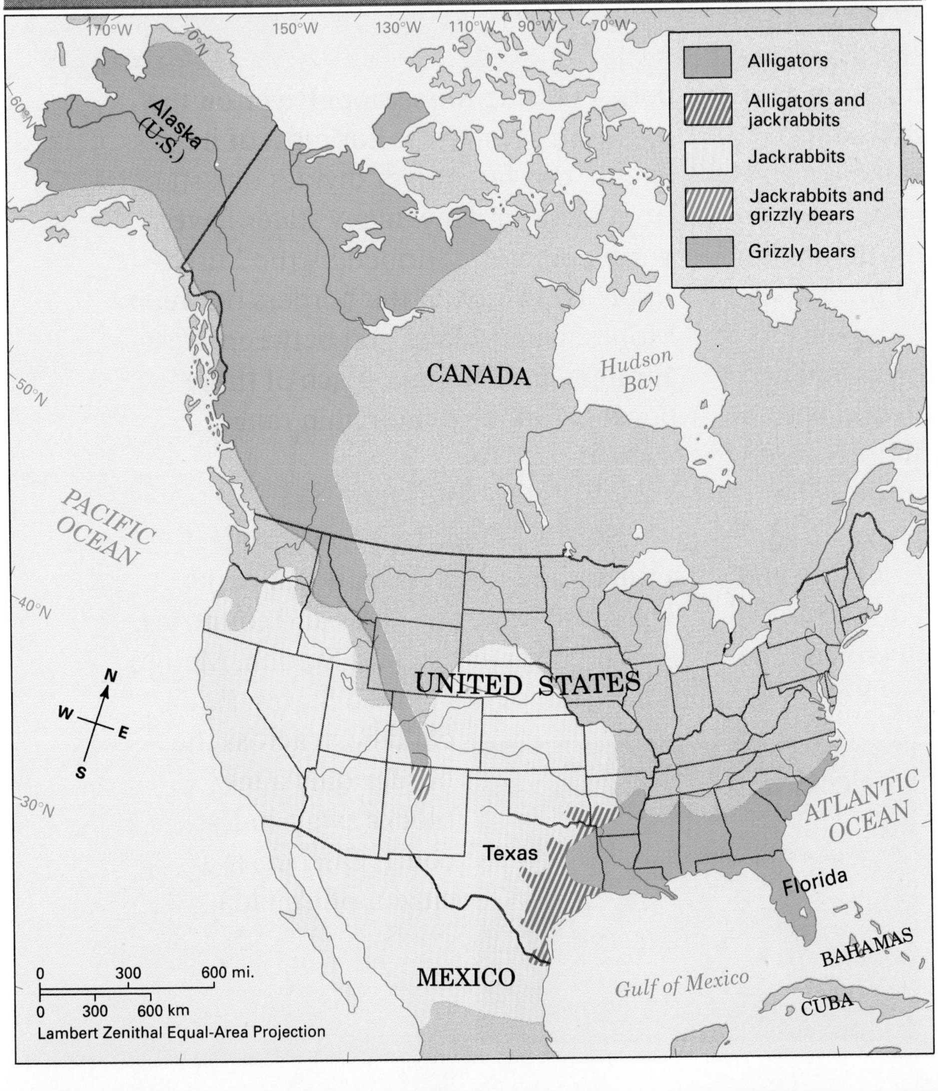

◄ *Name two states in each of the three animals' regions.*

Animal Regions of the United States and Canada

Legend:
- Alligators
- Alligators and jackrabbits
- Jackrabbits
- Jackrabbits and grizzly bears
- Grizzly bears

Map labels: 170°W, 150°W, 130°W, 110°W, 90°W, 70°W, 70°N, 60°N, 50°N, 40°N, 30°N, Alaska (U.S.), CANADA, Hudson Bay, PACIFIC OCEAN, UNITED STATES, Texas, ATLANTIC OCEAN, Florida, BAHAMAS, MEXICO, Gulf of Mexico, CUBA

Scale: 0 300 600 mi. / 0 300 600 km
Lambert Zenithal Equal-Area Projection

Regions and Borders

The Jack Rabbit Region

The map also shows where jack rabbits live. Much of this region is very dry. Most animals could not find enough food in such a dry place. But jack rabbits can eat the cactus, sagebrush, and other plants that grow in this dry area.

Jack rabbits have some very special skills. Because few tall trees and bushes grow in their region, jack rabbits have no place to hide when animals like coyotes and hawks chase them. Instead, they just sit still beside some sagebrush. Their gray-brown fur is almost the same color as sagebrush, so they blend right in with the plant. In this way they hide from the animal chasing them. Other times, they outrun an attacker. Jack rabbits can run as fast as 35 miles per hour and can jump 20 feet in a single leap.

The Grizzly Bear Region

The map on page 33 also shows the home of the grizzly bear. Grizzlies live in the forests that cover much of this

Can you spot the jack rabbit? Notice how it blends right in with the bushes and plants behind it.

UNDERSTANDING BORDERS

The swamps of Florida form a region. Like all regions, this region has a border where it ends and where another region begins. Some borders are natural. Rivers, mountains, and ocean shores are often borders of plant, animal, and weather regions.

Borders that divide towns, countries, and states are agreed upon by people. Sometimes these borders are lines that you see only on a map. For example, on the map on pages 42-43, find the border between Colorado and Wyoming. Without a sign or a marker, you would not know if you crossed the border between these two states.

Borders agreed upon by people can also be natural. Rivers, mountains, lakes, and oceans often act as bor-

ders. Find the Mississippi River on the map on pages 42-43. For most of its length, this large river divides one state from another. How many states have borders that are formed by the Mississippi? Now look at the borders between Montana and Idaho and between West Virginia and Virginia. Each of these borders follows a mountain range.

Why Borders Are Important

Borders made by people protect animals and plants in national parks. They also separate states and countries. A child born in Estcourt Station, Maine, is a citizen of the United States. But a child born across the border only a few blocks away, in Estcourt, Quebec, is a citizen of Canada.

cold, mountainous region. These bears eat nuts, berries, fish, and small animals. During the summer and fall, one bear can eat as much as 80 or 90 pounds of food each day to prepare for the cold winter months ahead. Grizzly bears can weigh as much as 700 pounds and stand as tall as eight feet.

Grizzly bears once lived in many parts of the West. But as people cleared new land to farm and settle, grizzly bears lost their homes. As a result, the grizzly bear region is much smaller today than it was 100 years ago. ■

◄ *Grizzly bears scoop fish right out of the water with their heavy paws or their strong jaws. They also eat berries, like the soapberries pictured below.*

■ *How is the grizzly bear region different from the alligator and jack rabbit regions?*

Where Regions Meet

On the map of animal regions, the end of each region is marked off by a line. This line is called a **border**. A fence around a yard is one kind of border. The line that divides two towns, states, or countries is another kind of border.

Some borders are hard to see. There are no fences or lines to show the border of the alligator region. But an alligator that traveled too far north would get too cold and return to its swamp. You could figure out what marks the border of the alligator region just by watching where the alligators go. One border does not always end where another begins. Sometimes two regions overlap. As the map shows, the alligator and jack rabbit regions overlap in one small area. ■

■ *What is a border?*

R E V I E W

1. **FOCUS** What is a region?
2. **CONNECT** Give an example of an animal region that either has a lot or a little rainfall. What kinds of animals can live in that region?
3. **GEOGRAPHY** Give an example of a landform that can act as a border.

4. **CRITICAL THINKING** Why do you think the jack rabbit's region is larger than the alligator's?
5. **ACTIVITY** Draw a poster showing an animal that lives in your region. Describe the climate of your region and the resources the animal uses to live.

Looking at Regions

Key Terms

- broadleaf tree
- needleleaf tree

At summer camp, you are sitting by a lake with a group of friends who come from different parts of the country. A small insect goes whizzing by. It looks like a blue-green toothpick with big eyes and four large wings. Your friend from the northeastern part of the country says, "Look at that beautiful darning needle!"

Your friend from the Southeast looks up. "I have never heard of a darning needle that flies. That insect was a mosquito hawk. We have lots of them where I live."

Your third friend, who comes from the middle of the country, says, "What are you two talking about? All I saw was a snake feeder."

Everyone turns to you. What do you think just flew by?

"I thought it was a dragonfly."

Who was correct?

Speech Regions

Everyone was correct. The dragonfly has different names in different parts of the country. People in different speech regions of the United States have their own ways of talking. What do you carry water in? A pail? You are from New England. A bucket? You probably live in the Midwest. Do you ride on a teeter-totter as children do in the North? Or do you get on a see-saw like children in the South? Do you get water from a spigot, a faucet, or a tap? These words are used in different parts of the country to name the same thing.

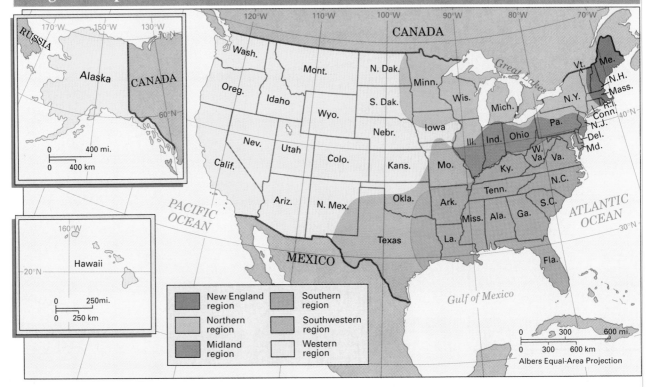

People not only name things differently in the different speech regions of the United States, they also say the same words differently. The different ways that people have of saying words are called accents. For example, look at the map above and find the New England speech region. Many people in this region drop the r sound from words. Try saying the word "farm" without the r sound. It sounds like *fahm*. People in other regions sometimes add the r sound to words not spelled with an r. In the Southwest speech region some people add the r sound. The word "wash" sounds like *warsh*.

People learn to speak from their family, friends, and neighbors. Today many children also learn to speak by listening to and watching television. Most actors and newspeople on television speak with the same accent and use the same words to name things. As a result, many people in different regions are beginning to sound and speak alike. The differences in the speech of various regions have become less noticeable. ■

▲ *Name the speech regions of the United States. For help in reading a regions map like this one, see page G11 in the* Map and Globe Handbook.

■ *Why are there differences in speech in the United States?*

Forest Regions

Another way to divide the United States into regions is by looking at the trees that grow in each part of the country. **Broadleaf trees** are trees with wide, flat leaves and include maples, oaks, and ashes. The leaves on broadleaf trees

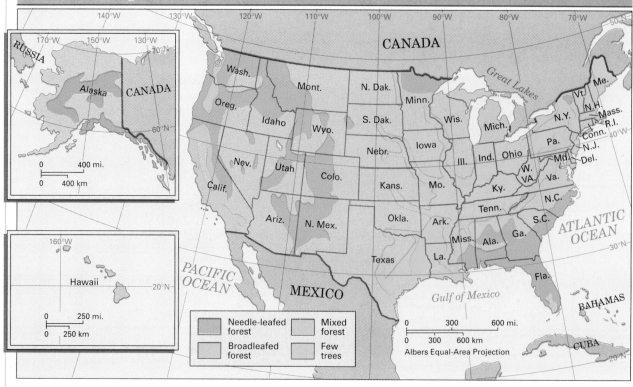

Needle-leafed forest

Broadleafed forest

Mixed forest

Few trees

Albers Equal-Area Projection

▲ *Which western state has broadleafed forests?*

usually turn beautiful colors and fall to the ground each autumn. These trees need two months without frost each year. The map on this page shows that the broadleaf tree region is in the Eastern United States.

Needleleaf trees include pines, spruces, firs, and other trees with very thin, narrow leaves. If you compare a sewing needle to a leaf from one of these trees, you will see how these leaves got their name. These trees usually stay green all year round. Most needleleaf trees grow well in the drier soil and cool climate of the northern regions and the mountains. Other kinds of needleleaf trees grow well in the warm and wet climate of the Southeast.

Climate, temperature, rainfall, and soil will tell what kind of trees will grow in an area. Both broadleaf trees and needleleaf trees will grow in some regions. These regions are often found in areas between two regions where only one type of tree is found. In other regions, very few trees grow at all. ■

➤ *Looking at these illustrations of a broadleaf and a needleleaf tree branch, it's easy to see where these trees got their names.*

■ *Why do the broadleaf tree and needleleaf tree regions overlap?*

Regions You Live In

▼ *Your home is a region within the region of your block, within the region of your neighborhood, within the region of your school district.*

The United States can be divided into regions in many other ways besides speech and the types of trees. Defining a region helps people group together places that share important features. This helps to compare the different parts of the country with each other. It also helps to understand how different people in the regions live.

The type of region you look at depends on what you want to know. Are you planning a winter vacation to a warm place? A map of climate regions will show you where the weather is warm. Do you want to know where the food you eat comes from? A map of the country's farming regions will help you find the answer.

The place where you live is part of many different kinds of regions. You live in a speech region, a forest region, a climate region, and a farming region. You also live in many smaller regions. For example, your block is a region. What features makes your block different from other blocks? Perhaps the houses on your block are all built in the same style. Or maybe a certain kind of tree grows on your block.

Your block is also part of a neighborhood region. The parks, trees, and houses are all things that define your neighborhood. Another region you live in is called a school district. This region is the area that includes the homes of all the students who go to your school. Wherever you live, you are part of many regions all at the same time. ■

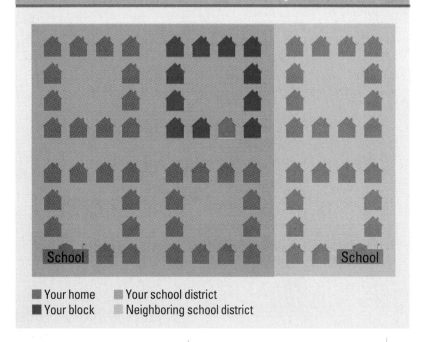

School Districts in Your Community

■ Your home   ■ Your school district
■ Your block   □ Neighboring school district

■ *Why is it helpful to divide the United States into regions?*

R E V I E W

1. **FOCUS** In what ways can the United States be divided into regions?
2. **CONNECT** What kind of trees are most common in the alligator region?
3. **CULTURE** Describe the features that set your neighborhood apart from other neighborhoods.
4. **CRITICAL THINKING** Compare the two maps in this lesson. What forest region covers most of the New England speech region?
5. **ACTIVITY** Draw a map of one region that you live in. Identify the borders and explain what makes this region different from other regions.

39

Regions of the United States

Key Term

• geography

➤ *If you were a creature from outer space and saw flowers blooming near a snow-covered mountain, what would you think? The picture shows avalanche lilies at Mount Rainier National Park in Washington.*

Imagine that five creatures from outer space beam down to earth to explore the United States. Each is sent to a different part of the country. After spending a day looking around, they report back to their leader.

"The United States is nothing but mountains. There are hardly any roads," says the first. "Besides a few cities on the coast, very few people seem to live there."

The second steps up. "Coast? I didn't see any coast. The country is as dry as dust. I do agree about the mountains. The land takes on many strange and beautiful shapes."

"You two are crazy," says the third. "There is no coast. And mountains? No way. The United States is flat, flat, flat. There are lots of people, and most of the land is farms."

"You are all wrong," interrupts the fourth. "The United States is wet and green. It rains all day long. I got lost in the woods and fell in a swamp. A fisherman caught me in his net. If I hadn't beamed up, I'd be soup right now."

As the four argue, the fifth creature smiles. "Leader, I don't know what country my friends went to, but let me tell you what the United States is really like. It's a huge city with millions of people, many tall buildings, and roads covered with cars."

The leader is confused. She does not know who to believe. "How can I learn what the United States is really like?" she wonders.

Dividing the Nation

How would you give the leader a clearer picture of the United States? After all, the creatures' reports leave a lot out. They don't mention thick forests, mountains of snow and ice, or huge fresh-water lakes. These are all part of the geography of the United States. **Geography** is the study of the land, water, plants, animals and climate of a region. It is also the study of how the people have used the land and its resources.

Dividing the Country Into Regions

In this book, you will learn about large groups of states that make up five regions of the United States. These regions are the Southeast, Northeast, Midwest, Southwest, and the West. You can see these regions, as well as the weather they have, in the Closer Look on page 42-43.

What makes these five groups of states regions? One way to answer that question is to look at the geography of the Southeast, the first region you will study in this book. The Southeast has three main landforms—the flat Coastal Plain, the hilly Piedmont, and the mountainous Appalachians. Many of the states in the Southeast have resources such as fish, lumber, coal, and rich farmland.

But it is not just landforms and resources that make the Southeast different from other regions. The climate and the ways people work with the land also help to define the Southeast as a region. For example, temperatures in the Southeast are warmer than in the Northeast. More rain falls in the Southeast than in much of the Southwest. The warm climate of the Southeast has made it a rich farming region as well as a popular vacation spot. The combination of many similar features such as land, climate, resources, and vegetation make the states in the Southeast one region. Other states sharing similar features can also be grouped into one region. ■

▲ *In the West, redwood trees can grow as high as a 30-story building and can live thousands of years. They are the largest and one of the oldest kinds of trees on earth.*

■ *What are some features that help to define a region of the United States?*

Weather in the Five Regions

It's a Saturday morning in October and you're ready to go outside and play. What's the weather like? That depends on which of the five regions you live in. This morning, some kids will be running out into the bright sunshine. Others will be leaping into ankle-deep snow. Take a look at this map to see what kids in all five regions are doing today.

Alaska

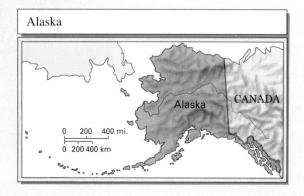

0   200   400 mi.

0 200 400 km

Alaska   CANADA

Pull! Pull! Pull! These California kids are having a tug-of-war. It's a little cloudy today. Moisture from the Pacific Ocean makes clouds and fog roll in along much of the West Coast. But the air is breezy and comfortable—warm enough to wear your shorts, but cool enough to play a tough game like this.

Washington

Oregon

Idaho

W E S T

Nevada

Utah

California

Arizona

Hawaii

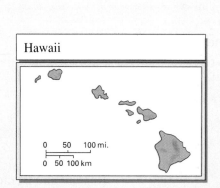

0   50   100 mi.

0 50 100 km

Snowball fight! Yesterday was warm, but last night temperatures dropped and the first snow fell in the upper Midwest. These Minnesota girls know what to do today.

Jack-o'-lanterns will appear in the windows tonight. October is harvest time in Vermont. On frosty fall mornings like this, many farms in the Northeast let you go into the fields and pick your own pumpkins or apples.

It still feels like summer along the Georgia coast. So these boys head for the beach to enjoy what's left of the hot weather. If they're lucky, the beach weather could last into November.

Montana
North Dakota
Minnesota
Michigan
Maine
Vt.
New York
N.H.
Mass.
NORTHEAST
Conn.
R.I.
South Dakota
Wisconsin
MIDWEST
Iowa
Pennsylvania
N.J.
Md.
Del.
Wyoming
Illinois
Indiana
Ohio
W. Va.
Virginia
Colorado
Nebraska
Kansas
Missouri
Kentucky
North Carolina
New Mexico
Oklahoma
Arkansas
Tennessee
SOUTHEAST
South Carolina
SOUTHWEST
Miss.
Alabama
Georgia
Texas
Louisiana
Florida
MEXICO

N
W E
S

0   200   400 mi.
0   200   400 km
Lambert Equal-Area Projection

Soccer, anyone? Kids in the Southwest can play outside just about anytime of the year. After a long, scorching summer, it has finally "cooled down" to about 80 degrees.

How People Use the Land

Across Time & Space

The work people do has changed a lot since the United States became a country in 1776. Then, almost everyone either worked on farms or made things for people who did. Today, about 2.9 million farm workers can produce enough food to feed all 250 million people in the United States, as well as millions of people in other countries.

➤ *A map can give you an idea of the geography of a region.*

You wouldn't open a ski shop in the middle of the desert. And you'd have a hard time growing oranges on a snowy mountaintop. It's easy, then, to see why people in each of the five regions make their living in different ways.

When settlers moved into the different regions, they looked at the land and resources there. In some places, people found the type of land and climate needed to farm. In others, they found forests with animals for hunting and flat grasslands for raising cattle. Some regions provided trees for logging or metals to be mined. Other regions had rivers for water power and for transporting factory goods.

As they have worked with a region's resources, people have often shaped and changed the land of a region. In the Southwest, people turned deserts into productive farmland by figuring out how to channel water from faraway rivers. The Northeast was once covered with forests. Today the land of this region is filled with cities, factories, and people because of the many enterprises in that region.

To understand the regions of the United States, you must look at the landforms, the climates, and the natural resources of these regions. You must also examine how people have shaped and formed their regions over time. This book will give you an opportunity to explore the history of the regions of the United States and to discover how those regions came to be what they are today. ■

■ *Name one way in which the five regions are all different.*

R E V I E W

1. **FOCUS** Why do we divide the United States into five different regions?

2. **CONNECT** Compare the map on page 38 with the map on pages 42-43. What kind of trees grow best in the Midwest?

3. **GEOGRAPHY** What are the five major regions of the United States?

4. **CRITICAL THINKING** List four things that people do that have changed the region you live in.

5. **ACTIVITY** Use the map on pages 42-43 to help you draw a map of your region. Label each of the states in your region.

Locating Places

Here's Why

Suppose you want to locate an unfamiliar city. You can do this by looking up the city in a gazetteer, at the back of this book or in an atlas. A gazetteer gives you the city's latitude and longitude which you can use to locate the city on a map.

Here's How

Look at the map on this page. Notice that the grid on this map is formed by latitude and longitude lines spaced 5 degrees apart. Find the latitude line for 30°N, drawn across the map from left to right. Run your finger along this line until you come to the longitude line for 90°W. New Orleans is located at the place where the line for 30°N and the line for 90°W come together. Therefore, we say the location of New Orleans is

30°N, 90°W. Notice that the latitude is always given first and then the longitude.

Try It

Look at the map again. Identify the cities that are found at these locations:
1. 40°N, 75°W.
2. 40°N, 90°W.
3. 40°N, 105°W
4. 35°N, 85°W

Next give the latitude and the longitude for Reno, St. Joseph, and Houston.

Apply It

Look up two state capitals, Augusta and Springfield, in the gazetteer on pages 411–413. Write down the latitude and the longitude for each one. Using this information, locate both cities on the map on pages 404–405. On that map, what is the city nearest to each of these capitals?

Eight Cities in the United States

Chapter Review

Reviewing Key Terms

A. Write the key term for each of the definitions below.
1. an area that has certain features, such as amount of rainfall, in common
2. a tree like maples, oaks, and ashes
3. the study of a region's land, climate, and resources and of the way people use the land and its resources
4. a tree like pines, spruces, and firs
5. a line on a map that divides two states or countries or marks off the edge of a region

B. Write the key terms that best complete the sentences in the paragraphs below.

The five major ____ in the United States are the Northeast, Southeast, Midwest, Southwest, and the West. Each area has special features of its own that set it apart from the others. Some areas have trees with large leaves that turn color and fall off each autumn. These ____ grow especially well in the East. Other areas have ____, the trees with narrow, thin leaves. In some regions, both types of trees grow well.

Look at a map to find the region in which you live. What ____ separate that area from the other regions?

Exploring Concepts

A. Copy the chart below on a separate piece of paper. Use information from this chapter to give examples of different kinds of regions.

B. Support each of the following statements with information from lessons in this chapter.
1. An area that has the same animal life or plant life can form a region.

Features that define a region	Examples discussed in this chapter
Where a type of animal lives	
The way people speak	
Types of trees	
The kind of weather	

2. Some borders between states and regions follow natural landforms, such as rivers and mountains.
3. The people in different speech regions may name the same thing differently.
4. The borders of different regions can overlap with each other.
5. It would be very difficult to describe the United States in just one single sentence.
6. The physical characteristics of a region can affect the region's history.
7. People consider a region's land and resources before deciding how to earn a living there.

Reviewing Skills

1. Look at the latitude and longitude lines on the map of Alaska to the right. Then answer the following questions.
   a. What city is located near 60°N, 150°W?
   b. What city is located near 65°N, 140°W?
   c. What is the latitude and the longitude of each of the following Alaskan cities: Ruby? Sitka?

2. Use the map on pages 404–405 of the Atlas to find the latitude and the longitude of a city in your state.

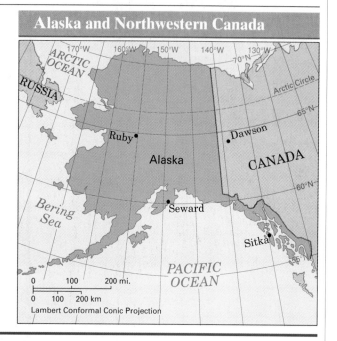

Alaska and Northwestern Canada

Using Critical Thinking

1. Each region in the United States is different. Consider what it would be like if all the regions were alike. Would the regions still be regions?

2. Why is it easier to study the geography of five regions, each made up of several states, than to study the geography of each of the 50 states individually?

Preparing for Citizenship

1. **ART ACTIVITY** Use maps from the Atlas, pages 404 – 410, to find out about the land, population, plant life, climate, and land use in the region in which you live. Then, use this information to draw a scene that shows what life in your region is like.

2. **INTERVIEWING** Interview someone who has moved to your region of the country from another region in the United States. Ask what differences the person notices between the regions. Find out what he or she likes as well as dislikes about each region.

3. **COLLABORATIVE LEARNING** As a class project, make a wall map of the five regions in the United States listed in Lesson 3. Use the map on pages 42– 43 as a model. Have students work in five groups to draw and label the states in each region. Color each region a different color. Use the Minipedia, pages 350 –399, to add information about each state. Choose two students to make a map legend naming each region and showing its color.

   Next, make a map quiz game. Each person in the class should write two questions about the map. Include questions such as the following: How many states are in the Midwest? For which region does the Pacific Ocean form a natural border? How many states share a border with California? Choose one person to ask the questions. Players should use the map to answer.

Unit 2

The Southeast

For hundreds of years, people stayed away from the Everglades. This Florida swamp is the kingdom of birds, reptiles, and insects. Hungry alligators cruise the waters and mosquitos fill the hot, humid air. The marsh is draped with Spanish moss. The Seminole Indians called this dark jungle Pahay-okee or "Grassy Water." Today, thousands of visitors marvel at the exotic plantlife and wildlife.

Everglades National Park in Florida.
Photograph Copyright David Muench.

The Southeast

A Sun-Splashed Land

Sun shines on the Southeast and warms the land. A long, sandy coastline surrounds much of the region. From the banks of the Mississippi River, to the warm mountain forests, to the flat and beautiful coastal plains, the Southeast is a comfortable, livable place. From the earliest times, the region's soil, trees, wildlife, and mineral resources have drawn people southward.

Magnolia blossoms
from Mississippi

Pine trees
from North Carolina

The Appalachian Mountains
in Kentucky

The Southeast

The 12 states of the region
- Alabama
- Arkansas
- Florida
- Georgia
- Kentucky
- Louisiana
- Mississippi
- North Carolina
- South Carolina
- Tennessee
- Virginia
- West Virginia

Why do birds head south for the winter? To come to the warm climate and beautiful wilderness of this sunny region. With mild winters and hot summers, the Southeast is home to millions of birds, animals, and insects. More than 600 kinds of fish fill the warm waters off the southern tip of Florida.

Population: 59,259,299
Size: 549,210 square miles. The region includes the continent's southernmost U.S. city: Key West, Florida.

Major resources: clay, coal, farmland, lumber, natural gas, oil, stone

One of the nation's longest rivers, the Mississippi, flows through the western part of the region. The rain that falls on about one million square miles of land drains into the Mississippi. The river starts in Minnesota, then widens as it runs for 2,350 miles, finally emptying into the Gulf of Mexico.

The Appalachian mountains form an unbroken chain from northern Alabama through Maryland. The Southeast lumber industry uses the evergreen and oak trees in the forests to make wood and paper products. Coal and other minerals are buried beneath these mountains.

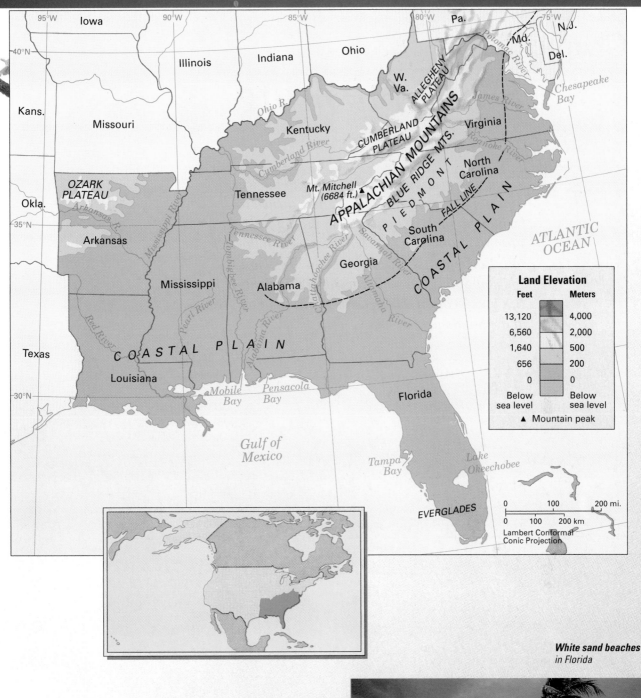

Iowa

95°W 90°W 85°W 80°W Pa.

Md. N.J.

40°N Illinois Indiana Ohio Del.

Kans. W. Va. ALLEGHENY PLATEAU Potomac River Chesapeake Bay

Missouri Kentucky CUMBERLAND PLATEAU James River

Ohio R. APPALACHIAN MOUNTAINS Virginia

OZARK PLATEAU Cumberland River Roanoke River

Okla. Arkansas R. BLUE RIDGE MTS. North Carolina

35°N Tennessee Mt. Mitchell (6684 ft.)▲ PIEDMONT FALL LINE

Arkansas Tennessee River South Carolina COASTAL PLAIN ATLANTIC OCEAN

Mississippi River Savannah River

Mississippi Chattahoochee River Georgia Altamaha River

Alabama Tombigbee River

Texas COASTAL PLAIN Alabama River

Red River Pearl River

Louisiana Mobile Bay Pensacola Bay Florida

30°N

Gulf of Mexico Tampa Bay Lake Okeechobee

EVERGLADES

Land Elevation

Feet	Meters
13,120	4,000
6,560	2,000
1,640	500
656	200
0	0
Below sea level	Below sea level

▲ Mountain peak

0 100 200 mi.

0 100 200 km

Lambert Conformal Conic Projection

Thousands of miles of coast surround the Southeast. The region has many important harbors. The waters of the Atlantic Ocean and the Gulf of Mexico provide good fishing. And the flat, sandy beaches draw many people to the coast.

White sand beaches in Florida

Chapter 3

Early Farming

When European settlers first came to the warm coastal plain of the Southeast, they turned to farming to make a living. First, the colonists in Virginia found that tobacco grew well in the rich soil. Later, people discovered that the swampy coast of South Carolina was ideal for planting rice. But it was cotton that became the king of all crops in the Southeast.

Slaves carried cotton in from the field at the end of the work-day. Notice the small children, who worked in the field with their parents. One woman holds a baby while she balances a cotton load on her head.

| 1580 | 1640 | 1700 |

1607

This painting shows Rice Hope, a South Carolina rice plantation. Like most rice plantations in South Carolina, Rice Hope covered acres and acres of land.

Music was important to the African slaves. This fiddle, made from a gourd, shows how slaves mixed African and English musical traditions.

1760

1820

1880

1840 The Southeast becomes the world's leading producer of cotton.

1865

L E S S O N   1

The Tobacco Fields

THINKING FOCUS

Why did tobacco farming spread in Virginia?

Key Terms

- colony
- cash crop

L and ho!" Excited voices spread the news. From the ships' decks, the distant Virginia coastline looked like a thin green ribbon of land. As the three wooden ships sailed closer, the settlers saw thick forests along the shore. The ships nosed into a big, calm bay. The water sparkled with fish. It looked like you could just scoop them up with a frying pan.

The ships entered the wide mouth of a river. Following the river inland, the settlers gazed at the green meadows that lined the riverbanks. This seemed to be the perfect spot to start the settlement they would call Jamestown. Jamestown is shown in the picture below.

Surely this land held other treasures. The men had heard of Spanish explorers finding gold and silver in the New World. Excited, they scooped up soil filled with shining specks and sent it back to England. But it was not gold. It was "fool's gold," just shiny pieces of worthless rock.

The settlers were disappointed. But in a few years, they would learn how valuable the rich soil was in other ways.

Tobacco Becomes Virginia's Gold

More disappointments came to the settlers of Jamestown. Many people became sick. The settlers in the new colony often ran out of food. A **colony** is a settlement or group of settlements far away from the home country. Even with help from England, life was still hard in Virginia.

One settler had an idea that would help the colony. John Rolfe had seen local Indians growing tobacco in their gardens. They smoked dried tobacco in wooden pipes. Rolfe knew that many English people also smoked tobacco. Maybe they would want to buy Virginia's tobacco.

The Indian's tobacco was too bitter. Rolfe needed to find a better-tasting plant. He filled his garden with different tobacco plants and worked to grow a plant that tasted good enough to send to England. When Rolfe's tobacco arrived in England, people rushed to buy it.

Soon many people in Jamestown were growing tobacco to send to England. Tobacco was a **cash crop**, a crop that farmers raised for money, not for their own use. With this money, farmers could buy land or fine clothes and furniture from England. Tobacco helped to make the colony rich. ■

▲ *John Rolfe brought tobacco seeds to Virginia from South America. Today, farmers in the Southeast grow four kinds of tobacco.*

■ *Why is tobacco said to be Virginia's gold?*

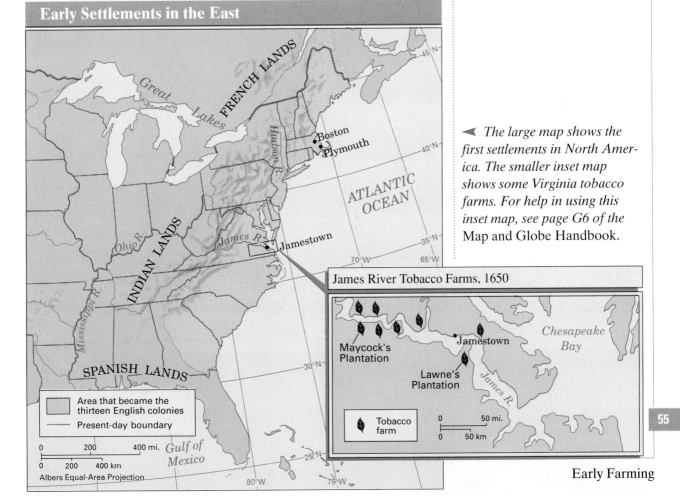

Early Settlements in the East

Great Lakes

FRENCH LANDS

Hudson R.

Boston
Plymouth

45°N

40°N

ATLANTIC OCEAN

70°W   65°W

Ohio R.

James R.   Jamestown

35°N

INDIAN LANDS

Mississippi R.

SPANISH LANDS

30°N

Area that became the thirteen English colonies

Present-day boundary

0   200   400 mi.   *Gulf of Mexico*
0   200   400 km

Albers Equal-Area Projection

80°W   75°W   25°N

◄ *The large map shows the first settlements in North America. The smaller inset map shows some Virginia tobacco farms. For help in using this inset map, see page G6 of the* Map and Globe Handbook.

James River Tobacco Farms, 1650

Maycock's Plantation

Jamestown   *Chesapeake Bay*

Lawne's Plantation

James R.

Tobacco farm

0   50 mi.
0   50 km

Early Farming

Raising Tobacco

Tobacco plants sprouted everywhere, even in dirt roads. Virginia turned out to be the perfect place to grow tobacco. The soil was rich and there was plenty of rainfall. Also, the weather was warm throughout the summer, when the tobacco plant grew. People started tobacco farms all along the James River, as the map on page 55 shows.

> *This 1750 illustration shows African slaves engaged in various stages of preparing tobacco for shipment from Virginia. The woman prepares the tobacco for packing in barrels.*

Tobacco plants take important minerals out of the soil. Because of this, tobacco does not grow well on the same land year after year. So farmers had to clear forests to add new, rich fields to their farms. As a result, tobacco farms became larger and larger.

The planters needed many workers to clear fields and grow tobacco. Growing tobacco was hard work and, as the graph below shows, took all year. In the early spring, workers knelt in the fields, planting each small plant by hand. In late summer, the tobacco ripened. Workers picked the leaves and took them to barns to dry. Finally, the leaves were packed in barrels. Some barrels weighed almost 1,000 pounds. Groups of men pulled the barrels to docks and loaded them onto ships headed for England.

Planters built docks on the riverbanks of their farms,

Across Time & Space

People in the 1600s did not know about the health dangers linked to smoking tobacco. Today, people know that tobacco smoking causes illnesses such as lung cancer and heart disease.

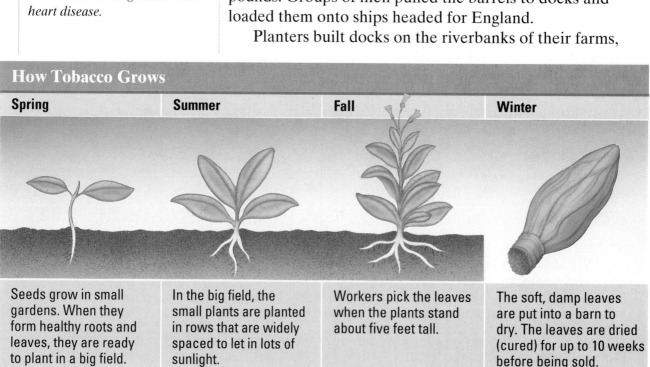

How Tobacco Grows

Spring	Summer	Fall	Winter
Seeds grow in small gardens. When they form healthy roots and leaves, they are ready to plant in a big field.	In the big field, the small plants are planted in rows that are widely spaced to let in lots of sunlight.	Workers pick the leaves when the plants stand about five feet tall.	The soft, damp leaves are put into a barn to dry. The leaves are dried (cured) for up to 10 weeks before being sold.

where English ships could load the tobacco. When the English ships arrived, workers unloaded supplies from England. Then they rolled the barrels of tobacco onto the ships.

Poor People Make a Deal

News of tobacco farms spread in England. Many people wanted to come to Virginia. But most of the people could not pay for the trip across the ocean. These people made a deal.

Planters would pay a person's fare to come from England. The person paid the planters back by working as a servant on their farms for five to seven years. The servant's "masters" gave him or her food and a place to live. One servant wrote about this difficult life in a poem:

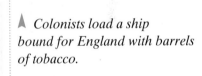

Colonists load a ship bound for England with barrels of tobacco.

N o Shoes nor stockings had I to wear,
Nor hat, nor cap, both head and feet were
bare,
Thus dress'd into the Field I nex[t] must go,
Amongst tobacco plants all day to hoe
At day break in the morn our work began
And so held to the setting of the Sun.

Most servants did not live long enough to be given their freedom. Those who did got an ax, a hoe, a suit of clothes, and a barrel of corn. It was hard to begin a farm with just these items, but for some people it was a start.

More people came to Virginia. As the tobacco trade grew, so did the colony. At the same time, nearby colonies discovered their own important cash crops, and also grew. ■

■ *What deal did some people make in order to come to Virginia?*

R E V I E W

1. **FOCUS** Why did tobacco farming spread in Virginia?
2. **CONNECT** Look at the climate map on page 408 and describe Virginia's climate.
3. **GEOGRAPHY** Why was the James River important to early tobacco farmers?
4. **CRITICAL THINKING** Why do you think some people would give up their freedom for five to

seven years to come to Virginia?

5. **WRITING ACTIVITY** Imagine that you live on a tobacco farm. Write a letter to a friend describing what happens when an English ship comes to your farm. What did the ship bring for you? What else did it bring for your family?

Early Farming

LESSON 2

A Rice Coast

Key Terms

- slave
- plantation

➤ *Rice plants grow to be two to six feet tall. As the grain ripens, the plants turn yellow.*

Imagine yourself working in a swampy field on a hot summer afternoon. The sun beats down on your head, making your hair feel like it's on fire. Sweat drips down your cheeks. Its salty taste stings your dry, cracked lips. When you look up to wipe your eyes, the sun blinds you. You wave back to another worker, maybe to your best friend or your mother. But with the blazing sun in your eyes, it is impossible to make out the bent shapes across the field. With stooping backs and lowered heads, workers sink their hoes again and again into the swampy field. "Come on, keep going, keep going," you say to yourself. "Just one more row."

Mosquitoes buzz around your ears, biting your neck, your arms, and any other part of you that is not covered. They like to swarm around your ankles, which are coated with mud. As you reach down to scratch a bite, you look out at the thousands of green rice plants.

Just one more row. Your aching feet slog through the mud. Soon you will be finished. Until tomorrow, when more rows of rice will be waiting to be hoed.

◄ *The flow of water into the rice fields always had to be controlled. Slaves are shown here filling in a break in a rice field bank.*

Rice Takes Hold

Workers toiled in rice fields like these in the Carolina colony. This colony started just south of Virginia, where North Carolina and South Carolina are today. In the 1700s, rice became an important crop for the region. People in England wanted rice from the Carolina colony just as they wanted tobacco from Virginia. Knowing that rice would bring good prices, the Carolina farmers planted more of it.

No one knows when settlers first began growing rice in the Southeast. They may have struggled for years to raise crops. But people do know when settlers grew the first large crops of rice. It was in the late 1600s, when Africans were brought to the Carolina colony.

The Africans had not come to the colonies by choice. They had been taken from their homes in Africa and brought by force to the colonies. There they were sold as slaves. A **slave** is a person whose rights or freedoms have been denied. Slaves and their children were owned by white planters.

Slaves worked the rice fields in the Carolina colony, and rice became a successful crop. The area had the perfect conditions for growing rice. It had a warm climate, with long, hot summers. Carolina also had plenty of rain, which rice needs to grow. Most important, swamps covered much of

■ *How did the African slaves contribute to growing rice?*

▼ *This painting shows a rice plantation called Mepkin in the Carolina Colony. The plantation boasted 3,000 acres of land.*

the Carolina coast. Slaves carved out rice fields from these swamps because rice plants grow best when their roots are under water. Planters used many slaves and workers to grow rice on large areas of land. Soon these **plantations**, or large farms, were common throughout the Carolina colony. ■

Life in the Lowlands

Springtime on Waverly plantation in the Carolina colony in the early 1800s meant a lot of work. The slaves' first job in the rice fields was to repair old ditches and make new ones. When the digging was done, the slaves planted the rice seeds. Then they let water in through the ditches to flood the fields.

As the rice grew, slaves flooded the fields, drained them, and hoed the soil over and over again throughout the summer. Working in the rice fields was hard. African men, women, and children who worked in the fields had to fight the heat and swarms of mosquitoes. Many of the slaves died from the heat and disease. What made life even harder was that most slave families could not stay together. Family members, even children, were sold to other plantation owners.

September was harvest time on the plantation. The slaves worked quickly to save the crops before flocks of shiny black bobolinks flew in from the north. These "rice birds" gobbled up the crops. After cutting down the six-foot-tall rice plants, the slaves pounded and shook the plants to remove the grain. Finally, they put the rice into large bags.

The rice trade helped Charles Town grow into a busy city. Many silversmiths made fine things such as this sugar bowl for Charles Town's wealthy residents.

Rice Develops a City

After the harvest, plantation owners shipped the rice down the rivers to Charles Town. This city, which is now Charleston, South Carolina, became an important port because of the rice trade. The Virginia colony's rivers were deep enough for English ships to sail directly to the docks of the tobacco plantations. But the large ships coming to Charles Town could not sail up the shallow Carolina rivers to the rice plantations. Instead, they docked in Charles Town's harbor to pick up the loads of rice that the plantation owners had brought in for them.

In addition to being the business center of the colony, Charles Town was a summer meeting place for planters and their families. While slaves tended the rice fields on the plantations, planters escaped the heat and the mosquitoes. On Charles Town's cool coast, they lived in fine homes surrounded by colorful gardens. Charles Town grew as more money came in from the abundant rice crops. Rice became the second crop to help settlement in the colonies. ■

■ *How did Charleston's location help it become a leading Southern city?*

R E V I E W

1. **FOCUS** What helped rice become an important crop in the Carolina colony?

2. **CONNECT** Why was the life of a slave more hopeless than that of a servant?

3. **GEOGRAPHY** What kind of land and climate did rice need to grow?

4. **CULTURE** How did the rice crop help Charleston develop into a major Southeastern city?

5. **ACTIVITY** Look up South Carolina in the Minipedia on page 389. Is rice still a major product of the area? List two major crops now grown in South Carolina.

Early Farming

L E S S O N 3

A Cotton Kingdom

THINKING FOCUS

What events helped the growing of cotton spread throughout the Southeast?

Key Terms

- invention
- growing season
- precipitation

▼ *A sample book showed English people the many types of cotton cloth they could buy.*

The heap of cotton looks like a mountain of white snow inside the barn. Slaves—men, women, boys, and girls—empty their sacks, adding more white fluff to the pile. The air is thick with dust. As the red sun sets over the wide, green fields, the cotton mountain grows higher and higher.

The slaves have been picking cotton since dawn, but their work is not over. After working all day in the fields, they must pick the seeds out of the cotton bolls. A cotton boll is about the size of a golf ball, and its shell is sharp and prickly. Inside the boll are seeds with white fibers, or little threads, growing from them. A cotton boll holds about 50 seeds. As the slaves handle hundreds of bolls, their hands get scratched and their fingers ache. Picking out cotton seeds is like having to get all the burrs out of your socks after you have walked through a weedy field. In the late 1700s, it could take a person as many as 10 hours to clean the seeds out of just one pound of cotton fiber.

Cotton's Beginnings

Somebody had to come up with a better and faster way to get the seeds out of the cotton. Planters knew that if they could clean cotton faster they would make more money. Like tobacco and rice, cotton was another southeastern crop that people in England wanted to buy.

A former teacher from New England finally solved the problem. In the 1790s, Eli Whitney moved to South Carolina, where he met Catherine Greene. Perhaps Mrs. Greene told him about the problem of cleaning cotton. Or maybe he saw for himself what a long job it was. Whitney decided to make a machine to separate cotton seeds from the fiber.

Whitney built a machine with wire teeth that would comb the seeds from the fiber. He called his invention the cotton gin. An **invention** is a new tool that helps people to do a task more quickly and more easily.

Whitney's invention was a great help to the cotton planters of the Southeast. Now they could keep up with the many orders of cotton coming in from England. The English wanted cotton because it made comfortable clothes. Cotton could also be washed easily and dyed beautiful colors.

There are two types of cotton—long-strand cotton and short-strand cotton. Long-strand cotton grows best in the wet soil of the coast and its seeds are taken out more easily. Short-strand cotton can be grown in many types of soil, but its seeds are harder to remove.

Using the cotton gin, a worker could clean as much short-strand cotton in one day as 50 workers could clean by hand. Farmers all over the Southeast began to grow short-strand cotton. Inland states such as Mississippi, Alabama, and Louisiana became important cotton-growing areas. The map on page 65 shows how cotton growing spread. ■

▼ *Eli Whitney and his cotton gin are shown here. The gin's white teeth combed the seeds out of the cotton.*

■ *How did Eli Whitney help the Southeast produce more cotton?*

King Cotton

Using the new cotton gin, so much cotton could be harvested and sold that cotton was called the "king" of the Southeast. Cotton plantations varied in size. Some were very big, with hundreds of slaves. Many more were smaller, with only family members and a small number of slaves working the fields. Most plantations had a main house, some small cabins where the slaves lived, and acres of cotton fields.

Life on the Plantation

The wife of the planter ran the household. She watched over the house slaves and nursed people when they were sick. The planter directed all the work on the plantation.

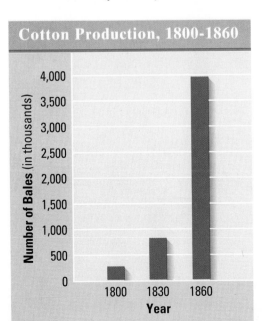

Cotton Production, 1800-1860

Number of Bales (in thousands)

4,000	
3,500	
3,000	
2,500	
2,000	
1,500	
1,000	
500	
0	1800 1830 1860

Year

◄ *The chart shows how cotton production increased after the invention of the cotton gin.*

Early Farming

Meanwhile, the slaves did the hard work in the fields. In her memoirs, Susan Dabney Smedes described life on a plantation in Mississippi, where she grew up in the 1840s and 1850s.

A Southern plantation, well managed, had nearly everything necessary to life within its bounds. At Burleigh there were two carpenters in the carpenter-shop; two blacksmiths in the blacksmith shop; . . . and usually five seamstresses in the house. In the laundry, there were two of the strongest . . . women on the plantation. Boys were kept about, ready to ride for the mail or take notes around the neighborhood.

The climate of the Southeast was perfect for growing cotton. The long, hot summers provided the long growing season that cotton needs. The **growing season** is the time between the last frost in the spring and the first frost in the fall. Cotton must have a growing season of at least six months.

Cotton also needs a certain amount of **precipitation**. Precipitation is any form of water that falls to the earth, such as rain or snow. Cotton needs between 20–60 inches of rain during its growing season. As the map on page 409 shows, many parts of the Southeast get this much rain.

Cotton planting began in the spring, after the danger of frost had passed. After planting the cotton, slaves hoed and weeded the fields during the late spring and summer months. In July, the plantations looked like a sea of cotton

▼ *This painting shows slaves working on a cotton plantation in late summer. The wagon is loaded with bales of cotton.*

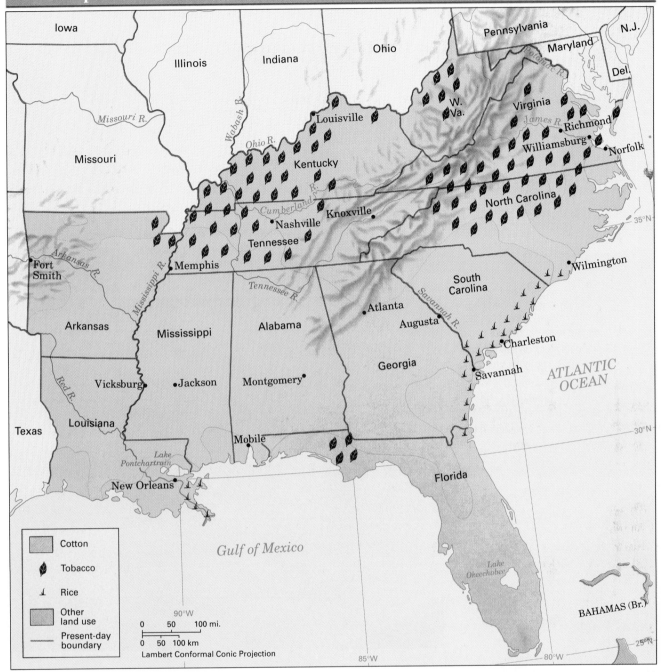

Cotton

Tobacco

Rice

Other land use

Present-day boundary

90°W

0   50   100 mi.

0   50 100 km

Lambert Conformal Conic Projection

blossoms. Finally, in August the cotton bolls started to burst open, showing white, fluffy fibers. Now the cotton plants looked like they were covered with snow.

When the first bolls opened in the late summer, the slaves began picking the cotton from the plants. The cotton had to be picked quickly, otherwise it would change color. When this happened, the crop brought a lower price. Because all the bolls did not open at the same time, picking continued through the fall. Some plantations were still harvesting in late December.

After harvesting the cotton, planters sent it to a nearby

▲ *This map shows where tobacco, rice, and cotton were grown in the Southeast. Can you see why the Southeast was called a cotton kingdom?*

65

A Trip to New Orleans

The cotton harvest is in. It's time to sell! But the busy cotton trading center of New Orleans, Louisiana, is more than 600 miles away from this plantation in Snow Lake, Arkansas. The planter prepares for a boat trip down the Mississippi River. Such a trip might last for over a week.

Cotton bales slide down the long wooden shoot and are stacked 15 feet high. Squawking chickens, fresh eggs, and smoked hams are packed on too. They'll be traded at a store downriver.

Sandbar ahead! Riverboat captains had to be careful not to get their boats stuck on sandbars. A boat could be grounded for days, or even weeks, waiting for the river to rise. Sometimes, if a boat caused a river traffic jam, groups of slaves would have to drag it off the sandbar.

Agents from the Cotton Exchange often met planters at the New Orleans wharf. An agent could answer the planter's many questions: What is the price for cotton today? Where is the best place to sell?

Goods from around the world are on the planter's list of things to buy. With the money from the cotton he's sold, he buys coffee from Mexico, furniture from France, and dishes from England.

city, such as New Orleans, to trade with other merchants. A Closer Look at a trip to New Orleans on page 66 tells more about this journey. The cotton market helped many cities to develop. Memphis, Tennessee, on the Mississippi River, became the greatest inland cotton market in the United States. Cotton was also shipped from coastal cities such as Savannah, Georgia; Mobile, Alabama; and Jacksonville, Florida.

▼ *This flag represented the Confederate states during the Civil War.*

Changes for All

Northerners and Southerners held different views about slavery. Southern plantation owners insisted that they needed slave labor. These owners believed each state had the right to decide whether to allow slavery. Some Northerners believed slavery was wrong. Others believed that slaves were no longer necessary in the South. Northern businesses and farms did not use slaves, but black workers were usually paid less than white workers.

The argument over slavery became more heated. Eleven Southern states decided to leave the rest of the states and form a separate country. As a result, a war broke out in 1861. At the end of the four terrible years of the Civil War, the North won. The country was united again. In 1865 slavery was abolished.

The Civil War left the South in ruins. Plantations and homes had been burned, and cities were destroyed. Thousands of Southern people, both black and white, had died. Many years passed before the Southeast recovered from the war. ■

■ *Describe a slave's life on a cotton plantation in spring, summer, and fall.*

R E V I E W

1. **FOCUS** What events helped the growing of cotton spread throughout the Southeast?

2. **CONNECT** In what ways was a rice plantation like a cotton plantation?

3. **ECONOMICS** Why did planters want to grow short-strand cotton?

4. **GEOGRAPHY** Why did cities such as Memphis, Tennessee, and New Orleans, Louisiana, become major cotton trading cities?

5. **ACTIVITY** Think of an invention that has changed people's lives. List three ways in which your life would be different without this invention.

Using Map Legends

Here's Why

You can learn many things about a region from special-purpose maps. The map in Lesson 3 showed you where tobacco, rice, and cotton were grown in areas of the Southeast. The legend in the lower left corner told you what the different colors and symbols on the map meant. You can use other maps to find out what conditions are best for growing tobacco, rice, or cotton. Use the legends to read these maps.

Here's How

Look at the map on this page. It tells you the kinds of soils found in different parts of the Southeast. Next to each of the six colors in the legend is a description of one type of soil.

Find Georgia on the map. What types of soils are found in Georgia? Look for the colors orange, yellow, and purple in the legend. By doing so, you can find out that Georgia has clay, sandy, and poorly drained soils.

What color are the largest areas of the map? Use the legend to find out what kinds of soils are found in these orange areas. From this information you can tell that most areas of the Southeast have clay soils.

What color is used to show upland soils? These soils are usually found on hillsides. You can see that the pink areas are in the Appalachian Mountain area.

Now look at the map on the next page. The legend tells you the number of frost-free days in different areas. Frost-free days are the days from the last frost in the spring to the first frost in the fall. This period is sometimes called a region's growing season.

The number of days without frost is one way to measure the climate of a region. In warm climates, there are many days without frost. Cooler climates can have fewer than 160 frost-free days.

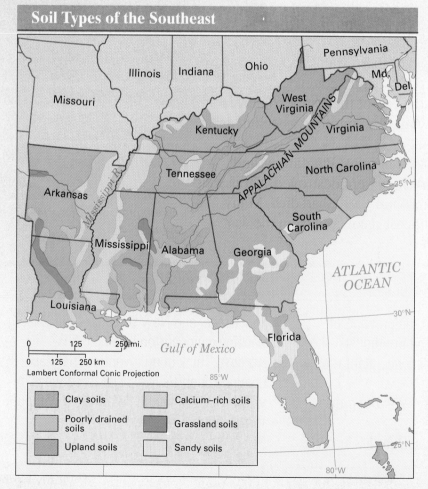

Soil Types of the Southeast

Clay soils
Poorly drained soils
Upland soils
Calcium–rich soils
Grassland soils
Sandy soils

Average Length of Frost-Free Periods

Legend:
- 120–160 days
- 160–200 days
- 200–240 days
- Over 240 days

0   125   250 mi.
0   125   250 km
Lambert Conformal Conic Projection

What color is used for areas with over 240 frost-free days? What parts of the map are this color? You can tell that all of Florida, and parts of six other states, have over 240 frost-free days each year.

Now you can work with these two maps and the map in Lesson 3. By comparing the information on them, you can find out what conditions are best for different crops.

Try It

Start with the map on page 65. Find the areas in which rice was the main crop. Which states are rice growers? Now look at the map showing soil types. What types of soils are found in the rice-growing areas? What do you think is the best soil for growing rice?

Now look at the map that shows frost-free days. Compare it with the tobacco-growing areas on the map in Lesson 3, page 65. Which states were tobacco growers. How many frost-free days are there in the tobacco-growing areas? Did tobacco grow in any areas that have fewer than 160 frost-free days? Did tobacco grow in areas where there were more than 200 frost-free days? What can you conclude, or figure out, about the climate needed for growing tobacco?

Apply It

Find the map in the Atlas on page 409 that shows Average Annual Precipitation. The annual precipitation of an area is the amount of rain or snow that falls in that area in a year. Use the legend to find out how much rain falls every year in different parts of the Southeast. Which states have the largest areas with more than 60 inches of rain each year? Which state has an area with 20–40 inches? Compare the amount of rain that the Southeast gets every year with that of the rest of the United States. Does the amount of rain the Southeast gets make for good growing conditions? Look at the map on page 409. What is the average annual precipitation where you live? Does this limit what grows there?

Chapter Review

Reviewing Key Terms

cash crop (p. 55)   plantation (p. 60)
colony (p. 55)   precipitation (p. 64)
growing season (p. 64) slave (p. 59)
invention (p. 63)

A. Choose the key term that best completes each sentence.
1. Eli Whitney's _____ , the cotton gin, was a machine that cleaned seeds out of cotton bolls.
2. Settlers from England set up a _____ in Virginia.
3. Tobacco grown in Virginia was a _____ that was sold to the English.
4. A _____ had no rights and was forced to work hard in the fields.
5. The _____ for cotton is more than six months long.
6. Rice and cotton were grown on southeastern _____.
7. The rains that come in spring and early summer provide the ideal amount of _____ for growing cotton.

B. Write the definition of each key term below. Then write two or three sentences telling how the four terms are related.
1. plantation
2. slave
3. cash crop
4. growing season

Exploring Concepts

A. Copy and complete the chart below on a separate piece of paper. Use details from the chapter to answer the questions.

B. For each of the following events, write one or two effects.
1. The cotton gin made it much easier to pick the seeds out of cotton bolls.
2. Many people in England who wanted to settle in Virginia could not pay for the voyage.
3. Carolina planters needed more workers to grow rice on their plantations.
4. English people rushed to buy the tobacco sent to England from the Jamestown colony.
5. Planters sent their rice crops to Charles Town so it could be picked up by English ships.

Crop	Name the states where each crop was grown.	Describe the work needed during the growing season.	What workers first grew it?	Where was it sold?
Tobacco				
Rice				
Cotton				

Chapter 3

Reviewing Skills

1. Look at the United States vegetation map on page 408 of the Atlas. This map shows the kinds of vegetation, or plant life, that grows in different areas of the United States. Use the map and the map legend to answer the following questions: How many regions are shown on the map? How do you know? What color stands for the grassland region? What color stands for the forest region?

2. Look at the United States climate map on page 408. How many climate regions does it show? How many climate regions are there in the southeastern states? How many climate regions are there in California? Name them.

3. Look at the United States map on pages 404–405. What parallel line forms part of the southern border of Tennessee? In which state would you be at 85°W, 30°N?

Using Critical Thinking

1. Think of the many men, women, and children who were bought and sold as slaves to work on southeastern plantations. What rights did they lack that you and your family have today?

2. While the Virginia colonists were encouraged to plant tobacco, today there are programs to discourage farmers from growing it. Farmers are encouraged to grow other crops instead. What do you think is the reason for this change?

3. One farming area grows tobacco. Another grows rice. A third area grows cotton. What might you expect to be different about the land and climate of these three farming areas?

Preparing for Citizenship

1. **WRITING ACTIVITY** Imagine you are an English worker in the tobacco field or an African slave on a rice or cotton plantation. Write a diary entry that describes a day in your life.

2. **ART ACTIVITY** Make a poster that shows how cotton or rice was grown in the Southeast. Use encyclopedias to find pictures of the plants. On the front, draw the crop growing in the field. On the back, list what was needed and what was done to raise the crop.

3. **COLLECTING INFORMATION** As a class, find out as much as you can about the early years of the Jamestown colony. Some students can make a timeline of important events. Others can find maps of Jamestown and the nearby bodies of water. Several students should use encyclopedias and books to make notes about daily life in the colony, contact with the Indians, health problems, food supplies, and the tobacco crop. Share your findings with each other.

4. **COLLABORATIVE LEARNING** As a class project, organize a discussion panel like those on radio or television. Choose one student to be the leader. Select other students to be these guests: Eli Whitney, plantation owners, African slaves. Have the rest of the students make up the audience. Each audience member should make up a question for one of the guests.

Chapter 4
From Field to Factory

*After the Civil War, the Southeast needed to rebuild.
The slaves were freed and the plantation system ended.
People had to find new ways to work the land. Farmers
tried new crops and new farming methods. People in
Appalachia discovered the richness of their coal fields.
And factories in the Southeast began to make cloth
from the huge supply of cotton.*

Freed slaves grew crops
for land owners and
tended small garden plots
to feed their families.

These miners are headed to work in
the coal mines of Appalachia.
Helmets like the one shown below
protected heads from falling rocks.

1850	1880	1910

1865

1890 In the late 1800s, the
United States passed Great
Britain as the leading producer of
coal in the world.

This group of girls smiled for the camera during a break in the workday at a Knoxville, Tennessee, cotton mill in the early 1900s.

Changes on the Farms

In what ways did farming in the Southeast change after the Civil War?

Key Terms

- agriculture
- sharecropper
- crop rotation

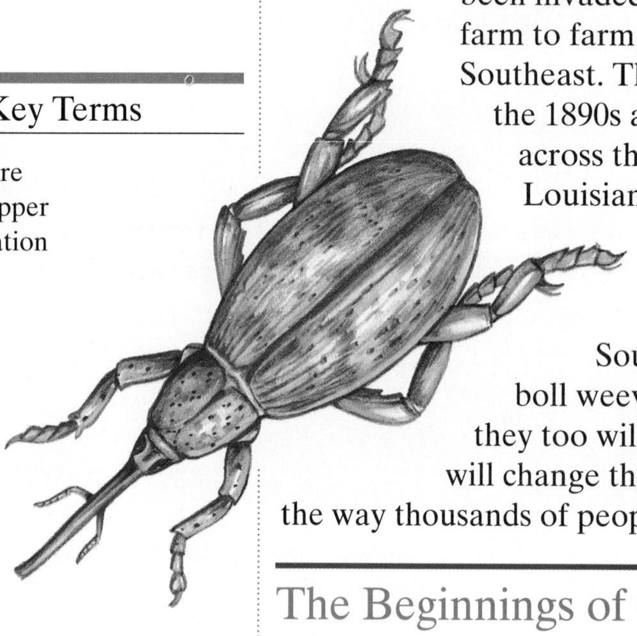

▲ *Hungry boll weevils came north from Mexico in the 1890s and ate their way through the cotton fields of the Southeast.*

Inside a two-room cabin in Alabama in 1914, a family sleeps peacefully. The summer night air surrounds them like a thick blanket.

Yet, out in the family's cotton fields, thousands of bugs are wide awake. The bugs, called boll weevils, creep along the cotton plants, chewing them up as they go along. The weevils eat the cotton fiber in the cotton boll, then creep on to the next plant.

The sleeping family does not yet know that its farm has been invaded. The weevils have crept from farm to farm, from state to state in the Southeast. They entered Texas from Mexico in the 1890s and started eating their way across the cotton fields of Arkansas, Louisiana, and Mississippi. Now they are in Alabama, and soon they will be in Georgia.

Cotton farmers across the Southeast are already fighting the boll weevil. When this family wakes up, they too will join the fight. The boll weevil will change their lives. This tiny bug will change the way thousands of people farm in the Southeast.

The Beginnings of Change

From the early days of tobacco, rice, and cotton plantations, many people in the Southeast farmed to earn a living. Farm work like growing crops and raising animals is called **agriculture**. The boll weevils were one of many problems for agriculture in the Southeast after the Civil War.

When the war ended, a new system of agriculture developed in the South. The slaves were free, but they owned no land to farm. Wealthy landowners still had their plantations, but they had no workers to run them.

As a result, owners divided up their plantations which were hundreds of acres or more. They kept a part for themselves. They split up the rest into small plots of 25 to 40 acres, each with a cabin. They rented the plots to farmers, both black and white. This type of farmer was called a **sharecropper**. In order to use the land, sharecroppers had to pay the landowner by giving him a share of the crops they raised each year.

◄ *A family of southern sharecroppers plow their cotton field.*

Nate Shaw and his family were former slaves who became sharecroppers in Alabama. In the spring, Shaw borrowed money from a landowner to buy seeds and tools.

UNDERSTANDING AGRICULTURE

*T*he many different activities done on a farm are all part of agriculture. Agriculture includes growing crops such as fruits and vegetables or raising animals for meat, milk, and eggs. Like lumbering, mining, and manufacturing, agriculture is a big business in the United States today. But unlike other businesses, only agriculture involves growing or raising food on the land.

The first settlers in America became farmers in order to survive. Clearing the land to plant crops was hard work. At first, the settlers could only grow enough to feed their own families. If they had a good year, they might have enough extra food to trade with other settlers.

Agriculture as a business didn't start until the settlers had cleared enough land and had enough labor and tools to grow large amounts of extra food. Family plots gave way to large plantations that needed more machines and more workers. Crops were then sold to pay for the costs of doing business and to make a profit. In this way, agriculture became much like any other business, such as making sneakers.

In one way, however, agriculture is a business with special importance. People can live without many products for a long time, even sneakers, but all people must eat.

Like many sharecroppers, he planted cotton. A big share of the cotton went to the landowner. He sold part to pay back the borrowed money. He used income from the rest of the crop to buy food for the family. Little, if anything, was left over. If the Shaws were lucky, they earned enough to pay back what they owed. If the crop did poorly, they had to borrow more money.

Part of the reason that made farming hard for sharecroppers was that they planted only one cash crop. If a plant disease or a bug like the boll weevil ruined that year's crop, the sharecropper lost everything. Planting the same crop in the same field every year took minerals out of the soil, so plants didn't grow as well. ■

■ *What was sharecropping?*

Better Ways to Farm

George Washington Carver, a scientist in Tuskegee, Alabama, wanted to help the sharecroppers. On market days, Carver often saw farmers driving to town with empty wagons. At the market, farmers bought vegetables for their families that they could have raised on their own farms.

Carver also knew about the problems that came from growing just one crop. So in 1892, he started a program to teach sharecroppers better farming methods, such as **crop rotation**. This is a method of planting different crops in a field every year to keep the soil rich. With this method, a farmer

▲ *George Washington Carver, pictured above right, found 300 uses for the peanut plant. Other farmers grew fruits and vegetables and sold them at fruitstands.*

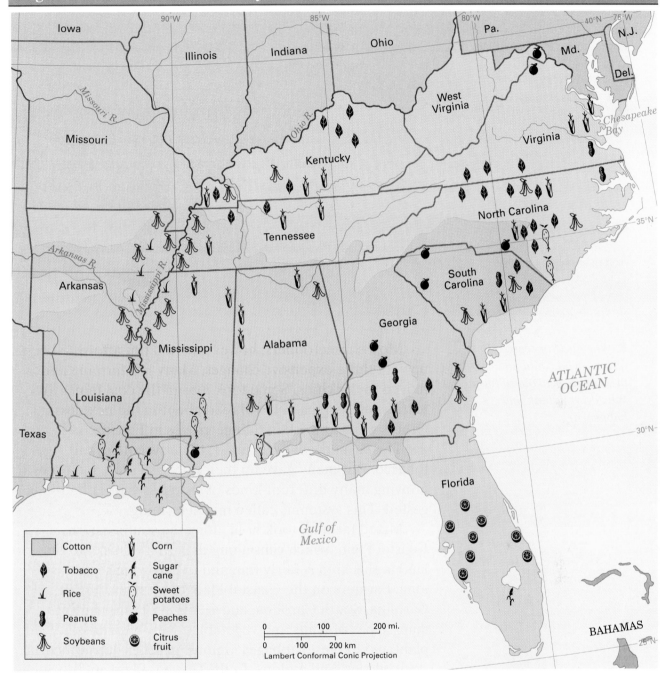

in Alabama, like Nate Shaw, might raise cotton in a field one year and beans the next year. Crop rotation produces more crops because it puts minerals that the plants need back into the soil.

More Crops and New Machines

During the 1920s and 1930s, something else came along to help farmers in the Southeast—the tractor. One new steam-powered tractor could do the work of ten sharecropping families. Tractors and other machines such as the cotton picker allowed farmers to produce more crops.

▲ *Which crops are grown over the largest part of the Southeast today? For help in understanding this product map, see page G12 of the* Map and Globe Handbook.

77

From Field to Factory

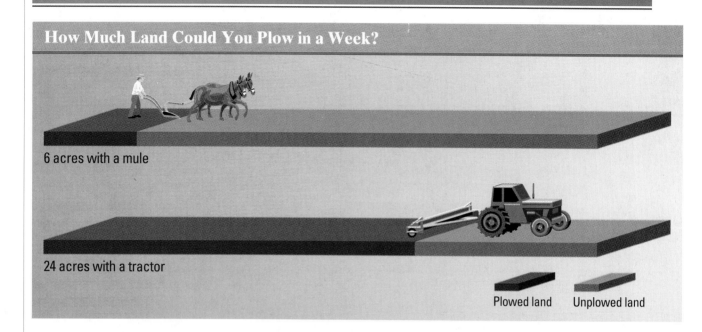

How Much Land Could You Plow in a Week?

6 acres with a mule

24 acres with a tractor

Plowed land   Unplowed land

▲ *When tractors came along, farmers who could not afford them often went out of business. Why do you think that happened?*

■ *In what ways did agriculture in the Southeast improve in the late 1800s and early 1900s?*

Most sharecroppers, however, could not afford to keep up with these expensive changes. Many left farming and moved to the cities. Some took jobs in the coal mines and textile mills, which you will read about in the next lessons. Others went to work in orange groves in Florida.

The farmers who remained still grew cotton and tobacco. But many gave up their one cash crop and began growing many different kinds of crops, as Carver had suggested. This system is called mixed farming.

Mixed farming took hold along the southeastern Coastal Plain, which runs along the Atlantic Ocean. The land in this area is fairly flat, and the growing season is long. Farmers on the Coastal Plain of Virginia, North Carolina, South Carolina, and Georgia began planting many types of fruits and vegetables. New machines helped plant and harvest cabbages, onions, peaches, lettuce, corn, strawberries, and melons. In the Coastal Plain and throughout the Southeast, mixed farming and machines like tractors made agriculture more successful than ever. ■

R E V I E W

1. **FOCUS** In what ways did agriculture in the Southeast change after the Civil War?
2. **CONNECT** Why did early southeastern farmers grow rice along the Coastal Plain?
3. **ECONOMICS** How did George Washington Carver try to help southeastern farmers?
4. **CRITICAL THINKING** If sharecropping was so hard, why do you think so many freed slaves tried to do it?
5. **WRITING ACTIVITY** Pretend you are writing a newspaper article about how machinery changes southeastern farming. In your article, interview a farm family from Virginia who has just bought a tractor. How do they feel?

Organizing Information

Here's Why

Organizing information on a chart will often help you to remember the new facts you have just learned. For example, you have just learned new facts in this lesson about the many kinds of crops grown in the Southeast.

Here's How

Look at the chart to the right. This chart is a way to organize the information in the map of southeastern crops on page 77. Six southeastern states are listed in the first column under the heading "States." The second column has the heading "Major Crops"and shows two major crops of each state.

Try It

You can make your own charts to help you organize, compare, and remember information. Start by copying the chart on this page. Leave plenty of room for additional information. Now use the map on page 77 to add more information to your chart. List as many other crops in these six states as you can find. In which column should you list them? Then look up each state in an encyclopedia to find other major crops grown there. Try to find as many as you can.

Now extend your chart by adding six more southeastern states to the first column in alphabetical order. In the second column, list the major crops for those states. Find them on the map on page 77 and in an encyclopedia.

Use the completed chart to answer the following questions:

1. What are the major crops grown in the state of Louisiana?

States	Major Crops
Alabama	Cotton, peanuts
Arkansas	Soybeans, cotton
Florida	Citrus fruit, sugar cane
Georgia	Peanuts, soybeans
Kentucky	Tobacco, corn
Louisiana	Soybeans, cotton

2. In which states is corn one of the leading crops?
3. Which crop is listed for only one of the states?
4. Which is the best title for your chart?
   a. Agriculture Today
   b. Major Crops Grown in the Southeast Region
   c. The Southeastern States

Apply It

Create new columns on your chart of the southeastern states. Use the heading "Manufacturing" for a third column. Use the heading "Largest Cities" for a fourth column. Find the information for these columns in the Minipedia in the back of the book. Give your chart a new title.

George Washington Carver

Anne Terry White

George Washington Carver was born a slave near Diamond, Missouri, in 1864. He eventually became a world famous scientist, known especially for his agricultural research. As you read this story, ask yourself, "Why was Carver so concerned about finding new ways to farm in the Southeast?"

You read in Lesson 1 about the role George Washington Carver played in introducing new farming practices to the Southeast. This selection describes Carver's attempts to find new and better ways to grow crops.

Going down on the train to Tuskegee, George Carver was all eyes. He had read and read about cotton, but he had never seen it. Now it was everywhere around him. Fields of coppery stalks and puffs of white slipped endlessly by the window. And here and there in the fields he could see the people of King Cotton's kingdom.

It was early October, cotton picking time. Everybody who could raise a hand to pick was in the fields. Backs bent a little above the rows, black hands reached for the white fluff. As the train passed, the backs would straighten for a moment, the hands hold still. The pickers looked curiously at the monster roaring through the cotton. And from the train window Carver looked curiously back at them.

"Cotton—that's all they know," he thought. "Cotton—that's all their life."

Whenever he caught sight of the miserable, unpainted shacks in which the people lived, his heart sank. Every roof sagged in the middle. The falling chimneys were propped by sticks. There wasn't a tree to give shade, there wasn't a flower in the dooryard. Once in a while a little patch of corn or sugar cane would appear near a cabin. But much more often the cotton came right up to the door—the cabin looked lost in the cotton.

The memory of Uncle Mose Carver's farm rose before him. That was a one-room house, too. But it wasn't like these shacks. He thought of the horses and the cows, the sheep and the poultry. He recalled the beehives and the fruit trees.

"Uncle Mose and Aunt Sue raised almost everything they needed," he thought. "They lived well, they had plenty. But these people raise nothing but cotton; so how can they live well? What do they eat?"

His heart sank even more when he saw the worn-out and wasted land. In many fields the cotton was stunted and bore very few white puffs. In others, because the top soil had been washed away, nothing would grow at all. The rolling country lay utterly bare, wrinkled and scarred with deep gullies.

Carver knew the reason for that. King Cotton had ruled over the South too long. Cotton had been planted on the same acres over and over again until all the good had been taken out of the soil. Then forests had been cut down to make more land for cotton. Once the trees were gone, there was nothing to hold the rain water. It ran off the surface, taking the top soil along with it.

"I can help my people only by healing their sick land," Carver thought. "And I can heal this sick land only through the people. It goes around in a circle like that. Where am I to begin?"

The problem was so big. What he saw out of the train window was just a tiny part of the cotton belt. If he traveled east and west for a thousand miles, he would see the same dirty, unpainted shacks, the same rain-gullied fields, the same straggling fences. Everywhere he would find the people just as poor, just as ill fed. They would be wearing the same jeans and dresses made out of feed bags. They would be doing the same drudging, monotonous work. He would find no flowers in their yards, no beauty or comfort in their houses.

"Where am I to begin?"

Carver completes his journey and goes to work at the Tuskegee Institute. There he begins to experiment with new ways of growing crops. Since most Southern farmers can't afford fertilizer, Carver tries to find other ways to enrich the soil.

Carver racked his brain what to do. Then early one morning he got an idea.

He was always up and in the woods at four o'clock in the morning to gather specimens and get close to the Creator. On his way home he generally passed the trash heaps, where very often he would pick up something for his laboratory. This morning, happening to look up to the top of the pile, he saw a large plant of some sort growing up on top. What was it?

He climbed up to see. The plant was a magnificent pumpkin vine growing right out of what looked to be a mass of tin cans. It was the very best pumpkin vine Carver had ever seen. It had seven runners nearly forty feet long, and each of them was loaded with big, healthy pumpkins.

When later in the day Carver met his students, he had a broad grin on his face.

"Boys," he said, "I have the answer to our problem." And he took them out on the dump.

"A pumpkin seed," he said, "somehow found its way into this waste. And look what happened. Is it not proof that rotted leaves and grass and rags and paper make very good fertilizer? We will level this trash pile down and rake it over and plant it with cantaloupe and watermelon and onions and potatoes. And at the same time we'll start a compost pile to serve our other fields."

He had the boys build a pen. Anything that would rot quickly was thrown into the pen. Leaves went in and paper and rags and grass—even street sweepings. On top of everything he had the boys throw rich earth from the woods and muck from the swamps. When the whole was well rotted, the students spread it over their fields.

"Now we are not taking an unfair advantage," Carver said. "Any farmer can do the same thing."

Any farmer could also plant the pea family.

"The pea family," Carver explained to the boys, "is the magician among plants. It can pluck nitrogen right out of the air—which is something no other plant can do. All others take nitrogen, which is their most important food, *out* of the soil. But the pea family puts nitrogen *into* the soil. Now we have to find out which member of the pea family does the best all around job."

So the students planted crimson clover and cowpeas and hairy vetch. They planted peanuts and velvet beans and soybeans. And they watched to see which would come out best.

When the cowpeas won, Carver put out a bulletin explaining why farmers should plant them. They were good food for man and for beast, he wrote. Besides, they would put $25 worth of nitrogen into every acre. At the end Carver gave eighteen different recipes for cooking cowpeas.

Further Reading

George Washington Carver, Scientist. Shirley Graham and George D. Lipscomb. This biography describes Carver's life and achievements.

Peanuts for Billy Ben. Lois Lenski. This book tells the story of a sharecropping family in the peanut growing region of Virginia.

Tuskegee and the Black Belt. Anne Kendrick Walker. This book tells the story of the Tuskegee Institute, which was founded in 1881 by Booker T. Washington.

LESSON 2

The Coal Mines

THINKING FOCUS

What effects did coal mining have on the Appalachian Mountain region?

Key Terms

- fuel
- labor union

▼ *Miners covered their faces with bandanas so they wouldn't breathe so much of the thick, black coal dust.*

> avid stepped boldly into the yawning mouth of the [mine]. . . . Around him the damp, dark walls glistened. The air in the tunnel was stale and smelled of coal dust. On both sides of the iron rails small streams ran by, making whispering sounds. An ice-cold drop of water fell from the ceiling and splashed against his face.
>
> David took another deep breath. He stepped forward one step along the cinder path between the two iron rails. Night, deep black night, came down all around him. But against the night, his miner's lamp glowed steadily and he could dimly see the path that lay ahead.
>
> *Journey to Jericho*, by Scott O'Dell

The Coal Rush

To nine-year-old David, going into the depths of a coal mine is an adventure. For his father, grandfather, and uncle, it is hard and dangerous work. They spend their days in the mines, digging coal out of the earth. Coal, a black, dusty, crumbling rock, is a valuable fuel. **Fuel** is a substance that can be burned to make heat or energy.

David comes from a coal-mining family in Kentucky. The tallest mountains in the East, the Appalachians, run through the states of Kentucky, Tennessee, Alabama, North and South Carolina, Virginia, and West Virginia. The mountain areas of these states have some of the best coal in North America. The map on page 85 shows where coal deposits are located in the Southeast.

The Appalachian Mountains have many narrow valleys. In the 1700s, farmers and hunters began to settle in these valleys. They lived on the rugged green land of the thick forests. Back then, the only people who really used coal were ironworkers, such as blacksmiths. They needed coal to make their fires burn very hot. Their needs were met by the coal from just a few mines.

But in the 1880s, the need for coal grew. Factories had begun to use machines to make their products. These machines needed coal to run. Ships and trains burned coal to power their steam engines. And coal was also used to make steel. As more and more coal was needed, new mining companies set up business in the Appalachians. The coal rush was on.

Mining companies quickly bought up farms and forests and dug coal mines beneath them. In places like Harlan County, Kentucky, green fields and wooded hillsides were covered by mining towns with new roads, railroad stations, and hotels. Each new train brought in carloads of miners and took away carloads of coal.

By the 1920s, coal mining had changed the Appalachian Mountain area from a quiet farming region to a place with

The Coal Belt of the Southeast

Coal

0   125   250 mi.
0   125   250 km
Lambert Conformal Conic Projection

90°W   85°W   80°W

Ohio   Penn.   40°N
Ill.   Ind.   Md.   Del.
Mo.   Ky.   W. Va.   Va.   James R.
Okla.   Ark.   Tenn.   Cumberland R.   N.C.   35°N
Arkansas R.   Tennessee R.   APPALACHIAN MOUNTAINS
Tex.   La.   Miss.   Ala.   Ga.   S.C.
Mississippi R.   Ohio R.   ATLANTIC OCEAN
Fla.   30°N

▲ *Both hard and soft coal is found in the Southeast.*

◄ *Rich coal deposits were found in the Appalachian Mountains of the Southeast.*

From Field to Factory

large companies and a growing population. One man who grew up in Harlan during this time, G. C. Jones, wrote about the many changes that had taken place so quickly in the region. ■

T alk of how fast the surrounding county was growing! New coal mining companies were coming into our county. It seemed like a mine would open up and be producing coal overnight, and all the workers were strangers to these hills. A lot of them came from as far away as Italy, and I met a few who said they were from Scotland, Ireland, and England. I tell you, these big thick seams of coal discovered here were being talked about all over the world.

from "Growing Up Hard in Harlan County"

How Do We Know?

HISTORY *In 1966, a group of high school students in Rabun Gap, Georgia, started a magazine called* Foxfire. *It tells the story of Appalachian life as the students' parents and grandparents remembered it. Their articles were later made into a series of books. The magazine also inspired a Broadway play about mountain life in Georgia.*

▼ *Mules pulled heavy carts from deep within the coal mines. Notice the black face of the miner standing with his arms at his sides.*

Working in the Coal Mines

By looking at a tree-covered hillside, you would never guess how much activity was going on deep within it. Miners tunneled into the sides of the Appalachians to reach the coal buried beneath layers of limestone and sandstone. The mines stretched for miles in all directions.

In the cold mountain mornings, when it was still dark, the miners' day began. Inside the mining tunnels, or shafts, miners worked by the light of small lanterns. Often the shafts were so small that miners could not stand up.

Miners swung picks all day long, earning very low pay for a 12-hour work day. They loaded the coal into wagons,

Entrance to Coal Store

which were on tracks. Mules often pulled the wagons from deep in the mines back up to the surface, where the coal was loaded onto railroad cars.

By nightfall, the miners' long day was over. They went home to small and poorly built houses that were owned by the mining company. These companies built whole towns for the miners, which included houses, schools, and stores. The stores, run by the mining companies, charged very high prices for food and clothing.

Children in mining towns did not go to school for very long. Girls helped their mothers tend the home and the family gardens. And boys as young as 11 were sent to work in the mines to earn money for the family.

People Join Together

Low pay and poor housing were not the only problems facing the miners. After years of breathing coal dust, many men developed black lung disease. Others were hurt in accidents and explosions. Sometimes tunnels collapsed, trapping miners inside.

During the 1890s, miners joined together to improve their working conditions. They formed a **labor union**. Members of the labor union met with company officials to demand changes.

The miners called their union the United Mine Workers of America. John L. Lewis, the son of Welsh immigrants, was the president of the union from 1919 to 1960. He led the workers in demanding changes such as better pay, health care, housing, and schools. The union fought to stop child labor in the mines and to make the tunnels safer. The United Mine Workers continues to help miners today. ■

◄ *Miners were paid with company scrip—fake money produced by the mining company to pay their workers. The only place where scrip was worth anything was the company store. Mining families had no choice but to pay the stores' high prices.*

■ *Why did miners form a labor union?*

R E V I E W

1. **FOCUS** What effects did coal mining have on the Appalachian Mountain region?
2. **CONNECT** Why did many sharecroppers move to the Appalachians?
3. **ECONOMICS** In what ways was coal used in the late 1800s?
4. **CRITICAL THINKING** Would you rather have been a sharecropper or a coal miner? Why?
5. **WRITING ACTIVITY** Imagine that you are working in the coal mine like David. Write a diary entry for one day in the mine.

From Field to Factory

Identifying Main Ideas

Here's Why

Suppose you want to learn more about a topic in this chapter. How can you remember the new information you read?

For example, you can read about other leaders of the union movement like John L. Lewis, discussed in Lesson 2. One such leader was Mary Jones, known as "Mother Jones." Her fiery speeches encouraged Appalachian miners to demand reform.

When you read about Mother Jones's life, you should not try to remember every detail. Concentrate on the most important ideas. Identifying main ideas will help you to organize information and to remember more of what you read.

Here's How

In a paragraph, one sentence often states the main idea or tells what the whole paragraph is about. The main idea in the paragraph below is stated in the first sentence: *Mother Jones spent her life*

organizing miners into labor unions. The main idea is often stated in the first sentence of a paragraph, but not always. The other sentences in the paragraph give details that support the main idea.

Mother Jones spent her life organizing miners into labor unions. She became famous by leading coal miners' strikes in West Virginia and Pennsylvania. Later, she disguised herself as a peddler so that she could visit mining towns in Colorado. The mine owners threw her off their property, but she came back again and again. She continued her work until she was nearly one hundred years old.

Try It

Read the paragraph below. Ask yourself these questions: What one idea is the whole paragraph about? Which sentence states the main idea? Which sentences give details that support the main idea?

Mother Jones's first job was teaching in a school that paid her $8 a month. Her husband and children all died when yellow fever broke out in Memphis. She then volunteered to help those who could not afford doctors. Later she worked as a dressmaker in Chicago. During the great Chicago fire, she lost everything she owned as did thousands of others. She began working for the unions because she knew how it felt to be poor.

Apply It

Now read the last paragraph on page 91. What is the whole paragraph about? Which sentence states the main idea? What details do the other sentences give to support the main idea?

L E S S O N   3

Turning Cotton into Cloth

Inside the tall and narrow wooden building, whole families are at work, turning fluffy white cotton into brightly colored cloth. The North Carolina sunshine streams through the windows, showing the tiny cotton fibers floating through the air. The cotton looks like snowflakes as it falls on the workers' hair and clothes. The machines rumble on, and the men, women, and children make what seems to be miles of cloth.

But slowly the noise of the clattering machines begins to fade. A small boy grins widely. More people begin to smile. They stretch their necks to look out the windows at the river that powers the machines.

"I can see her. There's Lily. Let's go!" someone shouts. Lily is the name that the workers have given to a big rock in the river that is usually covered with water. When the water is so low that you can see Lily, the machines have to stop until the water rises again. The people get a break from their work.

T H I N K I N G
F O C U S

Why did the textile industry grow in the Southeast?

Key Terms

- textile mill
- industry

◄ *Notice the many young children in this photograph taken around 1885 in front of Glencoe mills in North Carolina.*

From Field to Factory

Mills Come to the Southeast

Some children your age spent their days working in cotton mills in the early 1900s.

The people are working at a textile mill in Glencoe, North Carolina, in the early 1900s. Textile is another word for cloth. A mill is a place where people use machines to make a product. So a **textile mill** is a place where people use machines to make cloth.

Before the Civil War, most of the cotton grown in the Southeast was sent to textile mills in the Northeast or England. But after the war, many people in the Southeast wanted to build their own textile mills. "Why send our cotton away when we can make cloth here?" they said. Mills would bring more money and jobs to the region.

Like Glencoe, the first mills built in the Southeast used water power to run the machines. Many rivers run through the Piedmont region of the Southeast. Piedmont is an Italian word meaning "at the foot of the mountains." The Piedmont region is a strip of land between the farming area of the Coastal Plain and the mining area of the Appalachian Mountains. Find this area on the map on pages 406–407. Water power attracted textile mills to the Piedmont region of Virginia, North Carolina, and South Carolina.

Mills such as this one in Columbus, Georgia, were built near rivers. Rushing water provided power to run the spinning and weaving machines.

Later, mills switched from water to coal for power. The Piedmont was still a good spot for the mills because they could get coal from the nearby Appalachian coal fields.

By the 1920s, the textile industry had spread throughout

the Southeast. An **industry** is all the businesses that make one kind of product. You will learn about many industries in this book, including the steel, oil, dairy, logging, and airplane industries.

Like coal mining, textiles helped change the Piedmont from an agricultural region to an agricultural and industrial region. The Piedmont region became the world leader in the production of yarn and cloth. ■

■ *Why did the Southeast want a textile industry?*

Life in the Mill Town

In 1905, four-year-old Jessie Lee Carter and her family moved from their small farm in Tennessee to the Brandon Mill in Greensboro, North Carolina. Families like Jessie's lived in small wooden houses near the mills. Like the coal towns, textile mill towns were often built and run by companies. Company stores in the mill towns had the same high prices as those in the mining towns in the Appalachians to the west. To save money, families often grew their own food in small gardens next to their homes.

Inside the mill, workers ran the machines that made cotton into cloth. Machines cleaned and separated the fibers of the cotton boll. Then they straightened and twisted the fibers into threads. The threads were then woven into cloth, as shown in the illustration below.

While most mine workers were men and boys, whole families worked in the textile mills. Soon after Jessie's family moved to Greensboro, six of her older brothers and sisters went to work in the mill. When Jessie turned 12, she joined them. Young girls such as the one in A Moment In Time on the next page earned money for their families. In

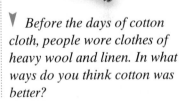

▼ *These tools were used in the cloth-making process.*

▼ *Before the days of cotton cloth, people wore clothes of heavy wool and linen. In what ways do you think cotton was better?*

Making Cotton into Cloth

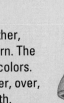

Today machines pick the fluffy cotton bolls.

The cotton is cleaned in a cotton gin to remove the seeds.

The cotton seeds are used to make many things, such as cooking oil and soap.

By twisting the cotton fibers together, machines make the cotton into yarn. The yarn can be dyed many beautiful colors. Then, weaving the yarn over, under, over, under, the cotton is made into cloth.

Ready to wear! The cloth is sewn into many kinds of clothes, such as this soft and comfortable T-shirt.

A Mill Girl

7:12 P.M., June 2, 1902
Outside a cotton mill in Charlotte, North Carolina

Cotton Blouse
A "hand-me-down" from her older sister, this is one of her two work blouses. She's glad that her sleeve didn't tear when it caught on the loom this morning.

Ball of Cotton
Tending machines for ten hours a day can get very boring. During her midday break she plays games with left-over balls of cotton yarn. She's taking this one home to her mom.

Wages
Pay day! Two dollars, her first week's wages! She was so proud to stand on the bobbin box and sign her name in the paymaster's book.

Handkerchief
She keeps a handkerchief tucked in her pocket while working at the mill. The vibrating looms and turning bobbins create cotton dust that makes her sneeze.

Shoes
After work, she likes to skip home, singing a little rhyme. Her shoes kick up the dust as she goes. The high laced shoes protect her feet during the day while she works near the looms.

◄ In today's mills, fast machines controlled by computers turn out more cloth than ever before.

the early 1900s, children as young as seven years of age worked with their parents.

Textiles Today

Jessie and her family would hardly recognize a textile mill today. By the 1930s, mills began to change. Newer, faster machines were added to the mills. They produced much more cloth and needed fewer workers to run them. New laws required children to go to school instead of work.

Cars brought other changes. Workers could live farther away from the mills. They no longer needed to live in the company houses. Mill owners sold the company houses or tore them down. A way of life had ended.

The textile industry itself changed. During the 1940s and 1950s, new types of cloth, like polyester, were invented. Today, the Southeast makes nearly all the textiles produced in the United States. Although the industry has changed over the years, textiles are still one of the Southeast's biggest industries. ■

■ *How did mill towns change between 1900 and the 1930s?*

R E V I E W

1. **FOCUS** Why did the textile industry grow in the Southeast?
2. **CONNECT** In what ways was a mill town similar to a coal town?
3. **GEOGRAPHY** Why were many textile mills built near rivers?
4. **CRITICAL THINKING** What do you think would be the advantages and disadvantages of working at the age of ten?
5. **ACTIVITY** Look at the labels of some of your clothes. Can you find out where they were made? Were they made in the United States or in another country?

Chapter Review

Reviewing Key Terms

agriculture (p. 74)
crop rotation (p. 76)
fuel (p. 84)
industry (p. 91)

labor union (p. 87)
sharecropper (p. 75)
textile mill (p. 90)

A. Write a sentence that includes each pair of words below:
1. sharecropper, landowner
2. crop rotation, George Washington Carver
3. fuel, coal
4. labor union, John L. Lewis
5. textile mill, cotton
6. agriculture, boll weevil
7. industry, textiles

B. Choose the key term that best completes each sentence.
1. Tractors and other machinery have helped make farming a modern _____.
2. _____ is the business of raising crops and animals for sale.
3. Coal is a type of _____ that is mined in the Appalachian Mountains.
4. When _____ rented farmland, they paid for it with some of their crops.
5. The United Mine Workers is a _____.
6. _____ helps farmers to put important minerals back into the soil.
7. Water power ran the first _____ built near rivers.

Exploring Concepts

A. Copy and complete the chart to the right on a separate sheet of paper. Describe how each problem listed in the chart was solved.

B. Write sentences that support each of the following statements with at least two details from this chapter.
1. Farming changed along the Southeast Coastal Plain after the Civil War.
2. Coal mining was both a difficult and a dangerous job.
3. After the Civil War, the Southeast became a center for the textile industry.
4. During the 1880s, industry's need for coal grew.
5. When it became too expensive to farm, many sharecroppers left farming to find other ways of earning a living.
6. The use of machinery brought many changes to agriculture in the Southeast.
7. Textile mills are built near a source of power so that it can run the machinery.

Problem	Solution
After the Civil War, farmers in the Southeast needed workers.	
Coal miners often had dangerous working conditions.	
Many young children worked full time in textile mills.	

Reviewing Skills

1. Read the paragraph below. Which sentence gives the main idea of the paragraph? Which sentences give details that support the main idea? **When the boll weevil first appeared in the United States, many southeastern farmers were growing cotton. Because the boll weevil destroyed their cotton plants, they had to plant other crops. Farmers found that crops such as peanuts could be as profitable as cotton. Also, growing crops like peanuts improved the soil. One could say that the boll weevil was responsible for mixed farming in the Southeast.**

2. Copy and complete the chart shown on the right. Add the name of your state to the first column. Then use information from the Minipedia, pages 350–399, to complete the other two columns.

3. Look at the map of the United States on pages 404–405 of the Atlas. What longitude line touches the eastern coast of Florida? If you were standing at the point 92° W, 35° N, in what state would you be?

State	Land Area	Population
Alabama		
Florida		
Georgia		
North Carolina		
Virginia		

Using Critical Thinking

1. How might life have been different for sharecroppers if they had owned the land they farmed?
2. What advantage did coal miners gain by joining a labor union to talk with mine owners about work conditions?
3. In what ways were the lives of textile workers and coal miners similar?

Preparing for Citizenship

1. **ART ACTIVITY** Build a clay model of the Appalachian Mountains. Start by looking at the physical map of the United States on pages 406–407. Then find a more detailed one in an atlas. First, trace the map onto posterboard and then build up the clay to form the physical features. Include tall mountains, narrow valleys, lakes, and rivers.

2. **INTERVIEWING** Work with a partner. Pretend that you are a television reporter and that your partner is a member of a sharecropping family who is leaving the land. Conduct a television interview. Where is the family going? How do they hope to make a new start?

3. **COLLABORATIVE LEARNING** As a class, plan a movie about the life of a coal miner and his family who live in a mining town in the 1930s. Work in small groups to plan scenes that describe the homes they live in and the mines they work in.

The Southeast Today

People of the Southeast can trace their roots back to many countries and many cultures. In these pages, you'll explore some places that celebrate the people and the traditions of this region. In Nashville, Tennessee, for instance, the city is alive with the stories and songs that entertain country music lovers all over the world. Tradition lives on in Kentucky's Bluegrass region, where people have been raising horses for 200 years. In Montgomery, Alabama, a monument honors some of the people who died in the struggle to gain equal rights. And in Florida, millions of people each year visit some of the most famous and fun places in the Southeast.

Exploring Country Music

It doesn't matter if you like classical music or rock and roll. You'll find yourself clapping your hands and stomping your feet in a wild night of country music at the Grand Ole Opry. "Opry" is slang for "opera." But this place has nothing to do with opera. It is in Nashville, Tennessee, the country music capital of the world.

The Opry is a giant music hall with over 4,400 seats. It is also the world's largest recording studio. Every weekend, the Opry broadcasts live country music shows featuring guitars, fiddles, banjos, and country music bands.

Country music dates back to the 1700s, when the Southeast was just being settled. It began as a blending of English, Irish, and Scottish tunes played by traveling musicians. Today, country music is popular in every region of the United States.

▲ Fiddles and harmonicas are main features in country music.

Iowa
Illinois
Indiana
Ohio
Pa.
N.J.
Md.
Del.
Potomac R.
Chesapeake Bay
West Virginia
Kans.
Missouri
Ohio R.
Louisville
Frankfort
Charleston
Richmond
Newport News
Lexington
Kentucky
Virginia
Norfolk
James R.
35°N
Arkansas
Nashville
Knoxville
Durham
Raleigh
Fort Smith
Tennessee
North Carolina
Little Rock
Memphis
Chattanooga
Charlotte
Okla.
Hot Springs
Columbia
South Carolina
Alabama
Atlanta
Greenville
Birmingham
Georgia
Charleston
Texas
Louisiana
Jackson
Montgomery
Savannah
ATLANTIC OCEAN
Mississippi
30°N
Mississippi R.
Baton Rouge
Biloxi
Mobile
Pensacola
Tallahassee
St. Augustine
New Orleans
Gulf of Mexico
Orlando
Cape Canaveral
Tampa
Florida
★ State capital
• Major city
— State boundary
90°W
85°W
0 100 200 mi.
0 100 200 km
Lambert Conformal Conic Projection
Miami
BAHAMAS
80°W
25°N

Exploring Kentucky's Horse Country

This is one of the world's most famous events. People all over the world come to see it. Jockeys and their horses prepare for many months for this event. And it's all over in about two minutes. The Kentucky Derby is a champion horse race held in Louisville, Kentucky, each year on the first Saturday in May. The derby has been run for more than 100 years.

Kentucky is famous for raising champion horses. There are more than 400 horse farms in Lexington, in the north-central part of the state. Horses, sheep, and cows graze on the grass-covered hills of this area. Tiny blue blossoms in the grass give it a blueish look. That's why Kentucky is nicknamed "the bluegrass state."

▼ *Some of the world's finest horses are raised in Kentucky.*

▶ *Montgomery's Civil Rights Memorial honors Americans who died for freedom.*

Exploring the Civil Rights Memorial

She was tired and her feet hurt. In 1955, Rosa Parks, a black woman in Montgomery, Alabama, didn't want to give up her seat on the bus to a white man.

At that time, black and white people had to sit in separate sections on the bus. Other places were divided too, such as restrooms, waiting rooms, movie theaters, and restaurants. Rosa Parks was tired and angry with this unfair system. She refused to give up her seat and was arrested by police. Many people joined Parks in her fight for equal rights for black Americans.

Today, in Montgomery, Alabama, you can visit a monument made in memory of the many people who died trying to gain equal rights. These rights are often called civil rights. The Civil Rights Memorial is a large round table of black granite carved with the names of 40 men, women, and children who died for freedom. Water pours from the center and flows over the names. Visitors are encouraged to put their hands in the water and to touch the names, remembering the people and their courage.

Exploring Tourism in Florida

Florida is one place where you won't say, "There's nothing to do." You can splash in the surf, visit a magical castle, take a ride on a glass-bottomed boat, pet a dolphin, and watch a rocket launch. Florida, the most populous state in the Southeast, attracts nearly 40 million visitors each year. With more than 110 state parks, gardens, nature preserves, amusement parks, beaches, and museums, the "Sunshine State" has something for everyone.

Tourism is Florida's leading industry. People visit the coastal beaches, the Everglades National Park, and the Kennedy Space Center. There are many amusement sites, including Walt Disney World, a 28,000-acre theme park in Orlando. Another popular place is the Florida Keys, a group of 52 islands that extend south from the state about 150 miles. The islands are connected by one highway that has 42 bridges spanning the clear blue sea.

Move Ahead

Now you're ready to find out more about the people and places of the Southeast. Encyclopedias, travel magazines, and library books will help you. Here are some questions to guide your research.

1. What is gospel music? Which people developed gospel music in the Southeast?
2. When did horses first come to America? How are horses raised on horse farms? What kind of training do champion horses get? Find information and pictures about your favorite kind of horse.
3. What role did Martin Luther King, Jr., play in the struggle for equal rights for all Americans? How is he remembered today?
4. What is a manatee? Where does this animal live? Why are people today concerned about manatees?

Explore Some More

Use your library to find out more about the interesting sites and people in your state or region. For example, what is the most popular tourist site nearest to you? How many people visit there each year? Is your region known for a special kind of music? How did it develop? Who developed it? Does your community have a monument to remember people who have died? Research the life of a person who is honored by a monument in your region. When did the person live? What is the person remembered for?

Millions of people spread their blankets on Florida beaches each year.

Unit 3

The Northeast

Fishing lines dropped overboard into the dark waters. Within minutes sailors had pulled in a five-foot codfish. John Winthrop reported this story in the early 1600s. The sailors on his ship caught 67 cod in 2 1/2 hours. The Atlantic Ocean offered rich fishing grounds to the settlers in the Northeast. Its waters also became a highway for ships carrying fish and other goods around the world.

1600

Acadia National Park in Maine.
Photograph Copyright David Muench.

2000

The Northeast

A Small and Scenic Land

The Northeast, the smallest region, shows that "good things come in small packages." Linked by a mountain range that runs like a backbone through the region, the states have much in common. Each new season brings real change to the Northeast—from freezing, snowy winters to blazing summer heat. Although the region has mountain wilderness and rolling farmland, much of the Northeast is covered with cities and roads.

Maple leaves
from Vermont

The Northeast

The 11 states of the region
- Connecticut
- Delaware
- Maine
- Maryland
- Massachusetts
- New Hampshire
- New Jersey
- New York
- Pennsylvania
- Rhode Island
- Vermont

The mountains seem to be on fire as maple and oak trees burst into their fall colors of red, orange, and yellow. In no other region is the arrival of autumn more beautiful than in the Northeast.

Population: 56,256,865. That includes New York City, the city with the highest population in the United States. The Northeast has more people living on each square mile of land than any other region.
Size: 181,397 square miles, the smallest region. In fact, the Northeast is smaller than Texas or Alaska.

Major resources: coal, fish, farmland, lumber, natural gas, sand, stone

Elevation
- Lowest: sea level along the coast
- Highest: Mount Washington, New Hampshire, 6,288 feet above sea level

Five different mountain ranges cover much of the Northeast. The Catskill, Allegheny, Green, and White mountains are all part of the Appalachian Mountains. The Adirondack mountains in northeastern New York stand alone.

Mount Katahdin
in Maine

The Atlantic coast
runs the entire length of the region. With its bays and wide river mouths, the coast offers many fine harbors.

Cape Cod
Massachusetts

Scallop shells
from the Atlantic Ocean

A series of rivers cut through the mountains on their way to the sea. These river valleys are filled with rich soil making them good for farming.

Granite
from the mountains of New Hampshire

Physical Map of the Northeast

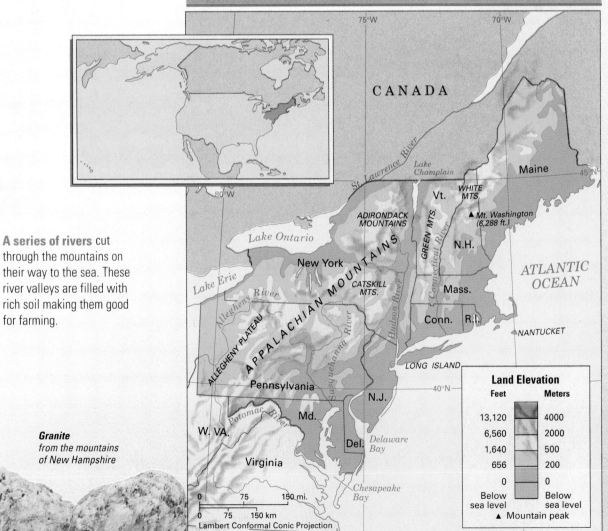

CANADA

St. Lawrence River
Lake Champlain
Maine
45°N

Vt.
WHITE MTS.

ADIRONDACK MOUNTAINS

GREEN MTS.

▲ Mt. Washington (6,288 ft.)

N.H.

Lake Ontario

New York

Connecticut River

ATLANTIC OCEAN

Allegheny River

Lake Erie

CATSKILL MTS.

Hudson River

Mass.

Conn.   R.I.

ALLEGHENY PLATEAU

A P P A L A C H I A N   M O U N T A I N S

Susquehanna River

NANTUCKET

LONG ISLAND

Pennsylvania

40°N

N.J.

Potomac River

Md.

W. VA.

Del.

Delaware Bay

Virginia

Chesapeake Bay

75°W   70°W

80°W

Land Elevation

Feet	Meters
13,120	4000
6,560	2000
1,640	500
656	200
0	0
Below sea level	Below sea level

▲ Mountain peak

0   75   150 mi.
0   75   150 km
Lambert Conformal Conic Projection

Chapter 5

Using Land and Sea

Water was at the center of life and business in the early settlements of the Northeast. Fur traders traveled up the rivers of New York to buy beaver skins from the Indians. Ships built along the coast were sent to buyers in England. And water power ran the new mills that ground wheat grown on Pennsylvania farms.

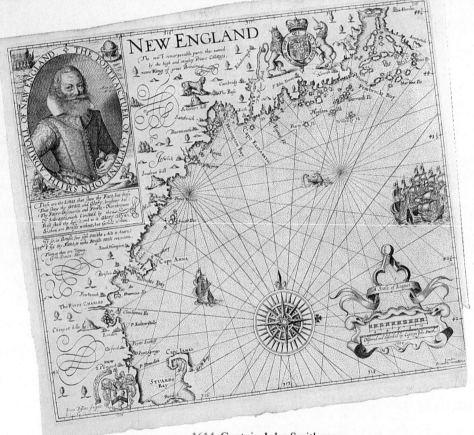

1614 Captain John Smith maps the coast of New England. Returning to England, he tells of the fish and furs in the Northeast.

1600	1640	1680

1600

1636 Settlers build a trading post at what is today Springfield, Massachusetts, to trade with Indians for beaver skins.

This ship flies the flags of the many nations it travels to. By 1800, goods from the Northeast were shipped all over the world.

Fishing was important to the people of the Northeast. Many people decorated their homes with items like this fish weathervane.

| 1720 | 1760 | 1800 |

1800

L E S S O N 1

Looking for Furs

THINKING FOCUS

How did the beaver trade affect the lives of people in the Northeast?

Key Terms

- trade
- manufactured goods

➤ *The Indians of the Northeast understood much about nature and the habits of the animals they hunted.*

I n a flash, a hot fire races across the forest floor. Yellow flames attack the low branches of trees. A small pine explodes in a smoky flash. Thick black smoke fills the air, blocking the sun.

Several Indians stand back to watch the blaze. They set the fire in order to burn off the underbrush. The big trees will be blackened but not damaged by the brush fire.

The ashes from the fire will enrich the soil. This will help new plants to grow. Within weeks green shoots will poke up through the charred brush. Rabbits, deer, and other forest animals will feed on the young plants. Because of these fires the animals will have plenty to eat, and the Indians' future hunts will be successful.

The Indians of the Northeast were skilled hunters. They knew every animal trail and every river and lake in the northeastern mountains. They knew the habits of the deer, the moose, the bear and the beaver. These animals provided the Indians with food and with skins to keep them warm during the winter. The Indians also made animal bones into needles and other kinds of tools.

The Fur Trade

Indian tribes lived throughout the thick forests that covered the Northeast. The first European settlers arrived in the 1600s. Most of them lived on the coast at the edge of the forest and fished the rich Atlantic Ocean. Soon these settlers began to explore the forest and learn more about the Indians of the region. What interested the settlers most were the Indians' beaver furs.

Pelts in the Northeast

Beavers built their houses, called lodges, in the rivers and streams of the Northeast. People in Europe wanted these beaver for their furry skins, or pelts. Hats made of beaver fur were very popular in Europe at that time. The beaver hats were warm and lasted for many years. The hats had become so popular that nearly all the beaver in Europe had been killed.

Europeans were glad to hear that there was more beaver in America. To get the beaver pelts, they set up a **trade**, or exchange of goods, with the settlers in the Northeast. The feature Understanding Trade on page 108 tells more about trade.

Life was hard for the early settlers. The food they got from farming and fishing was enough to keep them alive. But the settlers still needed **manufactured goods**, things such as cloth, iron tools, and other goods made by people. They could get these goods only from Europe. And the Europeans were interested in trading for beaver pelts.

The settlers were smart traders. Their pelts got them valuable goods from Europe. To get these pelts, settlers had to trade with Indians. Indians paddled to settlements in 15–or 16–foot birchbark canoes piled high with

The trade in beaver pelts involved Indians, settlers, and people in Europe.

Items Used in the Fur Trade

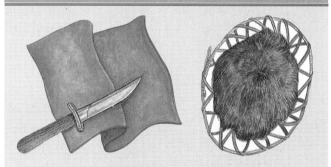

Settlers from Europe traded items such as cloth and knives with Indians in the Northeast. In return, Indians gave the settlers beaver pelts.

Settlers sent the pelts they got from the Indians to Europe. In return, people in Europe sent the settlers manufactured goods such as pots and pans. The settlers needed these goods because they could not make them themselves. They also used some of these goods to trade with the Indians.

Using Land and Sea

■ *Why did the people of the Northeast trade with Europe for goods rather than money?*

bundles of furs. In return for their pelts the Indians might choose one shirt, one yard of cloth, forty biscuits, or two small axes. At times these goods seemed so valuable to the Indians that one said, "The English have no sense." ■

▲ *Beaver hats were very strong and lasted many years. They were often handed down from parent to child.*

Spreading Settlements

People from many nations in Europe moved to the Northeast in the 1600s. They all needed manufactured goods from Europe. And the Europeans still wanted beaver pelts. However, after years of trapping, there were no longer many beavers left in the Northeast. For the settlers of the region, the search for the valuable animal began to seem like a search for gold.

Looking for the Great Lake

Settlers knew that beaver lived along rivers, streams, and lakes. One story told of a great lake where beaver lived by the millions. People believed this lake was in the land of the Iroquois *(IHR uh kwoy)* Indians. The map on page 109 shows where the Iroquois lived.

Many rivers were said to connect to this lake. Everyone wanted to be the first to find this new supply of beavers.

UNDERSTANDING TRADE

The early settlers in the Northeast exchanged the things they had for the goods they wanted without using money. They traded only goods.

Later, colonial merchants organized trade between the settlers and England. Some merchants, instead of trading only with England, also helped people trade with settlers in other colonies .

Merchants set up shops in the cities. A merchant's job was to buy goods, set their cash value or price, stock the goods, and then offer them for sale. Some merchants also shipped goods to and from colonies in both the North and the South. By serving as middle-men, merchants helped people trade.

Today cities of the Northeast still are important centers of trade. Goods from all regions of the United States are bought and sold. Goods also leave the Northeast for all parts of the world and arrive from other countries daily.

The shops of the colonial merchants have grown into companies trading goods every year worth billions of dollars. Of course goods no longer move by the sailing ships of colonial times. Airplanes, steamships, railroads, and trucks are all important methods of transportation for trade in the Northeast and in the world.

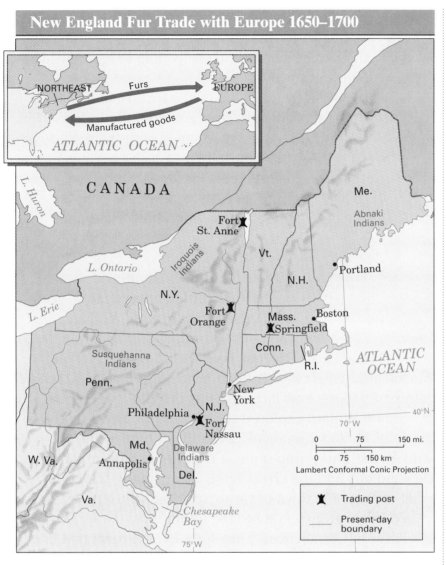

New England Fur Trade with Europe 1650–1700

NORTHEAST — Furs → EUROPE

Manufactured goods ←

ATLANTIC OCEAN

CANADA

L. Huron

L. Ontario

L. Erie

Iroquois Indians

N.Y.

Fort St. Anne ✗

Vt.

N.H.

Me.

Abnaki Indians

Portland

Fort Orange ✗

Mass. ✗ Springfield

Boston

Conn.

R.I.

ATLANTIC OCEAN

Susquehanna Indians

Penn.

Philadelphia

N.J.

New York

✗ Fort Nassau

40°N

70°W

Md.

Annapolis

Delaware Indians

Del.

W. Va.

Va.

Chesapeake Bay

75°W

| 0 | 75 | 150 mi. |
| 0 | 75 | 150 km |

Lambert Conformal Conic Projection

✗ Trading post

— Present-day boundary

◄ *Why do you think the trading posts shown are located on rivers or lakes away from the coast? You can figure out the distance traders had to travel between trading posts by using the map scale, which is explained on page G5 of the Map and Globe Handbook.*

Across Time & Space

The fur trade in the 1600s and 1700s killed nearly all the beaver in the Northeast. But today the beaver is coming back. You can find the furry animals in rivers, streams, ponds, and lakes all across the Northeast.

Settlers raced to explore the Connecticut, the Hudson, and the Delaware rivers.

As people canoed farther up the rivers, they set up trading posts where Indians could easily reach them. The traders set up posts on rivers that flowed to settlements on the ocean. From these settlements they could send the pelts to Europe in return for manufactured goods.

Settlements Along Rivers

As more people came to trade, the trading posts themselves grew into settlements. One of these was Fort Orange, which later became Albany, New York. The fort stood along the Hudson River. By 1680, it

▼ *Trading posts were the scene of much activity in the Northeast. Many grew into important cities.*

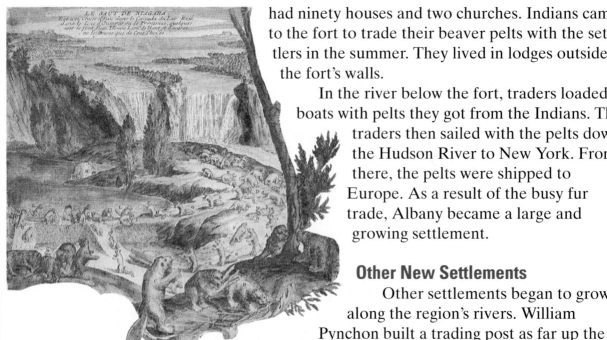

The artist who made this picture may have been thinking of a place like the Great Lake of the Iroquois.

Find examples from the text of how the beaver helped "draw the map of the Northeast."

had ninety houses and two churches. Indians came to the fort to trade their beaver pelts with the settlers in the summer. They lived in lodges outside the fort's walls.

In the river below the fort, traders loaded boats with pelts they got from the Indians. The traders then sailed with the pelts down the Hudson River to New York. From there, the pelts were shipped to Europe. As a result of the busy fur trade, Albany became a large and growing settlement.

Other New Settlements

Other settlements began to grow along the region's rivers. William Pynchon built a trading post as far up the Connecticut River as boats could go. Springfield, Massachusetts, grew up around his post. See page 370 in the Minipedia to see how large this city is today.

Simon Willard explored the Merrimack River in Massachusetts. He led a group of 12 families 17 miles into the wilderness. This group found a treasure in beaver pelts, but they did not find the Great Lake. They finally settled in what is today the town of Concord, Massachusetts.

Another group explored the Quinnipiac *(kwihn uh PEE ak)* River in Connecticut. They founded the town that later became New Haven.

The Great Lake of the Iroquois is still a mystery. Some believe it was actually Lake Champlain, on the border of Vermont and New York. Others think no such lake ever existed. But the search for the lake and its beaver pelts helped spread settlement of the Northeast from Maine to Delaware. In this way, it might be said that the beaver helped to draw the map of the Northeast. ■

R E V I E W

1. **FOCUS** How did the beaver trade affect the lives of people in the Northeast?
2. **CONNECT** Find an example from an earlier chapter of the importance of rivers to settlers.
3. **ECONOMICS** Why did the settlers of the Northeast have to depend on Europe?
4. **CRITICAL THINKING** How do you think the settlement of the region would have been different had there been no beaver in the Northeast?
5. **WRITING ACTIVITY** Imagine you are settling a new town in the Northeast. Write a letter to Europe asking for the goods you will need to live.

L E S S O N 2

Building Ships

"Thwack"—a man hits the tree with the back of his ax. The solid sound tells him that the tree is not hollow. He smiles as he orders his crew into action. Soon this great pine tree, which has stood for five hundred years or more, will fall.

Giant chips fly as two workers chop at the huge trunk from each side. Others cut smaller trees and spread them on the ground. They form a bed to soften the tree's fall. One last chop with the ax and a terrible creaking begins. Workers run for cover as twigs and branches rain down around them. Crashing and tearing, the pine thunders to the ground.

Much of the hard work is still ahead. Getting a 150-foot tree out of the forest takes great skill and strength. Using up to 100 oxen, the crew will haul the pine 20 miles to the nearest river. Workers will then float the tree downstream to the sea. From there it will be sent to England and traded to a shipbuilder.

THINKING
FOCUS

Why did shipbuilding become such a successful business in New England?

Key Terms

- craftsman
- raw material

◄ *The forests in the northern part of the Northeast are full of pine trees. Forests elsewhere in the region had more oak, maple, and other types of trees.*

111

Using the Land and Sea

Lumber and the Sea

The forests of New Hampshire and Maine had some of the biggest pine trees in the world. Shipbuilders could make a ship's mast using just one of these trees. These masts made from a single pine were much stronger than those made from two pieces joined together. These pines were so valuable that England wanted all of them for its own ships.

The Growth of Shipyards

Specially made ships were needed to carry the long masts to England. Shipyards in New England built these large "mast ships." Builders also made other kinds of ships. They built fishing boats called schooners that caught great amounts of fish in Georges Bank. They also built trade ships. Soon, ships carrying beaver pelts, lumber, and fish sailed daily from New England shipyards.

Workers in the Northeast became well known for building excellent ships. Their ships were cheaper than those made in England. This was partly because the wood they needed was nearby. Soon, even the English bought ships made in the Northeast. And as more people came to the shipyards to work, towns along the coast got bigger. ■

■ *How did the great mast pines help New England shipyards to grow?*

➤ *Why do you think most of the mast pines were cut near the coast?*

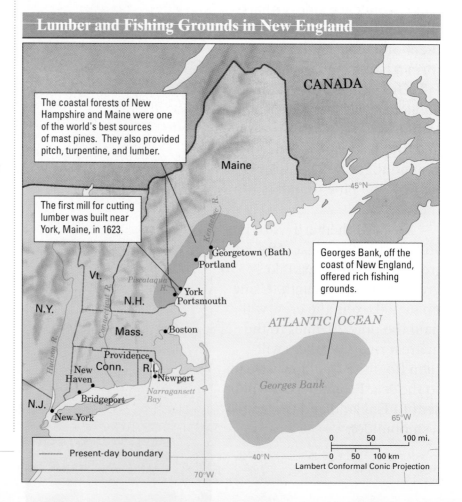

Lumber and Fishing Grounds in New England

The coastal forests of New Hampshire and Maine were one of the world's best sources of mast pines. They also provided pitch, turpentine, and lumber.

The first mill for cutting lumber was built near York, Maine, in 1623.

Georges Bank, off the coast of New England, offered rich fishing grounds.

CANADA

Maine

45°N

Georgetown (Bath)
Portland

Vt.
Piscataqua R.
York
Portsmouth

N.Y.

N.H.

Mass.
Boston

Providence
Conn.
R.I.
Newport

New Haven
Narragansett Bay

N.J.

Bridgeport

New York

ATLANTIC OCEAN

Georges Bank

65°W

——— Present-day boundary

0   50   100 mi.
0   50   100 km
Lambert Conformal Conic Projection

40°N

70°W

The Craft of Shipbuilding

A person who has learned a special skill is called a **craftsman**. In the early 1600s, there were few craftsmen in the Northeast. But then, growing shipyards brought many craftsmen to New England. Building a ship required many people with special skills. Blacksmiths made iron nuts, bolts, and braces. You can see how a blacksmith made these and other metal parts in A Moment in Time on page 114. Sailmakers sewed miles of canvas sails. Carpenters cut and shaped the ship's wooden hull.

Craftsmen had to build ships carefully. A ship might spend months or even years at sea. It had to be strong enough to sail through the wildest storm.

Each ship was planned by a master shipbuilder. He began by carving a wooden model of the hull, the ship's body. Using the model, he made exact drawings of the ship's parts. The builder then chose trees best suited for each part of the ship.

▼ *Craftsmen in New England shipyards had no power tools. They used hand tools like these to build ships.*

Once the builder got the wood, building began. Each part of the ship was made by hand. Dana Story's family once owned a New England shipyard. He recalled the skill of these craftsmen, who used large-headed axes:

> They "beat out" the timbers and frames with their broadaxes. These men could split a pencil line with a broadaxe and think nothing of it. The finished surface would look and feel as though it had been planed.
>
> Dana Story, *Frame Up!*

First, men cut oak logs into huge beams. These beams were joined together to make the keel. A keel is like a backbone for the ship, so it must be strong. It may be 100 feet long. Next, workers cut wood for the ship's frame, and

A Craftsman

2:30 P.M., September 14, 1810
A workshop on Nantucket, an island
off the Massachusetts coast

Hammer
The red-hot harpoon glows as the blacksmith prepares to strike. The metal has just been pulled from the forge fire. Years of experience tell the blacksmith when the heated metal has become soft enough to shape.

Apron and Gloves
The blacksmith wears an apron and gloves that were gifts to him when he opened his own shop. The tough leather, worn and burned from years of use, protects him from flying sparks and heat.

Harpoon
Anchors A-weigh! The whaler *John Jay* sets sail in two days. Bill Coffin, the ship's captain, will stop by today for this harpoon that he has ordered.

Anvil
Clang! On this 200-pound anvil, the blacksmith pounds red-hot iron into anchor chains and other fittings for ships.

attached it to the keel. As you can see in the picture on page 113, a ship's frame looks much like a person's ribs.

With great care, the ship came together like a jigsaw puzzle. A new group of carpenters began putting the final pieces together. They nailed planks to the framing ribs. Using a sharp tool called an adze, they trimmed each rib to size so it would fit snugly. Caulkers plugged any cracks with strips of tar-covered fibers called oakum. This sealed the hull and kept water out.

Once the hull was finished, carpenters built cabins inside using iron braces, brackets, and other fittings.

Next, workers put in the mast by tipping the boat on its side. For good luck they placed a silver coin under the mast. Finally, riggers climbed high to set the dozens of ropes that held the ship's sails. After perhaps two months of work, the ship was ready to sail. ■

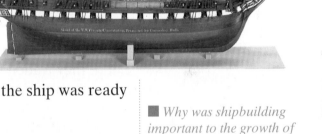

▼ *Every single piece of this ship had to be made by hand.*

■ *Why was shipbuilding important to the growth of skilled crafts in the Northeast?*

Uses of Ships

Settlers in the Northeast found many uses for the ships that were built in their ports. Two important uses were fishing and trade. Large fishing schooners sailed for the waters off the coast. Once there, small boats called dories rowed out from these schooners to set fishing lines. Rudyard Kipling, in his 1897 novel *Captains Courageous* wrote about these dories.

There must have been nearly a hundred of them, of every possible make and build . . . all bowing and curtseying one to the other. From every boat, dories were dropping away like bees from a crowded hive; and the clamour of voices, the rattling of ropes and blocks, and the splash of oars carried for miles across the heaving water.

From the dories fishermen hauled in large catches of codfish. They returned to their harbors where they salted and sold the fish. Merchants then loaded the cod onto their

115

Fishing and Shipping
Everything from fish netted by New England fishing ships to whale oil was shipped in wooden barrels. Craftsmen called coopers made these barrels. Coopers used wood cut by farmers during the winter, and hoops made by blacksmiths.

Whaling
Oil from whales helped light homes and streets in the Northeast. Hundreds of seamen hunted the whales.

Rope Making
New England ships used miles of heavy rope. Many people worked in long buildings called ropewalks making the rope.

▲ *The sea provided jobs for many in the Northeast—even for those who did not sail or fish.*

■ *Besides people who built ships, who earned their living from the sea?*

ships and sailed for faraway places, such as the West Indies. There they traded their fish for barrels of sugar, molasses, and coffee. You can locate the West Indies, a group of islands that include Cuba, the Bahamas, and other islands, on page 400–401 of the Atlas. They lie in the Caribbean Sea to the south and east of Florida.

Merchant ships also traded with towns along the Northeast coast for grain, wood, and other **raw materials**. A raw material is something that is taken from the earth to be made into something else. The merchant ships then carried these raw materials to Europe. There they traded for pottery, tools, cloth, silver, and other manufactured goods. After the ships returned to the Northeast, the goods were sold in the shops of the harbor towns.

The Northeast had much of value to trade. By helping the fishing and trade businesses to grow, shipbuilders helped the Northeast to grow as well. ■

R E V I E W

1. **FOCUS** Why did shipbuilding become such a successful business in the Northeast?
2. **CONNECT** Find an example from Lesson 1 of another important resource in the Northeast.
3. **GEOGRAPHY** Why did England place great value on the pine trees of New Hampshire and Maine?
4. **CRITICAL THINKING** Why was it so important for people to become craftsmen in the Northeast?
5. **WRITING ACTIVITY** Imagine that you lived in New England in 1750. Write a paragraph telling what job you would like to have.

116

Identifying Causes and Effects

Here's Why

An event that leads to other events is a cause. The events that happen as a result of the cause are its effects. Events in history are often related in a chain of causes and effects. For example, the people in New England saw that their tall pine trees made good masts for ships. One effect of this was that England took the best trees to build English ships. Identifying other causes and their effects will help you understand how events in history are connected.

Here's How

The diagram below shows that people's use of whale oil for lamps was a cause that led to other events. First, many New Englanders found jobs building whaling ships. That was one effect of the demand for whale oil. What other effects are shown in the diagram?

Asking the right questions can help you to identify causes and effects. To identify the possible causes of an event,

ask yourself, "Why did it happen?" To discover the effects of an event, ask, "What happened as a result?"

Word clues can also help you to identify causes and effects. The word clues *because*, *since*, *for*, and *in order to* often signal that a cause will follow. The words *so*, *therefore*, and *as a result* are often clues that an effect will follow.

Try It

Make a chart with two headings: "Causes" and "Effects." Then read the examples below. Write the cause and effect for each in the proper columns on your chart. Remember to look for word clues and to ask, "Why did it happen?" and "What happened as a result?"

1. Whaling towns became important centers of business and trade because of the money that whale oil and other whale products brought in.
2. Whales became increasingly scarce in the Atlantic, and as a result, the whalers began to look for whales in the Pacific Ocean.
3. People discovered that whalebone is springy, flexible, and strong. Therefore, they used it for items such as the handles of horse whips and the ribs of women's undergarments.
4. Because people found that oil could be pumped from the ground cheaply, the demand for whale oil decreased.

Apply It

Reread Lesson 1 in this chapter. Ask yourself what happened as a result of nearly all the beavers in Europe being killed. Make a list of the effects.

Cause

Effects

People used whale oil for their lamps.

More ships were built in New England shipyards.

Whaling seaports grew in size and importance.

Whale herds were wiped out.

LESSON 3

Farms and Mills

THINKING
FOCUS

Why did wheat farming become a successful business in the Northeast?

Key Terms

- river valley
- port

➤ *Women had many jobs on farms. Here they churn milk to make butter.*

Only a faint sliver of moon lights the country road near Lancaster, Pennsylvania. It is two hours before dawn. But the road is as crowded as the town center at noon. Horse-drawn wagons piled high with vegetables rumble by. Black buggies rattle up behind them with butter pails, cheeses, and chickens bouncing along in back. Young women ride on horseback. Bags of dried apples hang from behind their saddles.

The women have been riding all night. In the early morning, they will sell their goods at a stand in the town center. Baskets of peaches, boxes of eggs, and piles of vegetables will nearly spill over the edges of the table. Jars of jams, apple butter, and coleslaw will rise up in stacks.

As daylight comes, the market overflows with customers. Everyone knows these women bring in the best farm goods. By day's end, the stands are empty and spotless again. The women head home. They are tired but proud of their day's earnings.

Successful Farming

In the 1600s and 1700s, many farmers settled along the rivers that had first been traveled by fur traders. A **river valley** is the land through which a river passes. Over thousands of years, floods had deposited new soil in these river valleys. This new soil was fertile which helped crops to grow.

Farmland in the Susquehanna *(SUHS kwuh HAN uh)*, Hudson, and Delaware river valleys was the best in the Northeast. The flat land had rich soil and plenty of rainfall. This made Pennsylvania, New Jersey, and New York the best colonies for farming.

The women you just read about were farmers in Pennsylvania. William Penn founded this colony. In the late 1600s, Penn invited poor German farmers to come to Pennsylvania to farm. These farmers called themselves Deutsch *(doych)*, their word for "German." Other people thought they were saying "Dutch." So the German farmers became known as the Pennsylvania Dutch.

These farmers knew how to take good care of the soil because it was just like the soil they farmed in Germany. Each year they planted different crops on the land. This crop rotation kept the soil rich.

The Pennsylvania Dutch also grew fruit trees. The fruit from these trees was dried and saved for the winter months. Dairy cows provided milk and butter for the Pennsylvania Dutch. Huge two-story barns housed the cows and other farm animals. Most farms had many other buildings as well.

◄ *This painting shows the Margaret and Thomas Hillborn family doing chores on their farm. The picture stresses the values of family and hard work that were so important to Pennsylvania farmers.*

Using the Land and Sea

In a smokehouse, meat was smoked to preserve it for future use. A windmill ground grain into flour. The Pennsylvania Dutch became well known for their neat, clean farms. ■

Selling Wheat

Farmers in the fertile river valleys of the Northeast grew more wheat than they needed. They sent this extra wheat to the nearest port. A **port** is a place along a river or a coast where ships deliver and receive goods. At the port they traded the grain for manufacturered goods.

The Pennsylvania Dutch built Conestoga (*KAHN ih STOH guh*) wagons to carry their wheat. These big wagons were pulled by teams of four to six horses or oxen. By the early 1700s, hundreds of Conestoga wagons were rolling into Philadelphia from the farms of Pennsylvania and Delaware. Many farmers in New York State and New Jersey brought their wheat to New York City.

Some farmers in the Northeast sent their wheat down the rivers on flat boats called barges. Merchants in the port cities bought this wheat. The wheat was then milled, or ground into flour. The diagram on page 121 shows how the milling was done. After milling, workers loaded the flour into barrels. Merchants then shipped the flour to the West Indies and to Europe.

▲ The farms of the region produced a variety of fruits, vegetables, and dairy products.

■ *Give two reasons why the Pennsylvania Dutch were successful farmers.*

➤ *The Conestoga wagon would later be used to carry thousands of settlers to the western United States.*

Oliver Evans' Mill

Turning the stones of a mill to grind wheat took a lot of power. For this reason, mills were built on river banks. The river's flowing water turned a water wheel, which then turned the millstones. But even though water did much of the work, mill workers still had to carry the heavy sacks of grain to feed into the mill.

In the 1780s, a young man worked out a plan for a new kind of mill. Oliver Evans wanted to cut down on the human work in milling. So he set up a new type of mill near Philadelphia. Powered by water, a chain of buckets carried grain to the top of the mill. The grain then poured down to the millstones. There it was ground into flour. The flour moved on flat belts to be dried. Then it was poured into barrels and covered. Evans' mill needed few workers to keep running.

With the growth of farming, the wheat trade became as important as the trade in fish and furs. In the years to come, the Northeast would see even greater changes. People would soon use the ideas of Evans and others to build new factories and machines. These inventions changed the work and the trade of the Northeast and of the nation. ■

▼ Flour mills used the power of water to grind wheat.

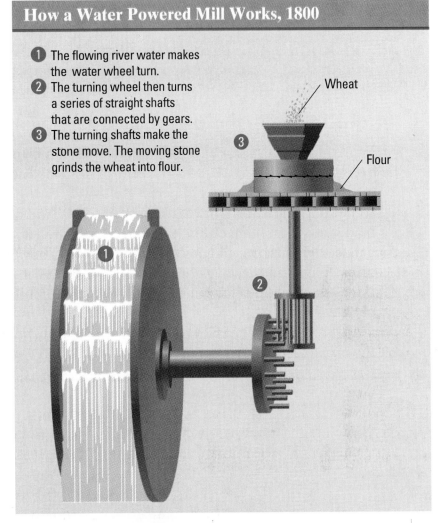

How a Water Powered Mill Works, 1800

1. The flowing river water makes the water wheel turn.
2. The turning wheel then turns a series of straight shafts that are connected by gears.
3. The turning shafts make the stone move. The moving stone grinds the wheat into flour.

Wheat

Flour

■ How did wheat help the farmers and merchants in the Northeast?

R E V I E W

1. **FOCUS** Why did wheat farming become a successful business in the Northeast?

2. **CONNECT** What crops were important in the Southeast that were not as important in the Northeast?

3. **GEOGRAPHY** Why was farming successful in the southern part of the Northeast?

4. **CRITICAL THINKING** For settlers in the Northeast, what did wheat have in common with beaver pelts and fish?

5. **ACTIVITY** Look up the Northeast states in the Minipedia, pages 350-399. Note the rank of agriculture today compared to other economic activities.

Chapter Review

Reviewing Key Terms

craftsman (p.113)
manufactured goods (p.107)
port (p.120)

raw material (p.116)
river valley (p.119)
trade (p.107)

A. Write the key term for each definition below.

1. a person who has learned a special skill
2. something taken from the earth to be made into something else
3. a place along a river or coast where ships deliver and receive goods
4. things that are made or put together by people
5. land through which a river passes
6. the exchange of one good for another

B. Choose the key term that best completes each sentence.

1. New England forests provided the basic _____ for ship building.
2. In return for beaver pelts, settlers gave the Indians _____ that were made in Europe.
3. Trading ships from England and other European countries sailed into _____ along the coast of the Northeast.
4. During the 1600s, it took a skilled_____ to build a ship.
5. _____ in beaver pelts helped to settle the Northeast.

Exploring Concepts

A. Complete the chart below on a separate piece of paper. Use information from this chapter.

Trade in the Northeast		
What was traded?	**Where did these goods come from?**	**What were these goods used for?**
Beaver pelts		
Pine trees		
Fish		
Wheat		

B. Write one or two sentences to answer each question below. Use information that you find in the chapter.

1. How did the Northeast become a center for beaver fur trade in the 1600s?
2. Why were so many ships built in the shipyards of the Northeast?
3. Where were trading posts located?
4. Why were German farmers so successful on their Pennsylvania farms?
5. How was wheat milled into flour in the 1700s?
6. Why did Oliver Evans decide to build a new kind of mill?

Reviewing Skills

1. Write the following sentences on a separate piece of paper. Draw a line under the part of the sentence that describes an effect. Circle words that signal a cause-and-effect relationship.
   a. Because of the raw materials nearby, New England ports had a large shipbuilding industry.
   b. Most men in Nantucket went to sea, and as a result, many of the town's stores were run by women.
   c. People found that whale oil burned with a bright, clean flame, so whale oil became very valuable.
2. Read the following paragraph. Which sentence gives the main idea of the paragraph? Which sentences give details that support the main idea?

The captain of a whaling ship needed to have many skills. He had to be an expert navigator, for his voyage might take him around the world. Because a ship stopped in many lands to trade, the captain had to know different languages and customs. Finally, the most successful captains developed the special ability of finding whales in the vast ocean.

3. Reread the paragraph above. Ask yourself which sentences contain both a cause and an effect. On a separate sheet of paper, list the causes under the heading *Causes*. List the effects under the heading *Effects*.

Using Critical Thinking

1. Most workers in shipbuilding, fishing, and the fur trade were men, not women. What jobs do women do today that they didn't do long ago?
2. Traders did not use money. They exchanged the goods they had for the goods they wanted. How would life be different today if people exchanged goods instead of using money?
3. If you were a craftsman who built ships, which job would you have liked to do? Why?

Preparing for Citizenship

1. ART ACTIVITY Draw a picture of a trade ship, a schooner, or a dory that was used in the Northeast. Include people working and a background. Write a caption for your picture.
2. GROUP ACTIVITY Work with a small group to find out about beavers. Find information about where they live and how they build their homes. Then make a poster about the beaver to share with another class. Using the poster, explain the life of the beaver and the part that it played long ago in the fur trade.
3. COLLABORATIVE LEARNING As a class project, plan a Trading Day. In one group, decide what kinds of items can be traded and how the exchanges will be made. In another group, draw up a list of rules to make sure the trades are fair. Have each group present its plan to the rest of the class. Then ask your classmates to bring in small inexpensive items that they would be willing to trade. On Trading Day, everyone in the class should take part in the trading.

Chapter 6
Industry Takes Over

At the dawn of the 1800s, the Northeast was on the move. New factories made a growing number of useful goods. Railroads and waterways helped the factories make even more goods to send around the growing nation. Business prospered, and as it did, the nearby cities grew out—and up toward the sky.

Steam engines help power the growth of the Northeast. The powerful machines are used to make goods and to move people and products.

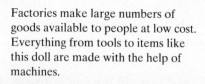

Factories make large numbers of goods available to people at low cost. Everything from tools to items like this doll are made with the help of machines.

1800	1840	1880

1800

1814 Francis Lowell's mill in Waltham, Massachusetts, uses machines to make cloth from start to finish.

The twin towers of the World Trade Center are a symbol of New York City's role as the home to thousands of businesses.

5th AVE for 34th St. B-16257
UNDERHILL, Photographer New York

1910 The Northeast becomes a region known for its large cities. Here people crowd a busy street in New York City.

1920	1960	2000

1976 Washington, D.C., becomes the most recent city of the Northeast to open a subway.

2000

LESSON 1

Factories Bring Change

How did machines change the lives of people in the Northeast?

Key Terms

- wage
- immigrant

➤ *This painting shows Samuel Slater's first mill. The water rushing over the waterfall supplied a great deal of power.*

I n September of 1789, a young man boarded a ship in England. Others on board did not notice him. He looked like an ordinary farmer. However, this man— Samuel Slater—carried something of great value. This valuable item was not in his bags. It was not in his pockets. It was in his mind.

Slater was one of a few people who knew how to build England's cotton-spinning machines. He had worked with the machines for seven years. He knew how to build them and how to use water power to drive them.

The English used the machines to spin cotton that they bought from plantations in the Southeast. The English wanted to be the only ones with these kinds of machines, so they did not allow people to take the machines, or the plans for them, out of England. They even tried to keep people who worked on them from leaving England. But, this did not stop Slater. Disguised as a farmer, he sailed for the United States with the plans for the machine in his head.

Growth of Factories

After reaching the United States, Slater found a spot along the Blackstone River in Pawtucket, Rhode Island. There he built a mill. The swift river gave the mill power.

Before Slater built his mill, people had spun yarn by hand. Making yarn in this way was a slow job. Slater's water-powered machines made yarn quickly. He needed only a few workers, so the cost of making yarn was low. People could buy it for less money than they had before.

Before long, other new factories were making goods of all kinds. Like Slater's yarn, these goods cost less to make and buy. These factories allowed people to make large amounts of manufactured goods.

The Need for Steam

The number of factories grew in the early 1800s. But places for new factories were getting hard to find. Many areas had no rivers swift enough to power a factory.

Steam engines did not need the power of flowing water. They allowed people to build factories away from rivers. Steam engines used the power made when water boils. If you watch a covered pot boil, you can see a small example of this power. Steam from the boiling water makes the lid move.

Workers in Pittsburgh, Pennsylvania, built many steam engines. The city was close to sources of iron, coal, and water needed to make the engines. As a result, Pittsburgh became a city of industry. In 1841, a visitor wrote about Pittsburgh's factories, telling how "the hissing of steam, the clanking of chains, the jarring and grinding of wheels and other machinery, and the glow of melted glass and iron, and burning coal beneath burst upon" his eyes and ears. ■

▼ *By the middle of the 1800s, factories were making goods of all kinds. This factory in Connecticut made hoops that women wore under their skirts.*

■ *What effect did the steam engine have on the location of factories in the Northeast?*

The First Wage-Earners

In 1800, most people were farmers. However, farm life was not easy in many areas. New England was such an area. Poor soil there made it hard to earn a living by farming.

127

Changes in Factory Production, 1769–1897

1784 Oliver Evans, seen on the right, invents a way to use water power for many flour mill jobs. He uses machines rather than people to move wheat through the mill.

| 1750 | 1775 | 1800 |

1769 English inventor Richard Arkwright develops the water frame, shown here. The machine is powered by a river or stream and spins thread quickly.

1789 Samuel Slater arrives in the United States with the secret of Arkwright's spinning machines.

▲ *The growth of factories started in England. It did not take long for factories to reach the Northeast.*

New England farm children saw that the factories paid good wages. A **wage** is money paid in return for work. Thousands of young people left the farm for factories. As a result, many parents had trouble running their farms. This story appeared in the April, 1837, *Old Farmer's Almanac:*

> My boys have all left me and turned shoe-peggers. I was in hopes to keep at least one of them to help carry on the farm; but they have all five gone. . . . If this is the way things are going on, our farms must soon run up to bushes.

▼ *The Morning Bell,* a painting by Winslow Homer, *shows that women played a central role in many early factories.*

In the early 1800s, factories sometimes hired many members of a single family. One group of New England mills hired only young women. These hard-working women also came from the region's farms.

Later, immigrants from Ireland, Germany, and other countries began taking the factory jobs. An **immigrant** is someone who moves to a new country. By the 1840s, ships were bringing thousands of immigrants to cities in the Northeast. Most of these immigrants came to find better jobs. In the late 1800s, these

1814 Francis Lowell builds a successful mill in Waltham, Massachusetts. Lowell's mill uses machines powered by flowing water to make cloth.

1850 Factories are making a great variety of goods in large numbers. These goods are inexpensive to make, so people can afford to buy them.

1825	1850	1875

1817 John Hall finds a way to make metal parts that are exactly the same. Hall's ideas are used to make products like clocks and sewing machines.

1870 Steam engines like this now provide much of the power in factories. The engines help build trains, farm machines, and many other large goods.

immigrants were joined by people from Italy, Greece, Poland, and other countries. See page 400 of the Atlas to locate these countries.

Factory Work

Inside the factory, work was a challenge. Workers stood at the machines 12 hours a day, six days a week. The machines were noisy. Some were dangerous. Factory owners wanted workers to work quickly and make more goods. Workers who wanted to keep their jobs had little choice but to do what the owners said.

Workers also had to get used to doing one job over and over. In shoe factories, some workers just cut soles. Others stitched, or nailed, or buffed. It was a big change from the days when one shoemaker made a whole shoe.

Of course, many men and women liked their jobs. They enjoyed the challenge of working in a factory. For these workers, the changes brought about by new and faster machines meant new opportunities. ■

Across Time & Space

In the 1800s, factories often hired very young children. The factories did so because they could pay the children less than they did older workers. Today, laws prevent the hiring of children under a certain age.

■ *What was one important way that factories changed how people worked?*

R E V I E W

1. **FOCUS** How did machines change the lives of people in the Northeast?
2. **CONNECT** Find an example from your earlier reading in this book of how an invention helped change the way people worked.
3. **HISTORY** Name two groups of people who

were affected by the growth of factories.
4. **CRITICAL THINKING** Why do you think England did not want other countries to know how to build their machines?
5. **ACTIVITY** Make a list of things you use every day that are made with the help of machines.

Making a Timeline

Here's Why

The timeline in Lesson 1 shows the years in which some events occurred that led to the spread of factories. A timeline shows the order of events. A timeline can help you to remember important dates. Making a timeline is a useful way to organize a list of events.

Here's How

The timeline below shows important events in the history of Newark, New Jersey. The timeline begins with the year 1790 and ends with 1840. You can see that it covers a period of 50 years and is divided into 5 sections of 10 years each. Each event on a timeline is placed at the year when it happened. If an event happened over several years, it should be placed near the middle of the period.

Try It

Copy the timeline of events that happened in Newark. Leave room for making the line longer. Then add the events listed below. Extend the timeline to cover years that are not included in the timeline on this page.

1. Leather tanning centers opened on Market Street in the 1730s.
2. Edward Weston established the first U.S. factory for making electrical machinery in 1877.
3. By 1846, Newark had more than 100 factories powered by steam engines.
4. First Newark iron forge was built in 1710.
5. In 1872, the Newark Industrial Exposition showed off the city's manufactured goods.
6. Between 1840 and 1860, many German immigrants settled in Newark.

Apply It

Make a timeline of important events in your family's history. Choose events you want to include and find out when they happened. Decide how many years your timeline will show in all. Share the timeline with a friend or relative.

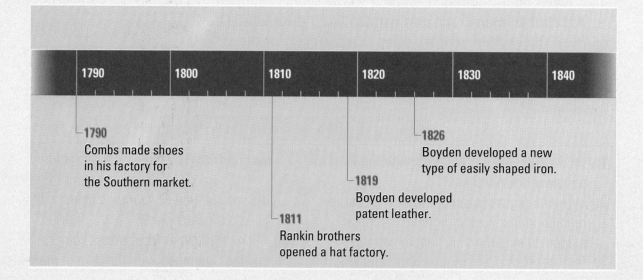

1790 · 1800 · 1810 · 1820 · 1830 · 1840

1790
Combs made shoes in his factory for the Southern market.

1811
Rankin brothers opened a hat factory.

1819
Boyden developed patent leather.

1826
Boyden developed a new type of easily shaped iron.

LESSON 2

Railways and Waterways

The year was 1827, and the city of Baltimore, Maryland, had a problem. New York and Pennsylvania were taking over much of the trade in the Northeast. Their factories were making and selling more goods than factories in Baltimore. The city's leaders looked into the future—and saw grass growing in the once-busy streets. They had to do something.

One February day, a group of 25 people met at the home of Baltimore merchant George Brown. The group was meeting to discuss ways to brighten Baltimore's future. Talk soon turned to a new invention from England. This invention used large cars that ran along a track. It was called a railroad. Maybe this was the way to bring more trade to Baltimore. They decided they would give the invention a try.

Three years later, members of that group sat in a railroad car. Before them stretched the first 13 miles of the new Baltimore and Ohio Railroad—the B & O. Attached to the front of the railroad car was a small steam engine on wheels. The engine was the first locomotive built in the United States. With the train's first chugs, recalled rider H. B. Latrobe, "The blower whistled, the steam blew off in vapory clouds, the pace increased, the passengers shouted, . . . and a great hurrah hailed the victory."

How did railroads, canals, and subways help the Northeast grow in the 1800s?

Key Terms

- transportation
- canal

▼ *With the B & O's success, railroads soon began to appear across the region.*

131

Industry Takes Over

▼ How did the number of miles of canals change between 1840 and 1880?

Building Waterways and Railroads

Factories grew quickly in the early 1800s. Transportation was needed to bring raw materials to the factories and also to ship manufactured goods to customers. **Transportation** is the way by which goods or people are moved from place to place.

One reason for Baltimore's problem in 1827 was that New York had better transportation. In 1825, New York opened the Erie Canal. A **canal** is a waterway made by people. A Closer Look on page 133 shows how people built the Erie Canal.

The Erie Canal linked the Hudson River to the Great Lakes. The Midwest sent raw materials such as coal to New York along the canal. Northeast factories used the raw materials to make goods. Merchants then shipped the goods on the canal to the Midwest.

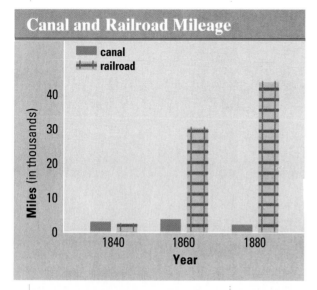

Canal and Railroad Mileage

Legend: canal, railroad

Miles (in thousands): 40, 30, 20, 10, 0

Year: 1840, 1860, 1880

➤ Notice how well railroads and canals covered the Northeast by 1860.

Across Time & Space

The New York Thruway is a highway that runs across the state. The Thruway runs alongside the route of the first Erie Canal. In some places, old, empty sections of the canal can be seen from the road.

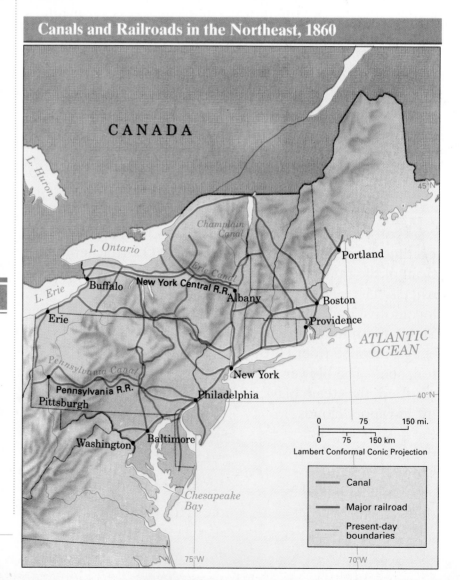

Canals and Railroads in the Northeast, 1860

CANADA

L. Huron

L. Ontario

Champlain Canal

Erie Canal

Portland

L. Erie

Buffalo

New York Central R.R.

Albany

Boston

Erie

Providence

ATLANTIC OCEAN

Pennsylvania Canal

Pennsylvania R.R.

Pittsburgh

New York

Philadelphia

40°N

45°N

0 75 150 mi.

0 75 150 km

Lambert Conformal Conic Projection

Washington

Baltimore

Chesapeake Bay

— Canal

— Major railroad

— Present-day boundaries

75°W

70°W

Building the Erie Canal

The 363-mile Erie Canal was the first major waterway built in the United States. After eight years of work, the canal made water travel possible between western New York and the Atlantic Ocean. Goods could be carried faster than ever before. Canal boats could haul 100 times more lumber or furs than a wagon and in half the time.

"Clinton's Big Ditch" is what people called it. They laughed at Dewitt Clinton's plan to build a canal between Lake Erie and the Hudson River. They thought the canal would cost too much and not increase trade as he predicted.

Over 3,000 workers cleared trees, leveled ground, and dug the ditch for the canal. The workers were mostly farmers and Irish immigrants. They earned 50 cents a day for their backbreaking work. How hard was it? It took three men with horses and oxen three months to dig one mile.

Cannons fired in New York towns from Buffalo to Long Island to celebrate the canal's opening in 1825. Clinton poured water from Lake Erie and the Atlantic Ocean into the canal to show the joining of the two bodies of water.

133

The Erie was not the region's only canal. For example, Pennsylvania built many canals. The Schuylkill Canal connected Philadelphia and Reading.

Railroads Take Over

Canals improved transportation. As a result, they helped factories make and sell more goods. But canals froze in winter. Even in summer, canal traffic was slow. Railroads were faster, so they carried more goods to and from factories. Railroads also worked all year long. By the 1840s, people in the Northeast were racing to build railroads. J. P. Kennedy of Baltimore spoke for many of these people. He said that his city should "imitate the spider; spread her lines [tracks] towards every point of the compass, and lodge in the center of them."

Railroads offered good transportation. They also became a well-loved part of the countryside. John Lewis discussed railroads in his 1851 book, *Across the Atlantic.* ■

■ *What advantages did railroads have over canals?*

A s for villages and country towns, it rattles right up their main streets, [often] stopping at the door of the hotel or in front of the church. . . .You might sometimes shake hands with the people . . . who stand at their shop fronts to see you go past.

▼ *W. Louis Sonntag painted this New York scene,* The Bowery at Night, *around 1895. This section of train tracks was built above the street.*

Getting People to Work

You have seen how railroads and canals helped factories grow. Their success was important to the Northeast. The literature selection at the end of this lesson will give you an idea of the affection people felt for the railroads and canals.

With the growing factories came more workers. The cities, where many factories were located, grew crowded. Each day the streets filled with horse-drawn carts and people. After work, factory workers walked to their homes nearby.

Coming to the City

Many people longed to escape the city crowds, but they could not move too far away. They had to live close enough to reach their jobs in the cities.

In the 1840s, companies began building a new kind of transportation system. The system used horse-drawn buses that ran on tracks. The buses traveled to areas beyond the cities. Now people could live outside the cities and still get to work. Of course, they could not move too far away. The speed of the buses was about five miles an hour. As a result, they only traveled a few miles from the city.

Beginning in the late 1800s, horse-drawn buses were replaced with electric streetcars. Streetcars were much faster than buses, so they reached areas farther away from the cities.

People loved the streetcars. They especially liked the open cars used in warm weather. Families sometimes rode them just for fun. They used streetcars to reach parks, zoos, and beaches, as well as their jobs.

The streetcars helped people get to work and to enjoy the cities. But the speed of the streetcars was a danger on busy streets. By the end of the 1800s, Boston and New York had plans to run their streetcars underground. These underground tracks are called subways.

Subways still play a big role in Northeastern cities. Millions of people depend on subways and buses to get to work each day. Like the railroads and canals in the 1800s, this form of transportation helps trade. And this helps businesses and cities grow. ■

▲ *Only women were allowed to ride on this 1909 New York subway car.*

▼ *In 1900, New York City's mayor used this silver shovel to dig the first load of dirt for the city's new subway line.*

■ *Find information to support this statement: Transportation for people is as important as transportation for products.*

R E V I E W

1. **FOCUS** How did railroads, canals, and subways help the Northeast grow in the 1800s?

2. **CONNECT** Before railroads and canals, how did people travel and ship goods?

3. **GEOGRAPHY** What might have happened in the cities if buses, streetcars, and subways had not been built?

4. **CRITICAL THINKING** Why do you think that railroads are less important today than they were in the 1800s?

5. **WRITING ACTIVITY** Imagine you are a mayor of a northeastern city in 1830. Write a speech about why you think the city needs a railroad.

John Henry

The sound of John Henry's hammer rings in many traditional folk tales and work songs. All the stories are based on the life of a real man, a black railroad worker in the 1870s. In this song, John Henry with his hammer races against a steam-powered drill. John Henry's story tells us about the early days of the railroads in this country. As you read, ask yourself, "How would it feel to tunnel through a mountain using only a hammer?"

John Henry was a little baby,
Sittin' on his gran'ma's knee,
Oh, he lift up a hammer and a little chunk of steel,
Said, "This hammer's gonna be the death of me. Lord, Lord.
Yes, this hammer's gonna be the death of me."

The captain says to John Henry,
Gonna bring a steam drill 'round,
Gonna take that drill out on the road,
Gonna drive that steel on down. Lord, Lord.
Gonna drive that steel on down.

John Henry drove through fourteen feet,
The steam drill only drove nine;
But he drove so hard that he broke his poor heart,
And he laid down his hammer and he died. Lord, Lord.
Yes, he laid down his hammer and he died.

They took John Henry to the graveyard
And they buried him deep in sand.
Now ev'ry train that comes a-chuggin' round
Says, "Here lies a steel-drivin' man." Lord, Lord.
Says, "Here lies a steel-drivin' man."

As you learned in Lesson 2, railroads and waterways linked the United States and brought about an exciting new age in transportation. But the people who did the everyday hard work of building and running the railroads and canals were often overloaded. These two songs tell about their contributions.

The Erie Canal

William S. Allen

In the early 1800s, barges filled with millions of tons of raw materials and finished goods made their slow but steady way through the Erie Canal and on to the Atlantic Ocean or the Great Lakes. Mule drivers, and their mules pulled the barges through the narrow canal that at some places was little larger than a drainage ditch. This is a song that the mule drivers sang as they rode. As you read, ask yourself, "What would it be like to drive a mule on the canal?"

I've got a mule, her name is Sal,
Fifteen years on the Erie Canal.
She's a good old worker and a good old pal,
Fifteen years on the Erie Canal.
We've hauled some barges in our day,
Filled with lumber, coal and hay,
And every inch of the way I know
From Albany to Buffalo.

Low Bridge, everybody down,
For it's Low Bridge, We're coming to a town!
You can always tell your neighbor,
You can always tell your pal,
If you've ever navigated on the Erie Canal.

We better get along on our way, old gal,
Fifteen miles on the Erie Canal.
Cause you bet your life I'd never part with Sal,
Fifteen miles on the Erie Canal.
Git up there, mule, here comes a lock,
We'll make Rome 'bout six o'clock.
One more trip and back we'll go
Right back home to Buffalo.

Further Reading

The Folk Songs of North America. Alan Lomax. This collection contains more than 300 folk songs.

L E S S O N 3

The Story of the Corporations

T H I N K I N G
F O C U S

What are corporations and why did they grow in the late 1800s?

Key Terms

- corporation
- invest

➤ *This picture shows how rush hour got its name. Rush hour happens twice a day, when people travel to work and when they leave to go home.*

It begins just after dawn. The silence of the night is broken by the gentle "whoosh" of a passing car. Within minutes, this almost peaceful sound has become a loud roar. The road is filling up with cars, trucks, and buses. Soon it will look like a river of traffic.

Meanwhile, the sidewalks of the city are also becoming crowded. Now and then, the doors of a subway station burst open. A flood of men and women pours into the street. Waiting for them are people selling newspapers or shoeshines. Most of the men and women walk quickly past. A few yell to passing cabs, which screech to a stop.

One by one people duck into the tall buildings along the street. They line up outside the shiny brass doors of the elevator. Once inside, they push the button for their floor. A short ride later, the doors open. Then it's down the hallway, in the door, and to the desk.

Another day at work is about to begin.

Growth of a Company

In Lesson 2, you read about the growth of the Northeast's factories and cities. You have just read about how people today get to work in a northeastern city. Which city? It could be any one of dozens in the region. How did the Northeast change from a region of small mills to one of tall buildings? One company's story will help to explain.

A Problem of Size

Running a railroad was much more difficult than running a small mill or factory, as the Pennsylvania Railroad found out. It takes a lot of money to buy equipment and pay the many people who work for you. In order to get money to run its business, a company can become a corporation. A **corporation** is a company that is allowed to raise money from the public. Corporations raise money by getting people to invest. To **invest** means to give a corporation money in return for a share of whatever the company earns. So the Pennsylvania Railroad became a corporation.

J. Edgar Thomson became president of the Pennsylvania Railroad in 1852. Thomson saw that no one person could run such a large company, so he broke the railroad into many small departments. Each department was in charge of one part of the railroad. For example, one department repaired track. Another bought equipment. One main office made decisions for the whole company. Each department took orders from this office.

People invest in corporations by buying stock. Papers like this one show that a person owns stock. Stock is bought and sold at a stock exchange, seen below.

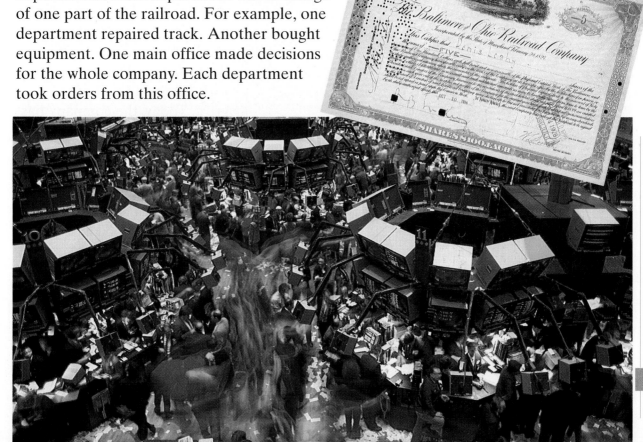

139

Thomson soon had the railroad running smoothly. Each department was able to concentrate on one job, so it did that job well. As a result, the Pennsylvania Railroad earned a lot of money. It grew to be a huge corporation.

Because the Pennsylvania Railroad was earning money, more people wanted to invest in it. The railroad used the money people invested to build more track. By the 1890s, the railroad had 5,000 miles of track and 50,000 workers. ■

Corporations in the Northeast

The Pennsylvania Railroad was a success. The ideas that helped it grow helped other companies too. The DuPont Company is one example.

DuPont began business in 1802 as a small mill on Delaware's Brandywine River. They made gunpowder. All through the 1800s, the DuPont Company grew. Improved transportation in the Northeast helped the company to sell its product to more and more markets.

DuPont used some of its money to buy new factories. Many of these factories made goods besides gunpowder. By the 1930s, DuPont was making paint, film, and many other goods. Just as the Pennsylvania Railroad had, DuPont set up many different departments. This organization helped DuPont to grow. Today, the company has 140,000 workers and hundreds of offices and factories.

A similar story could be told about many companies in the Northeast. These companies have helped cities and towns grow. Their workers fill the Northeast's offices, factories, and homes.

Building a Team
What is it like to work in a large corporation today? That's a hard question. Each

How did the Pennsylvania Railroad operate smoothly in spite of its size?

▼ *This map, along with the Minipedia on pages 350–399, shows that the people per square mile in many northeastern states is higher than in other regions. For help in using this population density map and the Minipedia, see pages G13 and G15 of the* Map and Globe Handbook.

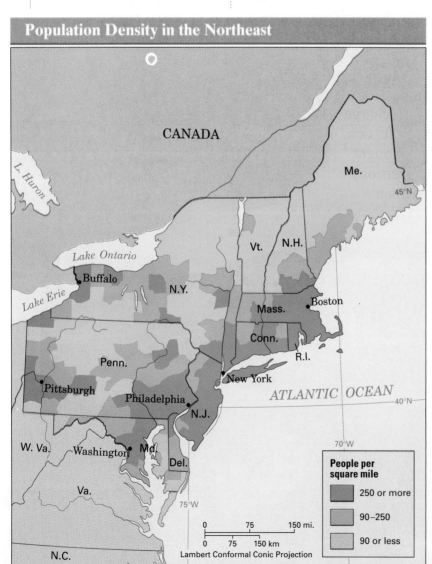

Population Density in the Northeast

CANADA

L. Huron

Lake Ontario

Buffalo

Lake Erie

N.Y.

Me.

45°N

Vt.   N.H.

Mass.   Boston

Conn.

R.I.

Penn.

Pittsburgh

Philadelphia

New York

ATLANTIC OCEAN

40°N

N.J.

W. Va.   Washington   Md.

Del.

Va.

70°W

75°W

People per square mile

250 or more

90–250

90 or less

0   75   150 mi.

0   75   150 km

Lambert Conformal Conic Projection

N.C.

The Many Offices of a Large Toy Corporation

Main Office
People in this office keep track of what all the other offices are doing. The president of Acme works here.

Factory and Shipping Office
Some people who work here run the machines that make Acme toys. Some keep track of how many toys they have ready to sell. Others pack up the toys and load them in the trucks.

Sales and Advertising Office
People in this office sell Acme toys to toy stores across the country. Another group here writes commercials for television and magazines.

New Product Development Office
These men and women try to think up new toys to make. They talk with people to find out what toys children want. Then they figure out how to make them.

corporation has many different jobs. One thing, however, is found in all good companies—teamwork. People can have different jobs, but they must work together in order for a company to succeed. Company leader James Treybig knows about the need for teamwork. He says that one key to building a good company is "bringing different ideas together and different kinds of people and working at it and letting it kind of grow."

Teamwork is also good for workers. People like being an important part of a successful team. That's why good companies make workers feel like partners in business. They ask workers to share their ideas with the company. Company leader Rene McPherson puts it this way: "You never stop listening. You never stop asking people what they think." In this way, people in every department can see that they make a difference.

As you have seen, people have made a big difference in the development of this region. From the fur trade to the factories to the corporations, people and businesses have built and shaped the cities of the Northeast. ■

This diagram shows how one company might have several different departments. People in these offices may have very different jobs but they are all still part of the same team.

■ *Why is teamwork an important part of the job in today's corporations?*

R E V I E W

1. **FOCUS** What are corporations and why did they grow in the late 1800s?
2. **CONNECT** Compare today's corporations with enterprises discussed in earlier chapters.
3. **GEOGRAPHY** Why might it be harder to run a business that is spread over many cities?
4. **CRITICAL THINKING** What factors might a person consider before investing in a corporation?
5. **ACTIVITY** As a class, discuss what might happen if all the workers in a company did not work as a team.

141

Chapter Review

Reviewing Key Terms

canal (p. 132)
corporation (p. 139)
immigrant (p. 128)
invest (p. 139)
transportation (p. 132)
wage (p. 128)

A. Write the key term for each definition below:
1. money paid in return for work
2. someone who moves to a new country
3. a kind of company that is allowed to raise money from the public
4. the process of moving something or someone from one place to another
5. to give a company money in hopes of getting more money back at a later time
6. a waterway made by people

B. Choose the key terms that best complete the sentences in each paragraph.

During the 1800s, thousands of European _____ came to the Northeast looking for work. Many found jobs in mills and other factories. They worked hard for the _____ they earned.

Factory goods were shipped by railroads and _____. These two methods of _____ helped factories grow. With so much business, the railroads grew also. By raising money for new growth, the Pennsylvania Railroad became a large _____. People who chose to _____ in the railroad helped pay for new trains, offices, and tracks.

Exploring Concepts

A. Complete the chart below on a separate piece of paper. Use information from your reading in this chapter to give an effect on industry for each one of the causes listed in the chart.

Cause	Effect on industry in the Northeast
Development of steam power	
Building of canals and railroads	
Building of streetcar and subway lines	
Growth of large corporations	

B. Support each statement below by writing another sentence. Use details from this chapter.
1. Samuel Slater's machines changed the way that yarn was made in the United States.
2. Thousands of young people gave up working on farms in order to take jobs in factories.
3. New York factories made good use of the Erie Canal.
4. Although canals had improved transportation, the railroads offered an even better way to travel.
5. Many city workers today depend on subways and buses.
6. Running a large corporation requires teamwork.

Reviewing Skills

1. The timeline on this page shows the dates for important developments in transportation. Copy the timeline on a separate piece of paper. Then add the dates for three other transportation developments mentioned in the chapter. Extend the timeline if necessary.

2. Make a chart with two headings: "Causes" and "Effects." Read the following sentences. Write the cause and the effect from each sentence in the appropriate columns of the chart.
   a. Because early factories used water power, they were built along rivers.
   b. People wanted to live outside the cities, so companies built transportation to get them to and from their jobs.
   c. There was not much land in the cities for new buildings, and as a result, businesses built skyscrapers.

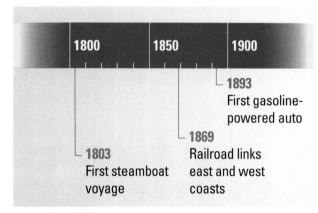

1800   1850   1900

1893
First gasoline-
powered auto

1869
Railroad links
east and west
coasts

1803
First steamboat
voyage

3. Look at the population map in the Atlas on page 410. Find the areas with the greatest population per square mile. Compare this map with the land use map on page 409. What conclusion can you draw about which land use goes together with high population?

Using Critical Thinking

1. In the 1800s, railroads and subways were new. What kinds of transportation might be developed for the future?
2. United States law does not allow children to work in factories. Why do you think those laws were made?
3. In the 1800s, railroads carried many products around the country. Today trucks carry more products than railroads do. Why do you think this is so?

Preparing for Citizenship

1. **GROUP ACTIVITY** Working in small groups, make a list of the kind of transportation available to factories and people today. Discuss how new transportation systems differ from railroads and canals. Then create posters showing each of these transportation methods.
2. **WRITING ACTIVITY** Write a story about a young factory worker during the 1800s. Include details about what factory work was like at that time.
3. **COLLABORATIVE LEARNING** Suppose that your class is starting a business to bake and sell cookies in your school. You have decided to become a corporation so that you can ask investors for the money you need to start your business. Divide the class into groups of four students to plan departments for your corporation. Besides departments for purchasing raw materials, making your product, marketing it, and attracting investors, what other departments should your corporation have? Each group should report to the rest of the class on their different jobs.

The Northeast Today

The Northeast is proud of its history. The region is home to many of the nation's oldest cities, as well as some of the first schools, libraries, and government buildings. It is known as the birthplace of the nation. The Northeast is also the birthplace of a great American sport—baseball. Springtime in the region brings not only the start of baseball season, but also of another Northeast tradition—maple sugaring.

Exploring Historic Philadelphia

"Welcome to Independence Hall. Please leave your chewing gum at the door and step inside." The park service guide in the green uniform motions you in. She closes the heavy wooden doors behind you, shutting out the traffic on the street. Suddenly you realize that you're standing right where Ben Franklin stood more than 200 years before.

Some of the most brilliant people in history once gathered in this room in the young city of Philadelphia, Pennsylvania. They met to discuss the forming of a new nation, which they would later call the United States of America. Many future presidents sat in these chairs—John Adams, Thomas Jefferson, and James Madison. On top of the wooden desks around the room lie their belongings—quill pens, reading glasses, and canes. It seems like they've just stepped away from their desks.

Near Independence Hall are many other historic sites, including the building that contains the 2,000-pound Liberty Bell.

▲ *In the center of Philadelphia stands Independence Hall. It appears on one side of half dollars made in 1976.*

Political Map of the Northeast

CANADA

Maine

80°W   75°W   70°W

48°N

Burlington   Vermont

Montpelier ★   Augusta ★

New Hampshire

L. Ontario

Rochester   Portland

Syracuse   Concord ★

Buffalo   Albany

L. Erie   New York   Mass.   ★Boston

Springfield

Hartford ★   ★Providence

Connecticut   Rhode Island

New Haven

Pennsylvania

Newark

Pittsburgh   Harrisburg   New York

Philadelphia   ★Trenton

New Jersey

Wilmington

W. Va.   Baltimore

Washington ⊛   ★Dover

Annapolis

Virginia   Delaware

Maryland   ATLANTIC OCEAN

40°N

	National capital
★	State capital
•	Major city
—	National boundary
—	State boundary

0   75   150 mi.

0   75   150 km

Lambert Conformal Conic Projection

Exploring Washington, D.C.

You never know who you might bump into in the nation's capital—maybe a senator, maybe an ambassador, maybe even the President of the United States.

In Washington, D.C., you can see the government at work. You can visit the Capitol and watch Congress making laws. And you can stroll through the White House, where the President lives and works.

The best place to get a view of the city is from the pencil-point top of the Washington Monument. You can climb the winding staircase up 555 feet or take the easy way

▼ *The Washington Monument provides visitors with an excellent view of Washington, D.C.*

by elevator. From there you can look out on the city of green parks, cherry trees, and brilliant white monuments.

Exploring Cooperstown, New York

An observer of life in the United States once wrote, "Whoever wants to know the heart and mind of America had better learn baseball." There is no better place to get to know baseball than in Cooperstown, New York.

Some people claim that baseball was invented in Cooperstown which today is baseball's hometown. The city is home to the National Baseball Hall of Fame. A visit to the Hall of Fame can tell you a lot about the United States. The photos, uniforms, and other displays give you a look at heroes such as Jackie Robinson, Hank Aaron, and Babe Ruth.

Baseball greats like Babe Ruth, Mickey Mantle, and Hank Aaron are paid tribute in the Baseball Hall of Fame in Cooperstown, New York.

Exploring Maple Sugar Country

For much of the United States, spring means baseball. In the forests of Vermont, spring is maple sugar season.

As the weather begins to warm, sap starts to flow in the trunks of maple trees. This sap can be collected by drilling small holes into the trees. The sap is then boiled. As the water in the sap boils away, maple syrup or sugar is left behind.

Factories have helped people in the Northeast make many goods quickly, but there is no fast way to make maple syrup. The process takes time, just as it did hundreds of years ago. Forty gallons of sap must boil away in order to leave one gallon of maple syrup.

Move Ahead

Now you're ready to find out more about the sights and history of the Northeast. Encyclopedias, travel magazines, and library books will help you. Here are some questions to guide your research.

1. What role did Philadelphia play as capital of the United States? Who were Benjamin Franklin and William Penn?
2. Why did the nation's leaders want to move the capital out of Philadelphia? Who was George Washington, and what role did he play in the founding of Washington, D.C.? What is the Smithsonian Institution?
3. How many players are honored in the Baseball Hall of Fame? What exhibits does the Hall of Fame have about old baseball leagues for black players and women?
4. Which states make the most maple syrup in this country? What kind of maple tree is used to make syrup?

Explore Some More

Now it's time to discover if your state or region has places like the ones you've read about here. Ask your librarian to help you learn about historic places near your home. If possible, plan a trip to visit these places. Also find out about famous people from history who have lived in your area.

Look in the Minipedia to find your state's capital. Then do research about when the city was founded and when the capitol building was built. Make a list of sports teams that play in your region. Find out about famous players from the team's past.

Finally, explore some of the crops and food products of your state. Does your state grow more of any product than any other state?

▼ *Making maple syrup is done today much as it was hundreds of years ago.*

147

Industry Takes Over

Unit 4
The Midwest

The French explorers of the early 1600s were puzzled by the unbroken stretch of blue water before them. It looked like an ocean, but it didn't taste salty like an ocean did. They sailed from one large body of water into another and again tasted the water. "Seas of sweet water" is what they called these lakes. What they had actually found were the Great Lakes, the largest group of freshwater lakes in the world. The French had entered the gateway to a new, unexplored region–the Midwest.

1750

148

Isle Royale National Park in Michigan.
Photograph Copyright David Muench.

2000

The Midwest

The Nation's Heartland

The Midwest lies at the very center of the United States. It is also the agricultural center, because it has the richest soil and the ideal climate for growing corn and wheat. With excellent water routes for shipping, the Midwest is an important trade center as well. Finally, the heartland is the nation's population center, the home to more people than any other region.

Iron ore
from Minnesota

The Midwest

The 12 states of the region

- Illinois
- Indiana
- Iowa
- Kansas
- Michigan
- Minnesota
- Missouri
- Nebraska
- North Dakota
- Ohio
- South Dakota
- Wisconsin

A land of trees and of no trees —forests cover the northern edge of the Great Lakes states. But to the west, the land flattens into the treeless Great Plains. Once covered by prairie grass and wildflowers, the 400-mile-wide plains are now a patchwork of farms.

Population: 59,668,632, more than any other region
Size: 766,364 square miles, not including the Great Lakes

Great Lakes: 94,510 square miles of water. The largest of the five, Lake Superior, is nearly the size of Maine. The elevation of the lakes drops from 600 feet to 245 feet, creating beautiful waterfalls.

Resources: coal, farmland, gold, iron ore, limestone

The nation's breadbasket —that's the nickname of the Midwest, because of the huge supply of corn, soybeans, wheat, and other grains grown there

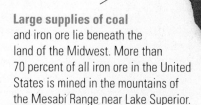

Large supplies of coal and iron ore lie beneath the land of the Midwest. More than 70 percent of all iron ore in the United States is mined in the mountains of the Mesabi Range near Lake Superior.

The Mississippi River Valley

Beginning as just a stream in Minnesota, the Mississippi becomes an important trade route as it is joined by other rivers farther south. Wheat, corn, and other Midwestern crops are shipped down river to southern ports.

Wheat
from Kansas

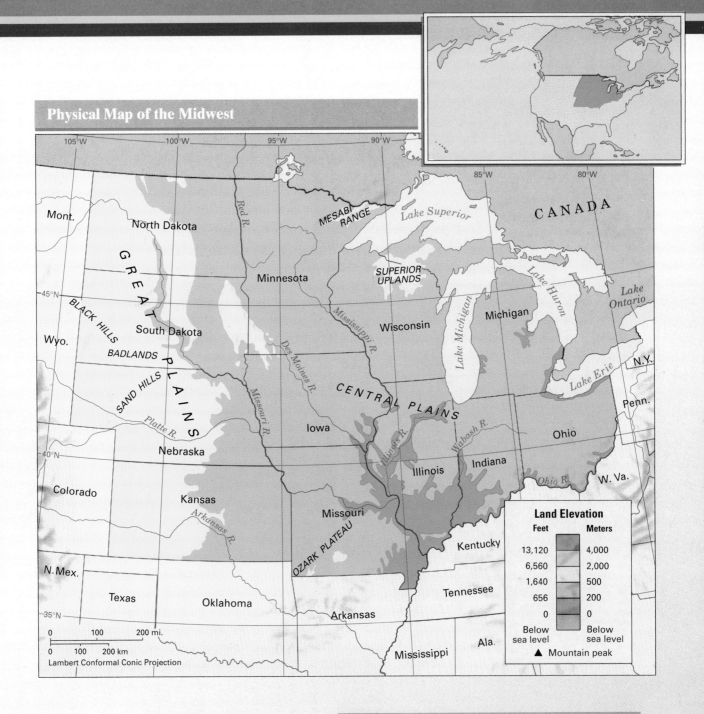

Physical Map of the Midwest

CANADA

Mont.
North Dakota
Red R.
MESABI RANGE
Lake Superior
SUPERIOR UPLANDS
Minnesota
Mississippi R.
Wisconsin
Lake Michigan
Michigan
Lake Huron
Lake Ontario
GREAT PLAINS
BLACK HILLS
South Dakota
BADLANDS
SAND HILLS
Des Moines R.
Missouri R.
Iowa
CENTRAL PLAINS
Illinois R.
Wabash R.
Ohio
Lake Erie
N.Y.
Wyo.
Platte R.
Nebraska
Illinois
Indiana
Penn.
Colorado
Kansas
Missouri
Ohio R.
W. Va.
Kentucky
Arkansas R.
OZARK PLATEAU
N. Mex.
Texas
Oklahoma
Arkansas
Tennessee
Mississippi
Ala.

105°W 100°W 95°W 90°W 85°W 80°W
45°N
40°N
35°N

Land Elevation

Feet		Meters
13,120		4,000
6,560		2,000
1,640		500
656		200
0		0
Below sea level		Below sea level

▲ Mountain peak

0   100   200 mi.
0   100   200 km
Lambert Conformal Conic Projection

Warm, wet summers on the Central Plains are good for growing corn. Before settlers began farming, Indians lived on the plains. Spears and arrowheads that the Indians used to hunt deer and buffalo can still be found in the fields today.

Indian arrowheads
from Ohio

Corn fields
in Wisconsin

151

Chapter 7

Living Off the Land

When families crossed the Appalachians into the Midwest, they cleared the thick forests to plant corn. Further west, on the Great Plains, settlers changed the grasslands into endless fields of wheat. More and more families came, eager to start farms on the richest land in the country.

Settlers traveled down the Ohio River on flatboats to reach the open spaces of the Midwest.

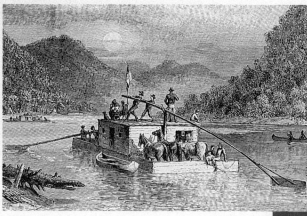

Few trees grew on the Great Plains. So people cut the sod, or grass-covered earth, into bricks to build houses, like this one in Nebraska.

1750	1780	1810

1750

Farmers planted corn and wheat in the Midwest. Later, farmers in some states like Wisconsin, began to raise cows.

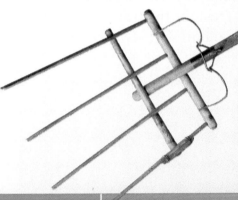

Settlers found that the grassy land was hard to plow with their wooden tools. Later, steel plows and machines made their work easier.

1840

1870

1900

1840 Cyrus McCormick's reaper is introduced to Midwest farmers. The machine could harvest wheat much more quickly than hand tools could.

1900

LESSON 1

Plains and Forest Indians

THINKING

FOCUS

How did Indians in the Midwest use the natural resources of the region?

Key Terms

• culture

▼ *What can you tell about the geography of the Great Plains from this painting of a buffalo hunt by George Catlin?*

F rom on top of a small hill an Indian boy looks out over the wide, flat, treeless land. This is his first buffalo hunt, and he is excited and proud. His father and his uncles watch with him there, but no one speaks. The hunters keep very still. The only sounds are the soft whinnying of their horses and the easy breeze blowing through the tall, dry grass.

Then, in the far distance, the boy spots a herd of buffalo grazing on the grassy plains. His heart races at the sight of these great shaggy beasts with their long sharp horns. The boy cries out and the hunters charge. The thundering hooves of the buffalo and the Indians' horses raise up a huge cloud of dust. Five mighty buffalo fall in the rain of the hunters' arrows.

It has been a good hunt. The tribe offers a prayer of thanks. Soon the women of the family will begin to clean the hides and prepare a great feast for the tribe. The Indian boy's mother will make a special buffalo-hide robe for him.

Buffalo Bill Historical Center, Cody, WY

Hunters on the Plains

A buffalo hunt like this one might have happened in the late 1700s on the Great Plains of the Midwest. Many Indian tribes lived on the Great Plains. The Sioux *(Soo)* were one of these tribes. They lived in what is now South Dakota.

Other Indian tribes made their homes in forested river valleys in other parts of the Midwest. The Miami lived in the wooded valleys of what is now Ohio and Indiana. In this lesson you will learn more about the Sioux and the Miami.

The huge herds of buffalo that fed on the grasses of the plains were the most important resource for the Sioux. The Sioux's whole culture was based on the buffalo. **Culture** is a people's way of life. It includes their food, clothing, shelter, activities, and beliefs. Each Sioux family lived in a buffalo-skin tent called a tipi *(TEE pee)*. The Sioux people dressed in buffalo skins, and ate buffalo meat. Horns and bones from the animal were made into tools and weapons

▼ *Walter McClintock took this picture of Black-feet Indian tipis. The Blackfeet were Plains Indians who lived near the Sioux. They decorated their tipis with buffalo, otter, and crow.*

UNDERSTANDING CULTURE

Your culture is as much a part of you as your hair or eyes. But unlike your body, culture is not something you are born with. Culture is something that you learn. You learn culture mostly from your parents, teachers, and friends. Culture includes all the customs, beliefs, and traditions they teach you. The foods you learn to eat and the songs you learn to sing are also part of your culture.

The culture of the Indians was based on a deep respect for nature. The Sioux and the Miami taught their children to value the land on which they lived.

When European settlers came to this country, they brought their own culture with them. Their clothing, food, and religious beliefs were not the same as those of the Indians. The way the settlers lived and the way they used the land was different.

Today we sing songs and celebrate holidays that come to us from people who lived here hundreds of years ago. These traditions are part of our culture. When you celebrate Thanksgiving Day, you are remembering the meal that European settlers and Indians once shared. Many people from different lands now live in the United States. They all enrich the culture of this country.

such as spoons and spearheads. Products made from buffalo and other plains animals supplied the Sioux with most of their daily needs. To learn about the culture of a different Indian people, the Chippewa, look at A Moment in Time on page 157.

The Sioux had no permanent homes. They moved often, always following the buffalo herds that roamed the plains. Sioux families could easily carry all of their belongings from place to place. A band, or group, of these Indians could break camp and move in two hours time.

The Sioux thought of the plains as a loving mother who fed and clothed them. They studied the natural world carefully. In 1933, Sioux chief Luther Standing Bear wrote of the Indian's love for nature in *Land of the Spotted Eagle*. ■

Farmers in the River Valleys

Bands of Sioux roamed across all the northern plains, on both sides of the great Missouri River. Far to the east lived another Indian people, the Miami. These people made their homes in the thick forests that grew in the valleys of

■ *Why did the lives of the Sioux depend on their frequently moving from place to place?*

▼ *Does this picture show the area where the Sioux or Miami lived?*

A Chippewa Gatherer

5:13 P.M., early Spring, 1750
A stand of maple trees near Cass Lake, Minnesota

Maple Sap
She will heat the sap by throwing hot stones from a fire into large wooden bowls of the sap. The heated sap will thicken into syrup. The tribe will use the syrup to make sweet drinks and season vegetables and meat.

Birchbark Container
She had placed the container at the foot of a maple tree in the early morning. Drop by drop sap had dribbled into the container from the tap she had cut into the tree.

Leather Food Pouch
A pouch filled with a mixture of dried blackberries and moose fat hangs from her belt by birch twine. She has been eating this all winter, and she'll be glad for warm weather—and fresh fruit!

Snowshoes
The wet snow of early spring is still deep. These snowshoes made of birch wood and beaver skin help her to move easily without sinking into the slushy snow.

Deerskin Clothing
She made her deerskin clothes, using cedar bark thread and a bone needle, while sitting by the fire during winter evenings. The rabbit fur in her robe helps to keep her warm in the cool evening air.

the Ohio and other smaller rivers. Look at the map on page 151 to help you locate the places where the Miami lived.

The Miami were hunters, like the Sioux. The Miami culture, however, was very different from that of the Sioux. Plentiful rains fell in the valleys where the Miami lived. The rain made the lands easier to farm than the dry and dusty plains of the Sioux. The culture of the Miami was based on farming as well as hunting.

Miami women grew corn, beans, and squash on large fields that had been cleared of trees. In forests and meadows, the men hunted deer and other animals for food and for skins. Men, women, and children gathered nuts and berries from the forests.

After clearing the fields of trees, the Miami Indians grew crops, like the acorn squash pictured above, on their farms.

A Forest Culture

Unlike the wandering Sioux, the Miami lived in permanent villages near their fields. Trees from the rich forests gave them plenty of wood to make their dome-shaped houses, or wigwams. Bark from the same trees made the walls of the wigwams. The Miami also used birch tree bark to build light, strong canoes. Fishing from these canoes in rivers near their villages was another important part of their culture.

The Midwest in the 1700s was a good home to many different Indian cultures, from the ever-moving buffalo hunters of the plains, to the settled farmers of the river valleys. Over the next 100 years, many settlers from the United States and Europe would also make their homes in this region. The way people in the Midwest used their land would soon change a great deal. ■

■ How did the cultures of the Miami and the Sioux differ?

R E V I E W

1. **FOCUS** How did Indians in the Midwest use the natural resources of the region?
2. **CONNECT** How was the culture of the Miami like the culture of the Indians in the Northeast?
3. **GEOGRAPHY** How did the geography of their lands influence the cultures of the Indians in the different parts of the Midwest?
4. **CRITICAL THINKING** One group of Native Americans often traded goods with another. What goods might Sioux and Miami Indians have exchanged if they had traded with each other?
5. **ACTIVITY** The painting on page 154 tells a lot about the geography of the Great Plains. Make a painting or drawing of your own that show's Miami farmers in their fields. What can you show about the geography of the Miami lands?

L E S S O N   2

Waves of Grain

It is a crisp, cool October evening. A full yellow moon shines brightly on the dense Ohio forest. In a small barn in a forest clearing, two groups of men, women, and children stand facing each other, very still and silent. A corn cob fire crackles in the doorway. The fire throws eerie shadows over two huge heaps of corn in the center of the floor.

A tiny old lady in a corner of the barn whistles once. Then laughing, singing, and banjo music fill the air. Corn flies everywhere as the two teams race to pull the husks, or coverings, off each ear. Only one team can win the game, but everybody has a lot of fun. When the husking is done, everyone sits down to share a delicious supper of corn bread, ham, and squirrel potpie.

T H I N K I N G
F O C U S

What helped pioneer farmers turn the Midwestern frontier into an important corn- and wheat-growing area?

Key Terms

- pioneer
- frontier
- prairie

◄ *A husking bee was just one part of life on a Midwest farm.*

Farm Families Move West

Yearly husking bees like this one gave farm families a chance to do their work and have some fun at the same time. By the late 1700s, most farmers in what is now Ohio were growing corn as their leading crop. These families had come to the Ohio Valley from crowded areas in the eastern

Living Off the Land

➤ *Pioneers traveled west in Conestoga wagons. Here settlers ride on the Pennsylvania Turnpike in the early 1800s.*

■ *What drew pioneers to the Midwestern frontier?*

parts of the young United States. The hilly fields and rocky soil in most of these eastern states were not good for growing many kinds of crops. A farm family that moved to the rich, flat fields of the Midwest would have a chance to own some land and start a successful farm. These pioneers followed rivers and old Indian paths through the Appalachian Mountains to reach the Midwest. A **pioneer** is someone who goes to a new place and shows the way for others to follow.

In the 1780s, the land that is now Ohio was a frontier. A **frontier** is land at the edge of a settled area. In the frontier forests of Ohio and Indiana, the pioneers' first task was chopping down the trees to clear the land for farming and building houses. Like the Miami Indians before them, pioneers then planted corn, and later, wheat. Some settlers, in fact, planted in "Indian fields," or fields the Indians had cleared many years before.

Joseph Hayes, a farmer who settled in southern Indiana in 1809, worked together with his family to build their farm. Hayes described the hard work of planting corn, just one of the many jobs on the farm. ■

The first field of corn I planted was about ten acres. I scratched it over with a plow. I then fixed a little crib on the plow. We placed our child in the crib. I furrowed out [plowed] the soil, and my wife dropped the corn . . . At noon she would take the child, go home, and get dinner. While she would be getting dinner, I took the hoe and would cover the corn. We continued this way—with the child riding on the plow—until we finished our ten acres.

Corn Covers the Prairie

By the 1820s, other pioneers like the Hayes family had pushed the frontier all the way to the prairies of western Indiana and Illinois. A **prairie** is a plain that is covered with tall grass. The Midwestern prairie also extends across much of what is now Iowa and Missouri. This entire prairie is called the Central Plains. Farm families soon found that this flat, grassy land with its rich, black soil would be an important resource for them.

As settlers moved west onto the prairies, there were fewer trees to be cleared. But farm families still faced a difficult challenge as they prepared the land for planting corn and other crops. The tall prairie grass had thick roots that grew five feet into the ground. The wooden plows that farmers had used in the eastern states could not break up the tough, dense roots in the prairie soil. Then a blacksmith named John Deere helped solve this problem.

Deere invented a new kind of steel plow, which farmers began using in the 1830s. This plow could easily cut through the thick roots of the prairie grasses. Planting crops on the prairie became much easier. Corn farms soon stretched across the Central Plains.

At first, frontier farmers grew only enough corn to feed their families and their animals. They soon found that corn grew very well in the plentiful rains of the long, hot prairie summers. Before long, many farm families were growing a lot of extra corn. They shipped much

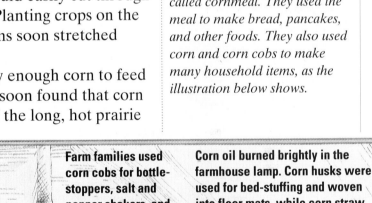

Settlers dried corn, then ground it into a coarse flour called cornmeal. They used the meal to make bread, pancakes, and other foods. They also used corn and corn cobs to make many household items, as the illustration below shows.

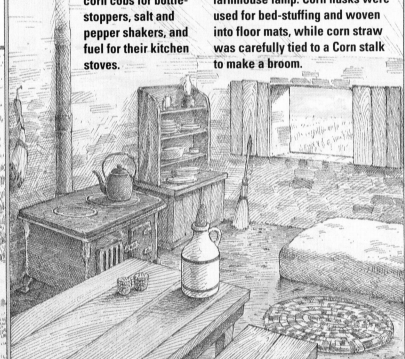

The corn field was protected from birds by a scarecrow made from corn husks.

Corn stalks helped strengthen the roof of a sod house and made a fence around the vegtable garden.

Farm families used corn cobs for bottle-stoppers, salt and pepper shakers, and fuel for their kitchen stoves.

Corn oil burned brightly in the farmhouse lamp. Corn husks were used for bed-stuffing and woven into floor mats, while corn straw was carefully tied to a Corn stalk to make a broom.

Why did the Midwest become such a good place to grow corn?

of this grain down the Ohio and Mississippi rivers to sell in New Orleans. To trace the routes of these rivers see the map on pages 404–405. The Midwest was on its way to becoming the country's corn-growing center. ■

Farmers Grow More Wheat

Some Midwestern farm families began to grow wheat as well as corn. European immigrant settlers especially enjoyed the taste of wheat bread, which they had eaten in their home countries. At first, farmers used hand-tools to harvest the wheat in their fields, but the work was hard and slow. One person could cut only two acres a day by hand. Then in the 1840s, a Virginian named Cyrus McCormick introduced a horse-drawn reaper for cutting grain. With this machine a farmer could cut five to six acres of wheat in a day. Now settlers could plant much larger fields of crops because they could harvest a lot of grain more quickly.

McCormick's reaper helped many farm families earn more money growing wheat. More and more farmers in the Midwest now turned to growing wheat instead of corn. Wheat growing became a booming business in northern Indiana and Illinois and southern Wisconsin and Michigan.

Wheat is a kind of grass that can be dried and ground into flour and used to make foods like whole-wheat bread. The reaper helped farmers harvest larger and larger fields of this valuable grain.

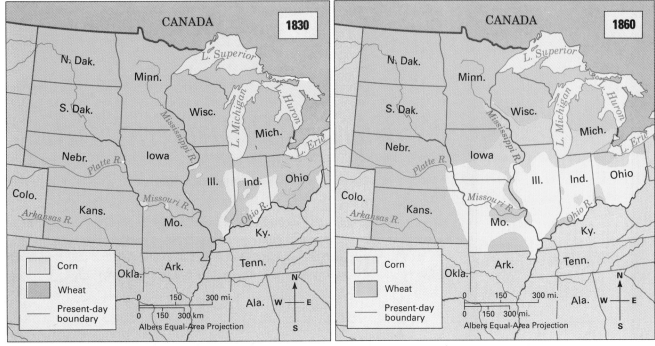

Corn and Wheat Spread West, 1830–1860

1830

CANADA

N. Dak., Minn., S. Dak., Wisc., Mich., Nebr., Iowa, Ill., Ind., Ohio, Colo., Kans., Mo., Ky., Okla., Ark., Tenn., Ala.

L. Superior, L. Michigan, L. Huron, L. Erie, Mississippi R., Platte R., Missouri R., Arkansas R., Ohio R.

Corn
Wheat
Present-day boundary

0   150   300 mi.
0 150 300 km
Albers Equal-Area Projection

1860

CANADA

N. Dak., Minn., S. Dak., Wisc., Mich., Nebr., Iowa, Ill., Ind., Ohio, Colo., Kans., Mo., Ky., Okla., Ark., Tenn., Ala.

L. Superior, L. Michigan, L. Huron, L. Erie, Mississippi R., Platte R., Missouri R., Arkansas R., Ohio R.

Corn
Wheat
Present-day boundary

0   150   300 mi.
0 150 300 mi.
Albers Equal-Area Projection

During the 1860s, settlers pushed farther west into the Great Plains of what are now Kansas, Nebraska, South Dakota, and North Dakota. This area has less rain and a shorter growing season than the rest of the Midwest. Frontier farmers found that under these conditions, wheat grew better than corn. Soon, wheat became the most important crop of the Great Plains.

Pioneer farm families faced many different challenges on the Plains and all over the Midwest. Storms, dry spells, and insects such as grasshoppers often ruined or damaged their crops. Despite these hardships, settlers made good use of the soil and the other natural resources in the area. Large, successful corn and wheat farms soon covered the rich land of the Midwest. ■

▲ *Compare these two maps to describe how different areas were changed by farm inventions such as the reaper and steel plow. For help in using the map's compass rose to describe where changes occurred, see page G4 of the Map and Globe Handbook.*

■ *Why did farmers on the prairies and Great Plains turn from growing corn to growing wheat?*

R E V I E W

1. **FOCUS** What helped pioneer farmers turn the Midwestern frontier into an important corn- and wheat-growing area?

2. **CONNECT** In what ways was the culture of the early frontier farmers in the Ohio Valley like the culture of the Miami Indians?

3. **GEOGRAPHY** Compare the map on this page with the climate map on page 408. How might the differences in the climate of the Great Plains and the climate of the Central Plains have affected the development of

corn- and wheat-growing in these areas?

4. **CRITICAL THINKING** How might Midwestern farming have developed differently if John Deere and Cyrus McCormick had not introduced the steel plow and the modern reaper?

5. **ACTIVITY** Imagine you are a new pioneer farmer in the Ohio Valley in 1800. Write a letter to your sister in New York, describing your life. Urge your sister to move to the frontier to join you.

Living Off the Land

Sarah, Plain and Tall

Patricia MacLachlan

Anna and Caleb's lives are happy except for one thing—they want a mother. Then one day their father tells them he has placed an advertisement for a wife. As you read, ask yourself, "What kind of personality and skills would a person need to make a good wife and mother to a prairie farm family?

Anna, Caleb, and their father have a farm on the midwestern prairie that you learned about in Lesson 2.

Papa leaned back in the chair. "I've placed an advertisement in the newspapers. For help."

"You mean a housekeeper?" I asked, surprised.

Caleb and I looked at each other and burst out laughing, remembering Hilly, our old housekeeper. She was round and slow and shuffling. She snored in a high whistle at night, like a teakettle, and let the fire go out.

"No," said Papa slowly, "Not a housekeeper." He paused. "A wife."

Caleb stared at Papa. "A wife? You mean a mother?"

Nick slid his face onto Papa's lap and Papa stroked his ears.

"That, too," said Papa. "Like Maggie."

Matthew, our neighbor to the south, had written to ask for a wife and mother for his children. And Maggie had come from Tennessee. Her hair was the color of turnips and she laughed.

Papa reached into his pocket and unfolded a letter written on white paper. "And I have received an answer." Papa read to us:

Dear Mr. Jacob Witting,

I am Sarah Wheaton from Maine as you will see from my letter. I am answering your advertisement. I have never been married, though I have been asked. I have lived with an older brother, William, who is about to be married. His wife-to-be is young and energetic.

I have always loved to live by the sea, but at this time I feel a move is necessary. And the truth is, the sea is as far east as I can go. My choice, as you can see, is limited. This should not be taken as an insult. I am strong and I work hard and I am willing to travel. But I am not mild mannered. If you should still care to write, I would be interested in your children and about where you live. And you.

Very truly yours,
Sarah Elisabeth Wheaton

P.S. Do you have opinions on cats? I have one.

No one spoke when Papa finished the letter. He kept looking at it in his hands, reading it over to himself. Finally I turned my head a bit to sneak a look at Caleb. He was smiling. I smiled, too.

"One thing," I said in the quiet of the room.

"What's that?" asked Papa, looking up.

I put my arm around Caleb.

"Ask her if she sings," I said.

Caleb and Papa and I wrote letters to Sarah, and before the ice and snow had melted from the fields, we all received answers. Mine came first.

Dear Anna,

Yes, I can braid hair and I can make stew and bake bread, though I prefer to build bookshelves and paint.

My favorite colors are the colors of the sea, blue and gray and green, depending on the weather. My brother William is a fisherman, and he tells me that when he is in the middle of a fog-bound sea the water is a color for which there is no name. He catches flounder and sea bass and bluefish. Sometimes he sees whales. And birds, too, of course. I am enclosing a book of sea birds so you will see what William and I see every day.

flounder, sea bass, bluefish three salt-water fish that are popular as food

Very truly yours,
Sarah Elisabeth Wheaton

Caleb read and read the letter so many times that the ink began to run and the folds tore. He read the book about sea birds over and over.

"Do you think she'll come?" asked Caleb. "And will she stay? What if she thinks we are loud and pesky?"

"You are loud and pesky," I told him. But I was worried, too. Sarah loved the sea, I could tell. Maybe she wouldn't leave there after all to come where there were fields and grass and sky and not much else.

"What if she comes and doesn't like our house?" Caleb asked. "I told her it was small. Maybe I shouldn't have told her it was small."

"Hush, Caleb. Hush."

Caleb's letter came soon after, with a picture of a cat drawn on the envelope.

Dear Caleb,

My cat's name is Seal because she is gray like the seals that swim offshore in Maine. She is glad that Lottie and Nick send their greetings. She likes dogs most of the time. She says their footprints are much larger than hers (which she is enclosing in return).

Your house sounds lovely, even though it is far out in the country with no close neighbors. My house is tall and the shingles are gray because of the salt from the sea. There are roses nearby.

Yes, I do like small rooms sometimes. Yes, I can keep a fire going at night. I do not know if I snore. Seal has never told me.

Very truly yours,
Sarah Elisabeth

"Did you really ask her about fires and snoring?" I asked, amazed.

"I wished to know," Caleb said.

He kept the letter with him, reading it in the barn and in the fields and by the cow pond. And always in bed at night.

One morning, early, Papa and Caleb and I were cleaning out the horse stalls and putting down new bedding. Papa stopped suddenly and leaned on his pitchfork.

"Sarah has said she will come for a month's time if we

wish her to," he said, his voice loud in the dark barn. "To see how it is. Just to see."

Caleb stood by the stall door and folded his arms across his chest.

"I think," he began. Then, "I think," he said slowly, "that it would be good—to say yes," he finished in a rush.

Papa looked at me.

"I say yes," I told him grinning.

"Yes," said Papa. "Then yes it is."

And the three of us, all smiling, went to work again.

The next day Papa went to town to mail his letter to Sarah. It was rainy for days, and the clouds followed. The house was cool and damp and quiet. Once I set four places at the table, then caught myself and put the extra plate away. Three lambs were born, one with a black face. And then Papa's letter came. It was very short.

Dear Jacob,
  I will come by train. I will wear a yellow bonnet.
I am plain and tall.

Sarah

"What's that?" asked Caleb excitedly, peering over Papa's shoulder. He pointed. "There, written at the bottom of the letter."

Papa read it to himself. Then he smiled holding up the letter for us to see.

Tell them I sing was all it said.

Further Reading

Dakota Dugout. Ann Warren Turner. A woman describes her experiences living with her husband in a sod house on the Dakota prairie.

Little House on the Prairie. On the Banks of Plum Creek. Laura Ingalls Wilder. These are the second and fourth books in Wilder's series about her life on the prairie.

My Prairie Year: Based on the Diary of Elenore Plaisted. Brett Harvey. This book tells about one year in the life of a young girl whose family moves to the prairie to live.

Measuring Distances on a Map

Here's Why

Suppose you want to find the distance between two cities. You can use a map to do this. But distances can look different on different maps. Look at the two U.S. maps on pages 402–403 and 404–405. The distance from the East Coast to the West Coast looks different on the two maps.

The distance doesn't actually change. These two maps are just drawn to different scales. On one map, an inch stands for 400 miles, but on the other map an inch stands for about 267 miles.

To figure out the distance between the two places, you need to use the scale for that map. For example, how far did a pioneer family travel up the Missouri River on their way to Sioux City, Iowa?

Here's How

Look at Map A below. It shows the path of the Missouri River from St. Louis to Sioux City. Find the map scale. A map scale is a straight line with distances marked on it. Each section of the map scale stands for a certain number of miles. On Map A, sections of the scale stand for 50 miles or 50 kilometers.

You can use the map scale to measure the distance between Omaha and Sioux City. Line up the edge of a piece of paper with the dots on the map that show the locations of the two cities. Then on the paper, make a pencil mark at the dot for Omaha and another pencil mark at the dot for Sioux City.

Now put the paper on the map scale. Place the first pencil mark on the 0. You will see that the second dot marks off about 100 miles. This shows that the distance between Omaha and Sioux City along a straight line is about 100 miles. Of course the Missouri River has many turns and bends. The actual distance the pioneer family traveled along the river was probably more than 100 miles.

Compare Map A with Map B. Map B was drawn to a different scale and shows more states. Find Omaha and Sioux City on Map B.

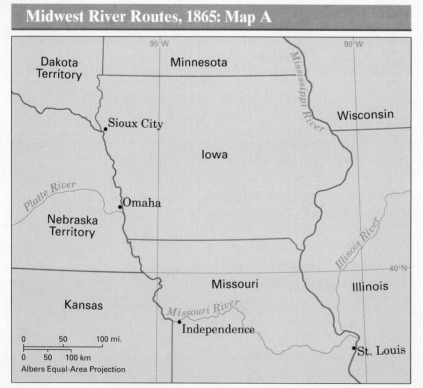

Midwest River Routes, 1865: Map A

Midwest River Routes, 1865: Map B

The distance between the two cities looks shorter on Map B than it does on Map A. But use the scale for Map B to find the distance between them. You will find that Omaha and Sioux City are about 100 miles apart on both maps.

Do not be fooled by the size of a map. Distances between places may look longer on one map than they do on another because maps are drawn to different scales. Always use the map scale to find the distance between places.

Try It

Frontier settlers made the trip along the Missouri, Mississippi, and Ohio rivers by paddle-wheel steamboats. Use the edge of a piece of paper and the scale on Map B to measure the distances for the following trips:

1. Bringing furs from Fort Pierre to St. Louis by boat.
2. Taking mail from Cincinnati to St. Louis, using first the Ohio River and next the Mississippi River.
3. Traveling from St. Louis up the Mississippi River to St. Paul.

Apply It

Suppose you want to plan a family trip from your community to some other place in the United States. Use the map of the United States on pages 404–405 of the Atlas. Find your community and the place you want to go. Use the scale to find the distance between them.

The Nation's Dairyland

THINKING
FOCUS

Why did the upper Midwest develop as an important dairy farming area?

Key Terms

- pasture
- dairy farming

Brown Swiss, Jersey, and Guernsey are breeds of cows often used for dairy farming.

Nearly two million years ago, the world began to get very, very cold. More and more snow fell, and less of it melted. Great masses of ice and snow, thousands of feet thick, formed near the North Pole. These glaciers began to creep south as the world grew colder. The glaciers were so powerful they could turn whole mountains into piles of earth and rock. They pushed this rocky soil hundreds of miles to the south.

Then, about 10,000 years ago, the ice began to thaw. As the air grew warmer, the glaciers melted away. Water began to run into the deep holes the glaciers had made in the earth. Lakes, rivers, and swamps appeared. The disappearing glaciers dumped millions of tons of rocks, sand, and clay on the land. The Great Lakes were formed by the actions of glaciers like these. Glaciers also shaped much of the hilly land in the upper Midwest. Modern scientists are still studying these great changes in the earth of long ago.

Pioneers Settle in the Upper Midwest

In the 1830s and 1840s, pioneers began moving into Wisconsin and Minnesota. These first farmers grew wheat in the rocky soil that the glaciers had left behind. They were able to make a great deal of money growing wheat at this time.

Nearly every farm family in the upper Midwest kept at least one cow to give them milk. A cow was an important possession. Every morning as the sun came up and again each evening, the cow gave milk. Most of the time, though, the cow ate grass in the pasture near the farmhouse. A **pasture** is a field where animals can graze, or eat grass. In winter, the cow moved into the barn and ate corn and hay.

A farm family's daughter often did the milking. When she finished she would let the milk stand in a pail for a few hours. Soon the cream rose and floated on top. The family would use the cream to make butter.

In *Little House in the Big Woods*, Laura Ingalls Wilder describes how a mother and her daughters make butter on a frontier farm. First they put some cream in a churn, a large wooden container with a hole in its top. Then Ma Ingalls uses pumping motions to stir the cream with a plunger-like tool called a dash:

> She churned for a long time. Mary could some-
> times churn while Ma rested, but the dash
> was too heavy for Laura.
> At first the splashes of cream showed thick and
> smooth around the little hole. After a long time, they
> began to look grainy. Then Ma churned more slowly,
> and on the dash there began to appear tiny grains of
> yellow butter.

Families like the Ingalls would drink some of their cow's fresh milk right away and use the rest to make cheese. Cheese-making involved many steps and was done over a number of days right on the farm.

Not only would a cow provide a family with milk, butter, and cheese, it would also give birth to a calf each spring. The family would keep some of the calves to build a small herd and then sell the others. In years when crops were poor, farm families depended even more heavily on their milk cows for food. ■

Farm families depended on cows for such food as cheese, butter, cottage cheese, and cream.

Across Time & Space

Margarine is a product that many people use instead of butter. When margarine first went on sale in the 1870s, dairy farmers feared they would sell less butter and make less money. They asked the government to put a tax on margarine so it would cost more and people might buy less of it. In Wisconsin, shoppers could not buy margarine at all until the 1960s.

■ *In what ways did frontier farmers depend on their milk cows?*

171

Living Off the Land

Wheat Fields Turn into Pastures

Wheat crops in the upper Midwest grew poorer as the years went on. Season after season of growing wheat in the same fields had worn out the soil. Pioneer farmers began earning less money. They were going through a very hard time. Luckily, they still had their dairy cows.

Leaders in Wisconsin were ready to help. The newspaperman William Dempster Hoard urged farmers to "substitute the cow for the plow." With slogans like "The cow is queen," Hoard encouraged farmers to change from wheat farming to dairy farming. **Dairy farming** is the business of raising cows for their milk and milk products such as butter and cheese. Look below to see how these products were made on farms. Many farmers made the change to milk. They found the rolling hills of Wisconsin were much better for dairy pastures than they had been for growing wheat. Grazing cows did not wear out the soil, either. Plenty of tender

A farm wife used a beautifully carved wooden butter mold to stamp a pattern on the surface of a container of homemade butter.

Pioneer families let milk stand in heavy wooden buckets until the cream rose to the top.

To milk their cows, these Wisconsin dairy farmers from the 1870s sat on low milking stools in the farmyard near their barn and their house.

Dairy farmers loaded their milk, cream, butter, and cheese onto horse-drawn wagons. They often sold their products in towns near their farms.

Settlers added fresh carrot juice to the churn to give the butter a yellow color.

grass grew for the dairy cows to eat.

Many of the settlers who came to the upper Midwest in the late 1800s were dairy farmers from New York and immigrants from northern Europe. These people brought special cows and farming skills with them.

Dairy farmers began to sell their products in the growing towns. New dairy farming methods, such as milking machines, helped farmers to produce more milk. Turning foods like milk and grain into products that people liked to eat was about to become a big business in the Midwest. ■

▲ *Describe the climate of the wheat, corn, and dairy regions.*

■ *Give some reasons why farmers in Wisconsin and Minnesota changed from wheat farming to dairy farming.*

R E V I E W

1. **FOCUS** Why did the upper Midwest develop as an important dairy farming area?

2. **CONNECT** How did the land of the upper Midwest differ from the land of the plains?

3. **ECONOMICS** Compare the map on this page with the map on page 199. Why did the dairy farming industry develop near growing cities like Chicago?

4. **CRITICAL THINKING** William Dempster Hoard and other leaders made statements like "the cow is queen." How did such statements affect the growth of dairy farming?

5. **WRITING ACTIVITY** Imagine that you are a dairy farmer. Write an advertisement for the cheese you make on your farm. Why might people like to buy your homemade products?

173

Living Off the Land

Chapter Review

Reviewing Key Terms

culture (p.155) pasture (p.170)
dairy farming (p.172) pioneer (p.160)
frontier (p.160) prairie (p.161)

A. Write the key term for each of the following definitions.
1. a people's way of life, including beliefs, foods, and type of shelter
2. a person who goes to a new place and leads the way for others to follow
3. a field where animals graze
4. land at or beyond the edge of a settled area
5. raising cows for their milk

B. Choose the key term that best completes each sentence.
1. _____ in Ohio and Indiana usually cleared some land to plant corn.
2. The _____ of the Sioux was based on the buffalo.
3. When wheat prices began to drop, some farmers turned to _____ .
4. Until John Deere invented a special plow, the tall grassland of the _____ was difficult to farm.
5. As more and more settlers came to the Midwest, the _____ moved west.

Exploring Concepts

A. Complete the cluster diagram below on a separate piece of paper. Add two or more details about the culture of each group of people in the Midwest.

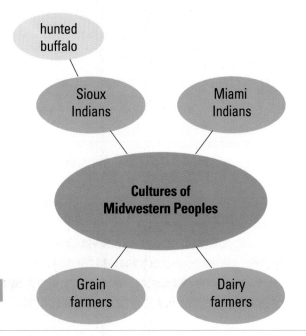

hunted buffalo

Sioux Indians

Miami Indians

Cultures of Midwestern Peoples

Grain farmers

Dairy farmers

B. Support each statement below with two details from this chapter.
1. Different customs showed that the Sioux and Miami lived in different geographic areas.
2. Farmers from the East moved to the Midwest to plant crops in the rich, flat fields there.
3. Corn and wheat became important crops in the Midwest.
4. In the mid 1800s, the McCormick reaper and the Deere plow helped make farming easier in the Midwest.
5. Many wheat farmers in Wisconsin turned to dairy farming.
6. The prairie soil, or sod, was a problem for pioneer families in one way but it helped them in another way.

Reviewing Skills

1. Why is a map scale useful?
2. Imagine it is 1865. You want to leave your home in St. Louis to settle in the Dakota Territory. You are going to travel along the Missouri River by steamboat to Bismarck. Use the map on page 169 to find the distance between St. Louis and Bismarck along a straight line.
3. Look at the map on page 199. Is the distance between St. Louis and Bismarck the same as it is on the map on page 169? Why does the distance look different on the two maps?
4. Inventions helped farmers grow their crops in the Midwest. Name two inventions described in this chapter and tell what effect each had on farming.
5. Copy the timeline on pages 152–153 on a separate piece of paper. Choose four events that you learned about in this chapter that are not already on this timeline. Add them to your timeline on the correct dates or periods of time.

Using Critical Thinking

1. "Nature is everything." What does that statement mean to you? What might it have meant to the Sioux and the Miami? To farmers in the Midwest?
2. Pioneer families helped build the Midwest. How might American agriculture have been different if these families had decided not to leave the East?
3. The frontier of the early 1800s was the Midwestern prairie. Where are the frontiers of today's world? In the United States? On the planet Earth? Explain your answer.

Preparing for Citizenship

1. **ART ACTIVITY** Make a shoe-box diorama of some part of the life of the Sioux, Miami, or Chippewa during the late 1700s. In your diorama, show the natural resources of the area where the Indians lived. Include pictures of their daily life.
2. **GROUP ACTIVITY** With the slogan "Substitute the cow for the plow," William Dempster Hoard helped settlers begin dairy farming in Wisconsin. Look under the heading "Economy" in the Minipedia to find out what the important products of your state are. Then make up advertising slogans like Hoard's about one or more of the products.
3. **WRITING ACTIVITY** Imagine that you are an immigrant arriving in New York in 1850. You are traveling to join your brother on his farm in Missouri. Write a diary of your trip. Note what cities you travel through, the activities of the people you meet, the transportation that you use, and the mountains and rivers that you cross.
4. **COLLABORATIVE LEARNING** As part of their culture, the Sioux celebrated successful buffalo hunts. Corn farmers worked and played at yearly husking bees. Make a book of celebrations that illustrates special events that are part of your local culture. In small groups, select the celebrations you want to include. Illustrate and write a paragraph about each one. Display your drawings and paragraphs.

Living Off the Land

Chapter 8

Developing
New Industries

In the late 1800s, Midwest factories were turning out new products that modernized the nation. Farmers sent their crops to factories in Minnesota and Wisconsin that made everything from cereal to cheese. Companies dug iron ore and coal from the hills to make steel. And with steel, the Midwest became famous as the car capital of the world.

Giant furnaces in steel plants were heated to temperatures of more than 2200 degrees. The furnaces melted minerals to make steel.

By the early 1900s, automobiles were sharing the roads with horse-drawn carriages.

1850	1880	1910

1850

1880 Gustavus Swift's refrigerated railroad car allows Midwest companies to ship fresh food around the country.

The future of the Midwest's auto industry depends on cars of the future, like this one displayed at an auto show in Detroit, Michigan.

Bridges with moving belts carry iron and other materials from place to place at a Ford automobile factory.

| | | 1940 | | 1970 | | 2000 |

1941 The United States enters World War II. The Midwest supplies much of the steel for the fighting planes, ships, and jeeps.

2000

L E S S O N   1

Food for the Nation

THINKING FOCUS

Why was the Midwest a good location for the growing food-processing industry?

Key Terms

- market
- livestock
- refrigeration

The invention of corn flakes changed what millions of people ate for breakfast.

Before the early 1900s, most people in the United States worked on farms. Each morning, they ate a big meal to give them plenty of energy for the busy day. Breakfast included meat, eggs, fried potatoes, and bread. Sometimes there was pie for dessert.

Then Will Kellogg had a new idea about breakfast. Kellogg was a businessman and an inventor who lived in Battle Creek, Michigan. In 1906, he began to develop a lighter breakfast food for people who did not need a heavy meal in the morning. First, Kellogg sliced the kernels off an ear of corn and cooked them. After adding vitamins and flavoring to the corn, Kellogg put it through heavy rollers that pressed it into flakes. Finally, he toasted the flakes until they were crisp.

Millions of people loved Kellogg's invention. Corn flakes swept the nation. Will Kellogg came to be known as the "King of Corn Flakes."

Flour Milling in Minnesota

Kellogg and others made a lot of money selling breakfast cereals. These products soon became an important part of the economy of the Midwest. Yet the cereal business was only a small part of a larger midwestern industry—food processing. Food processing turns raw foods such as corn, wheat, and milk into products like cereal, flour, and cheese. The Midwest today makes more food products than any other region in the nation. The story of Minnesota's flour industry will help explain the growth of food processing.

Years before Kellogg invented corn flakes, Charles Pillsbury bought one of the many flour mills in Minneapolis, Minnesota. The city had water power from the nearby Mississippi River and a huge supply of wheat from the Great Plains farms of neighboring North Dakota. These advantages made the city a perfect place for the flour industry to develop.

Before 1869, millers ground wheat into flour with large, slow millstones. Then Charles Pillsbury found a new way to grind wheat by using rollers. This process produced enormous amounts of excellent flour quickly and cheaply.

The new roller mills gave the Minneapolis flour business a great advantage over other companies. Soon, Pillsbury's roller mill was producing more flour than any other mill in the nation. The slow, old grist mills had only produced enough flour for local markets. Now Pillsbury could supply flour to markets all over the country. A **market** is an area where there are customers for a product.

Another key to the flour industry's success was the nation's growing railroad system. Trains carried wheat from farms in North and South Dakota, Nebraska, and Kansas to the mills of Minneapolis. From there, the railroads also carried Pillsbury's high-quality flour to markets throughout the country. ■

For much of the 1800s, cheese was made by hand on farms. Today it is made by machines in food-processing plants.

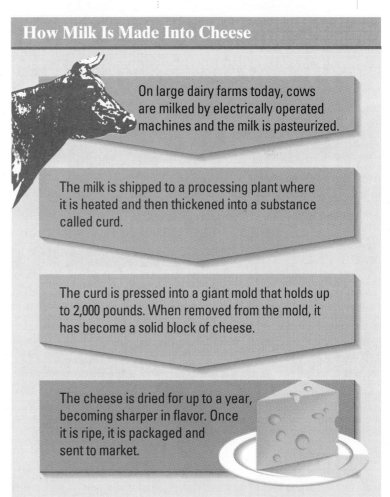

How Milk Is Made Into Cheese

On large dairy farms today, cows are milked by electrically operated machines and the milk is pasteurized.

The milk is shipped to a processing plant where it is heated and then thickened into a substance called curd.

The curd is pressed into a giant mold that holds up to 2,000 pounds. When removed from the mold, it has become a solid block of cheese.

The cheese is dried for up to a year, becoming sharper in flavor. Once it is ripe, it is packaged and sent to market.

■ *Why did flour milling grow to become an important industry in Minneapolis?*

Meat Packing in Chicago

Another new industry, meat packing, developed in Chicago at the same time as the flour-milling industry grew in Minnesota. Located at the southern tip of Lake Michigan, Chicago had become the transportation center of the country. This location helped make Chicago a good place for the new meat-packing industry to develop. From around the country, ranchers could easily ship their livestock to Chicago by railroad. **Livestock** are animals such as cows, hogs, and sheep that are raised on farms and ranches. At stockyards, Chicago meat packers prepared these animals for sale as meat and other products. Meat packers used railroads to send their products to distant markets, such as cities in the Northeast.

The meat-packing industry grew quickly. During the Civil War (1861–1865), Chicago stockyards supplied meat to millions of soldiers. Nine railroads ran directly into the huge, new Union Stockyards, which opened in 1865. In the late 1800s, meat packing and other industries drew many thousands of

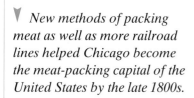

New methods of packing meat as well as more railroad lines helped Chicago become the meat-packing capital of the United States by the late 1800s.

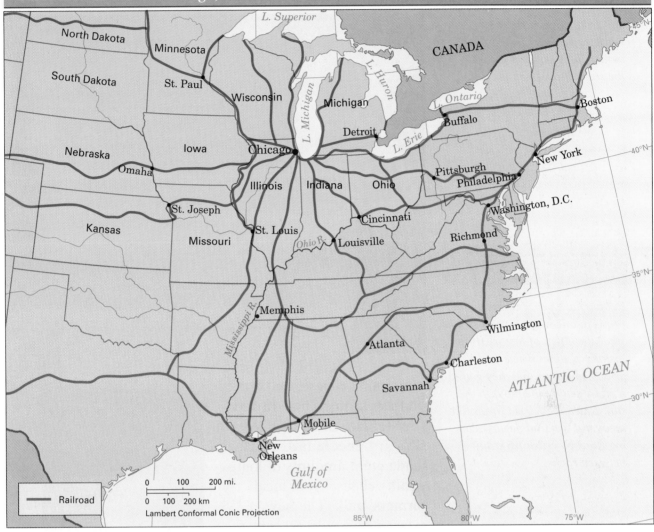

workers to Chicago. Many of them were blacks from the southern United States and immigrants seeking a better life.

Gustavus F. Swift and other business leaders helped Chicago grow into a big and important city. In the 1880s, Swift developed the refrigerated railroad car. **Refrigeration** means chilling food to keep it fresh.

Without refrigeration, meat spoils quickly. Before Swift's invention, packers could ship meat to distant markets only during the cold winter months. Swift's refrigerated railroad cars helped meat packers reach faraway markets all year-round. With these many new customers, the meat packing industry earned more money and grew rapidly. ■

■ *What helped Chicago become the center of the meat-packing industry in the United States?*

Cheesemaking in Wisconsin

Not far from Chicago, another new food-processing industry was developing in the rolling pasturelands of Wisconsin. Dairy farmers in this area were producing more and

181

Developing New Industries

➤ *To make cottage cheese, workers thicken milk to form curds. Here workers separate the solid curds from the liquid.*

Across Time & Space

People have processed raw foods in one way or another since the dawn of history. Prehistoric peoples dried the fruits, grains, and nuts that they gathered by setting them out in the sun. Later, they dried foods like meat and fish and began making flour by crushing grain between rocks.

more milk, cheese, and butter on their farms. Then, in 1864, Chester Hazen opened Wisconsin's first cheese factory. Hazen made great amounts of high-quality cheese from local farmers' milk. The new refrigerated railroad cars carried cheese products from Wisconsin factories to the Northeast. Some products, like cheese, were even shipped to Europe.

Today, Wisconsin produces more milk, butter, and cheese than any other state in the nation. The dairy business and other food-processing industries have brought great growth to all of the Midwest. ■

■ *Why did the dairy business develop in Wisconsin?*

R E V I E W

1. **FOCUS** Why was the Midwest a good location for the growing food-processing industry?

2. **CONNECT** Name some farm products you learned about in Chapter 7 that became important to the food-processing industries of the Midwest.

3. **ECONOMICS** How did refrigerated railroad cars help Chicago's meat-packing industry?

4. **CRITICAL THINKING** Look at the map on page 181. What city, other than Chicago, do you think would be a good place to open a meat-packing plant? Explain your answer.

5. **ACTIVITY** Use the Minipedia on pages 350–399 to find the main agricultural products of each state in the Midwest. Why do these products differ?

Chapter 8

L E S S O N   2

Steel Changes the Land

Elbert Gary gazed out over the Indiana shore of Lake Michigan in 1906. Gary saw the future in this deserted wasteland of rolling sandy hills and muddy marshes. He pictured the red glow of a modern steel plant here and a big city all around it.

Gary ran United States Steel Corporation. His company's new plant had to be near good water transportation, railroads, and the natural resources needed to make steel. Gary knew he had found the right place in Indiana.

The town of Gary, Indiana, was incorporated in 1906. Three years later, in 1909, a new steel plant opened in the new city. To build it, workers had leveled hills, filled in marshes, and even moved the path of a river. Elbert Gary's vision had become a reality.

THINKING FOCUS

How did the Midwest come to be the center for the nation's steel industry?

Key Terms

- iron ore
- smelting

◄ *In a little more than 10 years, Gary's population grew from zero to 55,000. To many people, it seemed "the city of the century."*

183

Steelworkers and Resources

▼ *The Midwest's natural resources made it an ideal place for steelmaking and for automobile manufacturing.*

The nearness of natural resources and transportation gave rise to steelmaking in Gary, much as the nearness of resources had led to the growth of the food-processing industry in the Midwest. The resources needed for steelmaking include iron ore, limestone, and coal. **Iron ore**—the rock from which iron is taken—came from the Mesabi Range in northern Minnesota. Huge ships called freighters carried the ore from Minnesota across the Great Lakes to Gary and other steel-producing centers. Trains brought limestone from Indiana and Michigan and coal from Illinois, Indiana, and Ohio to these centers. To find these places, look at the map below.

To produce steel, workers first melted iron ore to separate the pure iron, in a process called **smelting**. Then, this iron was combined with carbon from the coal to produce steel, a metal even stronger than iron. In the mid 1800s, European inventors improved the smelting process. These

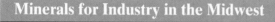

Minerals for Industry in the Midwest

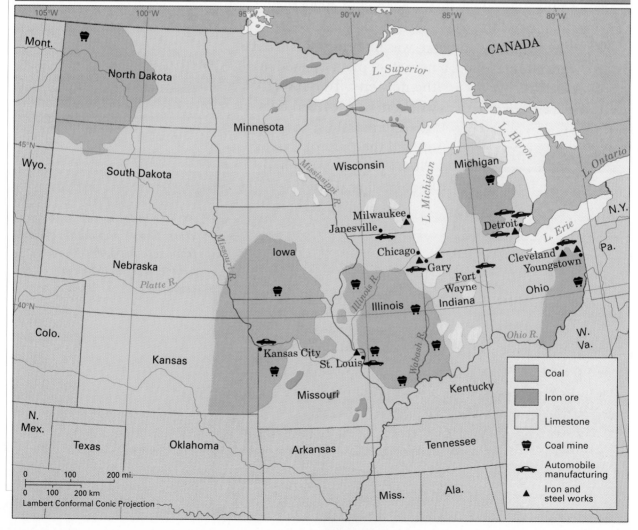

improvements helped steel factories in the United States produce huge amounts of high-quality steel for growing markets.

Steelworkers were another important resource of the Midwestern steel industry. Immigrants from Europe and Mexico made up much of the work force in Gary and the other midwestern steel centers. When World War I ended in 1918, blacks from the Southeast also came to the steel mills in great numbers.

Steelworkers worked long, hard hours in the steel plants. In her 1989 book, *No Star Nights*, Anna Egan Smucker described a busy steel mill. ■

▲ *New machines have made steelmaking more efficient than it was in the late 1800s. As people in the United States produced more steel, they also began to build larger and larger skyscrapers.*

T here was always something wonderful to watch. Through a huge open doorway we could see the mammoth open-hearth furnace. A giant ladle would tilt to give the fiery furnace a "drink" of orange, molten [hot, liquid] iron. Sometimes we would see the golden, liquid steel pouring out the bottom of the open hearth into enormous bucketlike ladles. The workers were just small dark figures made even smaller by the great size of the ladles and the furnace. The hot glow of the liquid steel made the dark mill light up as if the sun itself was being poured out. And standing on the bridge we could feel its awful heat.

■ *What resources contributed to the growth of the steel industry in Gary?*

Skyscrapers Made of Steel

Midwestern workers produced huge amounts of steel in the late 1800s and early 1900s. All over the growing United States, people needed more and more steel. The use of steel made it possible to build tall buildings and long bridges. With strong steel "skeletons," new buildings could rise higher than ever before. One of these buildings, Chicago's 10-story Home Insurance Building, became the world's first "skyscraper" in 1885.

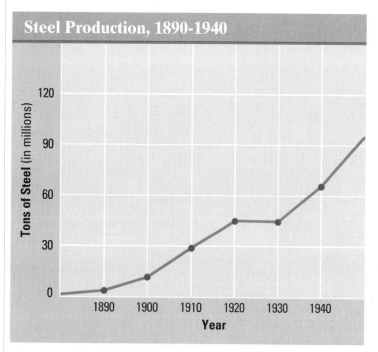

Steel Production, 1890-1940

Tons of Steel (in millions)

120
90
60
30
0

1890 1900 1910 1920 1930 1940

Year

▲ *Steel production in the United States began to rise rapidly in 1890. Steel was used to make, among other things, cars, fire engines, and even toys.*

In the 1940s, the need for steel increased. During World War II, the United States government needed steel for tanks, ships, and airplanes. Many men went overseas to fight, and steel mills hired women to take their place.

In the years following World War II, steelmakers in other countries, such as West Germany and Japan, began using new, modern equipment in their plants. Find these countries on the map on page 401.

Foreign mills were able to produce steel more cheaply than companies in the United States. Many factories that needed steel began to buy it from foreign countries. Some plants closed in the United States, and steel production began to fall off.

To deal with these problems, United States steelmakers began to make some of their plants more modern. Today, mills in Gary, Indiana, and other Midwestern cities still produce a lot of steel. ■

■ *What changes took place in the Midwestern steel industry in the 1900s?*

R E V I E W

1. **FOCUS** How did the Midwest come to be the center for the nation's steel industry?

2. **CONNECT** Compare the growth of the meatpacking industry in Chicago with the growth of the steel industry in Gary. What effect did the development of these two industries have on the populations of those cities?

3. **GEOGRAPHY** Why are the major steelmaking centers in the Midwest located on or near the Great Lakes?

4. **CRITICAL THINKING** How might the history of the steelmaking industry have been different if, in the years after World War II, mills in the United States had begun using modern equipment ?

5. **WRITING ACTIVITY** Imagine you are an African American who has migrated from the South to Gary, Indiana, in 1915, to work in the steel mills. Write a letter to your parents describing your life and work in this new city.

Seeing Changes Over Time

Here's Why

A line graph shows numbers in a way that is easy to read and understand. Line graphs are especially useful for seeing how things change over time. For example, in Lesson 2 a line graph showed you how steel production changed over a period of 50 years. Steel production increased when skyscrapers with steel frames were first built and continued to increase as new uses for steel were found.

Here's How

The graph on this page shows you the amount of steel produced in the United States between 1940 and 1990. The numbers along the left of the graph stand for millions of tons of steel. The numbers along the bottom of the graph are dates. To see how many millions of tons of steel were produced in 1940, find 1940 on the bottom of the graph. Follow the 1940 line up until you come to a dot on the line graph. You can see that this dot is just above the number 60 on the left. Steelworkers in the United States produced about 67 million tons of steel in 1940.

Now find the dot on the line graph for the year 1990. Look at the number to the left. What was the amount of steel produced in 1990?

You can use the line graph to see how steel production changed over a long period of time. The United States produced large amounts of steel during World War II. Notice that the line slants up between 1940 and 1950. How does the line slant between 1970 and 1990? The graph shows you that steel production decreased during these years.

Try It

Look at the line graph on the opposite page. What are the dates on the bottom? What do the numbers at the left represent? What facts does this graph give you about changes in steel production in the United States? How are these two graphs related?

Apply It

Look in a newspaper or magazine for a line graph. What is the title of the graph? What do the numbers along the left side of the graph stand for? What do those on the bottom stand for? Where does the line slant up or down? Is it level at any point? What changes do the lines show?

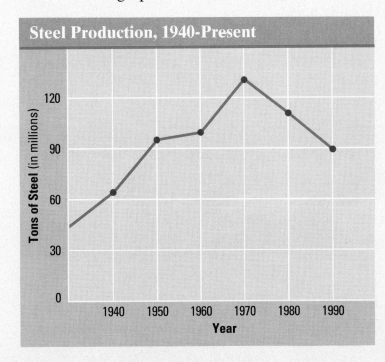

Steel Production, 1940-Present

LESSON 3

Autos for Everyone

THINKING
FOCUS

How did the Midwest develop as the center for the nation's automobile industry?

Key Terms

- assembly line

► *Henry Ford and his son Edsel are seated in the model F, produced about 1905.*

The man who puts in a bolt does not put on the nut; the man who puts on the nut does not tighten it. Every piece of work in the shop moves; it may move on hooks, on overhead chains . . . it may travel on a moving platform, or it may go by gravity, but the point is that there is no lifting or trucking. . . . No workman has anything to do with moving or lifting anything.

So said Henry Ford in 1913 of his new method of producing automobiles. Unfinished cars were hung on hooks attached to moving belts. Workers stood in one place and did not need to move—only the cars did. Each worker did one job and one job only, before the car moved on to the next worker in line. Ford got this idea from watching the methods of the meat-packing industry in Chicago. Ford used this method to produce many millions of cars quickly and cheaply.

A Modern Miracle

In the last years of the 1800s, automobile companies grew up in the Midwest. The many inventors and bold business leaders there led the way. The Midwest's supply of iron and steel helped the young industry grow. The excellent railroad and water transportation system also helped.

In 1896, a man from Lansing, Michigan, named Ransom Olds built one of the first cars in the United States. Olds's car company marked the beginning of the auto industry in this country.

The cars built by Olds cost over 1,000 dollars. This was more money than most people made in a year. Few people could afford them. Then Henry Ford in Detroit tried to build a cheaper, better car. His "Model T" of 1908 was easy to drive and simple to fix. Everybody wanted to buy one. But Ford could not sell the Model T for less than 850 dollars. He wanted to find a way to produce cars more cheaply.

To solve the problem, Ford thought of using assembly lines. At the beginning of this lesson you read how this system worked. In an **assembly line**, unfinished cars travel on a moving belt past workers and machines. Each worker or machine does a certain task. Using assembly lines, Ford lowered the cost of making a car. By 1914, the Model T cost 490 dollars. Two years later, the price fell to 360 dollars. Between 1908 to 1927, Ford sold millions of Model T's. ∎

▼ *Between 1915 and 1929, the factory sales of cars each year jumped from 895,000 to 4,455,000.*

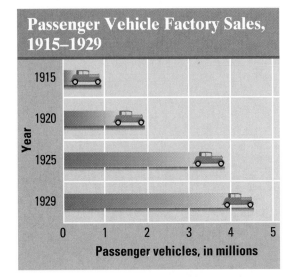

Passenger Vehicle Factory Sales, 1915–1929

What were some of the important developments in the early years of the automobile industry?

◄ *This photo shows a family with their 1915 Model T. To learn what driving was like in the early 1900s, read "Auto Trip in 1909" on pages 194 to 195.*

A Nation Takes to the Road

As more people started driving cars, life in the United States began to change. A farm family from Iowa used to travel many hours by horse and carriage to reach the nearest town. A trip that had taken three hours by horse now took only one hour by car. Life on the streets of cities such as St. Louis, Missouri, became more lively. Automobiles, trolley cars, and buses made it possible for workers to live farther from their jobs. Shopping, visiting, and vacationing became easier for people. At the same time, trucks joined trains as an important way to ship goods.

A Car Assembly Line

Using assembly lines in manufacturing helps factories produce goods quickly and cheaply. Most cars are built on assembly lines. Workers assemble cars step by step by adding parts as the car moves from one work station to the next.

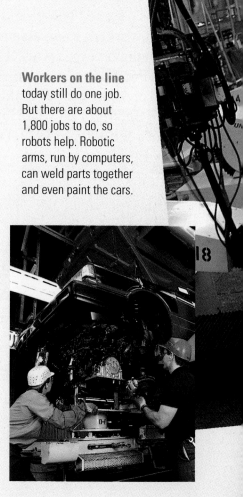

Workers on the line today still do one job. But there are about 1,800 jobs to do, so robots help. Robotic arms, run by computers, can weld parts together and even paint the cars.

Henry Ford introduced the moving assembly line to his car factory in 1913. By 1914, he had cut the time it took to build the steel frame for a Model T from 12½ hours to 1½ hours.

The automobile industry needed a great number of workers for its factories. European immigrants and blacks from the Southeast provided much of this labor. They streamed into busy Midwestern automobile centers, such as Detroit, Michigan, and Cleveland, Ohio.

During World War II, automobile companies made tanks, bomber planes, and other war supplies for the United States government. Many men left the car factories and went off to fight in the war. Automakers hired women to work on the assembly lines to take the place of the men. To learn more about a modern assembly line, see A Closer Look at a Car Assembly Line below.

Even robots can make mistakes. A factory worker must check to be sure that all 1,800 steps in assembling each car were done correctly.

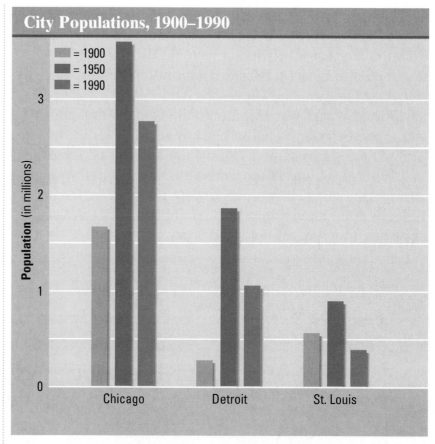

City Populations, 1900–1990

= 1900
= 1950
= 1990

Population (in millions)

3

2

1

0

Chicago   Detroit   St. Louis

➤ *From 1900 to 1950, industries such as food processing, steelmaking, and automobile manufacturing brought many people looking for jobs to midwestern cities. After 1950, people began to move out of these cities to nearby suburbs.*

Since the 1970s, the foreign car companies have been selling more and more cars in the United States. As a result, car manufacturers in the United States have sold fewer cars and have had to close plants. Today, Japan leads the world in the production of cars, trucks, and buses. Many people now work in car factories that the Japanese have opened in cities in the Midwest.

As you have seen, inventions like the steel plow and the reaper brought many changes to farming in the Midwest. Changes in the region continued as people developed the refrigerated railroad car and Model T. Life in the Midwest and the United States would never be the same. ■

■ *What changes has the growth of the automobile industry brought to the United States?*

R E V I E W

1. **FOCUS** How did the Midwest develop as the center for the nation's automobile industry?

2. **CONNECT** Look at the map that shows resources and manufacturing on page 184. Are automobile factories near the region's main steelmaking areas or far from them? What is the reason for this?

3. **ECONOMICS** Why did Henry Ford want to produce cars more cheaply?

4. **CRITICAL THINKING** What effect do you think the growing numbers of cars and trucks might have had on the railroads? Explain your answer.

5. **ACTIVITY** Make a list of Midwestern states that manufacture transportation equipment. Use the Minipedia to help you.

Conducting an Interview

Here's Why

Some of your relatives and neighbors may work in factories, such as automobile plants. Some of them may work at other kinds of jobs. Suppose you are writing a report on jobs and working. You can interview different people to learn about the work they do.

Here's How

You may have seen interviews given on television. An interview is a kind of conversation between two people. The interviewer asks questions, and the other person answers the questions.

In an interview, you must ask the right questions to get the information you want. Here are some guidelines to follow when you interview someone:

1. Make a plan. Decide what you want to learn.
2. Write down your questions based on what you want to know. Ask *Who? What? Where? When? Why?* and *How?* Do not ask a question that can be answered by simply saying "yes" or "no." Here are some good questions to begin with: Where do you work? What do you do there?
3. Begin your interview by telling the reason for it. Doing so will help the person think of specific answers that will answer your questions. One reason might be "I am writing a report on how people feel about their jobs."
4. Ask your questions clearly. Listen carefully to the answers. Show the person you are interested.
5. Take notes on the answers, but don't write down every word. Write only enough to help you remember the answers later.
6. If you don't understand an answer, ask more questions. Some answers may make you think of questions that you didn't prepare in advance. Ask these "follow-up" questions to learn more about specific topics.
7. Thank the person you interviewed.
8. Review your notes. Write a summary of the information that you can use in your report.

Try It

Work with a partner. Take turns interviewing each other about a favorite activity. Plan the interview, make up questions, and follow the guidelines for interviewing.

Apply It

Interview an older relative or neighbor about the jobs that he or she has had. Use questions such as these:

1. Why did you choose this job?
2. How did you you learn to do it?
3. What is the most interesting part of the job?
4. What do you like most about your job? Dislike the most?

Auto Trip in 1909

Paul G. Hoffman

In 1909, the Hoffman family set off on a long-awaited and carefully planned automobile trip between two small towns in Illinois. It was a "long" trip of 60 miles. Unfortunately, motor trips in the early days of the automobile did not always turn out as they were planned, as the Hoffmans discovered several days and many breakdowns later. As you read, ask yourself, "What would life be like today if modern cars still had the same problems they had in 1909?"

You read about the early days of the automobile industry in Lesson 3. In this story, Paul G. Hoffman, former president of the Studebaker Corporation, tells about early travel.

chassis (CHAS see) body of car
Rube Goldberg cartoonist who drew complicated, strange-looking machines
steering knuckle part of steering wheel
lugs bolts used to attach wheel to axle
casings tires
hamper picnic basket

I was the chauffeur on the first long motor trip of the Hoffman family. The car was a 1905 Pope-Toledo purchased secondhand by my father at a cost of approximately $1,500. It was an open car. The chassis would have done credit to Rube Goldberg. Advertisements called it the world's first mile-a-minute automobile. Tires cost from $75 to $90 apiece, were good for about 2,500 miles; punctures were frequent. A steering knuckle cost $30, and a new one was needed every so often. Springs, priced at about $30, broke every time you hit a bad bump. There were seven lugs on each wheel; to change a tire was a major operation. For touring we carried sixteen spark plugs, all available inner tubes, two extra casings, tools enough to outfit a small garage.

We lived in Western Springs, southwest of Chicago. Our trip, for which we had to wait until spring, had as its destination Sycamore, Illinois, approximately sixty miles away. Preparations were made weeks ahead. We started bright and early on Saturday morning, with five people and an enormous hamper of lunch. Our adventures, briefed, were as follows:

In the first few miles I changed four spark plugs. Otherwise, everything was lovely.

On the far side of the Fox River I tried to shift from third to second gear to climb a hill, and failed. When the car was out of gear there was no service brake. We started to roll backward. My aunt screamed, tossed out the lunch basket, and followed it herself in a flying leap. I stopped the car by backing into the bank.

After trying again and making the grade, we reached a fork in the road. Nobody knew which one to take, and we had no maps. Father said "Left" and Grandfather said "right." Grandpa had the more positive manner, and we went right. We should have gone left.

grade hill or slope

It began to rain. The road became a bog in which we finally sank. I cut brush to give the wheels traction. We got out of first mudhole, went a short way, sank again.

traction the way a rough surface allows wheels to grip the road without slipping

Night came on. I lighted the head lamps. Old-fashioned rock-carbide lamps, they flickered and flickered, went out. No help at all for seeing ahead. We slid into the ditch and were stuck for good. A neighboring farmer gave Mother and Aunt a bed for the night . . .

Next morning we managed to get out of the ditch under our own power. We had come forty-five miles and had had enough; we headed for home.

Presently the engine stopped cold. Trying to crank it, Grandpa gashed his forehead on the sharp toe of the radiator. The cut bled freely. My aunt and my mother began to weep.

crank start

I discovered what was wrong with the engine. A valve at the bottom of the crankcase had been turned when we were stuck in the ditch. The oil drained out, the engine "froze." I had extra oil and managed to start the engine, but we had burned out all the bearings, and found that the engine would die if the car speed dropped below thirty miles per hour.

crankcase part of the engine that holds moving parts

At St. Charles, where we had started to roll downhill the day before, the two ladies got on the streetcar and went home. The nearest garage was at Aurora, fourteen miles away. We three men headed for it. We struck at least fifty "thank-you-ma'ams" in the road between Aurora and St. Charles, taking them at thirty. Grandpa used most of his vivid vocabulary.

thank-you-ma'ams potholes

The car stayed in the Aurora garage about a month and was practically rebuilt. . .

Motoring was like that. . .

Further Reading

Roadbuilders. James E. Kelly. This nonfiction book describes the American highway system and explains how it was built.

Chapter Review

Reviewing Key Terms

assembly line (p. 189)   market (p.179)
iron ore (p. 184)   refrigeration (p.181)
livestock (p.180)   smelting (p.184)

A. Write a sentence for each pair of words below. Include details that give clues to the meaning of the first term in each pair.
1. livestock, stockyards
2. iron ore, steelworkers
3. assembly line, car
4. refrigeration, railroad cars

B. Write the key term that best completes each sentence.
1. The growing city of Chicago was an important ____ for Wisconsin dairy products.
2. ____ keeps meat fresher longer and helps meat packers ship meat over great distances.
3. ____, coal, and limestone are three resources which are often carried by freighters to steelmaking centers.
4. Workers on the ____ made millions of Model T cars quickly and cheaply.
5. Iron ore is heated to separate the metal from the ore in a process called ____.
6. Ranches all over the country shipped ____ to the meat packers of Chicago.

Exploring Concepts

A. Copy the chart below on a separate sheet of paper. Then complete the chart by filling in the blank boxes.

Midwestern Industries		
Industry	**Development**	**Effects**
flour milling	Pillsbury developed a new method of grinding wheat.	
meat packing		Fresh food can be shipped without spoiling year round.
dairy farming	Hazen developed the first cheese factory in Wisconsin.	
	Elbert Gary developed new steel mill in Gary, Indiana.	
auto making		Cars were built faster and more cheaply.

B. Write one or two sentences to answer each question below. Use details from this chapter to support your answers.
1. How did Charles Pillsbury build his flour business into an important national industry?
2. In what ways did the automobile industry help the growth of the Midwest?
3. How has steel produced in midwestern steel mills been used in the United States?
4. Why was Henry Ford able to sell millions of Model T's?

Reviewing Skills

1. Imagine you are going to interview a steelworker. What do you want to know about this job? Write a list of your questions. Include questions that follow the guidelines on page 193.
2. Look at this line graph. About how many cars were sold in 1940? In which ten-year period did automobile sales rise most sharply? What does the line graph show you about automobile sales between 1960 and 1990?
3. Use the scale on the map on page 184 to find out how far iron ore would need to travel by freighter from the tip of Lake Superior in northern Minnesota through lakes Huron and Michigan to the Gary, Indiana, steelworks.

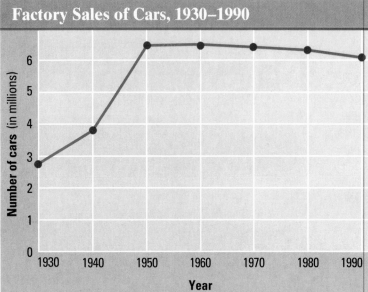

Factory Sales of Cars, 1930–1990

Number of cars (in millions) / Year

Using Critical Thinking

1. The food-processing, auto, and steel industries have created many new jobs for people in the Midwest. What are the reasons that these three industries developed in the Midwest?
2. People will go where they can find good jobs. Based on what you have learned in this chapter, do you agree with this statement? What special jobs do people do where you live?
3. Many cars sold in the United States today are made in Japan. Why do you think Japanese auto companies are opening factories in the United States?

Preparing for Citizenship

1. **WRITING ACTIVITY** Pretend that you are a newspaper reporter interviewing Will Kellogg or Henry Ford in the early 1900s. Decide which man you will interview and what questions you will ask. In your newspaper article, write details that answer your questions.
2. **COLLECTING INFORMTION** Gather information about the food-processing industry. In a notebook, make a list of processed food products that you find in your own home or a local store and those you see advertised in newspapers, in magazines, or on television. Then share your list with your classmates.
3. **COLLABORATIVE LEARNING** Work with the class to plan advertising projects for three industries in the Midwest—food processing, steel manufacturing, and automaking. Choose the products you want to advertise. Use both words and pictures to develop ads for newspapers, magazines, radio, and television. Then present the ads to the class.

197

The Midwest Today

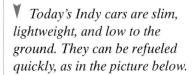Y ou can take it fast or slow in the Midwest. For a pulse-pounding event, get a seat at the Indianapolis 500, one of the world's most famous auto races. If you prefer a slower pace, how about a smooth sail on Lake Superior or a steamboat ride down the Mississippi? And for a sight that you'll simply want to stand and gaze at, you can visit the carved stone faces of the Presidents at South Dakota's magnificent Mount Rushmore.

Exploring the Indy 500

"Drivers, start your engines." Thirty-three powerful cars come to life at once. The cars begin circling the two-and-a-half-mile track, following the pace car. Then the green flag waves, the pace car pulls aside, and they're off!

The Indianapolis 500 is 500 miles of pure speed. You may have seen the auto race on television. But the only way you can truly sense how fast these cars go is to see them roar right by you at speeds of up to 200 miles an hour.

More than 300,000 people come each year to see the Indy 500 on the Sunday before Memorial Day. The race was first held in 1911, when the automobile industry was barely 10 years old. In the early days, cars bounced around a track made of brick. Today, cars hug the smooth turns at high speeds. Special safety equipment protects

▼ *Today's Indy cars are slim, lightweight, and low to the ground. They can be refueled quickly, as in the picture below.*

drivers in accidents. In the pit stops, crews can refuel a car, make minor repairs, or change tires in seconds. The first driver to reach the checkered flag on the 200th lap of the Indy 500 wins more than $600,000.

Exploring the Great Lakes

The people of Mackinaw City, Michigan, say this is the only place where you can watch the sun rise over one Great Lake and set over another. The city sits where Lake Michigan and Lake Huron meet.

Although the Midwest states do not border an ocean, they have plenty of beautiful shorelines and water views. The coastline of Michigan alone is longer than the whole East Coast from Maine to Florida. That's because the state borders four of the five Great Lakes.

The lakes—Superior, Michigan, Huron, Erie, and Ontario—are the largest group of freshwater lakes in the

▲ *Boats sail by skyscrapers in cities along the shores of the Great Lakes.*

Political Map of the Midwest

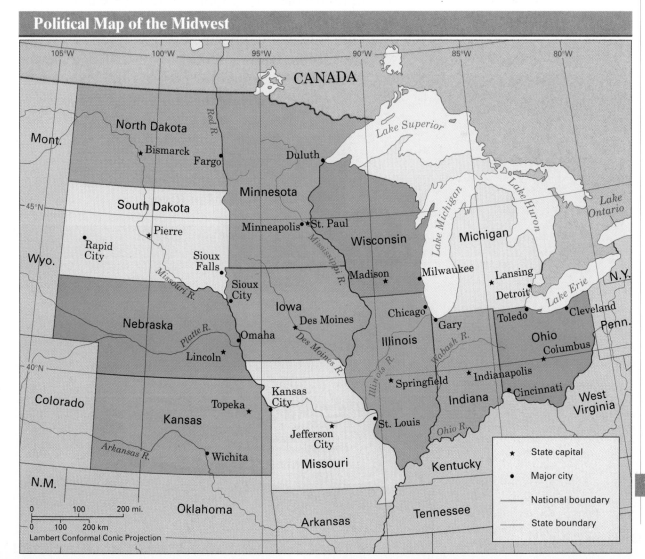

- ★ State capital
- • Major city
- — National boundary
- — State boundary

Lambert Conformal Conic Projection

199

world. If you stand on the shore of any one of them and look across it, you think you're looking out on a great ocean. Storms sweep along Lake Erie for 200 miles, gathering force and pushing 20-foot waves in front of them. The waves slam into Ohio's ragged shoreline, where the Marblehead Lighthouse has stood since 1821.

Ships, barges, sailboats, and fishing boats all share the lakes. In fact, the United States and Canada share the Great Lakes, because the two countries' border runs right down the middle of the waters.

Exploring the Mississippi

Look up. Look at the birds. There are thousands of them—hawks, ducks, swans, and geese. Where are they going? They're following the Mississippi River.

The Mississippi isn't just a famous shipping route. It is also the most heavily traveled flyway for birds in North America. The wide, winding river acts as a road map for birds heading south for the winter.

You can follow the Mississippi too. Just drive along the Great River Road as it hugs the muddy banks from Minnesota southward. Imagine the days when steamships carried lumber and coal downriver to New Orleans. Stop along the way at famous sites, like Hannibal, Missouri. Hannibal was the hometown of writer Mark Twain, who worked on the river in the 1850s and wrote many books and short stories about life on the "Ole Man River."

▼ *Put on your captain's hat and take an old-time paddleboat ride down the wide Mississippi.*

Exploring Mount Rushmore

For more than 50 years, these four faces have never blinked. That's because they're made of pure stone. Do you recognize them? They are four of our most famous Presidents.

When you visit the Black Hills of South Dakota, you can see that the faces are part of the hills themselves, carved out of the steep stone slopes. Each face is as tall as a five-story building, and together they make the largest sculpture in the world.

The sculptures were designed by Gutzon Borglum, whose family came from Denmark. When Borglum died, his son carried on his work. After 14 years, the great stone pictures were finally finished in 1941.

▼ *The faces of George Washington, Thomas Jefferson, Theodore Roosevelt, and Abraham Lincoln gaze outward from a hilltop in South Dakota.*

Move Ahead

Use encyclopedias and other books to find out more about these interesting places and events in the Midwest. These questions may guide your research:

1. Who are some winners of the Indy 500? What kinds of cars did they race? Who was the first woman to enter?
2. What waterfalls connect the Great Lakes? How do ships avoid the falls as they pass from lake to lake?
3. What does Mark Twain's book *The Adventures of Tom Sawyer* tell about life on the Mississippi River?
4. What tools did workers use in carving Mount Rushmore? What dangers did they face?

Explore Some More

Now you can find out what your state or region has in common with the Midwest. For example, are there any auto races in your area? What kinds of cars are driven?

Or explore the rivers and lakes of your state. Are the waters used for business purposes, such as shipping, or for fishing and swimming? You may want to research the national monuments or memorials in your state. Whom or what do they honor?

The Southwest

It must have looked like the river of no return. In 1869, John Wesley Powell and nine other men headed down the Colorado River to explore Arizona's Grand Canyon. The red canyon walls rose to almost one mile above them in awesome beauty. For nearly a month they floated through this "vast wilderness of rocks." Their wooden boats bobbed like toys on the "mad, white foam" of the river. There were dangers around every corner—boulders, whirlpools, and plunging waterfalls. But at last, the river floated them to safety.

1600

Grand Canyon National Park in Arizona.
Photograph Copyright Jerry Jacka Photography.

2000

The Southwest

A Land Like No Other

The wide-open land of the Southwest casts a spell on many newcomers. Much of the region's magic lies in how different it is from the rest of the nation. Its deep canyons, flat-topped hills, and towering rock sculptures make the geography unusual and rugged. Even the names of its plants and wildlife—yucca plants, saguaro cacti, mesquite trees, armadillos, and Gila monsters make you wonder about this region.

Monument Valley
in Arizona

The Southwest

The 4 states of the region
- Arizona
- Oklahoma
- New Mexico
- Texas

Hot and dry, hot and sticky—if you drove from Tucson, Arizona, to Houston, Texas, you'd feel a big change in climate. Cities like Tucson were built on the bone-dry desert. They need water from large rivers like the Colorado. When you reach the east Texas coast, the air is soaked with moisture from the Gulf of Mexico.

Population: 25,312,392. The population of the Southwest nearly doubled between 1950 and 1980.
Size: 567,897 square miles. The state of Texas alone is larger than the entire Northeast region. The smallest state in the region, Oklahoma, is larger than any state east of the Mississippi River.

Major resources: oil, natural gas, copper, uranium, gold, silver, stone, sand, gravel, water power

Climate: Temperatures in the Southwest often top 100 degrees (F) during the summer months. The region's record high temperature, 127 degrees (F), was recorded at Parker, Arizona, on July 7, 1905.

The average rainfall in most of the Southwest is only 10 to 20 inches a year. Desert areas receive less than 10 inches of rain each year. To live in this dry climate, the most famous of desert plants, the cactus, stores water in its large stems.

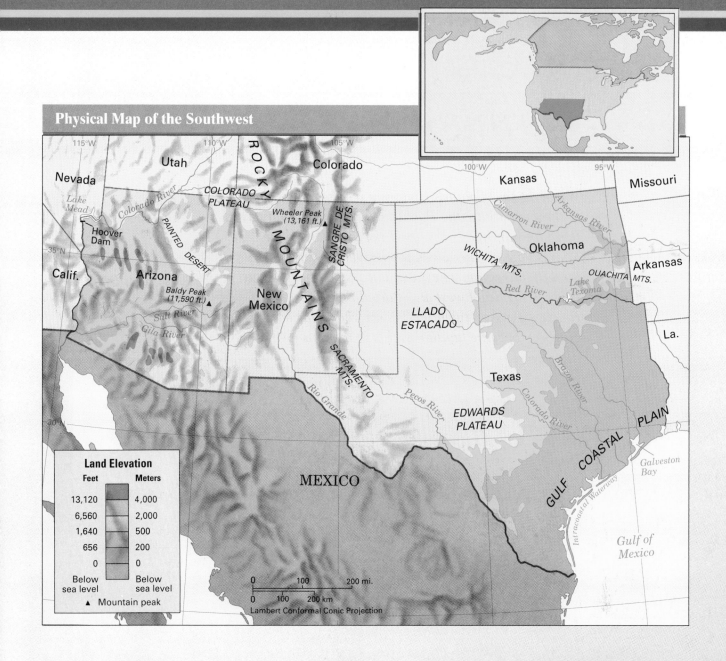

Physical Map of the Southwest

Utah
Nevada
Colorado
ROCKY
COLORADO
PLATEAU
Lake
Mead
Hoover
Dam
35°N
Calif.
Arizona
Baldy Peak
(11,590 ft.)
Salt River
Gila River
Colorado River
PAINTED DESERT
MOUNTAINS
Wheeler Peak
(13,161 ft.)
SANGRE DE
CRISTO MTS.
New
Mexico
SACRAMENTO
MTS.
Rio Grande
30°N
MEXICO

Kansas
Missouri
100°W
95°W
Cimarron River
Arkansas River
Oklahoma
Arkansas
WICHITA MTS.
OUACHITA MTS.
Red River
Lake
Texoma
La.
LLADO
ESTACADO
Texas
Brazos River
Pecos River
EDWARDS
PLATEAU
Colorado River
GULF COASTAL PLAIN
Galveston
Bay
Intracoastal Waterway
Gulf of
Mexico

Land Elevation

Feet	Meters
13,120	4,000
6,560	2,000
1,640	500
656	200
0	0
Below sea level	Below sea level

▲ Mountain peak

0   100   200 mi.
0   100   200 km
Lambert Conformal Conic Projection

Not all deserts in the Southwest are brown and bare. For example, the Painted Desert of Arizona lives up to its name each day at dawn. When the morning sun hits the rocks in this desert, they reflect the colors of the rainbow.

Texas coast
along the Gulf of Mexico

Turquoise stone
from New Mexico

The coastal plain of southeastern Texas is similar to the land and climate of the Southeast. The land here is flat or gently rolling, and it is often swampy. The climate is good for farming.

Chapter 9

Farming and Ranching

When the first Spanish explorers reached the Southwest in the early 1500s, the Pueblo people had already lived there for hundreds of years. Like the Pueblo, the Spanish drew water away from rivers to farm the dry land of the region. They also introduced horses and cattle to the Southwest and started the region's first ranches. As American settlers arrived in the early 1800s, cowboys became familiar sights in the Southwest.

The Zuñi, a Pueblo people, used beautifully decorated pots for storing dried corn.

1610 Santa Fe is founded, 10 years before the Pilgrims land in Massachusetts. Santa Fe later became the capital of the state of New Mexico.

1500

1580

1660

1500

1540 Francisco Vasquez de Coronado begins two-year exploration of the Southwest.

Frederic Remington captured the action and danger of a stampede in this 1908 painting.

Bells rang many times each day at the Spanish missions. They signaled the start of different activities.

1836 Battle of the Alamo is fought during the Texas war of independence from Mexico.

1740

1820

1900

1900

LESSON 1

Corn in the Desert

THINKING FOCUS

How did the Pueblo tribes learn to live in the dry, treeless land of the Southwest?

Key Terms

- mesa
- pueblo
- adobe
- irrigation

Zuñi *(ZOO nyee)* Indians tell many stories about corn. One of these legends describes how the first human beings got corn. The Zuñi called these first humans the Ashiwi.

In this legend, two spirits brought corn seeds to the Ashiwi to keep them from starving. The spirits planted the seeds at night. And by the morning, the corn stood in tall, green rows. The spirits called to the Ashiwi to come and look at the corn. The people came, and all day they stared in wonder as the corn grew.

By the time evening came, the corn was ripe and ready to be harvested. Again the spirits called out to the Ashiwi. But this time, they invited the people to eat the corn.

The Ashiwi started to eat the corn. However, it tasted hot to them, like chili peppers. The people did not like the corn because it was too hot. They told the spirits that they would not eat it.

The spirits heard what the Ashiwi said. So one at a time, they called to the crow, the owl, and the coyote *(ky OH tee)*. These three creatures came and tasted the crop. And as the birds and the coyote ate, the corn began to taste more and more mild. The Ashiwi, seeing what was happening, again tried the corn. Now it tasted just right to them.

By teaching them about corn, the spirits had helped the Ashiwi find a good source of food. But the spirits also let the crows, owls, and coyotes know how good the food tasted. So from that time on, the people who grew corn had to defend their crops against the animals.

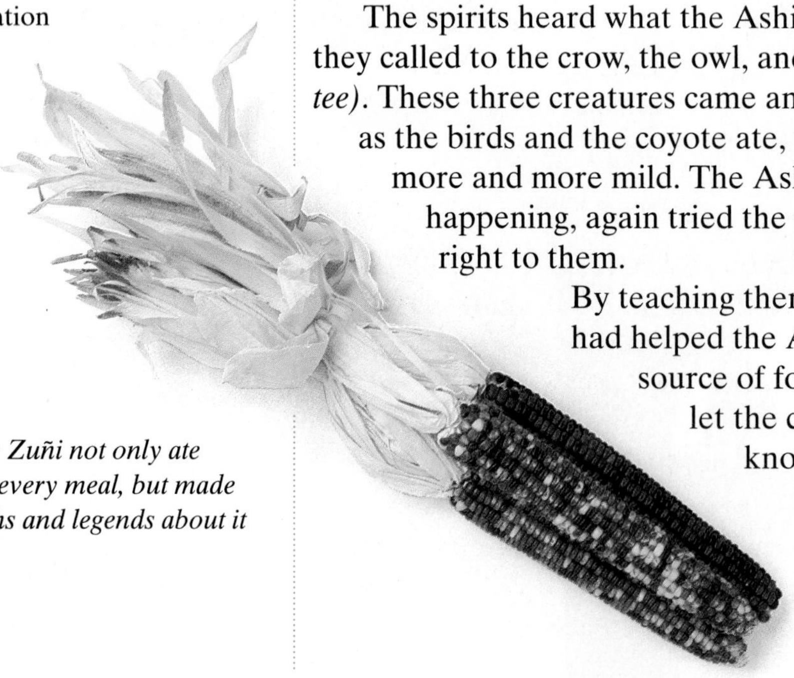

The Zuñi not only ate corn at every meal, but made up myths and legends about it as well.

Living in a Dry Land

In the 1500s, the Zuñi were one of many Indian tribes that lived in the deserts of what is now Arizona and New Mexico. These Indians made their homes in a rugged, treeless land of deep canyons and steep, flat-topped hills. This kind of hill is called a **mesa** *(MAY suh)*.

The Zuñi were part of a larger group of Indians known as the Pueblo *(PWEHB loh)* Indians. **Pueblo** is also the word for a Pueblo village.

The Hopi *(HOH pee)*, Acoma, Laguna, and Taos *(TOWS)* are also Pueblo tribes. These tribes lived apart from each other and spoke different languages. However, they all shared the same way of life. They all farmed and lived in the same type of buildings in their pueblos.

Because few trees grew in the desert, the Pueblo built their homes out of stone or adobe *(uh DOH bee)*. **Adobe** is a kind of brick that is made of mud and straw and dried in the sun. Pueblo houses had thick walls and small windows. The walls and windows helped keep people cool during the blazing summers and warm during winter.

Farming the Desert

The Pueblo also found ways to farm in the dry climate. These methods were important because some parts of the Southwest get less than 10 inches of rain in a year, as the map on page 409 shows.

The Pueblo used every drop of water carefully. They planted seeds deep in the ground where the soil stayed wetter. The ground also protected the seeds from the hot sun. Some Pueblo planted crops near mesas so that the crops could catch rainwater as it ran down the cliffs. Others dug ditches from nearby rivers to water their fields. Bringing rainwater to a field by means of ditches or pipes is called **irrigation.** ■

▼ *Pueblo homes were up to five stories high. All the buildings in a pueblo were connected. Indians went from level to level using ladders.*

Across Time & Space

Many of the buildings in New Mexico today are made of adobe, the same mud and straw mixture that the Pueblo used to build their villages hundreds of years ago.

■ *What methods did the Pueblo use to live and farm successfully in the dry climate of the Southwest?*

209

Farming and Ranching

The Central Role of Corn

By using water carefully and practicing irrigation, the Pueblo were able to grow cotton, squash, sunflower, and beans. But corn was by far their most important crop.

The Pueblo's corn was different from corn grown in the Midwest. It had long roots that reached the wet soil deep in the earth. As a result, the corn grew well in the Southwest's hot, dry climate.

The Pueblo depended on corn and ate it with every meal. In fact, corn was as important to the Pueblo as buffalo was to the Plains Indians. Their culture centered around corn and it was their main source of food.

Corn gave the Pueblo a steady food supply, which allowed them to live in one place. Many other Indian groups were hunters and gatherers. To get food, they had to follow game animals from place to place as the seasons changed. The Pueblo traded their corn and other crops with these Indians. Over the years, this trade made the Pueblo wealthy and powerful.

Corn and Everyday Life

A pueblo was a busy place. Much of the activity in the pueblo centered around corn. Each day, people gathered on

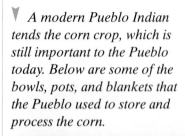

▼ *A modern Pueblo Indian tends the corn crop, which is still important to the Pueblo today. Below are some of the bowls, pots, and blankets that the Pueblo used to store and process the corn.*

the flat roofs of their houses for daily chores. Men wove cloth from cotton. Women ground corn into meal between two stones. Then they cooked the meal in one of 40 different dishes. Corn bread, corn pancakes, and corn dumplings were just some of the foods the Pueblo made with corn.

In the fields, workers planted seeds and dug ditches with simple tools. They tended and harvested the crops. After the harvest, the Pueblo husked and then dried the corn. Pueblo women wove delicate baskets and made beautiful clay jars for storing the corn.

Corn was more than just a good source of food to the Pueblo. It was also an important part of their culture and religion. The Pueblo tribes had colorful ceremonies to thank their gods for corn and other crops. Many Pueblo myths, songs, and legends tell about corn. You read about one of these legends at the beginning of the lesson. Tribal dances and ceremonies having to do with corn continue among Pueblo today. ■

■ *In what ways was corn important to the Pueblo?*

R E V I E W

1. **FOCUS** How did the Pueblo tribes learn to live in the dry, treeless land of the Southwest?

2. **CONNECT** In what sense was corn as important to the Pueblo tribes as buffalo was to the Plains Indians?

3. **GEOGRAPHY** Why is farming in the Southwest so difficult?

4. **CRITICAL THINKING** How do you think Pueblo Indians living in 1500 would have responded if no rain fell in a long time? Explain.

5. **WRITING ACTIVITY** Imagine you are preparing to interview a Zuñi. Write five questions you want to ask about Zuñi villages, homes and legends.

LESSON 2

Spanish Missions and Ranches

Key Terms

- padre
- mission
- rancho
- vaquero

➤ *This Southwest Indian wall painting in the Canyon del Muerto in Arizona shows the Spanish arriving on their horses in search of riches.*

For many years, people in Mexico had heard stories about Seven Cities of Gold to the north. There, the stories said, "chieftains sprinkled themselves . . . with gold dust every day and rode in chariots of silver." When these stories reached Spain, leaders there decided to locate these legendary cities.

In March 1539, the Spanish king sent Marcos de Niza *(NEE zuh)*, a priest in the Catholic Church, to find riches in the land of the Pueblo.

After weeks of traveling, Marcos reached the land where the Pueblo lived. While Marcos's group stopped to rest, he sent a black slave named Estéban to go on ahead. Estéban became the first person from across the Atlantic Ocean to meet the Pueblo. Estéban found no gold, but he did learn that the place Marcos was looking for was called Cibola *(SEE boh lah)*. Marcos returned to Spain with this news.

Exploring the Southwest

The following year, Francisco Vasquez *(vas KWEHZ)* de Coronado led another group through the Southwest. Coronado spent two years searching for Cibola. He never found it. Instead, he found Indian farmers living in dusty villages made of adobe. The golden cities that people reported seeing may only have been distant Indian villages shining in the bright sun.

Though Coronado failed to find Cibola, he did claim new land for Spain. The map below shows the route of Coronado's expedition. His group crossed deserts of cactus and tumbleweed and climbed over several mountain ranges. Once, a small party of Coronado's men stumbled upon the Grand Canyon. With wonder they gazed into this giant

Which Indian tribes might Oñate and Coronado have met as they traveled through the Southwest?

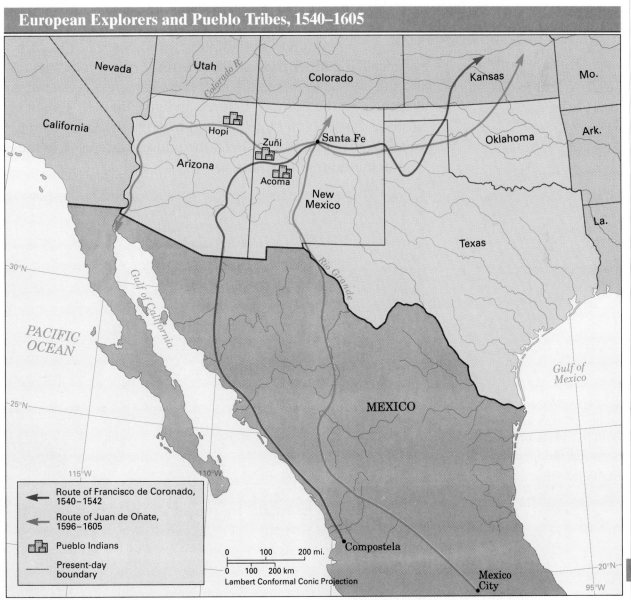

European Explorers and Pueblo Tribes, 1540–1605

Route of Francisco de Coronado, 1540–1542

Route of Juan de Oñate, 1596–1605

Pueblo Indians

Present-day boundary

0   100   200 mi.

0   100   200 km

Lambert Conformal Conic Projection

Farming and Ranching

Spanish explorers in the 1700s used pocket compasses, like the ivory compass pictured here.

opening carved out of the earth in what is now Arizona.

Coronado's expedition also traveled through what is now New Mexico, Texas, Oklahoma, and Kansas. When Coronado returned to Mexico, he brought no gold or silver. However, he did bring new knowledge about the beautiful land of the Southwest.

In 1598, the king of Spain decided to start Spanish settlements in this land. He chose Juan de Oñate *(aw NYAH tee)* to lead a group of settlers into New Mexico. They founded the Southwest's first Spanish settlement at what is today San Juan Pueblo. Then in 1610, the Spanish founded Santa Fe, which later became the capital of New Mexico. Santa Fe is the oldest capital city in the United States.

Along with the settlers, the king of Spain also sent priests to spread the Catholic religion to the Southwest Indians. The priests were called **padres,** the Spanish word for priest. The Indians did not always welcome the padres. Many Indians did not want to join the Catholic Church and give up their Indian customs. In 1680, the Pueblo tried to drive the Spanish out of the Southwest. But by 1692, the padres were back in the region building settlements. ■

■ *What led to the first Spanish settlements in the Southwest?*

➤ *This settlement, built in San Antonio, Texas, around 1768, looks like many of the settlements that the Spanish built in the Southwest.*

214

Working the Land

The settlements the padres started were called **missions**. One purpose of these missions was to bring Indians into the Catholic Church. The Spanish wanted to give more than a new religion to the Indians, however. They wanted to teach them new customs as well.

Farming on the Missions

Religion was the most important part of mission life. But farming was the activity that helped these small settlements survive.

Although the Pueblo had farmed before, the padres showed them new farming methods. The padres showed the Indians how to use plows and other tools. They introduced the Indians to new crops and animals. For the first time Indians grew peas, onions, peppers, watermelons, and wheat. They also learned to ride horses and to herd sheep and cattle.

Indians lived at the missions with the Spanish people. Some worked in storerooms and workshops behind the high walls. Others worked in the fields. They cared for herds of sheep and cattle in nearby pastures. And, as they had done in the past, they dug ditches to bring water to their crops.

One of the most famous of the padres of the Southwest was Father Eusebio *(yoo ZAY byoh)* Francisco Kino *(KEE noh)*. He started three missions in Arizona in the late 1600s and early 1700s. In his notes, Father Kino described one of these missions.

> **T**his mission has . . . a great many large and small cattle, oxen, fields, a garden with various kinds of garden crops. . . . It has a forge for blacksmiths, a carpenter shop, a pack train, water mill, many kinds of grain, and . . . other things, including horse and mule herds.

The Beginnings of Ranching

Father Kino was not only a priest. He was also a mapmaker, explorer, and rancher. He brought herds of sheep, cattle, and horses to the missions. These herds helped to start ranching in Arizona.

Raising cattle was well-suited to the region's large areas

▼ Chili peppers and beans were two of the crops the Spanish grew at their missions.

How Do We Know?

GEOGRAPHY *As a map maker and explorer, Father Kino helped many of the explorers and historians who followed him. His map of southern Arizona and northern Mexico was the most useful one for more than 100 years.*

A Vaquera

2:00 P.M., October 3, 1820
A roundup near San Antonio in South Texas.

Carne Seca (Dried Beef)
She carries half a piece of tough dried beef in her leather pouch. The other half she ate for lunch while in the saddle.

La Reata (Lariat)
She twirls the rawhide lariat and aims for the calf's neck. When she pulls the calf to the ground, other vaqueros will brand it MM.

Chaparreras (Chaps)
Thorns tore into these leather coverings when the vaquera chased the calf through the thick underbrush.

Silla (Saddle)
The vaquera digs her knees into the saddle. Her father gave her this saddle when she became the first woman on the rancho to work with the vaqueros.

Mustang
His hooves pound across the valley. The vaquera broke this wild horse herself, teaching him to stop, turn, and gallop.

of dry grazing land. The vegetation map on page 408 shows how much grazing land there is in the Southwest. Many Spanish settlers in the region replaced their crops with cattle. They sold their cattle's hide for leather. They also sold tallow, or fat, for making candles and soap. As more Spanish settlers arrived in the late 1700s, large ranches developed. The Spanish called these large ranches **ranchos.**

The owners of the ranchos hired workers to tend their large herds of cattle. These workers were called **vaqueros**. Like early cowboys, they rode horses and roped and herded cattle with great skill. Many grew up on the ranchos and learned to ride as soon as they were old enough to sit on a horse. As young children, vaqueros practiced for hours with their *reatas*, ropes that were often about 60 feet long. Most vaqueros made their own *reata* by braiding together four to eight strands of rawhide—the untanned leather of cattle.

As adults, vaqueros often spent most of their days in the saddle, riding for hours across the open land. They often traveled hundreds of miles to gather up the rancho owner's cattle. The Moment in Time on page 216 shows a female cowhand, a vaquera, at work on a rancho. Many of the vaquero's words, and much of their clothing and equipment, were used later by cowboys of the American West.

The growth of the ranchos helped change life in the Southwest. Ranching became the most important enterprise in the region. The spur, saddle, and horse became a major part of life for the vaqueros and cowboys who lived there. ■

▼ *In this painting by August Ferran, vaqueros rope stray cattle. A good vaquero could lasso, or rope, a running calf at 30 feet.*

■ *What impact did missions have on the growth of farming and ranching in the Southwest?*

The vegetation map on page 408

R E V I E W

1. **FOCUS** In what ways did Spanish settlements change the Southwest?

2. **CONNECT** How was Spanish farming both similar to and different from that of the Pueblo?

3. **CULTURE** How did the Spanish vaquero influence the later cowboy?

4. **CRITICAL THINKING** What do you think was the major religion in Spain in the 1500s?

5. **ACTIVITY** Using the information in the chapter, make a list of all the activities that might have taken place at a mission. Share your list with the class.

The Cowboys Arrive

THINKING FOCUS

How did cattle ranching become such an important business in the Southwest?

Key Terms

- cattle drive
- roundup
- stampede

▼ *All a cowboy needs to do his job is a good horse and a strong rope.*

As ranching grew in the Southwest in the mid 1800s, a new figure arose—the cowboy. Many cowboy stories tell about brave men who captured wild horses by day and told jokes around campfires at night. But real cowboys worked long hours for little pay. They risked their lives in blizzards to guard herds on the open prairies. They rounded up cattle and branded them by burning their ranch's mark into the animals' hides. And the cowboys drove cattle hundreds of miles to railroads so that they could be shipped across the country.

Over time, the cowboy came to be a symbol of the adventurous and independent spirit of the West. The following lines from a cowboy song capture this spirit:

I'm bound to follow the longhorn cows
    until I git too old,
    It's well I work for wages, boys,
    I git my pay in gold.
My bosses, they all like me well,
    they say I'm hard to beat,
Because I give 'em the bold stand-off, they know I've
    got the cheek [self-confidence].

Yes, I'm a rowdy cowboy,
    just off the stormy plains,
My trade is cinchin' [putting on] saddles and pullin'
    bridle reins,
O I can tip the lasso, boys, it is with graceful ease,
I can rope a streak of lightnin'
    and ride it where I please.

Settlers in Texas

In the early 1800s, the Southwest was home to Indians and Spanish people from Mexico. But the Southwest was about to change. Pioneer families from the United States had begun settling along the Mississippi River. New states such as Missouri, Louisiana, and Mississippi were attracting settlers from the eastern United States. Many of these settlers hoped to move farther west into land that belonged to Mexico.

In 1821, Mexico began allowing these settlers to buy Mexican land in what is now the state of Texas. By 1830, up to 30,000 people from the United States had come to live in Texas.

The new settlers in Texas soon decided that they did not want to be a part of Mexico. After a short conflict, the settlers gained control of Texas. In 1845, Texas became a state. ■

▼ *In 1836, settlers from the United States declared Texas a republic, independent of Mexico. For nine years, before it became a state, Texas was its own country.*

■ *Why did United States citizens begin to settle in Texas in the 1820s?*

Cattle Country

In the days of Spanish and Mexican rule, cattle often wandered away from the ranchos. Over the years, these cattle formed large wild herds. New settlers in Texas rounded up many of these cattle, called longhorns. They used these longhorns to build up the size of their herds. In this way, the longhorn helped Texas ranchers such as Charles Goodnight succeed.

Settlers and Ranching

Charles Goodnight was ten years old when his family moved from Illinois to Texas in 1846. Goodnight was amazed by the longhorn he saw. He quickly decided that he would be a rancher.

In 1856, Goodnight started out in the ranching business working as a cowboy. By 1860, Goodnight and his stepbrother had a herd of 180 cattle. In five years, that number grew to 8,000. Goodnight was on his way to becoming one of the most successful cattlemen in the Southwest.

All through the 1850s, ranches like Goodnight's spread across the Southwest. The new ranchers looked for good grazing land. They also needed large water supplies, because each animal drank about 30 gallons of water a day. The ranchers also relied on cowboys, who they hired to look after the herds of cattle on the open plains.

The Great Cattle Drives

Raising cattle was only one part of the ranching business. The cattle also had to be shipped around the country. This required good transportation. So when railroad lines reached into the Midwest in the 1860s, ranchers sent their cattle north to meet them. Getting cattle to the railroads was called a **cattle drive**.

Before the cattle drive could begin, cowboys had to gather cattle from the open plains. This gathering of cattle is called a **roundup.** Cowboys then branded the cattle with the ranch's symbol. In this way, cowboys could tell their cattle apart from others.

A cattle drive often involved six to twelve cowboys and a herd of 1,000 to 3,000 cattle. A trail boss led the drive. Most drives also had a wrangler. This person's job was to look after the herd of extra horses. A cook served beans, salt pork, pancakes, and biscuits to the hungry workers. The cook's kitchen was called the chuck wagon. The illustration below shows where everyone rode during a cattle drive.

Cowboys on cattle drives faced many dangers. These included cattle thieves, snakes, lightning, and floods. Perhaps the worst danger was the stampede. A **stampede**

A hat protected cowboys from long days under a hot sun. Chaps kept them from getting saddle-sore and from being scratched by trees. A cowboy used his spurs to control his horse.

How a Cattle Drive Works

The **trail boss** was the leader of the cattle drive. The **chuck wagon**, the drive's traveling kitchen, was driven by the cook. A team of cowboys guarded the herd of **long-horn cattle**. These cowboys rode in various positions around the herd, including **point**, **swing**, **flank**, and **drag**. A less experienced cowboy called a **wrangler** watched over the herd of extra horses, called the **remuda**.

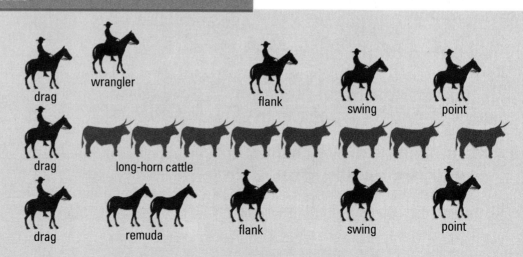

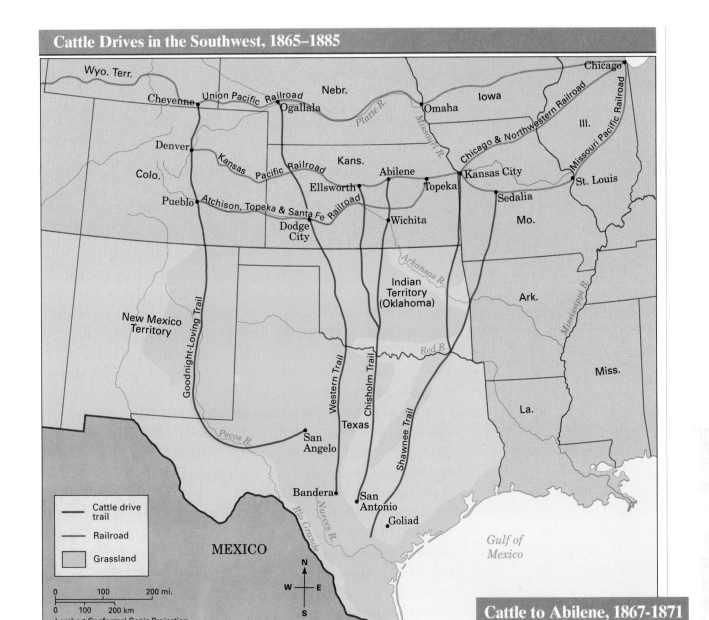

Cattle Drives in the Southwest, 1865–1885

Wyo. Terr.

Cheyenne · Union Pacific Railroad · Ogallala
Nebr.
Iowa
Chicago

Union Pacific Railroad

Platte R.

Missouri R.

Omaha

Chicago & Northwestern Railroad

Missouri Pacific Railroad

Denver
Kansas Pacific Railroad
Kans.
Abilene
Kansas City
St. Louis
Ill.

Colo.
Ellsworth
Topeka
Sedalia

Pueblo · Atchison, Topeka & Santa Fe Railroad
Dodge City
Wichita
Mo.

Arkansas R.

New Mexico Territory

Goodnight-Loving Trail

Indian Territory (Oklahoma)
Ark.

Red R.

Mississippi R.

Western Trail

Chisholm Trail

Miss.

Pecos R.
San Angelo
Texas
Shawnee Trail
La.

Bandera
San Antonio
Goliad

Rio Grande

Nueces R.

Gulf of Mexico

MEXICO

Legend:
— Cattle drive trail
— Railroad
▨ Grassland

0   100   200 mi.
0   100   200 km
Lambert Conformal Conic Projection

N
W   E
S

occurred when one cow was frightened and began to run. When this happened, the other cattle followed. A stampede was a terrifying experience. One person who had the experience of being in a stampede wrote "The earth trembled under the clatter of hoofs, horns clanged, and a great heat was generated." To stop a stampede, cowboys had to ride in front of the cattle and try to turn them until they ran in a circle. Even after the cowboys stopped the stampede and the cattle settled down, the danger of a stampede starting again was high.

Once they reached the railroad,

chuck wagon

trail boss

Cattle to Abilene, 1867-1871

Year	Number of Cattle
1867	35,000
1868	75,000
1869	350,000
1870	300,000
1871	700,000

▲ Cowboys drove cattle through the grasslands of Texas north to the railroads. The chart shows how many more cattle were rounded up in just 4 years.

221

Farming and Ranching

Buffalo Bill Historical Center, Cody, WY

▲ *This 1923 painting by W.H.D. Koerner shows the trail boss leading a cattle drive across Wyoming.*

many cattle were sent to states in the East. In the crowded eastern cities, far from the Texas ranches, people were willing to pay much higher prices for meat. In the late 1860s, cattle worth five dollars in Texas sold for forty dollars in the East.

The large numbers of cowboys and railroad workers helped towns near the railroads grow up almost overnight. Dodge City and Abilene *(AB uh leen)* in Kansas are two examples of such cities. See the map on page 221 to locate these towns and the cattle trails.

By the 1880s, many pioneers had set up new farms in the Midwest. Many of these farmers put up barbed-wire fences to mark the edges of their property. The fences blocked many cattle trails and made it harder for cattle to be driven across the open land. But cattle drives to distant rail lines became unnecessary when the railroads built lines to Texas. Then, most of the long cattle drives stopped.

The death of the cattle drive was not the end of the cattle business. Ranching is still a big part of the Southwest's economy. To see how important it is, look up the states of the Southwest in the Minipedia starting on page 350. Notice the rank of cattle in the list of agricultural products for each of the states. ■

■ *What led to the rise and fall of the great cattle drives?*

R E V I E W

1. **FOCUS** How did cattle ranching become such an important business in the Southwest?
2. **CONNECT** Would the growth of ranching in the Southwest have been possible without the Spanish?
3. **HISTORY** Why did long cattle drives stop when railroads were built in Texas?

4. **CRITICAL THINKING** If the Spanish had kept all settlers out of Texas in the 1820s, how might the history of Texas have been different?
5. **WRITING ACTIVITY** Imagine you are a cowboy on a cattle drive. Keep a diary for a week describing your adventures. Read your diary entries to the class.

Using the Card Catalog

Here's Why

Suppose you want to find out more about the cowboys in Lesson 3. Knowing how to use the library's card catalog will help you find the books you need.

Here's How

The card catalog is a cabinet with many small drawers. Each drawer contains cards in alphabetical order. On the front of each drawer are one or more letters that tell what cards are inside. For example, a drawer marked *V* contains all cards beginning with the letter *V*. Each library book has at least three cards in the catalog—a title card, an author card, and one or more subject cards.

To find books on the subject of cowboys, look in the card catalog under the letter *C*. You might find a subject card like the front card below. What are the title and the author of the book on this subject card?

Suppose you had started out looking for *The Life and Legend of George McJunkin.* You would look for the title card under the letter *L*. (If a title begins with *A, An,* or *The,* look under the first letter of the second word.) A title card looks like the middle card below.

What if you want to find more books by Franklin Folsom? Look for the author card. It is filed by the first letter of the author's last name, *Folsom,* in the drawer labeled *F*. An author card looks like the back card below.

Once you find the card for the book you want, how do you find the book? Letters or call numbers appear on the left side of most cards to tell the section of the library where you can find the book. The call number matches a number on the book and a place on the shelf.

Try It

Try your skill at using the card catalog by answering these questions.

1. Which kind of catalog card would help you find books about the Chisholm Trail? In which drawer would you look first?
2. Which kind of card would help you find a book written by Nat Love? In which drawer would you find this card?
3. Which kind of catalog card would help you find the book *Hurry Sundown*? In which drawer would you find this card?

Apply It

Find three books about ranching in the card catalog. Copy the title, author, and call number for each book. Then find the books on the shelves.

Folsom, Franklin

j 920
F73f
Famous Pioneers; illus. by Joseph Papin

The Life and Legend of George McJunkin

jB
M189foL
Folsom, Franklin
The Life and Legend of George McJunkin: Black Cowboy

COWBOYS

jB
M189foL
Folsom, Franklin
The Life and Legend of George McJunkin: Black Cowboy

Thomas Nelson Inc., Nashville, Tenn. 1973, 162 pp. Illus.

George McJunkin Cowboy

Franklin Folsom

In the late 1800s and early 1900s, George McJunkin was one of the most colorful figures on the Western frontier. He was born into slavery in Texas, but after the Civil War, he found freedom and an exciting life as a cowboy in northern New Mexico. As you read about McJunkin, ask yourself, "What was life like for a cowboy?"

George McJunkin was a legend among the cowboys you read about in Lesson 3. He was one of the best riders, ropers, shooters, fiddlers and storytellers of the Old West.

dismounted got off
lariat rope used by a cowboy
halter straps that fit around an animal's head and can be used to lead it

freighters drivers of wagons carrying freight, or goods

After a meal of hot corn bread and bacon, George thanked the woman and rode on to a place where she told him he'd find plenty of grass for his mule. It was still daylight when he dismounted and tied one end of his lariat to the mule's halter and the other end to a bush. That way she could eat but not wander away while George slept.

He unrolled his blanket and lay down in the sweet-smelling grass. The night was warm. No need to use any of his precious matches to make a fire. He just lay on his back and looked up at the stars. From nearby came the swishing sound of water in the river. Far away he heard dogs barking, and once he heard a coyote howl.

At first the night was dark, except for the stars. Then the moon rose and lit up the meadow. George lay especially quiet when he saw the black and white stripes of a mother skunk, followed by five youngsters, waddling down toward the edge of the water.

An owl hooted, and hooted again. Once in a while a mockingbird seemed to be singing in its sleep.

George had thought he would feel very much alone this first night by himself. But aloneness wasn't what he felt so much as excitement. He was in a new place—in a new night, and the night was full of wonder. He was on the road to living a new life—his own life.

Next day George met more freighters, some black and

some white. All of them were hauling smelly loads of buffalo hides, and two also had supplies of dried buffalo meat. Jerky, they called it. They were glad to give George strips of the tough stuff, which was hard to chew but tasted good, and it kept him from being hungry.

Finally George turned away from the Brazos and headed for the Leon. Here and there along the wagon tracks, a solitary man, or a man and his wife, had cut chunks of sod out of the prairie and piled them up, brick-fashion, to form the walls of a house. The people who lived in these soddies fed him, too. One of them even paid him to help dig a well. When the job was done, George wrapped a strip of cloth around a fistful of quarters that the man had given him. It was the first money he had ever earned, and he wanted to take good care of it.

A little cluster of houses made up the town of Comanche, the place that the freighter had told him about. "Anybody around here looking for cowboys?" George asked a man on the street. The man was white. There were no blacks anywhere.

"There's a trail herd forming west of town," the man told him. "But I doubt if they will take you on."

"They won't hire blacks," George thought. Then he had another idea. Maybe they just didn't hire blacks who were barefoot. The man was looking at George's feet.

Boots and just about everything else were for sale at a store in town. George tied his mule to a post at the back of the store where he knew blacks would have to go.

The boots he got felt strange. Until now he had always gone barefoot, and he walked clumsily in the secondhand pair that his handful of quarters had bought. Men lounging against the building stared at him with hard eyes as he went down the street. He was glad to get out of Comanche.

[George continues his journey until he reaches the place where the trail herd is forming. The trail boss offers him a job as the drive's wrangler, the person who looks after the horses and helps the cook. George had hoped to be a cowboy, so he is a little disappointed. But he agrees to take the wrangler job anyway, because he thinks the experience will help him to get cowboy work in the future.]

And so George turned his mule loose on the prairie and before dawn the next day the cook called him to start the fire for coffee.

Every day, after that, George drove the remuda, some-

Brazos a river in Texas
Leon a river in Texas
solitary single, alone

remuda herd of horses

225

times ahead of the cattle, sometimes well off to one side. But if he got a late start, he had to follow along behind the herd in clouds of dust so thick he couldn't breathe unless he covered his nose and mouth with his bandanna.

When he could see through the dust, he was fascinated by a trick the dragman had. This cowboy, whose job it was to keep the cattle from lagging behind or straying, had made his lariat into a whip. With the loop end in his hand, he snapped out the other end and flicked the backs of the animals that weren't keeping up. Leather strips attached to the end of the lariat cracked like a shot each time. George soon learned the trick, and he spent a lot of time snapping his rope.

Every morning the chuck wagon went out ahead of the herd and stopped near some grassy place before noon. Then the cook, with George helping, prepared the big meal of the day. Often he stewed potatoes and some fresh-killed beef and made sourdough biscuits in iron pots called Dutch ovens. Usually he served coffee, sweetened with molasses, and stewed dried fruit or a rice-and-raisin pudding that the men called spotted pup.

The nooning—the midday stop—was a time of rest for cowboys and cattle and horses, but not for George. He had to wash the tin plates and cups, which the cowboys had thrown into what they called the wreck pan. At the same time he had to keep an eye on the remuda to make sure the horses did not wander off too far. At the end of the long day he helped the cook prepare son-of-a-gun stew, a concoction of all the leftovers from the midday meal plus anything else the cook felt like throwing into the pot. Then came more dishwashing. When he crawled into his bedroll at last, it was usually well after dark. If he wasn't too tired to think about it, he was glad then that he would not have to get up in the middle of the night to take a turn riding around the herd the way the other hands did.

"How do you know when your turn is over?" he asked a waddy one evening.

The cowboy pointed to the eastern horizon and the stars just above it. Different stars, he said, would be showing there in two hours, still others in another two hours, and so on through the night.

Once in a while George woke up when he heard the riders changing the watch, and he got into the habit of looking with one sleepy eye to see what stars were showing in the

bandanna scarf used by cowboys

concoction mixture

waddy cowboy

226

low edge of the sky to the east. At other times he also noticed where the handle of the Big Dipper was pointing. That was another way of telling time at night. Sometimes the night sky made him feel he was on the edge of a world countless times larger than the one he already knew.

This stargazing habit George got into on the trail drive would stay with him for the rest of his life. In time his wonderment about planets and constellations and the Milky Way would link up with curiosity about other things in the natural world. But at the moment his interest was purely practical.

Then one night when he threw his bedroll on the ground, not a star was in sight. Clouds covered the sky.

"Looks like a storm," the trail boss said to George. "Keep a horse saddled. If the cattle get spooked, we'll need you to help."

spooked frightened

Later a clap of thunder woke George. At the same time rain started to fall—and the ground began to shake.

"Stampede!" the cook shouted to George. "Ride with the herd. We'll try to get it circling."

George was on his feet in an instant, his heart pounding with excitement—and fear. The night was so dark that he had to feel for the stirrup before he could swing into the saddle and turn toward the thundering hooves. His horse seemed to see well enough, however, even to enjoy racing the swiftfooted longhorns, which had been frightened by the storm. A sudden flash of lightning revealed the herd. Two cowboys were forcing cattle toward the left, so George swung his rope and yelled and urged his horse in that direction.

Gradually the frenzied creatures began to wheel in a great circle. The riders had succeeded in driving the head of the herd around until it joined the tail. Now the danger was over. Most of the herd, at least, had been kept together, and the cattle would not run off the edge of some bluff and kill themselves. George relaxed in the dark and patted his horse's neck, enjoying the feel of the animal's thumping heart against his legs.

frenzied terrified

Reading Further

Pecos Bill, The Greatest Cowboy of All Time. James Cloyd Bowman. This is the story of the famous fictional cowboy, Pecos Bill.
Duster: The Story of a Texas Cattle Drive. Frank Roderus. When his family needs money, young Doug Dorwood takes a job as a hired hand on a cattle drive.

Chapter Review

Reviewing Key Terms

adobe (p. 209)
cattle drive (p. 220)
irrigation (p. 209)
mesa (p. 209)
mission (p. 215)
padre (p. 214)

pueblo (p. 209)
rancho (p. 217)
roundup (p. 220)
stampede (p. 220)
vaquero (p. 217)

A. Write the key term for each definition below.

1. a ranch in the Southwest
2. a Spanish priest
3. one of the first cowboys
4. a steep, flat-topped hill
5. a mud-and-straw brick
6. the gathering of cattle from the open plains
7. a sudden rush of frightened cattle

B. Choose the key term that best completes each sentence.

1. Cowboys gathered cattle and drove them to the railroads on a _____ .
2. Spanish priests built _____ to teach the Catholic religion to the Indians.
3. The Zuñi and Hopi lived in villages called _____.
4. The Indians of the Southwest used a system of _____ to water their farmland.
5. Thick walls made of _____ kept the desert homes of the Pueblo Indians cool in the summer.
6. Some Pueblo Indians built their villages on top of steep _____.

Exploring Concepts

A. Make a copy of the chart shown below on a separate sheet of paper. Then fill in the blank spaces under *How They Made a Living*.

B. Support each of the statements to the right with two details from this chapter.

People of the Southwest	
Groups of People	**How They Made a Living**
Pueblo Indians	
Spanish settlers	
Pioneer families from the United States	

1. In search of gold and silver, Spanish explorers traveled through the Southwest in the 1500s.
2. Pueblo Indians farmed the deserts of Arizona and New Mexico.
3. When the padres set up missions, the Indians' way of life changed.
4. In 1835 settlers in Texas from the East did not want Mexico to control their land.
5. The railroads helped cattle ranching become a big business in the Southwest.
6. Cowboys and vaqueros had similar jobs.
7. Events important to Texas state history happened in the years 1836 and 1845.

Reviewing Skills

1. Look at the library catalog card at the right. What type of card is it? Under which letter of the alphabet would you find this card in the catalog?

2. Suppose you need information about the Texas war of independence. Which type of card will help you find a book with this information? What word should you look for at the top of this card? Under which letter of the alphabet would you find this card?

3. Look at the map in the Atlas on pages 404–405. Use the scale to find out how far a cattle drive would travel from Austin, Texas, to Wichita, Kansas.

Bolton, Herbert E.

973.16B   *The Story of Coronado*
University of New Mexico Press,
Albuquerque, NM, 1964
491 pp.

4. In some parts of the Southwest, cowboys still tend the cattle on ranches. Make up a list of questions that you would use to interview one of these modern cowboys.

Using Critical Thinking

1. When two cultures come together, each learns something from the other. What might the Indians and the padres on the missions have learned from each other? How do you learn about the cultures of other people today?

2. A line from an old cowboy song says, "A cowboy's life is a weary thing." Why do you think a cowboy's life was a "weary thing" at times?

3. If the Spanish explorers had found gold and silver in the Southwest, how might the history of the region have been different?

Preparing for Citizenship

1. **ART ACTIVITY** The English words *mesa*, *adobe*, *pueblo*, *taco*, *lasso*, *fiesta*, *rodeo*, *chili*, and *tortilla* come to us from the Spanish language. Make a picture dictionary by writing down each word and its definition. Then draw a picture to illustrate each one. Compare your dictionary with that of a classmate.

2. **GROUP ACTIVITY** In this chapter, you learned that Santa Fe, the capital of New Mexico, is the oldest capital city in the United States. Work with a classmate to list all the states and their capitals. Use the Minipedia, which begins on page 350, for help. After memorizing the names on your list, have a State Capital Quiz with another pair of students.

3. **COLLABORATIVE LEARNING** As a class project, make a mural showing what daily life was like in an Indian pueblo and on a Spanish mission. Work in two teams—a pueblo team and a mission team. Find information from this chapter that will help you illustrate the setting, people, and activities of a pueblo and a mission. Write captions for the pictures you draw. Then, as a class, compare life in an Indian pueblo to life on a Spanish mission.

Chapter 10

From Agriculture to Industry

The Southwest was still a region of small farms and cattle ranches in 1900. Two resources, water and oil, changed all that. Large dams helped farmers to bring water to the dry land and to build agriculture into a big business. Modern industry in the Southwest had its beginnings in 1901 with the discovery of oil. The oil boom brought new cities a~~~~l new factories to this land of cactus and cattle.

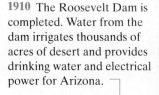

1910 The Roosevelt Dam is completed. Water from the dam irrigates thousands of acres of desert and provides drinking water and electrical power for Arizona.

| 1900 | 1920 | 1940 |

1900

Thomas Hart Benton's painting,
Boom Town, illustrates the
growth of a Southwest town after
oil was discovered.

Today cattle ranching and the oil industry
continue to be two of the Southwest's most
important activities.

	1960		1980		2000

2000

L E S S O N   1

Water in a Dry Land

T H I N K I N G
F O C U S

Why was water so important to the growth and development of the Southwest?

Key Terms

- dam
- reservoir
- aqueduct

➤ *This 1890 photograph shows a bustling downtown Phoenix. The city continued to grow, and by 1990, more than a million people lived in what had once been a quiet desert town.*

By the time Jack Swilling wandered into the Salt River Valley in 1867, the Hohokam Indians were long gone. Hundreds of years earlier, this tribe had lived in the desert valley of central Arizona. They used water from the Salt River to irrigate their crops.

As Swilling stood under the hot sun, studying the half-buried ditches of the Hohokam irrigation system, he got an idea. If the Hohokam could grow crops on the dry land by

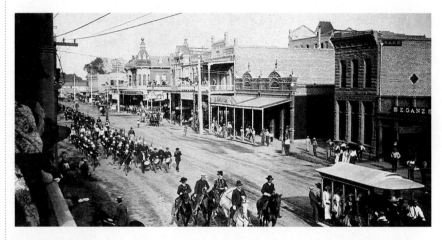

using irrigation, why couldn't other farmers? He knew that if he helped irrigate the valley, farmers would settle there. So he found a partner and started an irrigation company.

Soon, 30 farmers had settled along Swilling's irrigation ditch. Someone named the tiny settlement Phoenix, after a bird of Greek myth. The phoenix was said to burn itself to ashes every 500 years and then rise to life again. People hoped that a great city would rise on the desert land.

A Growing Demand for Water

Much of the land in the Southwest is as dry as the Salt River Valley. As the map on page 409 shows, many parts of the Southwest get less than 20 inches of rain each year. For this reason, irrigation has always been important to the region. In the past, Pueblo Indians dug ditches and canals to irrigate their crops. On the missions, Spanish priests often used irrigation to bring water to their small farms.

In the late 1800s, more and more settlers from the United States made their way into the Southwest. The canals and ditches carrying water from nearby rivers could not supply the many newcomers with enough water. People had to find new ways to bring water to the growing region.

A geologist named John Wesley Powell helped find a way to bring more water to the Southwest. Powell believed dams would solve the water problem. A **dam** is a wall built across a river to stop the flow of water. The stored water held back by the dam can be used for irrigation and for drinking water. The force of water falling over a dam's high walls can also be used to produce electrical power. People realized that the Southwest's future depended on dams.

Building Large Dams

To build large and costly dams, the Southwest would need the help of the nation's government. This turned out to be no problem. President Theodore Roosevelt wanted the dry regions of the nation to grow and prosper. For this to happen the regions would need large amounts of water to irrigate the land. So Roosevelt set up a government agency to plan and carry out irrigation projects.

Across Time & Space

By 1970, Arizona needed to bring more water to its cities. Congress provided funds for the Central Arizona Project, which was completed in the 1980s. Three great aqueducts were built to carry water from the Colorado River to Phoenix and Tucson. Look at page 404 to find the location of the Colorado River and of Phoenix and Tucson.

▼ *The dam's wall holds back a large pool of water. This water flows down from the mountain through long pipes and irrigates faraway fields.*

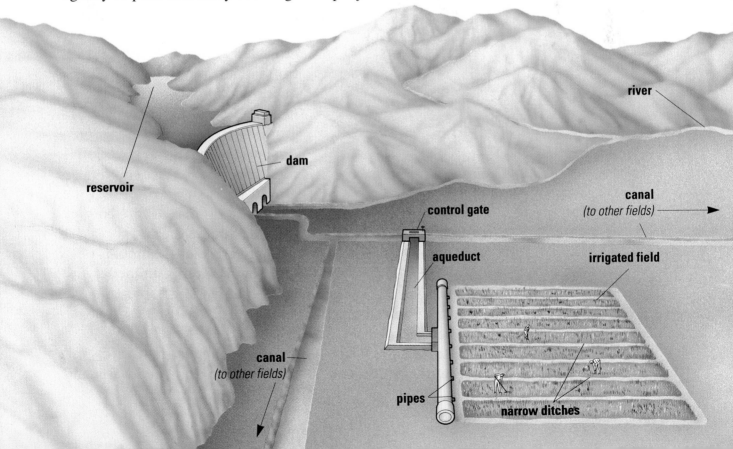

reservoir

dam

river

control gate

canal *(to other fields)*

aqueduct

irrigated field

canal *(to other fields)*

pipes

narrow ditches

In 1906, Roosevelt's new agency set out to build a dam on the Salt River in the mountains above Phoenix. Building this huge dam was a long, hard job. Before work could even begin, a 60-mile road had to be built through the mountains. The road was needed to carry tools and supplies to the dam site. Because the dam was so far from cities and towns, some materials had to be made on site. For this purpose, a lumber mill and cement mill were also built for the project.

Work on the dam finished in 1911. The Roosevelt Dam was the largest dam in the United States. The wall of the huge dam held back a large pool of water called a **reservoir**. Long pipes called **aqueducts** carried water from the reservoir to farms in the Salt River Valley. The water provided by the dam helped turn the desert valley into farmland.

The Roosevelt Dam was the first of many dams to be built in the Southwest. Dams were also built in New Mexico, Texas, and Oklahoma. The taming of the Southwest's wild rivers changed the region. ■

■ Why did the Southwest need to build many large dams in the early 1900s?

Water and Power Bring Growth

Before 1900, most farms in the Southwest were small. Farmers used irrigation only to grow crops to feed their families. But with the building of large dams, millions of new acres of desert land could be farmed. Agriculture soon became a big business in the Southwest.

Irrigation allowed farmers to grow new crops on larger fields. Cotton had always been an important crop in Texas and Oklahoma, but it had never grown well in the dry climate of Arizona. With large supplies of water, farmers in Arizona could grow the valuable crop. Today the Southwest produces more cotton than the Southeast.

▲ Farm workers harvest cotton on a Corpus Christi, Texas, farm in 1942.

Farmers also used irrigation to grow large amounts of fruits, vegetables, wheat, and peanuts. Trains shipped these crops to markets all around the country. Vegetables and fruit trees grew on land that had only been used for ranching before.

Large dams also helped cities and industries to grow in the Southwest. People needed water to drink and wash, and

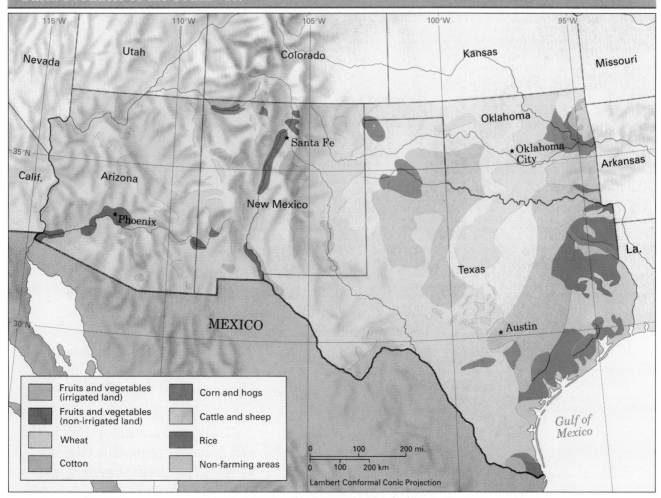

Map Legend:
- Fruits and vegetables (irrigated land)
- Fruits and vegetables (non-irrigated land)
- Wheat
- Cotton
- Corn and hogs
- Cattle and sheep
- Rice
- Non-farming areas

0   100   200 mi.
0   100   200 km
Lambert Conformal Conic Projection

power for light, heat, and cooking. A town like Phoenix would never have become a big city if the Roosevelt Dam had not been built. Water and power from other dams built in the Southwest helped cities such as San Antonio, Texas; Tucson, Arizona; and Albuquerque, New Mexico, to grow.

Factories also needed large amounts of water and power to run machines. The building of dams helped the rubber, machinery, and food processing industries to develop in the region. Without the resources provided by large dams, agriculture and industry would never have grown in the Southwest. ■

▲ How did irrigation change the types of crops grown in the Southwest?

■ How did large dams affect the growth of agriculture and industry in the Southwest?

R E V I E W

1. **FOCUS** Why was water so important to the growth and development of the Southwest?

2. **CONNECT** How is farming in the Southwest today different from farming as practiced by the Pueblo Indians or the Spanish?

3. **POLITICS** What role did the nation's government play in the growth of the Southwest?

4. **CRITICAL THINKING** If the Southwest had not built large dams in the early 1900s, how do you think the area would be different today?

5. **ACTIVITY** Look at the physical map of the United States on pages 406 and 407. Then make a list of all the major rivers in each state of the Southwest.

235

From Agriculture to Industry

LESSON 2

The Oil Boom

THINKING
FOCUS

How did the discovery of oil and natural gas change the Southwest?

Key Terms

- petroleum
- natural gas

➤ *The Spindletop gusher rose 200 feet into the air and could be seen for miles. When it blew on January 10, 1901, the people of Beaumont rushed to the hill. Men ran out of barber shops half-shaven, women left food cooking on the stove, and children deserted their classrooms.*

Before 1901, the people of Beaumont, Texas, would never have guessed that their little town was about to wake up to one of the biggest events in the history of the Southwest. How could they know that a big hill overlooking their town would soon make worldwide headlines?

Everyone thought Pattillo Higgins was crazy when he started drilling for oil at Spindletop Hill in the early 1890s. But Higgins kept up his search. The smell of gas, an odd taste to the water, and a strange feel to the soil all told him that oil flowed in the ground below. So while the town laughed, Higgins continued drilling. But for nearly 10 years, the drill came up dry at well after well.

By 1901, the workers at Spindletop were fed up. The well they had been drilling on for over a year had given them nothing but trouble. Then came the biggest headache of all. Without warning, a river of mud exploded from the ground, throwing six tons of pipe into the air. Disgusted, the tired workers began to clean up.

Within seconds, a roar like a cannon blast stopped them in their tracks. The frightened men looked up to see a black gusher of oil shooting into the air. They didn't know it, but they had just struck what was the world's largest oil field.

Black Gold

In the late 1800s, **petroleum,** or oil, as it was also called, had become so valuable that people began to call it black gold. The nation kept finding more and more uses for the thick, black liquid found deep in the earth. New machines and new industries needed oil to operate. Trains, ships, and farm machines used fuel made from petroleum. And people used oil to heat their houses and power their stoves.

By far the biggest user of petroleum was the automobile, which was invented in 1892. It quickly became a big part of life in the United States. By 1920, there were nine million cars on American roads. With so many cars, the country needed all the gasoline the oil industry could produce.

▲ *The man shown above made his fortune in Texas oil.*

Drilling for Oil

Before the late 1800s, most oil in the United States had been found in the East. Many people in the oil industry doubted that oil could be found in the Southwest. One Standard Oil Company executive was so sure of this that he promised to "drink every gallon of oil found west of the Mississippi River."

The oil experts were wrong. Even before the famous gusher at Spindletop, oil had been found in Red Fork, Oklahoma, on lands owned by the Osage and Creek Indians. In Texas, rich oil fields were found in West Columbia, Saratoga, and Sour Lake. In 1927, two very large fields were found in east and west Texas. Later, the oil industry would find ways to drill beneath the ocean floor. A Closer Look at Offshore Drilling on page 238 will show you more about this new method of drilling for oil.

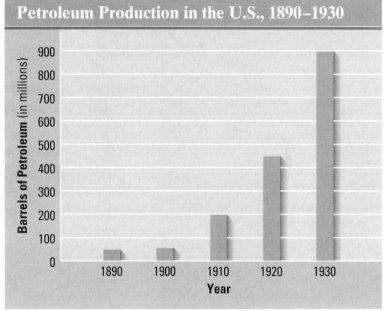

With the discovery of so many fields, thousands of people wanted to make their fortunes in oil. But success was not easy. First you had to dig a well. Usually that meant buying expensive machinery and paying a team of workers. Then you would drill hundreds of feet into the ground. Most of the time, the drill hit nothing but mud and rocks.

There was always the question of where to drill. Some people just guessed. Others spent years studying the land.

▲ *Automobiles, new industries, and new machines created a great demand for oil in the early 1900s. Production rose from 50 million barrels in 1890 to 900 million barrels in 1930.*

From Agriculture to Industry

An Offshore Oil Rig

To reach rich deposits of oil in the Gulf of Mexico, off shore oil rigs drill wells. Working on an oil rig several hundred miles off the coast of Texas is like living on an island. Supply boats deliver food, and a helicopter drops the crew on the rig for a week at a time. Workers use radio phones to talk to people on shore. Off duty, the crew sleeps, writes letters, or plays ping-pong below deck.

The crew is never far from the constant humming and vibrating of drillpipes and pumps.

revolving crane

helicopter

A rescue boat is ready to help in an emergency. There is always the risk of an accident in a fire, in stormy seas, or with the machinery.

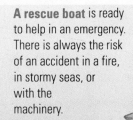

A submarine carrying divers plunges down 2,000 feet to make repairs to the drilling pipe. The submarine has a camera to take pictures underwater and a remote control arm to collect samples of sand and water.

Steel pipeline carries the oil from a hole drilled in the bottom of the ocean floor to storage tanks on the rig. A crew of 100 people work to keep the oil pumping safely.

Still others hired fortune tellers. But for every person who struck it rich in oil, hundreds more never made a penny. In the end, people often did better by opening stores and selling food and goods to the people looking for oil.

Boom Towns

Before oil was discovered in the Southwest, the big industries were cattle ranching and farming. But as more and more wells began to dot the land, oil soon became the most important industry. This new industry changed the region. Almost overnight, towns grew up on land that had only known dirt and cows. And small, quiet towns grew quickly into busy, crowded cities.

When Higgins found oil at Spindletop, the little town of Beaumont changed instantly and forever. Within days of the strike, people from all over the country raced to the booming town. The streets of Beaumont looked like a circus. Men walked around with signs on their hats advertising land deals. People pushed through the crowded streets, shouting "Howdy, Boomer" to everyone they met.

In six months, Beaumont's population rose from 9,000 to 50,000. Each day, hundreds of newcomers arrived. Some stayed in tents pitched on the edge of town. Others slept on pool tables, in barber chairs, or on rooftops. Water was so scarce it sold for six dollars a barrel. Oil, on the other hand, cost only three cents a barrel.

Beaumont was just one of many boom towns that grew up in the early 1900s. Others were Houston, Texas, and Oklahoma City and Tulsa in Oklahoma. All of these boom towns continued to grow and are now big cities. ■

▼ *These two photographs of Tulsa, Oklahoma, show how quickly this boom town grew. The first was taken in 1897. The second shows the town 13 years later.*

■ *Why did the discovery of oil at Spindletop cause such a rush of people to the Southwest?*

From Agriculture to Industry

The Natural Gas Bonus

When oil strikers drilled oil from the ground, they unearthed another valuable resource—**natural gas**. As the diagram on this page shows, natural gas is found where oil is found. Oil is a liquid, and natural gas is more like air. In a book called *Oil Notes*, the main character, a petroleum geologist, describes the difference between gas and oil:

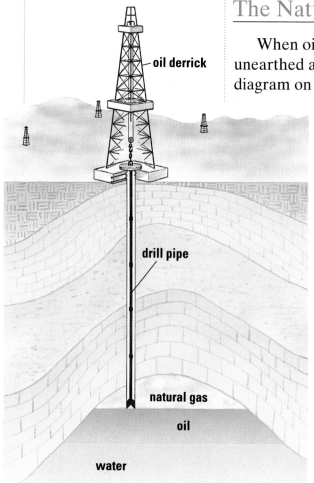

oil derrick

drill pipe

natural gas

oil

water

Pockets of natural gas collect deep in the earth above pools of oil.

What made it possible for people to take advantage of natural gas as a valuable resource?

You can't see gas, can't . . . peer at its hot, black sticky sweetness, but it smells good, and is more impressive to me than oil, in its own strong way.

It hisses. . . . It's not like anything you've ever heard. I could say it's like a jet, like a comet, but it's not like anything else.

It's easy to pour oil into a barrel, but how do you put gas into a container? That was the problem that the oil industry faced. For hundreds of years, people had known that natural gas was valuable. But no one could figure out how to contain it so that it could be used. At oil field after oil field, workers just burned the valuable gas away so they could get down to the oil.

In the late 1920s, new, stronger steel pipe made it possible to carry gas from a plant in Texas to cities in the Midwest. Many pipelines ran over 1,000 miles long. Now people in homes across the country used gas for heating, cooking, and air conditioning. The Southwest became the major supplier of this useful fuel to the nation. ■

R E V I E W

1. **FOCUS** How did the discovery of oil and natural gas change the Southwest?

2. **CONNECT** Explain how the growth of Beaumont, Texas, and the growth of Phoenix, Arizona, both depended on natural resources.

3. **HISTORY** How did the invention of the automobile affect the young oil industry in the early 1900s?

4. **CRITICAL THINKING** What are some good changes and bad changes that might have resulted from Beaumont's rapid growth after the workers struck oil at Spindletop?

5. **WRITING ACTIVITY** Imagine you are a reporter visiting Spindletop, Texas, on January 10, 1901. Write an article about the events of the day for your city or town's newspaper.

Drawing Conclusions

Here's Why

When you read, you should try thinking about new facts and ideas to develop ideas of your own. This process is called drawing conclusions. By drawing conclusions, you can understand more about what you read. For example, you can better understand new developments in the oil industry by combining what you already know with new information.

Here's How

To draw conclusions, you connect the new facts and ideas you read in books to what you already know about the topic. The diagram below shows how to draw a conclusion about an effect science has had on the oil industry. You already know that early oil drillers used hunches and guesswork to pick a spot to drill for oil. Recently, scientists found out how to use sound waves to study the layers of rock under the earth. Sound waves can now detect where a big pool of oil is. What conclusion can you draw about the way oil companies look for oil today? Check the diagram to see if your conclusion is right.

Try It

Read each statement below to learn more about the oil industry today. Think about what you already know about each topic from reading Lesson 2. Then draw a conclusion by combining what you already know with the information in each statement given below.

1. The U.S. oil industry began in Pennsylvania, but today oil companies drill for oil in Texas, Louisiana, California, Oklahoma, and Alaska.
2. Present-day methods bring to the surface only about a third of the oil in most oil fields.
3. Scientists have recently found out how to drill for oil on the bottom of the Gulf of Mexico.

Apply It

Think about the gasoline stations in your town or city. Suppose you are planning to open up a new one. What makes a gasoline station convenient? How can you attract customers? Why are particular gasoline stations successful? What conclusions can you draw about the best location for your new gasoline station?

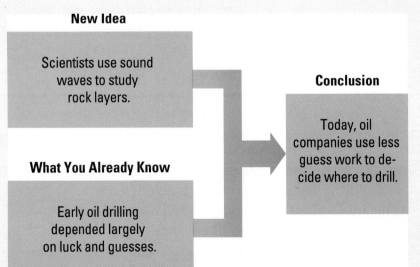

New Idea

Scientists use sound waves to study rock layers.

What You Already Know

Early oil drilling depended largely on luck and guesses.

Conclusion

Today, oil companies use less guess work to decide where to drill.

L E S S O N 3

Modern Industries Grow Up

THINKING FOCUS

What industries did the mineral resources of the Southwest help to create?

Key Terms

- refinery
- petrochemical
- conservation

➤ *Many toys, including the rubber balls shown here, are made from petrochemicals.*

You already know that the gasoline for cars comes from petroleum. But did you know that football helmets, lipstick, and insect sprays are made from oil, too? Or that oil is used in making record albums, nylon stockings, and perfume? Even the ink used to print this book has some petroleum in it.

In fact, from the moment you wake up in the morning until your head hits the pillow at night, you are using products made from petroleum. You brush your teeth with them. You wash your hair with them. You drink your soda from them. And you often wear them as clothes.

How could all these different products come from oil? The answer lies in the chemicals that are made from oil. These chemicals are used to make thousands of the objects you use every day. During the past 50 years, they have greatly changed the way people live.

It's no surprise that these chemicals have also helped to change the Southwest. Their discovery has led to the growth of one of the most important industries in the region.

From Oil to Petrochemicals

The raw petroleum that comes from the ground is called crude oil. Before crude oil can power cars, heat homes, or make other products, it must go through a special process. This takes place at a factory called an oil **refinery**.

An oil refinery looks like something you might see in a science fiction story. Its tall, rocket-like towers, mazes of pipes, and huge tanks often cover hundreds of acres of land.

242

Chapter 10

At night, when it is lit by thousands of lights and burning flames, an oil refinery can look very mysterious—like a city from another planet.

At the many refineries in the Southwest, petroleum and natural gas are changed into dozens of useful chemicals. Scientists boil crude oil at very high temperatures to separate it into different liquids and gases. These liquids and gases are then mixed in new and different ways. The mixtures are called **petrochemicals**. Petrochemicals are used to make such products as clothing, plastics, and paints.

The Petrochemical Industry

Scientists learned to make petrochemicals around 1915. By the beginning of World War II in 1939, the production of petrochemicals had become a major industry in the region.

During the war, the country badly needed rubber to make tires and parts for airplanes, tanks, and jeeps. Natural rubber is made from the juice of certain trees. Not enough could be made to meet the demand. Using petrochemicals, scientists invented a product that looked, felt, and worked just like rubber.

At the same time, scientists developed other products that could take the place of natural materials. Nylon could be used in place of cotton and silk. Plastic could be used in place of glass and tin. After the war, these new materials, and many others like them, became widely used.

Unfortunately, all of these products made from petrochemicals soon became too much of a good thing. In the

▼ *The city of Houston owes its enormous growth to the rise of the oil and petrochemical industries. Many people in the region, including the worker shown here, depend on these industries to make a living.*

243

magazine *Outdoor Life*, writer Lonnie Williamson talks about the amount of plastics used in the modern world:

A ll of that plastic coming through the front door means that a lot is going out the back as garbage. About 133 million tons, or 1,100 pounds per person, are discarded each year. Everything from plastic packaging to broken hula hoops is tossed to the garbage engineer and largely forgotten.

Today, people are finding ways to protect nature from the plastics that damage our lands and oceans. Protecting the environment is called **conservation**. The petrochemical industry is helping with conservation by inventing new plastics that can be reused instead of thrown away. ■

■ How has the rise of the petrochemical industry affected the Southwest?

▲ *People have used copper to make money and tools for almost 10,000 years.*

Minerals Bring Growth

In addition to oil and natural gas, minerals have also helped to bring growth to the Southwest. For example, more than half the nation's supply of copper comes from Arizona. The mining of this mineral has brought income and new jobs to the state.

During the 1900s, inventors found many new uses for copper. As a result, the mineral became more valuable.

UNDERSTANDING CONSERVATION

I n the United States, people use more energy than in any other country in the world. Most of this energy comes from oil, gas, and coal. But the fuels drilled, dug, and pumped every day will not last forever.

People can practice conservation by reducing use of these fuels. Conservation means saving energy sources—but also includes saving resources such as wetlands and drinking water. People can conserve wetlands by not building houses on them. They can save water for drinking by washing cars less often.

People in the United States have already begun to cut down on energy use by building smaller cars that burn less fuel. You and your family can save energy too. You can walk more and drive less. You can buy more energy-saving appliances and turn your heat down at night in the winter.

Another important way for people to conserve limited energy supplies will be to depend on other sources of power, such as the sun, wind, and waves. Unlike oil, gas, and coal, these energy sources will not run out.

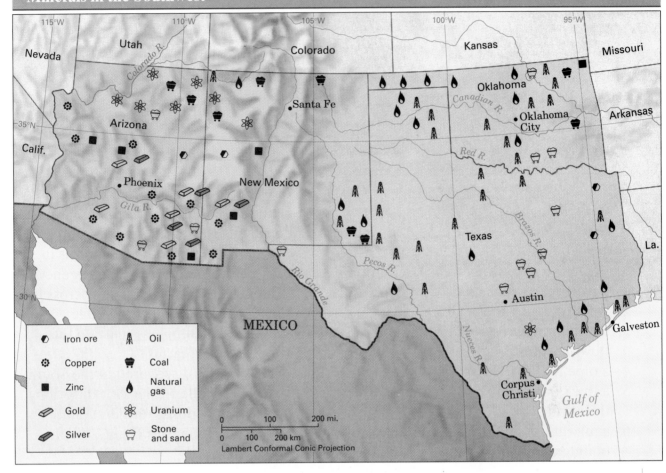

Minerals in the Southwest

Today, copper is used in making the pennies in your pockets, the wires and pipes in your home, and some of the medicines you take. It is also used to make machines such as refrigerators, dishwashers, and televisions. Over half of the nation's supply of copper comes from Arizona.

Other minerals in the Southwest have also helped the region grow. Uranium, found in New Mexico, helps to power nuclear power plants. Stone, sand, and gravel from all four Southwestern states are used by the building industry.

Clearly, the Southwest is rich with many different resources. The water, oil, and minerals found in the land have brought jobs, income, and new people to the area. All help to make the Southwest a rich and growing region. ■

▲ *If you were looking for a place to mine gold and silver, which two states would you start in?*

■ *How have minerals other than oil and natural gas helped the growth of the Southwest?*

R E V I E W

1. **FOCUS** What industries did the mineral resources of the Southwest help to create?

2. **CONNECT** In what way is the process of refining oil similar to the process of making steel?

3. **GEOGRAPHY** Why did the petrochemical industry develop in the Southwest instead of some other region of the country?

4. **CRITICAL THINKING** How would your life be different if petrochemicals did not exist?

5. **ACTIVITY** Make a list of 15 objects or products made from plastic that you use each day. Share your list with the class.

Chapter Review

Reviewing Key Terms

aqueduct (p. 234)
conservation (p. 244)
dam (p. 233)
natural gas (p. 240)
petrochemical (p. 243)
petroleum (p. 237)
refinery (p. 242)
reservoir (p. 234)

A. Write the key term for each definition.
1. a factory in which crude oil is processed
2. ways of saving the environment
3. a wall built across a river to stop the flow of water
4. a pipe that carries water a long way
5. a thick, black liquid found deep within the earth
6. a mixture of liquids and gases made by boiling crude oil

B. Choose the key terms that best complete the sentences in each paragraph.
1. President Roosevelt wanted to provide a supply of water to irrigate farms in the Southwest. He created an agency that built the Roosevelt ____ across the Salt River. Water filled the huge ____ behind the dam. _____ carried the water to desert farms.
2. When ___ was discovered in the Southwest, it was called "black gold." Along with the oil deposits, drillers found ____. Huge refineries change oil and natural gas into _____.

Exploring Concepts

A. Complete the chart below on a separate paper by adding the effects. Each effect should tell what type of growth took place in the Southwest as a result of people's using each resource.

B. Write a sentence to answer each of the following questions.
1. How does irrigation change the land?

Type of Growth	Cause	Effect
Agricultural	water	
Industrial	oil	
	gas	
	other minerals	

2. Why did the demand for petroleum increase in the early 1900s?
3. Why do people build large dams across rivers?
4. How has the geography of the Southwest created a need for aqueducts?
5. What caused boomtowns in the Southwest in the late 1800s and early 1900s?
6. What happens at an oil refinery?
7. What was necessary for cotton to become a major crop in Arizona?
8. Why did workers at oil fields just burn away natural gas before 1920?
9. What kinds of jobs are done on an offshore oil rig?
10. What was the major effect of World War II on the petrochemical industry?

Reviewing Skills

1. Draw one conclusion from each pair of statements below. Use what you have learned in the chapter to help draw your conclusions.

   a. President Roosevelt provided money to help the Southwest to grow. Today, the country gets many farm products and minerals from the Southwest.

   b. In the 1970s, many people in the United States began driving smaller, lighter cars. Small cars use less gasoline than big cars.

   c. Between 1950 and 1990, copper became a much more valuable and high-priced mineral. Arizona produces more copper than any other state.

2. Which kind of library catalog card would help you find a book about the life of songwriter Woody Guthrie? In which drawer would you find this card?

3. Look on page 409 at the map of annual precipitation in the United States. Which parts of the Southwest receive the greatest amount of precipitation? Which parts receive the least?

Using Critical Thinking

1. There are millions of automobiles in the United States. They run on gas and oil, two petroleum products. What do you think are the good and bad effects of using so much petroleum?

2. Long before the Southwest was irrigated by the building of dams, the Southwest Indians had irrigated their land. What else have people learned about land use in other regions from studying the Indians' ways?

3. What are some reasons besides jobs that people would want to move to the Southwest?

4. Phoenix might never have become a large, important city without the Roosevelt Dam. Explain why this statement is true.

Preparing for Citizenship

1. **COLLECTING INFORMATION** Start a notebook with pictures of petroleum products used today. Include pictures of plastics that are of all kinds. Write captions for your pictures.

2. **ART ACTIVITY** Pretend that you have written a book called *Pollution from Plastics*. Design a cover for the book. On the front, write and illustrate the title. On the back, write a paragraph that explains what the book is about.

3. **COLLABORATIVE LEARNING** As a class project, make a Conservation bulletin board. First, list our natural resources, such as oil, natural gas, and water. Next, research methods of conserving these resources. Finally, draw pictures and write captions about conservation for the bulletin board.

4. **COLLABORATIVE LEARNING** Work in a group of four or five students to find out about your community's supply of drinking water. Ask your families about the source of water for each of your homes. Have one student call the town or city hall to ask if water is brought to your community from far away or from a nearby source. Make an oral report to your class.

The Southwest Today

isitors to the Southwest are often amazed by the mix of people and cultures they find there. For example, many of the region's rivers and towns bear Indian or Spanish names. Houses and churches also show both the Indian and Spanish influence. And much of the art, jewelry, and clothing found in the region today were inspired by Indian, Spanish, or Mexican styles. Visitors can also see the role different groups of people played in the history of the region. The ancient homes of the Indians, the missions of the Spanish, and the ranches of the settlers of the 1800s are all part of the story of the Southwest.

▲ *The descendants of the Cliff Dwellers, the Pueblo Indians, still live in northern Arizona and New Mexico today.*

Exploring the Cliff Dwellings

The early Spanish explorers thought they were seeing things. How could an entire village be perched halfway up the straight side of a mountain? But there was no one around to answer their question. By the 1500s, when the Spanish arrived, the cliff dwellings had stood empty for two hundred years.

Today, guides explain some of these mysteries when you visit these dwellings in northern New Mexico and Arizona. An Indian tribe called the Cliff Dwellers lived in the hill country. Starting around the year 1000, they built homes from adobe bricks on ledges high up on cliff walls. Some of their villages could house more than 5,000 people.

Narrow trails lead you along the cliffs. You can climb up and down the ladders to peer into the adobe houses on different levels. Far below lies the land where the Cliff Dwellers farmed and hunted.

Political Map of the Southwest

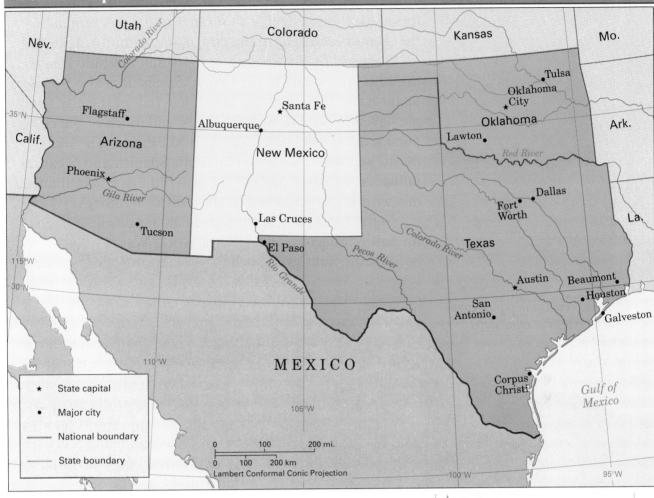

Exploring San Antonio

"Remember the Alamo!" Texans cried as they fought for their independence from Mexico in 1836. The Alamo was built as a Spanish mission and was later used as a fort.

From behind its high walls, a small band of Texans fought and lost a famous battle against a large force of Mexican soldiers. The defeat caused the Texas rebels to fight even harder. Two months later, Mexico granted Texas

▲ *Which river forms the boundary between Oklahoma and Texas?*

◄ *Among the men who died defending the Alamo was the famous frontiersman, Davy Crockett.*

249

From Agriculture to Industry

its independence. Today, thousands of visitors remember the Alamo each year in the city of San Antonio, Texas.

Founded by the Spanish in 1718, San Antonio is now the 10th-largest city in the United States. It is also the most Spanish city in the nation. More than half of the city's people have Mexican or Spanish roots, and much of the city's population speaks both Spanish and English. The food, music, and art of the city reflect this Spanish and Mexican influence. In many parts of the city, old Spanish buildings mix with skyscrapers and modern office buildings.

In the 1860s, San Antonio was an important stop along the cattle trails to Kansas. Since World War II, it has become the Southwest's leading center of trade.

Exploring the Grand Canyon

"Don't worry," the guides tell you. "The mules have walked this path a million times. They could do it in their sleep." Don't worry? Your mule is making its way along a narrow, rocky path. Only a few feet away from you is a very steep, very deep drop into the canyon. You're so high up that even airplanes and helicopters are flying below you through the breathtaking beauty of the Grand Canyon.

Since the time of John Wesley Powell's famous journey, millions of people have visited the 277-mile-long Grand Canyon. Each year thousands of people hike or ride on mules to the bottom of the canyon. Visitors are overwhelmed by the size, colors, and beauty of this natural wonder.

Grand Canyon National Park attracts scientists as well as tourists. The layers of rock and fossils that form the canyon's walls tell the story of plants and animals that lived in the area millions of years ago. More than 275 species of birds have been observed in the canyon. A few animals, such as the white-tailed Kaibab squirrel and the pink Grand Canyon rattlesnake, live nowhere else in the world.

Exploring Rodeos

The chute door flies open. A moment later, a bucking, kicking bronco rushes out. The horse rears into the air, then whirls around in circles. After a few seconds, the bronco

Guides tell you to pull up on the reins if your mule starts to stumble.

hurls the rider to the ground.

Welcome to the rodeo, where cowboys and cowgirls test their riding and roping skills. Besides bronco riding, rodeos also feature bull riding, calf roping, and steer wrestling. Altogether, there are eight exciting events at most rodeos.

From the earliest days, cowboys showed off their skills in competitions among themselves. But in 1883, Pecos, Texas, held the first rodeo for an audience. Before long, rodeos had become one of the Southwest's most popular sports. These events recapture the spirit of the Old West.

▲ *The cowgirl pictured here is competing in a barrel racing event.*

Move Ahead

Now you're ready to find out more about things to see and do in the Southwest. Encyclopedias, travel magazines, and library books will help you. Here are some questions to guide your research:

1. How did the Cliff Dwellers build their villages? What was the purpose of the underground rooms called kivas?
2. Why did Spain want to establish the settlement of San Antonio? What countries has San Antonio been part of since its founding?
3. Did anyone live in the Grand Canyon before the arrival of the first Europeans? Find out more about John Wesley Powell's trip through the canyon.
4. What is the difference between rough stock events and timed events at rodeos? What is barrel racing?

Explore Some More

Use your school or local library to find out about interesting places to visit in your state or region. For example, are there any historic sites devoted to Indian life in your area? Who founded the largest city in your state? What helped this city to grow? What is the most famous natural wonder in your region? What are the most popular sports or recreational activities in your region?

From Agriculture to Industry

Unit 6

The West

Poor John Colter. In 1807, he explored the area around the Yellowstone River, where Wyoming is today. He saw mysterious sights. Hot water shot up into the air from holes in the snowy ground. Ponds boiled and churned. Rock formations looked like frozen waterfalls. When he got back home to St. Louis and described what he had seen, nobody believed him. In years to come, millions of people headed West to see the land they had heard of. Then they believed.

1740

Yellowstone National Park in Wyoming.
Photograph Copyright Tom Algire, SuperStock.

2000

The West

A Land of Opposites

Just a quick look at these pictures tells you that this region has many different types of land—high and low, wet and dry, green and white and brown. What you can't see are the valuable resources that lie below these mountains and deserts. The West is a treasure chest of gold, oil, and other resources. They are spread out over the 11 states of this huge region.

Sitka spruce
Alaska's state tree

Orange blossom
in California

A lot of rain falls in some parts of the West. With moisture and rich soil, the West has a spectacular variety of plant life, more than any other region.

Kaimu Black Sand Beach
on the volcanic island of Hawaii

The West

The 11 states of the region

• Alaska	• Idaho	• Utah
• California	• Montana	• Washington
• Colorado	• Nevada	• Wyoming
• Hawaii	• Oregon	

No region has more types of landforms than the West—from the glaciers of Montana, to the volcanoes of Hawaii, to the Idaho desert.

Population: 47,587,785. That includes the state with the nation's highest population, California.
Size: 1,549,363 square miles, the largest region

Major resources: oil, natural gas, timber, minerals and salts, water power, wildlife

Annual rainfall
• About 2 inches in California's Death Valley
• 460 inches in Hawaii's Mount Waialeale

Elevation
• Death Valley, nation's lowest point, at 282 feet below sea level
• Alaska's Mount McKinley, nation's highest point, at 20,320 feet

Some of the largest and oldest trees in the world grow in Oregon and Washington, an area known as the Pacific Northwest. Pacific Ocean breezes bring rain to the thick forests along the coast, from northern California all the way up to Alaska.

Physical Map of the West

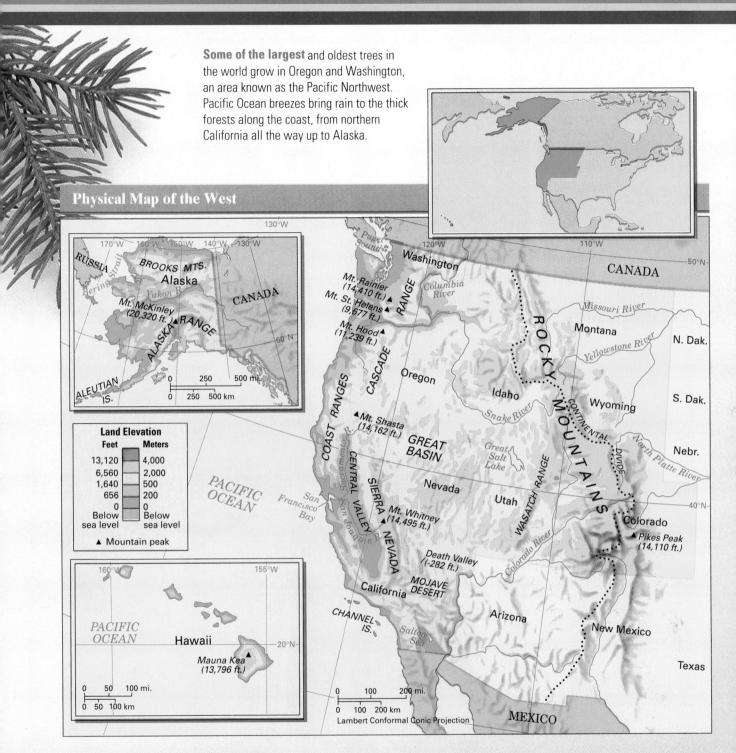

RUSSIA

BROOKS MTS.
Alaska

CANADA

Bering Strait
Yukon R.

Mt. McKinley
(20,320 ft.)

ALASKA RANGE

ALEUTIAN IS.

170°W 160°W 150°W 140°W 130°W
60°N

0   250   500 mi.
0   250   500 km

Land Elevation

Feet	Meters
13,120	4,000
6,560	2,000
1,640	500
656	200
0	0
Below sea level	Below sea level

▲ Mountain peak

PACIFIC OCEAN

PACIFIC OCEAN

Hawaii

Mauna Kea
(13,796 ft.)

160°W   155°W
20°N

0   50   100 mi.
0   50   100 km

Puget Sound

Washington

Mt. Rainier
(14,410 ft.) ▲

Mt. St. Helens
(9,677 ft.)

Mt. Hood ▲
(11,239 ft.)

COAST RANGES

CASCADE RANGE

Columbia River

Oregon

Idaho

▲ Mt. Shasta
(14,162 ft.)

GREAT BASIN

Snake River

Great Salt Lake

Nevada

Utah

CENTRAL VALLEY

Sacramento

San Joaquin

SIERRA NEVADA

▲ Mt. Whitney
(14,495 ft.)

San Francisco Bay

Death Valley
(-282 ft.)

Colorado River

WASATCH RANGE

ROCKY MOUNTAINS

CONTINENTAL DIVIDE

Montana

Wyoming

Yellowstone River

Missouri River

North Platte River

CANADA

MEXICO

California

MOJAVE DESERT

Arizona

New Mexico

Texas

CHANNEL IS.

Salton Sea

Colorado

▲ Pikes Peak
(14,110 ft.)

N. Dak.

S. Dak.

Nebr.

130°W   120°W   110°W   50°N

40°N

0   100   200 mi.
0   100   200 km
Lambert Conformal Conic Projection

Red Canyon Creek
in Wyoming

The lowest and driest land in the country lies between the Rocky Mountains and the Sierra Nevada. This huge bowl-shaped piece of land is called the Great Basin. It has rough, treeless mountains and very little water. Many of the West's natural resources, such as stone, metals, and natural gas, are found in the basin.

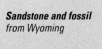

255

Sandstone and fossil
from Wyoming

Chapter 11
A Changing Frontier

For hundreds of years, Indians lived in the forests and the deserts of the West. But in 1848, one event changed the West forever. A handful of gold dust was discovered in a California stream. During the next 50 years, two million white settlers came to the West. The newcomers dug mines in the mountains and built a railroad to link them to the East.

This woman's home, clothes, and basket are made from natural resources. Indians of the Pacific Northwest held many ceremonies to celebrate the resources of their region. The mask shown here was worn by a singer during tribal ceremonies.

1740	1765	1790	1815

1750

1826 Fur trapper Jedediah Smith explores the West. His writings about the region's great resources attract other settlers.

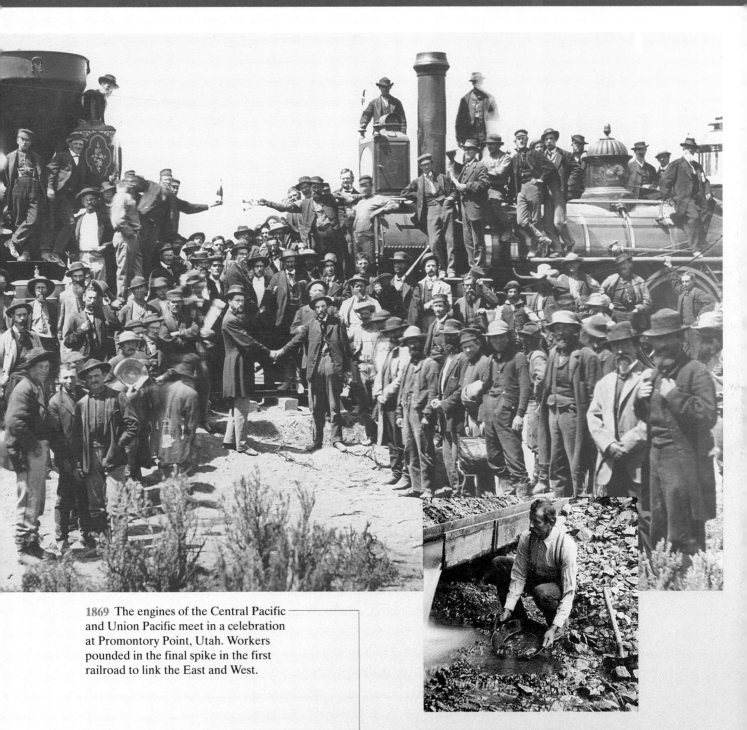

1869 The engines of the Central Pacific and Union Pacific meet in a celebration at Promontory Point, Utah. Workers pounded in the final spike in the first railroad to link the East and West.

Gold miners headed for the streams and rivers of California, hoping to strike it rich.

| 1840 | 1865 | 1890 | 1915 |

1897 The last major mining rush in the United States, the Alaska gold rush, begins.

1910

L E S S O N   1

Indians and the Land

THINKING
FOCUS

How did the lives of the Indians of the West change as new settlers came to the region?

Key Terms

- environment
- barrier

▼ *Northwest Coast Indians gave gifts of copper at occasions like weddings. Copper was a sign of wealth.*

The dark spot gliding across the surface of the water looks like the shadow of a cloud. The eight Makah Indians in the canoe paddle silently, watchfully. The chief stands up and raises his harpoon, ready to strike. Suddenly, the black form bursts through the waves like some great sea monster. Water spouts from the top of the whale's powerful body as it lets out a deep breath of air.

The chief sends his harpoon flying with deadly aim. The weapon's mussel-shell point pierces the thick skin of the humpback whale. The Makah quickly paddle the canoe backward so that they will not be clubbed by the harpoon sticking in the thrashing animal's side. When the whale's movements slow down, the Makah tie the great beast to their canoe and tow it to shore.

On the beach, the Makah chief holds a secret, solemn ceremony. The people pray and give thanks for the 40-foot humpback, which will provide a huge supply of food and oil. They sing songs to honor the spirit of the whale.

Tribes Use Their Resources

Whale hunting was an important part of the Makah culture. Whale oil, which they ate like butter, helped them get through the wet and cold winters when other food was scarce. The Makah were one of many groups that lived along the coast of the Pacific Northwest. The map on page 259 shows where the Makah and other groups of the West lived.

The region near the coast was rich with resources. Indians caught whales in the Pacific Ocean and salmon in the Columbia River. The huge trees in the forests provided wood for building houses and canoes. The forests were also home to many kinds of wildlife. Animals such as deer, bear, and moose provided food and clothing for the Indians. The Indians gathered roots and berries and used them for food and medicine. In fact, they used nearly everything in nature. Any resources that they could not use right away were stored for the winter.

The Shoshone used simple tools like this stone to grind seeds and nuts.

Living with Less

To the east of the Pacific coast, beyond the high peaks of the Cascades and the Sierra Nevada, stretches a large desert region called the Great Basin. The basin spreads across the state of Nevada and reaches into Oregon, California, Utah, Wyoming, and Idaho. The **environment**, or natural surroundings, of the Great Basin region seems too harsh for most people. Yet, for thousands of years many Indian groups lived in the Great Basin.

Compare this map of Indian groups to the climate map on page 408. In what kinds of climates did these groups live?

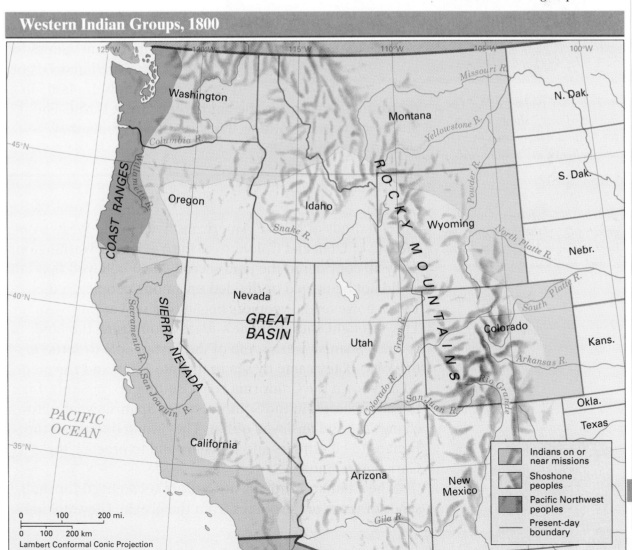

Western Indian Groups, 1800

Legend:
- Indians on or near missions
- Shoshone peoples
- Pacific Northwest peoples
- Present-day boundary

0   100   200 mi.
0   100   200 km
Lambert Conformal Conic Projection

This 1872 photograph, "The Basket Maker," shows a Great Basin Indian woman in front of her shelter of dry scrub brush.

■ *How did differences in the geography of the West affect the lives of the Indian groups living there?*

The Shoshone Indians roamed through the area in small bands, looking for food. Because they traveled so much, they did not build permanent homes, and they had few belongings.

The Shoshone survived in the hot, dry environment of the Great Basin because they knew where to find food. They ate roots that they tore from the ground with digging sticks. They also ate grasshoppers and knew when these creatures would be plentiful.

The Shoshone also tracked and hunted the rabbits, pronghorn, and antelopes that came down into the mountain valleys to graze. They ate hundreds of different kinds of plants that they found growing on the land of the Great Basin. The Shoshone wasted nothing. They used everything they caught or gathered. ■

Settlers Change Western Life

Hundreds of Native Americans lived in the West, from the Ute of Utah and Colorado to the Yakima of Washington. They all considered the land sacred. Most believed that land could not be owned or divided up among people. In the 1700s, however, newcomers began to discover the West. They brought with them new ideas about using the land.

The Spanish were some of the first people to settle in the West. They came by sea in the late 1700s and traveled up and down the California coast, setting up missions. Like the missionaries in the Southwest, the Spanish wanted to change the Indians' way of life. They wanted to teach the Indians to be farmers and ranchers and to practice the Christian religion.

The Chumash Indians of California had lived for thousands of years on resources from the ocean. They ate crabs, shellfish, and large fish, which they caught with hooks made from cactus needles. After the Spanish missionaries came, the Chumash began to grow crops and tend cattle and sheep. However, many could not adapt to this new and very different way of life. Within a hundred years, much of the Chumash group had died out.

Easterners Arrive

People from the East did not travel west because the Rocky Mountains acted as a geographical **barrier**, or natural wall, to keep them out. This barrier protected the Indians in the Great Basin and their way of life for many years. But in the early 1800s, the barrier could no longer keep the Easterners out. Explorers, looking for new land and new opportunities, started making the dangerous trip across the mountains and the wide Great Basin.

Jedediah Smith was one of the first pioneers to make the trip overland. In 1826, he set out to explore the rivers and forests of the West, looking for beaver to trap. In his journals, he described the places he saw, such as the Great Salt Lake, the Sierra Nevada, and the California coast. The writings of Smith and other pioneers made many more people want to come to this land of new opportunities.

By the early 1800s, small streams of pioneers were coming to the region. They saw the West as a new place to set up farms, ranches, and businesses. They wanted to take the resources of the region, like furs, and trade them to make money. Soon these settlers would discover a hidden resource of the West—gold. ■

▼ *Harvey Dunn's painting,* Jedediah Smith in the Badlands, *gives an idea of some of the difficulties of horseback travel in the rugged land of the frontier.*

SOUTH DAKOTA ART MUSEUM, BROOKINGS

■ *Why were the early settlers interested in the resources of the West?*

R E V I E W

1. **FOCUS** How did the lives of the Indians of the West change as new settlers came to the region?
2. **CONNECT** Compare the life of the Great Basin Shoshone with that of the Great Plains Sioux.
3. **GEOGRAPHY** Why did few Easterners come to the West until the 1800s?
4. **CRITICAL THINKING** Why do you think the settlers wanted to change the Indians?
5. **WRITING ACTIVITY** Using the map on pages 406 and 407, describe the geography of the Great Basin.

261

A Changing Frontier

Recognizing Fact and Opinion

Here's Why

When someone is trying to persuade you to do or think something, it is important for you to recognize the difference between fact and opinion. In the mid 1800s, John and Jessie Frémont wanted to persuade Easterners to go west and settle the land.

Like the Indians you read about in Lesson 1, the Frémonts recognized the value of the West and its rich resources. John C. Frémont made several exploring trips through the West. When he returned, his wife Jessie helped him rewrite his notes into books. Sometimes they reported the facts. At other times they gave their opinions. Jessie admitted that she "left out the shadows," for she and her husband wanted to paint a bright picture of the West.

Here's How

A fact is a statement that is true. It can be checked or tested. An opinion is a statement that one person believes to be true. An opinion cannot be checked.

Read the two sentences below.

1. Jessie Benton Frémont was the daughter of U.S. Senator Thomas Hart Benton.
2. I thought the Great Salt Lake was the most beautiful place we visited.

The first sentence states a fact. You can check the statement by looking in an encyclopedia. The second sentence states an opinion. It tells what one person believes to be true.

Words like *I think*, *I believe*, *agree*, *disagree*, *should*, and *most* can be clues that a sentence is an opinion. In the second sentence above, the words *I thought* are a clue. They show that this statement is what one person believes to be true. Others may or may not disagree.

Try It

Read the sentences below and decide whether each statement is a fact or an opinion. Ask yourself if you could check whether the statement is true. Also look for word clues that show that a statement is an opinion.

1. On the trip, we brought extra mules to carry supplies.
2. I believe that no other person ever traveled in better company.
3. The Sacramento River should supply enough water for growing wheat.
4. The two rivers meet in the Valley of the Sacramento.
5. Most of the Indians in California will be willing to work for the farmers.

Apply It

Look in a newspaper. Find two sentences that state facts and two sentences that state opinions. Bring your sentences to class. Have a classmate decide which of your statements are facts and which statements are opinions.

LESSON 2

The Rush for Gold

From my father's letters, I'd expected a magic city whose streets were paved with gold, shining in the sun like a fairy story, but all I could see was a flat gray stretch of sand with little shacks like packing boxes scattered helter-skelter along it, and an ugly blanket of soft-coal smoke hanging low over everything. I was so disappointed I felt like crying, but I didn't want Mother to know.

In *Daughter of the Gold Rush*, Klondy Nelson describes her arrival in Nome, Alaska, in 1902 to meet her father. He had come in search of gold. Like many miners, he couldn't think about anything but gold. In fact, he named his daughter after the Klondike gold mining region in Canada. For her middle name, Klondy's dad wanted the name of a mining camp he had worked at in South Dakota. But Klondy's mother said that was going too far. The name of the camp was Blacktail Gulch.

THINKING FOCUS

How did mining affect the population of the West?

Key Terms

- forty-niner
- claim

◄ *From this photograph of Nome in 1900, you'd never know how beautiful the state of Alaska is. No wonder Klondy felt like crying when she came to this rundown mining camp.*

263

A Changing Frontier

Mining Rushes in the West

The Alaskan gold rush was one of several "rushes" in the West. When gold or silver was discovered in an area, thousands of men and women rushed in hoping to make their fortunes. The timeline below shows the major mining rushes in the West.

The first big discovery of gold in the region was at Sutter's Mill in northern California. One day in 1848, Sutter's carpenter, James W. Marshall, walked down to the river near the mill. A yellow flash in the water caught his eye. Gold! The news spread quickly. Thousands of Easterners hurried to California. They were called **forty-niners** because they began their journey to find gold in 1849. A Moment in Time on page 266 tells about the life of a forty-niner.

Easterners Rush to the West

Until the California gold rush, people had settled mostly in the forests of the West, where there were furs and trees, or in the areas with good soil for farming. Parts of the Sierra Nevada, the Great Basin, and the Rockies had been thought of as wasteland. But this changed when waves of people traveled west to make their fortunes. These settlers built new towns in many parts of the region in the late 1800s.

At first, the miners headed for the rivers, where gold

Across Time & Space

In the gold rush states of Alaska and California, an even bigger resource was found in the 1900s —oil. At the same time, mountain states like Colorado discovered value in a white treasure—snow! Skiing is now a major enterprise in old mining towns, like Aspen. See the Minipedia, pages 351, 354, and 355, for more on these states' industries today.

Mining Rushes in the West, 1848–1897

1848, California
This gold nugget, found at Sutter's Mill, sets off the gold rush the next year. The miner below weighs his gold. He is one of 250,000 "forty-niners" who head west. This is the most famous of five major mining rushes in the West.

1859, Rocky Mountains
Gold and silver are found in Colorado. Since this state is closer to the East, it attracts great numbers of people.

1845 1855 1865

1859, The Great Basin
The Comstock Lode, a big silver discovery in Nevada, draws miners to the Great Basin. New exploration brings gold discoveries in Idaho and Oregon.

from the mountains was swept downstream. They used pans to scoop up dirt along the riverbeds. Then they swirled the dirt and water around in the pan. The heavy gold dust stayed in the pan while the dirt washed away.

Miners worked alone or in small groups. Soon they had gotten most of the gold from the rivers. More gold, silver, and other minerals lay buried in layers of rock beneath the mountains. In the 1870s, companies with new machinery came west to mine these buried treasures. They dug mining tunnels and carved out huge chunks of rock from far beneath the ground. At factories, machines crushed the rock to take out the gold, silver, copper, and other minerals. ■

■ *How did the gold and silver rushes of the middle and late 1800s affect the land of the West?*

Life in a Mining Town

When a miner found gold or silver, he quickly marked the boundaries of the land he wanted to mine. That land was called his **claim**. Word of a new claim brought people rushing to an area. A big discovery could turn a lonely mountain into a city overnight. Sometimes the gold would suddenly run out. Then the people would vanish, leaving behind a ghost town of empty buildings.

The way towns came and went could be confusing. For example, in 1879, four miners staked out claims along the Roaring Fork River at the bottom of Aspen Mountain in

1875, Mountains of the West
Small gold-mining claims have mostly run dry. Companies come West to mine silver, copper, and lead. The companies bring in the new equipment, shown below, to dig deep inside mountains.

1875	1885	1895

1896, Alaska
Gold is found in the Yukon River Valley of Alaska. Thousands of miners leave their old claims and head north. At first, most of the new arrivals are men. They write letters to stay in touch with their families. If their claims are successful, their families join them later.

A Forty-niner

2:30 P.M., August 15, 1850
A mountain stream near Sacramento

Blistered Hand

Swinging his pick since dawn has raised new blisters on this miner's rough hands. He was a bookkeeper from Maine, and all this stooping and digging is harder work than he thought it would be.

Wild Grapes

He found these grapes as he moved downstream to get away from other miners. His food is rarely exciting — flapjacks and bacon every day.

Backpack

He bought this pack in San Francisco for 50 dollars — 10 times what it would have cost back East. Strapped to the top are the first letters he's received from home.

Nugget

"Yahoo! Now that's more like it!" This is the biggest nugget he's ever seen. He'll build a lean-to right here, set up camp, and stake his claim.

Goldmining Pan

He has been working on his twenty-sixth panful of dirt since this morning. The cloudy water just cleared. Until now, he has only seen flakes of gold at the bottom of the pan.

Boots

His cold toes are pressed against soaking wet leather. These boots haven't been dry in weeks.

Colorado. Stories about their silver claim spread quickly. By the fall, other miners had set up camps along the river. Read the literature on pages 268–271, "Jamoka Jack," to learn more about life in a mining camp.

Henry B. Gillespie, a bookkeeper in Boulder County, heard the stories. He came to the Roaring Fork and bought two claims from the first miners. He wanted to start a town beside the river and name it Ute City. He went to Washington, D.C., to ask the government to set up a post office in Ute City. This would be the first step toward making the town official. While he was gone, someone came along and stole his claims. That person renamed the town Aspen, which it is called today.

A new town like Aspen needed services. Blacksmiths, carpenters, and shopkeepers rushed in to meet the need. In three years, Aspen had several hotels and restaurants, a newspaper, a playhouse, and a fire department. By 1887, Aspen was a roaring city of 12,000 people.

Towns like Aspen boomed throughout the West, and then died out just as fast. By 1930, Aspen's population had dropped to only 750 people. The people had spread out to other parts of the West. But mining did not disappear completely. It continues to be important in the West today. But it is especially important because it brought so many new people to the mountains and valleys of the region. ■

▲ *The top photograph, called "The Dinner Hour," shows Colorado miners on their claim. These tent cities often grew into major cities, such as Aspen, shown in the lower photograph in about 1890.*

■ *Why did mining towns grow so quickly?*

R E V I E W

1. **FOCUS** How did mining affect the population of the West?
2. **CONNECT** How was the Indians' view of land different from the miners' view of land?
3. **HISTORY** Use the timeline on pages 264–265 to describe some of the areas in the West where mining boomed.
4. **CRITICAL THINKING** Do you think the gold rush was good for the West? Explain your answer.
5. **WRITING ACTIVITY** Pretend you are the forty-niner in A Moment in Time. Write a letter to a friend in the East describing your experience.

A Changing Frontier

Jamoka Jack

Sid Fleischman

The story of Jamoka Jack comes from By the Great Horn Spoon! *by Sid Fleischman. The tale tells of the adventures of a boy named Jack Flagg and his butler Praiseworthy. They leave Boston to try their luck in the gold fields of California. As you read this story, ask yourself, "What was life like in a mining town in California during the gold rush?"*

You read in Lesson 2 about how mining towns could form almost overnight and then disappear as soon as the gold ran out. This story shows what life was like in a mining town.

skewer stick through

jackboots heavy boots that extend above the knee

The stagecoach climbed as if it were part mountain goat. It lurched, it halted, it bucked, it leaped and it clung. At times there was a sheer drop to one side of the trail. Far below, the pine trees looked to Jack like sharp green lances waiting to skewer them if they slipped. He only looked once in a while.

They were almost at the diggings, he told himself—he'd been telling himself that for days. But at last, the stagecoach arrived, bringing a cloud of summer dust all the way from Sacramento City.

"Hangtown, gents!" the driver snapped, with a final crack of his whip. "Looks mighty quiet today. Don't see nobody standin' under a pine limb with his boots off the ground."

A dog greeted them at the end of the street and barked them all the way up to the Empire Hotel. The passengers got out. There was road dust in Jack's eyebrows, in his ears and down his neck. Now that they had arrived he had gold fever so bad that he didn't see how he could wait another five minutes to get his shovel in the ground.

Hangtown!

Everywhere he looked there were men in jackboots and colored shirts. There wasn't a woman to be seen. The miners were coming-and-going or standing-and-talking or sitting-and-whittling. Blue freight wagons were being unloaded. Blindfolded mules were being loaded. The store shacks on both sides of the street were raised on wood pilings, like short legs, and looked as if they had just walked to town.

Jack shouldered the shovel and Praiseworthy shouldered the pick. On the roof of the stage the driver was throwing down trunks and hand luggage.

"What's the best hotel in town?" asked Praiseworthy.

"The Empire."

Praiseworthy glanced at Jack. "Unless I miss my guess there's only one hotel in town—the Empire."

It was exactly one hour and five minutes before Jack saw the diggings. First Praiseworthy registered at the hotel. They washed. Immediately Praiseworthy wrote a letter to Dr. Buckbee, advising him that Cut-Eye Higgins was in Hangtown, but that the map had fallen into the hands of a gang of highwaymen.

"Can we go now?" said Jack, fidgeting. He had polished his horn spoon so much he could see his nose in it.

"Go where?"

"The diggings."

"Oh, the diggings will still be there after lunch, Master Jack."

Praiseworthy's patience was a marvel—and an exasperation. They had come more than 15,000 miles and now they had to stop to eat. Jack didn't care if they passed up eating for a week. A month, even. He wondered if he could ever grow up to be as easygoing as Praiseworthy.

But once they sat down in the hotel restaurant Jack discovered he was so hungry that he ordered bear steak. The only other item on the menu was sowbelly-and-beans, and Jack figured you had to be starving to order that.

"You and the boy want bread with your grub?" asked the waiter. He was a big fellow in floppy boots.

"Why not?" answered Praiseworthy.

"It's a dollar a slice."

The butler slowly arched an eyebrow.

"Two dollars with butter on it."

Praiseworthy peered at Jack, and then smiled. "Hang the cost, sir. We're celebrating our arrival. Bread and butter, if you please!"

The bear steak was greasy and stringy, but something to write home about. Jack forced it down. After they left the restaurant Praiseworthy bought a pair of buckskin pouches at the general merchandise store and emptied the gold dust out of his glove. The index finger was springing a leak. Jack liked the new leather smell of the pouch. He tucked it under his belt, next to the horn spoon, and was beginning to feel like a miner. Then, with tin washbasins under their arms and the pick and shovel across their shoulders, they set out for the diggings.

The day was hot and sweaty. When they reached running water they saw miners crouched everywhere along the banks. They were washing gold out of the dirt in everything from wooden bowls to frying pans.

"Anybody digging here" asked Praiseworthy when they came to a bare spot.

"Shore is," came the answer. "That's Buffalo John's claim."

The butler and the boy moved on upstream. Here and there miners were shoveling dirt into long wooden troughs, set in running water, to catch the flakes of gold.

"Anybody digging here?" asked Praiseworthy.

"Yup," came the answer. "That's Jimmie-from-Town's claim."

On and on they went, looking for a place to dig. They passed miners in blue shirts and red shirts and checked shirts and some in no shirts at all. Picks assaulted the earth and shovels flew. Weathered tents were staked to the hillsides and the smell of boiling coffee drifted through the air. After they had walked a mile and a half Jack began to think they would never find a patch of ground that wasn't spoken for.

Suddenly a pistol shot cracked the mountain air. Praiseworthy's washbasin rang like a bell and leaped from his arm and went clattering away.

"You there!" a voice from behind bellowed.

Praiseworthy turned. His eyes narrowed slowly. "Are you talking to me sir?"

"Talkin' and shootin'. What you doin' with my washpan under your arm?"

Jack stared at the man. He had a thick, tangled beard and his ears were bent over under the weight of his slouch hat.

"Needless to say, you're mistaken," Praiseworthy answered. "Until this moment I've had the good fortune never to set eyes on you or your washpan, sir."

"We don't take kindly to thievery in these parts," growled the miner, stepping forward. "A man steals around here, we lop off his ears. That's miners' law."

troughs (trawfs) containers used as strainers

slouch hat a soft hat with a broad brim

270

"Do you have any laws against shooting at strangers?"

"Nope."

Jack couldn't imagine Praiseworthy with his ears lopped off. He took a grip on the handle of the shovel as the miner came closer. His heart beat a little faster and he waited for a signal from Praiseworthy.

The miner belted his pistol and picked up the washpan. He crimped an eye and looked it over.

"It's mine, all right."

"You're either near-sighted or a scoundrel," said Praiseworthy.

Jack was ready to fight, if not for their lives—at least for Praiseworthy's ears. Just then, a flash of tin in the sunlight, from a pile of wet rocks, caught Jack's eye. He dropped the shovel and went for it.

"Is this your pan?" Jack said.

The miner's bushy eyebrows shot up like birds taking wing. "It is at that, ain't it?" Then he laughed as if the joke were on him. "I'd forget my boots if I didn't have 'em on."

Praiseworthy peered at the man. Apparently, shooting at strangers by mistake didn't amount to anything in the diggings. The miner hardly gave it another thought.

crimped wrinkled up

scoundrel an evil person

Further Reading

The Golden Venture. Jane Flory. This is the story of a young girl who stows away in her father's wagon when he travels to California to look for gold.

The Bandit of Mok Hill. Evelyn Sibley Lampman. An orphan boy from San Francisco joins a friendly family in the gold fields. This book takes a realistic look at life in the gold rush days.

Coarse Gold Gulch. Marion Garthwaite. Two children from Vermont come to California to search for their father. The children have exciting adventures with Californios, Indians, and Chinese immigrants.

California Gold Rush: Search for Treasure. Catherine Chambers.

LESSON 3

The Railroad Race

THINKING FOCUS

What effect did the transcontinental railroad have on the development of the West?

Key Terms

- transcontinental
- technology

➤ *The walls of Utah's Echo Canyon are 800 to 1,200 feet high. There was only one way for the railroad to go—through the walls. The illustration on page 274 shows how tunnels were dug through the mountainsides.*

It is very cold and very dark. You are deep in the belly of a long tunnel. The tunnel runs under a mountain so high that clouds hide its peak. It seems like the weight of the mighty mountain might fall on you at any minute. But you know it won't do you any good to worry about such things right now.

Clink, clink, clink. Splinters of granite rock fly this way and that as you swing your 12-pound steel pickaxe at the wall of solid rock in front of you. You're boring your way through to the other side, blow by blow, like a termite chewing through a thick log.

Clink, clink, clink. You and the other workers can make about 8 inches in 24 hours. At this rate, will you ever see the other side of this mountain? Will you get out of here alive? Clink, clink, clink. Who came up with the crazy idea of tunneling through a mountain anyway?

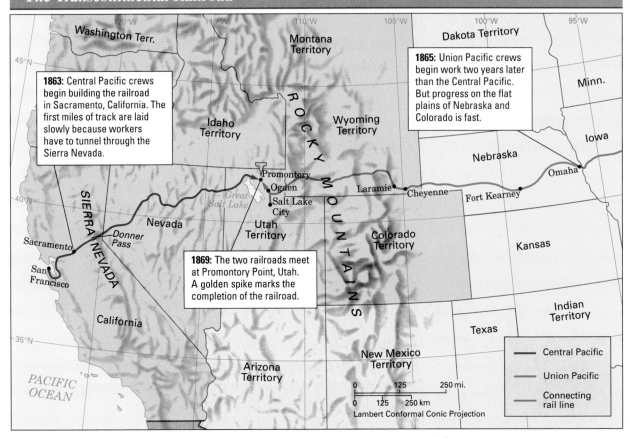

1863: Central Pacific crews begin building the railroad in Sacramento, California. The first miles of track are laid slowly because workers have to tunnel through the Sierra Nevada.

1865: Union Pacific crews begin work two years later than the Central Pacific. But progress on the flat plains of Nebraska and Colorado is fast.

1869: The two railroads meet at Promontory Point, Utah. A golden spike marks the completion of the railroad.

Central Pacific
Union Pacific
Connecting rail line

0   125   250 mi.
0   125   250 km
Lambert Conformal Conic Projection

"We Need a Railroad"

The man with the crazy idea was Theodore Judah. With more miners and businesspeople coming to the West every year, Judah knew that better transportation from the East was needed. It took six months to travel overland from coast to coast. Ships from New York had to sail all the way around the tip of South America before heading north to California. You can trace this long route by sea on the map on page 400.

The long trip was not just a problem for travelers. Most food, clothing, tools, and other goods came from the East. Sending them to the West cost a lot of money. This meant that Westerners had to pay more for these items than Easterners did. And at the same time, it was expensive to ship Western goods to Eastern markets.

Judah Works for His Dream

Judah dreamed of building a **transcontinental** railroad. The tracks of this railroad would travel from one coast of the United States to another, stretching across the North American continent. To most people, the idea seemed impossible. How could you build a railroad through the

From looking at this map, why do you think most people believed that a transcontinental railroad was impossible?

How Do We Know?

HISTORY *The official railroad photographer, A.J. Russell, took more than 800 pictures of the transcontinental railroad project, including the one on page 272. Among other things, his photographs show workers climbing mountain cliffs, executives signing papers, and the final celebration of the railroad's completion. These pictures also show how difficult this huge project was.*

273

A Changing Frontier

steep mountains of the Sierra Nevada and the Rocky Mountains? How could you build bridges over the deep valleys? Would you run tracks over the high peaks or wind them around the mountainsides? And what about the storms that pounded the mountains through the winter months, leaving tons of snow? Judah wanted to answer these questions.

> **E**verything he did from the time he went to California to the day of his death was for the great continental Pacific Railway. . . . It was the burden of his thought day and night, largely of his conversation, till it used to be said, "Judah's Pacific Railroad crazy."
>
> Anna Judah, Theodore's wife

Judah mapped out a route through the mountains that would not rise too steeply or cross too many deep valleys. In one two-mile stretch high in the Sierra Nevada, seven tunnels had to be built. ■

The Great Race

In 1862, the United States Congress gave two companies permission to build the railroad. The Central Pacific was to build east from Sacramento, California. The Union Pacific would start from Omaha, Nebraska, and build west. The race was on!

Workers for the Central Pacific had the hardest job, building over and through the Sierra Nevada. In the first year, only 20 miles of track were laid. To make the work go faster, new technology was needed.

Technology is the science, skills,

■ *Why was a transcontinental railroad needed?*

▼ *Crews started digging on both sides of a mountain, tunneling toward each other. A third crew blasted its way down to the middle of the mountain to speed up the work.*

and materials used to solve problems or do certain jobs. To build the transcontinental railroad, new tunneling technology replaced picks and shovels. Workers now used explosives to blast through the mountains. They dangled over steep cliffs in baskets, drilling into the mountainsides and stuffing the holes with dynamite. Many men were killed by the blasts.

▼ *Workers swung heavy pick-axes to chip through mountains of granite.*

Chinese Get the Job Done

Finding brave and hard-working people to build the railroad was not easy. Many workers signed on just to get to the gold and silver mines. Then they quit. But one group of workers saved the railroad—the Chinese. More than 60,000 men, most of them Chinese, worked in the mountains of the Sierra Nevada through the terrible winter of 1866. The Chinese worked quickly and with great skill in the cold and snow.

At the same time, 10,000 workers of the Union Pacific pushed across the Great Plains. These workers also had to cut through cliffs of granite as they laid track through the Rocky Mountains. When both companies reached the flat stretches of Utah, the work began to go faster and faster.

UNDERSTANDING TECHNOLOGY

Railroad workers dug tunnels through the Sierra Nevada with simple hand tools like picks and shovels. They also used dynamite to blast through the mountains. They had little other technology to help them. Technology is the machines and methods used to do or to make something. Hand tools and dynamite were the technology of tunneling in the 1880s.

Today technology can make jobs safer and improve our lives. Computers help people do things quickly. Medical x-rays help people live longer.

Engineers who recently designed a new tunnel for a superhighway in Seattle used large machines to push hollow cement tubes into the mountainside. Then giant cutting machines

dug out the dirt inside each tube.

But machines are not the only part of technology that has improved. There are also new ways of doing things and new ways of looking at problems. And people can use new technology to try to come up with more creative solutions to old problems.

275

> *The transcontinental railroad speeds its passengers to the East, while a wagon train slowly works its way westward near Promontory Point, Utah.*

▲ *Easterners packed their trunks and headed west by train in the late 1800s.*

■ *What problems did the two companies face in building the railroad?*

In one day, Chinese workers laid 10 miles of track, or 3,500 rails. This record has never been broken.

The scene looked like an assembly line in the desert. Some workers laid the wooden ties, others followed with the steel rails, and still others pounded metal spikes to hold them in place. A locomotive carrying supplies moved along the newly laid track, mile by mile, day after day.

Finally, on May 10, 1869, at Promontory Point, Utah, two trains, one from each railroad, stood facing each other. In a big ceremony, the last spikes were driven into the rails. The race was over.

Judah's dream, the transcontinental railroad, made the resources of the West open to all. New rail lines soon cut north through Montana and into the Pacific Northwest. Others crossed the southern Great Basin and traveled to Los Angeles, California. Farmers, ranchers, and other settlers built new towns in the wilderness. A new way of life had begun. ■

R E V I E W

1. **FOCUS** What effect did the transcontinental railroad have on the development of the West?

2. **CONNECT** What did Theodore Judah have in common with Jedediah Smith?

3. **HISTORY** Why were the Chinese so important to the building of the railroad?

4. **CRITICAL THINKING** How do you think the railroad helped the mining industry?

5. **ACTIVITY** Snowstorms were a big problem for the railroad builders. Design and draw your own technology to keep snow off the railroad tracks.

Chapter 11

Reading a Time Zone Map

Here's Why

The earth rotates from west to east. As it rotates, sunlight hits different places at different times. Each day, sunlight hits the East Coast of the United States three hours earlier than it hits the West Coast.

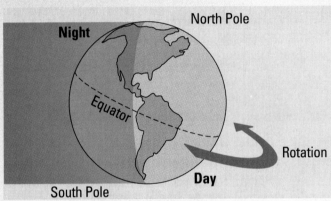

In the 1800s, each city and town set its own clocks by the sun. Clocks in different places did not agree. This system was confusing, and problems arose. When the transcontinental railroad was finished in 1869, the trains needed to run on a set time schedule. Finally, in 1883, the United States was divided into four time zones. The clocks in one zone all said the same time. This system solved the railroad's time-schedule problem. By understanding time zones on a map, you can figure out what time it is in different parts of the country.

Here's How

There are four time zones in the mainland of the United States. They are the Eastern, Central, Mountain, and Pacific Time Zones. Alaska and Hawaii also have time zones. Look at the time zone map on page 410 of the Atlas. It shows which states are in each of the time zones. The clock in the Eastern Time Zone says 7:00. The clock in the Central Time Zone says 6:00. It is one hour earlier. As you go west from the Eastern Time Zone, subtract one hour for the Central Time Zone, one more hour for Mountain Time, and another hour for Pacific Time. There is a difference of three hours between the East and West Coasts.

Try It

Look at the time zone map on page 410 and answer the questions below:

1. Name one state in each time zone.
2. Name three states that are in more than one time zone.
3. Name the time zone that is just to the east of the Mountain Time Zone.
4. When it is 7:00 A.M. in Iowa, what time is it in Vermont? Louisiana? Colorado? Nevada? New York?
5. As you go east from Sacramento, does the time get earlier or later?

Apply It

Plan a trip to six U.S. towns or cities. Begin in Portland, Oregon, and end up in Washington, D.C. Include places in each time zone. Trace your route on the map on pages 404–405. If it is 4:00 P.M. when you arrive in Washington, D.C., what time is it in each of the other cities?

Chapter Review

Reviewing Key Terms

barrier (p. 261)
claim (p. 265)
environment (p. 259)
forty-niner (p. 264)
technology (p. 274)
transcontinental (p. 273)

A. Write a sentence for each pair of words below.
1. environment, Shoshone
2. forty-niners, California
3. barrier, Rocky Mountains
4. transcontinental, travel
5. technology, railroad
6. claim, nugget

B. Write the key term that best completes each of the following sentences.
1. The Makah Indians made good use of the natural resources in their _____.
2. Two companies built the _____ railroad, linking the East Coast with the West Coast.
3. When gold was discovered in the West, many Easterners rushed there to find gold and stake a _____.
4. Chinese workers used new _____, like explosives, to tunnel through the Sierra Nevada.
5. The _____ searched the rivers and streams of California for gold nugget and flakes.
6. While building the transcontinental railroad, workers had to cross each _____ that blocked their way.

Exploring Concepts

A. Copy the chart below on a separate piece of paper. Complete the chart by telling how each group of people wanted to use the land.

Groups	How did they want to use the land?
Indian tribes	
Jedediah Smith and other pioneers of the 1800s	
Gold rush miners and mining companies	
Theodore Judah and the railroad companies	

B. Write sentences that support each of the following statements with two details from this chapter.
1. Jedediah Smith led the way westward for other pioneers from the East.
2. Spanish missionaries in the West changed the way of life for the Chumash of California.
3. The discovery of gold in California led to a population boom in the West.
4. May 10, 1869, was an important date in the history of the United States.
5. The most dangerous work on the transcontinental railroad was done by Chinese workers.
6. Until the early 1800s, the geography of the West kept most Easterners away.

Reviewing Skills

1. Read the sentences below. Which sentences state a fact and which state an opinion? Write a sentence to explain your reason for each answer.
   a. The Shoshone used their knowledge of plants and animals to survive.
   b. I believe that the Indians should not have moved to the Spanish missions.
   c. Most of the miners should have stayed home instead of chasing all over the West for gold.
   d. After building the railroad over the Sierra Nevada, the work went faster.
2. Look at the time zone map on page 410 and answer the following questions.
   a. In which time zone do you live?
   b. As you go west from Washington, D.C., does the time get earlier or later?
   c. When it is 8:00 A.M. in Denver, what time is it in New York? In Houston? In Seattle? In your community?
3. Read the following paragraph:
   Chief Joseph was a leader of the Nez Percé, a group of Northwest Indians. He agreed not to fight white settlers. In return, the U.S. government promised to let the Nez Percé remain in the Northwest. Later, however, the Nez Percé were forced to leave Oregon and go to Oklahoma.
   Think about what you know about the settlers of the Northwest. Now draw a conclusion about why the U.S. government broke its promise.

Using Critical Thinking

1. If not for the dreams of people like Theodore Judah, the transcontinental railroad might not have been built when it was. Why is it important for a country to have dreamers like Judah?
2. Imagine that gold is discovered in a forest or a national park in your state. New mining activities would be good for the growth of the state but would tear up the land and harm the environment. Should the mining be allowed? Would you want to go there and pan for gold? Explain your answers.
3. What effect do you think the transcontinental railroad had on the Indian tribes in the West?

Preparing for Citizenship

1. **ART ACTIVITY** Imagine that you could plan your own gold rush town. Decide what human and natural resources your town will need. Draw a map of the town. Use map symbols and a legend and give your town a name. Then draw pictures that show what life there is like .
2. **COLLABORATIVE LEARNING** Work as a class to make imaginary television news reports about two major events in the 1800s—the discovery of gold in California and the completion of the transcontinental railroad. Have half the class do a broadcast from Sutter's Mill and the other half broadcast the ceremony at Promontory Point, Utah. Research your event in the library. Choose students to be TV reporters who will interview other students playing the parts of people like Sutter, forty-niners, railroad workers, government officials, and bystanders. Rehearse your broadcasts and perform them for each other.

Chapter 12

New People, New Industries

Thousands of people followed the miners to the West. They settled in the California desert and turned it into an irrigated garden. They logged the giant forests of the Pacific Northwest. In the early 1900s, most people still lived in the countryside. But as more people came to the West, new industries drew them into the cities. One of the biggest new enterprises was the airplane and spacecraft industry.

Loggers and family members stand with giant saws in front of a log cabin near Puget Sound in Washington. Logging brought new people and helped many cities to grow in the Pacific Northwest.

Farmers began growing hundreds of kinds of fruits and vegetables in California's Central Valley. The state became the nation's leader in agriculture.

1850

1880

1910

1900 Washington becomes the country's leading lumber state.

1850

The *X-15* was the first plane to fly faster than the speed of sound. The building and testing of airplanes became very important in the West during the 1950s.

1940

1970

2000

1958 The country's space program begins. Western companies start building and testing spacecraft.

2000

L E S S O N   1

Plowing the Earth

Why did farming become an important business in the West?

Key Terms

- produce
- migrant workers

They claim to raise sizeable potatoes around here

Twelve pumpkins raised in Los Angeles weighed over 1,500 pounds.. . . Mr. Caldwell raised a sweet potato weighing 23 pounds. Mr. Smith raised a beet measuring three feet six inches [around].

Truth or fiction? The story above was printed in a gardening magazine in 1857. Another report told of a farmer in San Jose, California, who grew a 20-pound onion—about the size of a basketball. And there were stories of a 5 1/2-pound tomato and a monster squash weighing 131 pounds.

Farming in California

No wonder so many Eastern farmers threw down their hoes and headed west. With the gold rush and the transcontinental railroad, many newcomers moved to the West in the middle and late 1800s. All these people needed to eat. They were hungry for any food that farmers could grow.

Farmers had many good reasons to set up farms in California. The state had millions of acres of rich farmland. Crops could grow year-round in the warm and sunny climate. But often there was not enough rain. Farmers needed to find ways to bring more water to their fields.

Harriet Russell Strong was one farmer who had great success in bringing water to her crops. She owned a large ranch on very dry land in southern California. In 1887, Strong designed a system of dams that stored the floodwaters that came with the winter rains. In the dry summer months, she used the stored water to irrigate her crops.

Strong also tried planting different crops to see what grew best in the hot, dry climate. She found that many kinds of fruits and vegetables, or **produce** *(PRO doos)*, could grow in the region. Soon, farmers in the area began to grow such produce as grapefruits, avocados, and walnuts.

California's Farm Belt

Farmers in central California also needed water for their crops. In the Central Valley, a long belt of flat land in the middle of California, this problem was soon solved. Two long and large rivers, the San Joaquin *(waw KEEN)* and the Sacramento, run through this area. These rivers provided farmers with the water they needed to irrigate their farms.

With irrigation, the Central Valley became an area of rich farmland. By the 1920s, California had become a leader in agriculture. Californians shipped produce such as lettuce, oranges, and plums across the nation and around the world.

◄ American eating habits changed as California produce was shipped across the country. In 1919, the average person ate 16 pounds of oranges each year. By 1940, that number had risen to 52 pounds. People were eating three times as many oranges.

▼ By the 1920s, Harriet Russell Strong was not only a successful farmer, she was also an important member of her community. Below, a farmer irrigates the desert land of California's Imperial Valley about 1910.

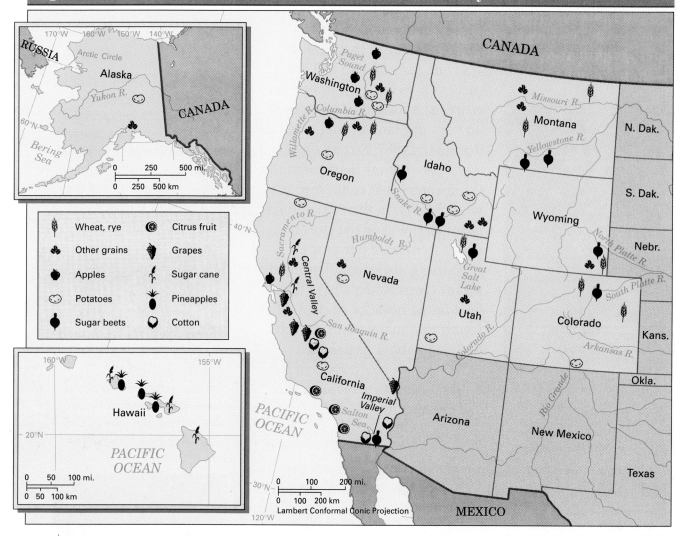

▲ *Compare this map with the map on page 408. Can you tell which crops might grow better in a warm, sunny climate and which might grow better in a wet climate?*

■ *What helped California become the nation's biggest farm state?*

By the 1940s, you could drive through the Central Valley and see huge farms spreading for miles across land as flat as a tabletop. The sharp scent of onions, the sweet tang of oranges, and the fresh smell of lettuce drifted through the air. Piles of newly picked carrots, peppers, and broccoli waited to be packed in crates.

The owners of these large farms hired migrant workers to harvest crops. **Migrant workers** moved from farm to farm with the seasons, picking ripe crops. They slept in shacks or in the fields. By 1940, most migrant workers in California came from Mexico. Along with irrigation, these low-paid and hardworking people helped turn California's desert land into green gardens. ■

Farming in the West

By the 1980s, California was growing 250 different crops. The state led the nation in almost 60 crops, including lemons, garlic, and grapes. Other Western states were becoming famous for just one or two special crops. Climate and geography of an area determined which crop or crops grew best in these different states.

Hawaii, an island chain in the Pacific Ocean, is known the world over for its pineapples. No one knows for sure how the first pineapple got to Hawaii. Some stories say that crates of pineapples from a Spanish shipwreck floated to the islands in the 1700s.

A pineapple takes about two years of frost-free days to grow. Hawaii's warm and humid climate made it a perfect place to grow the delicious fruit. Like most fruit, pineapples spoil quickly. Before the days of airplanes, growers had a hard time getting their fresh fruit to faraway markets. For this reason, most pineapples were canned. Now, fresh and canned pineapple is flown all over the world.

Other crops grow well in areas of the West that have a different climate and geography. In eastern Oregon, for example, farmers grow wheat on land where there is little rain and few rivers for irrigation. In the cooler, wetter climate of Washington, apples and cherries are important crops. Idaho farmers grow more potatoes in their rich sandy soil than in any other state. Beginning with the railroad and continuing with trucks and airplanes today, farmers of the West can ship their produce to dinner tables across the country. ■

▼ *Pineapples spread for acres on a farm in Maui, Hawaii. Other important Western crops are Wyoming beets and Oregon raspberries.*

■ *How was farming in states like Hawaii and Idaho different from farming in California?*

R E V I E W

1. **FOCUS** Why did farming become an important business in the West?

2. **CONNECT** How do you think the transcontinental railroad helped Western farmers?

3. **GEOGRAPHY** How did climate affect which crops became important in different Western states?

4. **CRITICAL THINKING** Why do you think farmers first settled near mining towns?

5. **ACTIVITY** Draw a picture of California's Central Valley during the 1940s. Show the different kinds of fruits and vegetables growing on the farms.

LESSON 2

Harvesting the Forests

Why did logging become a big business in the Northwest?

Key Terms

- timber
- lumber

▼ *Even Paul Bunyan might have fit into these enormous boots worn by loggers for over 100 years. The metal points keep loggers from slipping on logs and rough land.*

Paul Bunyan was a hero of tall tales told by loggers. He was said to be the biggest lumberjack who ever lived. When he walked through the woods, carrying his mighty axe, his head peeked out above the treetops. He cleared whole forests at a time, with the help of his giant blue ox, Babe. But even Paul Bunyan could not believe the stories about the big trees that grew in Oregon. So he decided to go and see for himself.

> Paul went down into Oregon because he had heard of the large trees in that part of the country. He soon found that the reports were true. Those were without doubt the largest trees he had ever seen. In some places the trees were so tall that you could only see the tops on a very clear day. …It took an ordinary man a week to see the top…
>
> Dell McCormick, *Tall Timber Tales: More Paul Bunyan Stories*

Well, maybe it didn't take a person a whole week to see the top, but these were very, very tall trees. Some reached as high as 300 feet into the sky. The trees grew so thick that in some places, the sun's rays had not touched the forest floor in hundreds of years. Forests of redwoods, spruce, and Douglas fir stopped only at the shores of the Pacific Ocean.

Life in the Logging Camps

In the 1860s, farmers introduced new crops to the West. At the same time, loggers made use of another resource that had grown in the northern parts of the region for thousands of years. Magnificent trees covered much of the Pacific Northwest, an area made up of Oregon and Washington. In places like the Cascade Mountains nature provides the perfect conditions for trees to grow tall and strong. Rain falls as often as 150 days each year and leaves up to 130 inches of water.

Early lumberjacks set up the first logging camps near rivers. There loggers could chop down trees, cut them into logs, and float them to the nearest sawmill. Later, machines were invented to carry logs from the forest to the rivers. This meant that loggers could make camps farther out in the wilderness. By the late 1800s, the forests echoed with sounds of chopping and sawing and trees falling.

Hard Work in the Woods

The wake-up bell in a logging camp of the late 1800s rings at 5:00 AM. One lumberjack climbs out of bed and pulls on his damp boots. As usual, it's raining outside. He rubs some grease on his only pair of pants to keep them dry. But he knows it won't help much. With a yawn, he steps out into the cold rain, joining other sleepy lumberjacks. They head toward the main cabin for breakfast. Each day, the camp cook serves up 1,000 pounds of meat, 2,000 pounds of fruits and vegetables, and nearly 3,000 eggs to 1,000 men.

After breakfast, the lumberjack heads to the river with

▼ *This diagram shows how logging was done in the Pacific Northwest in the early 1900s.*

From the Forests to the Cities

From the Logging Camp...

❶ Two strong men heave their sharp steel axes at an eight-foot-thick Douglas fir. For six long hours the wood chips fly as the lumberjacks make two deep cuts in the tree. That will make it fall exactly where they want.

❸ A dozen newly cut logs are chained together. Then a team of 16 oxen drags the five-ton load to a nearby river.

❷ Timber! The 1,000-year-old tree snaps and gives way. It is the height of a 25-story building, and it rocks the ground when it hits.

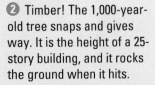

...to the Sawmill

❹ Hundreds of logs are rolled into a river. Workers known as "river pigs" use long poles to loosen the logs stuck in mud or on rocks. One trapped log could cause a logjam that might take weeks to clear.

❺ At the sawmill, the bark is stripped and the tree moves into the jaw of huge whirling saws. The cut boards are ready to ship to market.

❻ Carpenters build houses and mansions out of wood from the Pacific Northwest forests.

▼ *Workers around 1900 guide logs down an Oregon river to the sawmill See page 386 to see how important lumber is today.*

■ *What did it take to get trees from the forest to the sawmills?*

other workers. There they float newly cut logs downriver to a sawmill. On "river drives," logs race across roaring water like speeding canoes, whipping around bends in the river.

At first the work goes smoothly. Suddenly, one worker shouts "Logjam!" A log has hit some sharp rocks and jerked to a stop. Instantly, other logs slam into it. Within seconds there is a pileup. The logs snap like toothpicks as they toss this way and that.

Logjams were a logger's nightmare. Men could drown trying to break up a jam. It might take weeks of dangerous work to untangle the mess, even using dynamite to blast it apart.

Today, the lumberjack and his fellow workers are lucky. They manage to clear the jam by nightfall. They return to camp, almost too tired to eat dinner. The lumberjack eats quickly. Then he goes back to his tent and sinks into his wooden bunk. Tomorrow, he'll start all over again. ■

Lumber Builds the Northwest

The trees that the lumberjacks cut down were very valuable. The West was growing faster every day, and people needed wood to build new buildings. Oregon grew so fast that its population jumped from 50,000 in 1860 to 300,000 in 1890. Also, the East and Midwest needed wood from Northwest forests. These regions were running out of trees.

After a tree was chopped down, it was cut into several sections. Roughly cut logs, called **timber,** were used in the 1860s to build mining tunnels in Colorado and railroad tunnels through the Sierra Nevada. Timber was also used to make fence posts for farmers in Idaho and ship masts for shipbuilders in San Francisco.

➤ *This sawmill in Washington uses modern equipment and technology to turn timber into lumber.*

At sawmills, logs were sawed into boards. The boards, called **lumber**, were used to build homes, schools, and businesses. In the late 1800s, towns grew all over the West.

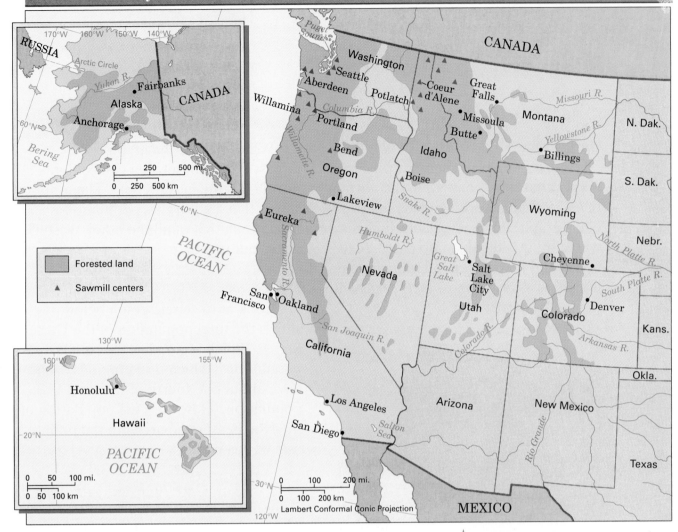

Lumber Industry in the West, 1910

Forested land

▲ Sawmill centers

So many trees were cut that it was common to see rivers choked with thousands of freshly cut logs. Mountains all over the Cascades looked like sheared sheep. By the early 1900s, Washington led the nation in lumber production.

Soon chainsaws took the place of axes and saws. A big tree now could be chopped down in minutes. Instead of oxen teams, trains and trucks hauled huge loads of logs out of the forests. Today, helicopters carry loggers into forests too thick to be reached by land. If Paul Bunyan wandered into a lumber camp today he would be mighty surprised. ■

▲ *Name five states that were good places to log in 1910.*

■ *Why were the forests of the Northwest being cut down so fast?*

R E V I E W

1. **FOCUS** Why did logging become a big business in the Northwest?
2. **CONNECT** How do you think the transcontinental railroad might have affected the logging industry in the Northwest?
3. **HISTORY** What were some uses for the timber

   and lumber from the Northwest forests?
4. **CRITICAL THINKING** The lumberjacks of the late 1800s called the big trees "green gold." How do you think the trees were like gold?
5. **ACTIVITY** Make an illustrated poster showing products that are made from wood.

Comparing Parts of a Whole

Here's Why

In Lesson 3 you will read two circle graphs that show changes in the portion of Californians working in agriculture. A circle graph shows at a glance how a whole thing is divided into parts. Textbooks and newspapers often use circle graphs as a way to show facts easily without words or numbers.

Population of the West, 1990

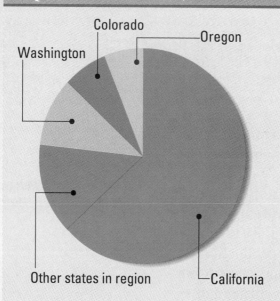

Here's How

A circle graph is sometimes called a "pie chart," because it looks like a pie that has been cut into pieces. A large piece represents a bigger part of the whole thing. A small piece represents a tinier part of the whole thing. Look at the graph above. The whole that this graph shows is the total population of the Western states. Four parts show the population of the four largest states in the West. The fifth part shows the population of the rest of the West.

Which part of the graph is the largest? You can see at a glance that California has the most people. The graph shows that California's population is larger than that of all the other Western states put together.

Try It

Look at the circle graph below. It shows the total population of the United States. Which region has the smallest population? Which three regions each have about one fourth of the total U.S. population? How does the population of the Northeast compare with the population of the West?

United States Population, 1990

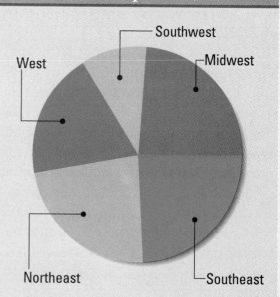

Apply It

Look for other circle graphs in encyclopedias. Find graphs that show your own state as one of the parts. What whole does the graph show? What are its parts? How do the parts compare in size?

L E S S O N   3

Taking to the Skies

J ackie Cochran wasn't trying to prove anything to
anybody when she set out to be the first woman to
fly faster than the speed of sound. She didn't have to.
She had already broken so many flying records that
she had made her mark as a world class pilot. Cochran
wanted to fly faster than the speed of sound because she
loved flying and she loved the feeling of speed.

Lifting off from Edwards Air Force Base in California,
Cochran pushed her plane into a steep climb. As the plane
rose higher, the sky became a deep dark blue. Ten miles up,
she could see stars in the sky, even though it was only noon.

Pointing the plane into a nose dive, Cochran zoomed toward the earth. As she neared the speed of sound, her plane
shook. Suddenly, she felt as if she were flying inside an
explosion. Strangely, she could not hear the plane's engine.
"You hear just fine up there, but you don't hear the sound
of your plane," she recalled. "That sound passes behind you
because you are going faster than sound can travel."

THINKING FOCUS

*How did air and space flight
change the West?*

Key Terms

- aviation
- aerospace

The Resources to Make Planes

Jackie Cochran flew faster than the speed of sound in
1953. At that time, **aviation**, or the building and flying of
aircraft, was already a major industry in
the West. Runways and testing centers
had been built in the deserts of southern
California, Utah, and Nevada. The flat,
open land and warm, dry climate in the
states were perfect for testing new types
of aircraft. Because the skies were clear
year round, pilots could fly on almost any
day of the year. More important, new aircraft could be safely flown and tested
because so few people lived in the desert.

▼ *In the 1930s and 1940s,
Jackie Cochran became world
famous for breaking records in
both men's and women's racing
categories.*

Between 1935 and 1960, the portion of Californians working in agriculture dropped from more than 50 to 9 percent. More people worked in industries like aerospace and manufacturing.

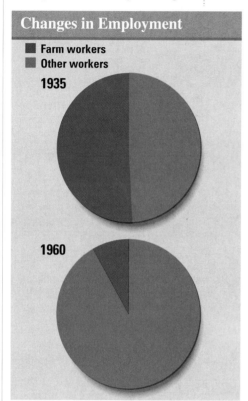

Changes in Employment

■ Farm workers
■ Other workers

1935

1960

From Lumber to Aluminum

The climate and geography of the Pacific Northwest also helped aviation develop. Natural resources in Washington helped that state to become the center of airplane manufacturing. It began when airplanes were invented in the early 1900s. These first airplanes were made out of wood. Many were built from the light, sturdy wood of the spruce tree. These trees grow in great numbers in many of Washington's forests. Because of this, many airplane manufacturing companies started in the area. They wanted to be close to this large supply of wood.

By the 1940s, however, airplanes were being made from a metal called aluminum. It takes huge amounts of electric power to make this strong metal. Washington was one of the few places that could provide that power. The Columbia River runs along the border of Washington and Oregon. Dams along this fast-flowing river produce electricity. Using this power, plants began to make aluminum.

Airplane Manufacturing

The resources of this region encouraged many new airplane manufacturing companies to develop in Washington. The Boeing Company started building airplanes in 1916. Today, it builds the world's largest jet airplanes. Boeing's manufacturing center in Everett, Washington, is the largest building in the world.

On one side of the enormous building, motorized doors open to let in tractors hauling the nose section of the airplane. Giant cranes lift parts weighing as much as 20 tons and fit

▶ *Each of these giant airplanes is made up of 4½ million parts. All these parts are assembled into four or five big pieces, which are put together in this huge building.*

Chapter 12

them into place. The 600 employees working in this assembly plant are just a small part of the company. Over 100,000 people in Washington work in airplane manufacturing. Other manufacturing companies in the area also provide many jobs in the aviation industry for the people of the state. ■

Aerospace Changes the West

In the late 1950s, aviation took a giant leap as the United States began to explore space. It was natural that Western aircraft companies would begin building and testing spacecraft as well. Many aviation companies became aerospace companies. **Aerospace** was the new word that described the design, manufacturing, and testing of aircraft and spacecraft. To learn about one important part of aerospace, see A Closer Look at the Space Shuttle on page 294.

The growth of the aerospace industry has had a big effect on life in the West. Aviation and aerospace in Washington brought thousands of people to Seattle. From its early days as a lumber and shipping city, Seattle has grown into one of the major cities of the United States. Now when visitors come to Seattle, they can see huge aircraft hangars as well as the smokestacks of the sawmills.

Another city that was changed by aerospace was Lompoc *(LOM pohk)*, California. In the late 1950s, Vandenberg Air Force Base was built on the central California coast. Life in nearby Lompoc changed forever. The population

▲ *As aerospace takes people higher and higher into space, they see the world in a whole new way. This picture shows the coastline of southern California.*

■ *Why did the aviation industry grow in the West?*

How Do We Know?

HISTORY *In 1961, President John F. Kennedy gave a speech about the importance of exploring space. He said that the United States should make it a goal to send a person to the moon within 10 years. The country reached this goal even sooner. In 1969, people watched on television as two men walked on the moon.*

293

New People, New Industries

The Space Shuttle

The first space shuttle thundered into space April, 1981. The shuttle lifts off the launch pad like a rocket, but lands like a plane. It is the largest vehicle to be flown in space. The shuttle's cargo bay, which carries telescopes and satellites, is as big as a railroad boxcar.

Outside the shuttle, astronauts float in space. They test equipment such as jet-packs and new spacesuits.

Blast off! The shuttle is launched with two rocket boosters. The force of these boosters is equal to 30 jumbo-jets. In orbit, the shuttle travels at 17,500 miles an hour and crosses North America in eight minutes!

A crew of seven people pilot the shuttle. Astronauts, like Sally Ride, use computers to contact Edwards Air Force Base and guide the shuttle to a safe landing.

◄ A dry lake bed serves as a runway and landing place at Edwards Air Force Base. This flat stretch of land provides plenty of room for space shuttles to land.

grew from about 6,000 people in 1957 to 18,500 in 1962. In just a few years, the quiet town that was famous for raising flower seeds leaped into the space age. Colorful fields of brilliant flowers trembled as powerful missiles and spacecraft blasted off. Today, about half the people in Lompoc work in agriculture and the other half work in aerospace.

The aerospace industry is important all over the West. Many of the parts for the space shuttles were built by manufacturing companies in states like California, Utah, and Colorado. In the Los Angeles area alone, one in four people works in the aerospace industry. It could be said that aerospace is the West's most important industry.

You have seen how, from the early days, people explored the unknown lands of the West. Minerals, farmland, and forests drew settlers to this vast region. Later, industries such as aerospace brought people to the cities of Seattle and Los Angeles. Today, pioneers in the aerospace industry explore the unknown regions of space. ■

■ *How has the aerospace industry changed the West?*

R E V I E W

1. **FOCUS** How did air and space flight change the West?
2. **CONNECT** Compare the work of building an airplane to that of assembling an automobile.
3. **GEOGRAPHY** Why is Lompoc a good example of old and new industry in the West?
4. **CRITICAL THINKING** How do you think manu-

facturing industries like aerospace affected western cities?

5. **ACTIVITY** Use the Minipedia to learn the populations of Los Angeles (page 354) and Seattle (page 396). Which city is larger, and by how many people?

295

Agriculture and Industry

Chapter Review

Reviewing Key Terms

aerospace (p. 293)   migrant workers (p. 284)
aviation (p. 291)   produce (p. 283)
lumber (p. 288)   timber (p. 288)

A. Write the key term for each definition below:
1. the design, manufacturing, and testing of aircraft and spacecraft
2. fruits and vegetables
3. sawed boards that are used to build homes
4. people who move from farm to farm to harvest crops
5. roughly cut logs

B. Choose the key term that best completes each sentence.
1. At sawmills, _____ is sawed into lumber, which is used to build houses.
2. Using irrigation, farmers in California's Central Valley grow oranges, tomatoes, and other kinds of _____.
3. Airplane test pilots like Jackie Cochran played an exciting part in the growth of _____ during the 1950s.
4. Owners of large farms in California used _____ to pick their crops.
5. Logging by _____ companies spread throughout the Northwestern forests.

Exploring Concepts

A. Copy the chart below. Fill in the chart by answering the questions across the top. Use information from the chapter in your answer.

B. Write two or three sentences to answer each of the following questions. Use details from this chapter to support your answers.
1. How has the aerospace industry helped to change the West?

2. Why might a logger from 1910 be surprised if he visited a logging camp in the Pacific Northwest today?
3. What is the main difference between farming in California and in the other Western states?
4. How is irrigation important to agriculture in the West?
5. How did the early aviation industry of the West develop into the aerospace industry of today?

Industry	Where has it developed?	What natural resources does it depend on?
Agriculture		
Logging		
Aerospace		

Chapter 12

Reviewing Skills

1. Look at the circle graph at the right. Write the answers to these questions: What is the whole that is divided into parts? How many parts are shown? What does the graph tell you about the age group to which you belong? Which age group makes up the largest part of the population? Are there more people over 64 years old or more people under 5 years old?

2. Which of the sentences below state facts and which state opinions. Write a sentence to explain each of your answers.
   a. I think Jackie Cochran was the bravest pilot in California.
   b. About half the people in Lompoc, California, work in aerospace.
   c. People should visit the Pacific Northwest to see the huge trees.

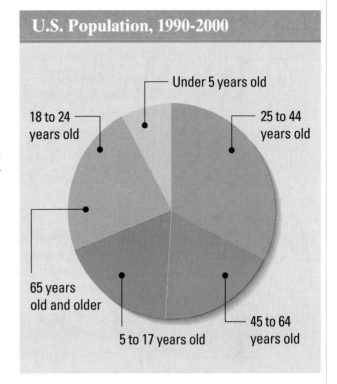

U.S. Population, 1990-2000

Under 5 years old
18 to 24 years old
25 to 44 years old
65 years old and older
5 to 17 years old
45 to 64 years old

Using Critical Thinking

1. Early lumberjacks called trees of the Northwestern forest "green gold." Why? How does the lumber industry in the late 1800s compare with the mining rushes in the West?

2. Farmers moved west after hearing wild stories about California agriculture. When they got there, they found that there were many challenges for farmers. Why did many of them stay instead of going back to the East?

Preparing for Citizenship

1. **GROUP ACTIVITY** Loggers often sang songs to keep their minds off their hard labor. Work with a partner to write a song about logging in the Northwest. Your song can sing the praises of logging or show the need to preserve the forests. Use a favorite tune or write your own melody. Perform your song for the class.

2. **COLLABORATIVE LEARNING** As a class project, make a mural that shows the jobs provided by the agriculture, lumber, and aerospace industries in the West. Before you begin, divide into three groups, one for each industry. Using information from this chapter and from library books, plan your part of the mural. Include drawings of several workers in the industry doing different jobs. Add captions that tell what the workers are doing.

The West Today

There are places in the West where you can see this region the way it was when the Indians roamed its mountains and deserts. One place is in a national park. However, much of the region has changed greatly from the early days. Today, old pioneer towns like Salt Lake City, Utah, are gleaming cities in the middle of the desert. Immigrants like the Chinese have helped to change the West, just as they helped build the railroads. In San Francisco's Chinatown you'll discover how immigrants have affected modern life in the West. Another example of change is in Hollywood, California. There you can see how an old chicken ranch grew into the movie capital of the world. In these pages you'll explore a little of the West today.

Exploring National Parks

You stand at the mouth of a dark, creepy-looking cave. Are you going in? No way! You look out at the land around you. The ground is pure black for as far as you can see. Tiny flowers poke up between the cracks of the smooth, hard volcanic lava. But there are no trees or animals on this hot hillside. Have you landed on some other planet?

This is Craters of the Moon National Monument, in southern Idaho. It is one of many national parks in the West. This region has more parkland than any other. It has the nation's first national park, Yellowstone, and another of the most famous, Yosemite (*yoh SEHM uh tee*). Many parks have strangely beautiful sights. In Alaska and Montana there are moving sheets of ice called glaciers.

▼ *Lava gushes from an erupting volcano. In the Hawaii Volcanoes National Park you can touch rocks that formed as the fiery lava cooled and hardened.*

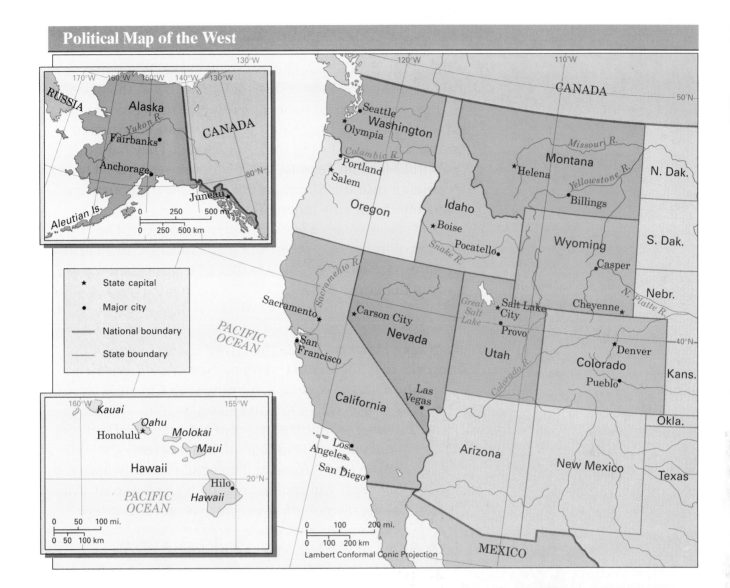

In Colorado there are old, Indian cliff dwellings that were suddenly and mysteriously abandoned.

Many beautiful creatures roam these parks, from grizzly bears and bighorn rams in the high mountains to the rare California condors and the tropical birds of Hawaii.

Exploring Salt Lake City

"Look, Mom—no hands!" Just lean back and float like a boat on the surface of Utah's Great Salt Lake. This famous lake is saltier than the ocean. The salt makes you float without even trying.

The city on the shores of this unusual lake is very beautiful. Salt Lake City lies in the Great Basin desert, surrounded by mountains. It was founded in 1847 by a religious group called the Mormons. The Mormons came from the East, where they had been treated badly because of their beliefs. They were looking for a "land that nobody

▲ *There are many major cities throughout the West today, as you can see from the map above. Salt Lake City, in Utah, is a main stopping place for people traveling across the Great Basin.*

299

New People, New Industries

wanted," so people would leave them alone. When they arrived in this hot, bare valley, they knew it was the place.

Few people would believe that the Mormons could have survived here. But they built the first irrigation system in the West and soon began to farm the land. They built the beautiful Mormon Temple, which you can see today. During the mining rush the Mormons dug gold, silver, copper, and lead from the nearby mountains.

Today the area is a leading mineral producer. The city also has oil refineries, sheep and cattle ranches, and a growing aerospace industry. It is a center of transportation and trade in the Great Basin.

Exploring Chinatown

"Gung Hay Fat Choy!" the crowd cheers as exploding fireworks rock the ground. "Happy New Year!" It is February, and everyone in San Francisco's Chinatown is in the streets celebrating the first day of the Chinese calendar. A roaring, red-jeweled dragon 60 feet long dances down the middle of Grant Street. The dragon leads a loud and colorful parade, which you can see if you can find a good high spot to sit. All along the parade route there is much to eat, to buy, and to look at.

If you like a place with lots of people and energy, you'll love Chinatown. About 70,000 Chinese people live within a few blocks. Few other neighborhoods in the country have so many people squeezed into such a small place.

It's easy to see why people would want to come to this warm, hilly city by the sea. Chinese immigrants came during the 1800s and provided services like restaurants and laundries that the miners needed. They brought new foods and customs to the West. Today, even the street signs and telephone booths are decorated in Chinese style, with fancy red roofs, bells, and carvings.

Exploring Hollywood

You feel warm breath on the back of your neck. Somebody screams. You turn around in your seat to come face-to-face with a 30-foot gorilla. King Kong! He throws his head back and roars, showing his sharp teeth. Then he reaches for you with his giant paw, missing by only a few inches.

How can you tell that this picture was taken in Chinatown? The Chinese writing below says Happy New Year. How is the writing different from the writing in this textbook?

This computer-controlled beast is one of the movie characters you meet when you tour Universal Studios, in California. For nearly 100 years, southern California has been the movie-making capital of the world. When movies were new, many young film-makers came to the small desert city of Hollywood. There the warm weather and beautiful landscapes were good for filming. Hollywood became the home of many famous stars, from Shirley Temple to Mickey Mouse. Today you can visit the homes of the stars and the studios where they worked.

Move Ahead

Now you're ready to find out more about these wonderful places of the West. Encyclopedias, travel magazines, and library books will help you. Here are some questions to guide your research:

1. Who was John Muir? What part did he play in creating national parks? What interesting plants, animals, and landforms can you find in these parks?
2. What part did Mormon leader Brigham Young play in building Salt Lake City? What famous choir and pipe organ are in this city?
3. What kinds of foods, celebrations, and building designs can you find in Chinatown?
4. Who was Walt Disney? What was his role in the cartoon and movie industries?

Explore Some More

Use your library to find out if your state or region has places like the ones you've read about here. For example, what national parks are nearest to you? What kind of trees and wildlife would you find there? Does your state have a big immigrant community, like Chinatown? Choose a city in your state and find out what people founded it. Then find out what immigrant groups came to the city and how they affected its growth. Or see if movies or television shows are made in your state or region. Are there movies about your state? What do they tell you about the land and the people?

When you go to the movies, there's a good chance you're watching something made in Hollywood, California. Many cartoon characters, outer-space aliens, and young movie stars became famous in this filmmaking city.

301

New People, New Industries

One Nation,
One Globe

*Imagine a giant game of connect the dots. The dots
are cities. They are connected by transportation lines,
like highways, railroads, and airplane routes. They
are connected by communication lines too, like the
telephone wires that stretch from city to city. With
modern technology, we have now connected the dots
around the world. What is the picture we've drawn in
our dot game? It shows a world that is joined closer
together today than ever before.*

1875

*Junction of Interstate 980, Interstate 880, and Highway 24 in
Oakland, California. Photograph Copyright Steve Proehl.*

2000

Chapter 13
Linking the Regions

As the five regions grew and developed, so did the links that joined them together. Roads connected states and cities. New inventions like the telephone and television drew people closer together. These changes in transportation and communication helped to unite the nation.

Thanks to the highways that crisscross the United States, people in all five regions can enjoy goods from thousands of miles away.

1875 | 1900 | 1925

1875

1915 The first transcontinental telephone service links San Francisco and New York.

The Golden Gate Bridge is a beautiful example of how roadways have helped link different parts of the nation.

You can watch your team play in cities across the country by turning on the television.

| 1950 | 1975 | 2000 |

1939 The first regular television broadcasts begin in the Northeast.

2000

Open Highways

THINKING
FOCUS

What effect has the Interstate Highway System had on the United States?

Key Terms

- network
- interstate highways
- commute

How would life on earth look if you visited from another planet and hovered above a busy highway? In "Southbound on the Freeway," May Swenson imagines what an alien might see.

A tourist came in from Orbitville,
parked in the air, and said:

The creatures of this star
are made of metal and glass.

Through the transparent parts
you can see their guts.

Their feet are round and roll
on diagrams or long

measuring tapes, dark
with white lines.

They have four eyes.
The two in back are red.

Sometimes you can see a five-eyed
one, with a red eye turning

on the top of his head.
He must be special—

the others respect him
and go slow

when he passes, winding
among them from behind.

They all hiss as they glide,
like inches, down the marked

tapes. Those soft shapes
shadowy inside

the hard bodies—are they
their guts or their brains?

▶ *This photograph shows just a thin strip of a 12-lane freeway in California.*

Highways Connect People

In May Swenson's poem, the automobiles rushing back and forth on this busy highway confuse the visitor. Not surprisingly, the space traveler thinks these cars are the planet's people.

"Southbound on the Freeway" might make you smile, but it has a serious meaning, too. Of course, automobiles are not really the "creatures of this star." But today cars are important to the lives of people all over the world. Without motor vehicles, life in the United States would be very different from what it is like today.

If you have ever flown in an airplane, you've probably looked down and seen a web of highways crisscrossing the countryside. This system of roads connects 48 states and looks something like the one on the map below. It is this giant web that helps to bind the country's different regions into a single nation.

From Indian Trails to Roads

Many roads began as American Indian trails. In the late 1800s, these trails were widened, first for carriages and then for cars. But they were still just dirt roads, and not paved over. Early motorists traveled over deep ruts, around tree stumps, and through mud and underbrush. Albert A. Pope,

▼ *The web of highways that cross the United States can take you from Boston, Massachusetts, to Los Angeles, California, in as few as six days. Signs like the ones above help you find your way.*

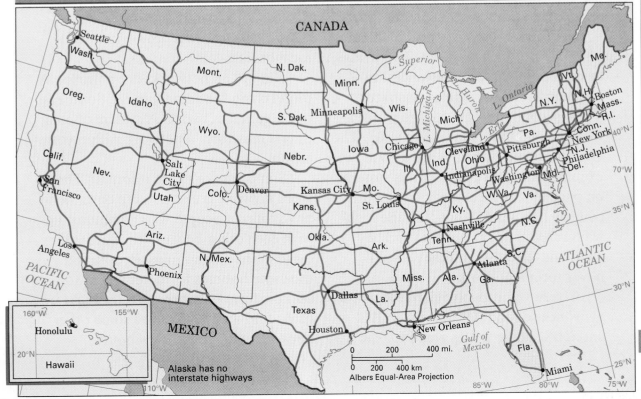

The National System of Interstate Highways

The man and woman in this 1920 photograph don't look very happy. Their Model T has gotten itself stuck in the mud.

an automaker in the early 1900s, said of these conditions: "The American who buys an automobile must pick between bad roads and worse."

To improve the nation's roads, Congress passed the Federal Highway Act in 1921. This allowed states to use money from the federal government to build new roads in the 1920s and 1930s. Many of these were excellent local roads. But the country still did not have a web of paved highways to link different states and regions. Long-distance travel by car or truck remained slow and difficult. What the country needed was a network of highways that would connect all the major cities of the nation. A **network** is made up of many parts or routes that cross each other and connect with each other. A network of highways traveling across the country would connect all the states except for Hawaii and Alaska.

UNDERSTANDING NETWORKS

One meaning of the word *network* is the same as the meaning of net. Picture a fishing net. The strings, or cords, cross at even distances. In between the strings are open spaces.

A second meaning for the word *network* is something that is like a net. The U.S. interstate highways are a good example. Look at a map of this system on page 307. Notice how it covers the country like a net. What if all the highways ran just north and south? They would never cross, and they would never form a network.

You have probably heard the word *network* used to refer to ABC, NBC, and CBS. These letters stand for the names of radio and television companies. These national networks link all local broadcasting stations.

But not all networks are national. A motel chain found only in the Southeast is a regional network. A system of computers may form a network within your school.

Some networks are informal. The word *network* is also used to describe any group of people who communicate with each other because they are interested in the same things. People with the same hobbies form networks. Job seekers form networks to help each other find work. What are some other networks that you know about?

From Roads to Highways

The story of a highway network in the United States goes back to 1917. That year the country entered World War I. A young army captain named Dwight Eisenhower led a group of soldiers and military trucks on a journey across the country from San Francisco to New York. There the trucks would be shipped to the war fields in France.

The cross-country trip turned out to be slow and rough. Eisenhower soon realized that the United States needed a system of **interstate highways**. These broad, paved roads would cross state lines and connect the country's regions.

Eisenhower later became a five-star general, and in 1952, he was elected President of the United States. He never forgot the lesson of his cross-country journey. In 1956, under Eisenhower's leadership, Congress voted for the money to build an Interstate Highway System. Soon after, work began on the greatest highway project in history. Eisenhower's 39-year-old dream was coming true. ■

■ *What problem did the Interstate Highway System help to solve?*

Highways Change People's Lives

Traveling in cars for family vacations began soon after the invention of the automobile. Interstate highways made these vacations easier. Today people from every state travel hundreds, even thousands of miles in their cars. They visit the many places of natural beauty and special interest in the United States, like Yellowstone National Park in Wyoming and the nation's capital in Washington, D.C.

Once, trips like these could take weeks. The distance across the country is about 3,000 miles. On an interstate highway, people often travel 500 miles or more in one day. Now a traveler can drive across country in as little as 6 days.

▼ *In 110 years, travel time across the country has decreased from 6 months to just 6 hours. The advertisement below is from the 1950s, when the De Soto was a popular car.*

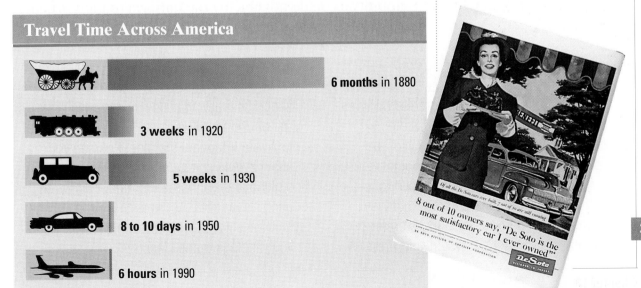

Travel Time Across America

	6 months in 1880
	3 weeks in 1920
	5 weeks in 1930
	8 to 10 days in 1950
	6 hours in 1990

8 out of 10 owners say, "De Soto is the most satisfactory car I ever owned"

De Soto

➤ *Workers in Chapel Hill, North Carolina, work on building I-95, an interstate highway.*

Across Time & Space

Those who plan for the future tell us to expect changes in our highways, including new and better traffic control. Radar and computers will be used to guide motor vehicles. They will help traffic to flow smoothly and will prevent accidents.

■ *How have highways changed the everyday lives of people in the United States?*

Family automobile vacations help connect people of various regions. While spending time in another region, you can learn about its geography and its history. You can also meet people who live in the region and discover how their customs and routines differ from your own.

The Interstate Highway System has also changed people's daily lives. People now can live farther away from where they work. Many people **commute** to work. That means they drive long distances to their jobs. They commute into the city or to other towns to work. They take buses to school or college. People who work in sales and deliveries spend their workday in cars, vans, or trucks.

Of course, people still travel in trains, airplanes, and boats. But cars are by far the most popular way to travel. They give people the freedom to move easily from one place to another whenever they want. This easy movement, or mobility, is made possible by the nation's roads, particularly the roads of the Interstate Highway System. ■

REVIEW

1. **FOCUS** What effect has the Interstate Highway System had on the United States?

2. **CONNECT** Name one place in each of the country's five regions that you would choose to visit on a family automobile vacation.

3. **HISTORY** How did the Interstate Highway System fulfill a future President's dream?

4. **CRITICAL THINKING** How would your life change if motor vehicles disappeared from the earth tomorrow?

5. **ACTIVITY** Interview the oldest person you know in your community. Ask what roads and highways in your area were built during that person's lifetime. Ask how those roads and highways have affected people's lives. Report your findings to the class.

LESSON 2

Sharing Ideas

W atson, come here. I want you!" Alexander Graham Bell said these words on March 10, 1875. They were the first words ever spoken over a telephone.

Bell, a teacher of the deaf who was born in Scotland, had moved to the United States in 1871. He was not an inventor by profession, but a man of great curiosity and imagination. His special interests were human speech and language. His goal was to find a way for human beings to communicate across great distances.

One day, Bell was working in his laboratory trying to perfect the telephone. He was preparing to test his latest transmitter, or sending device. His assistant, Thomas A. Watson, was waiting in another room to test the receiver.

Suddenly, Bell spilled acid on himself and called for Watson, speaking the famous words above. Excited, Watson rushed into the other room: "Mr. Bell, I heard every word you said—distinctly." That day marks the invention of the world's first successful telephone.

THINKING
FOCUS

How do telephones, televisions, and computers link regions of the United States?

Key Terms

- communications
- satellite

◄ *Early telephones looked like this. People spoke into the mouthpiece, and listened through the earpiece hanging on the side.*

Telephone Links

Today telephone lines and cables crisscross the nation. These lines and cables form a vast communications network. **Communications** is the technology of carrying information and ideas. By telephone, you are linked to your friend next door, to the corner store, and to your cousin who lives 2,000 miles away.

You pick up the telephone to save time. Is the library open yet? Does the supermarket have fresh strawberries?

311

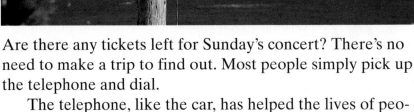

Are there any tickets left for Sunday's concert? There's no need to make a trip to find out. Most people simply pick up the telephone and dial.

The telephone, like the car, has helped the lives of people in rural areas. They can now talk to friends in town or relatives in faraway cities whenever they want. In emergencies, they can reach doctors, ambulances, firefighters, and police at a moment's notice.

Over the past 50 years, telephone service has made great advances. Public telephones are now located almost everywhere. People can walk out into the yard and continue a conversation on a cordless phone. People can even make telephone calls from an airplane or a car.

How Telephones Affect People's Lives

Until recent decades, many people used the mail to send personal messages. In today's society, far fewer people write letters. Instead, they pick up the telephone to tell the latest news, to hear the time, to invite someone to lunch, or to talk with a friend far away. The telephone is the most personal way to communicate from a long distance.

Telephones have become more important in the work world, too. Talking to people in other states, and even other countries, has become a normal part of the workday for many people. Today many businesses would have to close down if they did not have telephones. ■

Across Time & Space

In 1915, Bell and Watson took part in a ceremony opening the first transcontinental telephone service. In New York, Bell repeated his words of 39 years earlier: "Mr. Watson, come here. I want you!" From San Francisco, Watson said that he'd be happy to come, but it would take him a week.

■ *What effect has the telephone had on the lives of people in the United States?*

Television Links

Television also links people in the United States in important ways. Like the telephone, it forms a vast communications network. Television links people by spreading knowledge about other regions. Through television, people can discover how the Everglades, the Rocky Mountains, and Death Valley actually look. And they can learn about how people live and work in other parts of the country.

Television also links people by allowing them to share the experience of major events. When the President gives an important speech, the country shares the experience by watching the speech at the same time. When a space shuttle is sent up into space, millions of people watch the launching from living rooms across the country. Besides these major events, television programs broadcast every week provide people across the country with another shared experience.

Satellites are small machines that circle the earth and collect information. The use of these machines has made it possible for television to bring a live event to many more people. In addition to taking pictures of the earth's surface, tracking storms, and studying stars, satellites can send television pictures across great distances. As the Closer Look on pages 314-315 shows, a satellite can carry a sporting event in Alaska to television sets across the United States.

Many of the programs and commercials on television are the same all over the United States. One effect of these shared programs and advertisements has been to make our clothes, cars, and foods more alike. As a result, the differences between regions are no longer as great. Or to look at it another way, television has helped unite the country's regions into a single nation. ■

■ *How does television make Americans and the nation's regions more alike?*

▼ *People around the world watched when the Berlin Wall (left) opened up in November, 1989, after separating East Germany from West Germany for almost 30 years. Below, the opening ceremonies of the 1988 Olympic games in Seoul, Korea. The games reach televisions all over the world.*

A Television Broadcast

People all over the United States watch the finish of the Iditarod Trail Sled Dog Race in Alaska. How do the pictures and sounds get to TV sets across the country?

Nome

TV station in Anchorage, Alaska

TV camera

TV truck

Which picture should we send out? There are many cameras at the finish line. Each camera is sending a different picture to the truck. People in the truck quickly decide which camera is taking the best picture. They send that picture to a TV station in Anchorage, Alaska.

Here they come! One of the teams of dogs is about to cross the finish line and win the race to Nome, Alaska. A TV camera films the picture. Picture and sound travel along a wire to the TV truck.

TV station in Honolulu, Hawaii

314

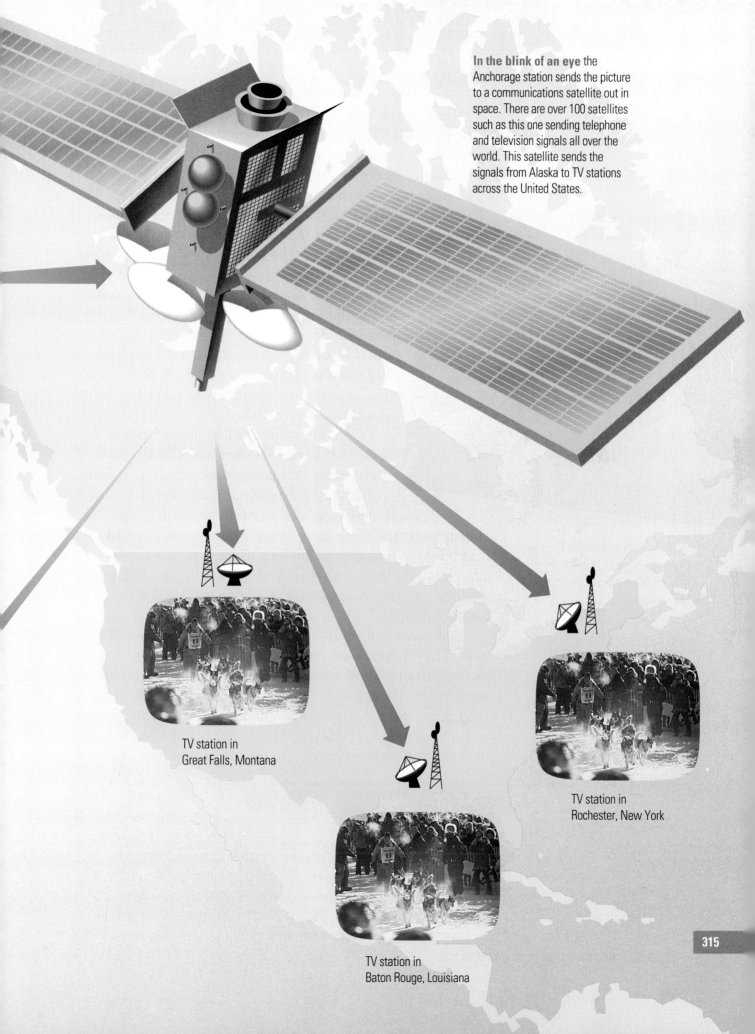

In the blink of an eye the Anchorage station sends the picture to a communications satellite out in space. There are over 100 satellites such as this one sending telephone and television signals all over the world. This satellite sends the signals from Alaska to TV stations across the United States.

TV station in
Great Falls, Montana

TV station in
Rochester, New York

TV station in
Baton Rouge, Louisiana

Computer Links

Many of you may have been introduced to computers through your television set. You might have used them to play video games. Later you may have used computers at your public library, at school, or at home.

Unlike you and your friends, your parents probably first used computers in high school or later on. They may have learned to use them at night school or at work. The computer is the newest and most important tool for improving communication.

Computer networks now link the regions of the United States. One example of such a network is in the computer systems used by most banks. Banking machines and a plastic bank card allow a person on vacation in New York City to withdraw money from his or her bank account in North Dakota.

Computers are used in many types of businesses and in homes across the nation. Publishing companies use computers to publish books. Businesspeople travel in airplanes working with computers on their laps. Hairdressers use computers to see what hairstyles looks best on their customers. Children use computers to play games and do their schoolwork. And families use computers to keep records, make up shopping lists, and save cooking recipes.

Today computers affect nearly every part of people's lives. They help people find library books and keep track of bank accounts. They operate complicated medical equipment. They direct robots to paint and assemble new cars. And they send messages to people around the world. Along with telephones and television, computers have become one of the country's most important means of communication. ■

▲ *This tiny ant holds the even tiner computer chip in its mouth. The chip is the brain of the computer.*

■ *How do computers affect our daily lives?*

R E V I E W

1. **FOCUS:** How do telephones, televisions, and computers link regions of the United States?

2. **CONNECT:** Transportation networks carry people and goods. What do communications networks carry?

3. **HISTORY:** Describe the well-known event that marked the invention of the telephone.

4. **CRITICAL THINKING:** Explain how a computer might make it easier to run a bookstore.

5. **ACTIVITY:** With a partner, role-play a debate between your telephone and your television set. Each should try to prove that it is more important in your life.

L E S S O N 3

Goods Across the Nation

On the day before Thanksgiving, most supermarkets are packed. Kitchen counters are piled high with groceries. On Thanksgiving, many families serve the same food at their tables. Some of these foods were served at the first Thanksgiving dinner in Plymouth, Massachusetts. In 1621, the Pilgrims shared a three-day harvest feast with the Wampanoag (*WAHMP uh nawg*) Indians. The menu included deer, wild goose, turkey, lobster, clams, oysters, and fish, as well as cornmeal bread. The Indians had taught the Pilgrims to dry wild fruits. Dried gooseberries, strawberries, plums, and cherries also colored the festive tables.

Most people no longer grow the food they eat on Thanksgiving. Instead, they buy it in supermarkets. The turkey isn't wild, but was raised on a turkey farm in North Carolina. The potatoes grew in Idaho, and the sweet potatoes in Louisiana. The green beans are from Michigan, the peas from Illinois, and the onions from Oregon. The apples for the pies grew in Washington. A Thanksgiving dinner, then, shows how tightly the country's regions are linked.

THINKING FOCUS

How do the nation's networks affect the way people live?

Key Terms

- interdependent
- economy

◄ *Poultry farms raise millions of turkeys for Thanksgiving dinners.*

317

Linking the Regions

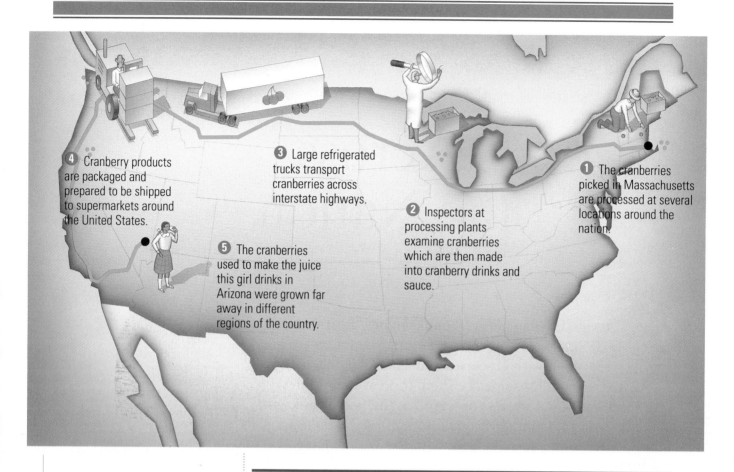

4 Cranberry products are packaged and prepared to be shipped to supermarkets around the United States.

3 Large refrigerated trucks transport cranberries across interstate highways.

5 The cranberries used to make the juice this girl drinks in Arizona were grown far away in different regions of the country.

2 Inspectors at processing plants examine cranberries which are then made into cranberry drinks and sauce.

1 The cranberries picked in Massachusetts are processed at several locations around the nation.

The Cranberry Story

Today people in the United States often eat cranberries at holiday meals. They eat cranberry sauce, cranberry relish, and cranberry nut bread. Many people also drink cranberry juice at all times of the year. Only a few people grow the cranberries they eat. Most buy them at the supermarket—fresh, canned, or frozen.

The story of cranberries is one example of how people use the country's resources. It is also an example of how the nation's regions are **interdependent**. This means that each region depends on other regions for its food supply as well as for many other goods and services. Much of the food you eat, the clothes you wear, and products you use in your daily life are produced in other regions.

Economy of the Regions

You have already learned about the crops and manufactured goods that each region in the United States produces. The **economy** of each region is the way a region produces and sells its resources, goods, and services. As the cranberry story shows, the economy of each region is linked by networks. Each region has products that other regions do not grow or produce. The network linking the economies of the five regions brings you wheat grown on farms in the Midwest, oranges grown in orchards of the West, clothes made from the cotton of the Southeast, books published in the Northeast, and fuel from the oil fields of the Southwest.

The network linking the regions' economies depends on other kinds of networks. Transportation is probably the most important network. Airplanes fly pineapples from Hawaii to stores in Maine, trains carry coal from the Southeast to furnaces in Wisconsin, and ships transport freight oil drilled off the coast of the Southwest to gasoline stations in Virginia. Perhaps most important are the trucks that travel day and night across the network of interstate highways. These huge vehicles cart every kind of food, product, and equipment that you can think of.

The network of the regions' economies also depends on communications. Supermarket managers use telephones to order food products and computers to keep track of them. An executive in New York City can send important papers to an office in Los Angeles using an overnight mail carrier. Also, many companies use television to advertise their products or services. ■

Linking Economies

A trip through the five regions can give you a good idea of how the economy of each region is linked to the economies of the other regions. Imagine that you and your family are driving from Baltimore, Maryland, to Yellowstone National Park in Wyoming for a vacation. When you pull off the interstate highway for food and gas, you will probably see many familiar signs. Some are for the same fast-food restaurants you eat in at home. Others are for gas stations that your parents use near your house. The same signs will greet you whether you stop in Cleveland, Chicago, or a small town in North Dakota.

During your journey, you will need to stop several times to sleep for the night. More often

■ *How does the cranberry story illustrate the interdependence of the country's regions?*

▼ *Trucks carry fruits, vegetables, oil, gasoline, furniture, and many other products from region to region across the Interstate Highway System.*

319

▲ *The John Davis House is a pioneer homestead in the Great Smoky Mountains National Park. The homestead and the park, which lies on the border of North Carolina and Tennessee, are two things that set the Southeast apart from other regions.*

■ *How do economic networks help to link regions in the United States?*

than not, you will stay in one of the nation's large motel chains. You may even stay in the same kind of motel every night. If you forget your toothpaste or your shampoo, you may find yourself buying these products in the same drugstore chain you use back in Baltimore.

As you can see from your vacation, this network linking the regions' economies helps to unite the nation. It is also very important to the nation's economy. Like the transportation and communications networks, this network reduces the differences between regions. In growing numbers, people in the United States eat in the same restaurants, stay in the same motels, and shop in the same stores.

Although they are more alike than they used to be, the regions of the United States are still very different. As you have seen in this book, each region has its own landscapes, its own products, and even its own way of speaking. Much of what makes the country's regions interesting and different cannot be seen from an interstate highway. You have to travel on back roads to discover the real character of a region. But even in the out-of-the-way places, you will find many examples of the networks that bind the United States into one nation and one people. ■

R E V I E W

1. **FOCUS** How do the nation's networks affect the way people live?

2. **CONNECT** How are the networks linking the regions' economies helped by the transportation and communications networks?

3. **HISTORY** Compare and contrast the first Thanksgiving with Thanksgiving at your house.

4. **CRITICAL THINKING** Do you think it is good or bad for Americans to become more alike? Could it be both good and bad? Explain.

5. **ACTIVITY** Make a list of the fast-food restaurants, gas stations, and motels you might see while traveling on an interstate highway. Share your list with the class.

Chapter 13

Making a Bar Graph

Here's Why

If you present lots of numbers in a chart it can sometimes seem confusing. You can make a bar graph instead. A bar graph can help compare amounts of something, such as the amounts of cranberries produced in different states.

Cranberry Harvesting	
State	**Barrels of Cranberries**
Massachusetts	1.7 million
New Jersey	0.3 million
Oregon	0.1 million
Washington	0.1 million
Wisconsin	1.2 million

Here's How

The chart above lists the five states where cranberries are grown for sale. It also shows how many barrels of cranberries each state grows per year. A barrel contains 100 pounds of cranberries. In the bar graph, at the right, the names of three of these states appear at the bottom. The numbers on the left side of the graph stand for millions of barrels. The bars show how many barrels each state produces. Find the top of the bar for Massachusetts between the lines for 1.6 and 1.8 million barrels. This bar tells you that Massachusetts produces 1.7 million barrels of cranberries a year.

Suppose you want to add facts about Wisconsin to the bar graph. At the bottom of the graph, you would write Wisconsin. From the chart, you know that Wisconsin raises 1.2 million barrels of cranberries. You would draw the bar for Wisconsin so that it comes just up to the line for 1.2 million.

Try It

Copy the bar graph below on a sheet of paper. Then use the information in the chart to add bars for both Washington and Wisconsin. Which of the five states produces the most cranberries? Which state ranks second in cranberry production?

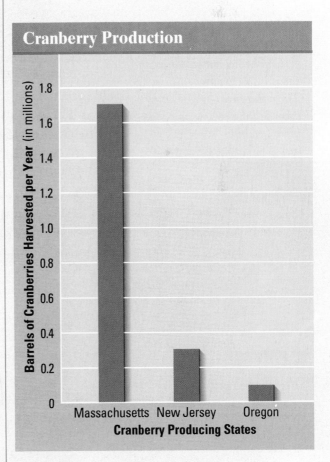

Apply It

Make a bar graph that shows how many students in your class have blue eyes, brown eyes, or green eyes.

321

Trolleys or Cars?

> A merica lives on wheels, and we have to provide the highways to keep . . . the kind and form of life we want.
>
> Former Treasury Secretary
> George M. Humphrey,
> 1956

> N early everyone was sure highways were the only answer to transportation problems. . . . But we were wrong.
>
> Former Massachusetts
> Governor Francis Sargent,
> 1970

▼ *Chicago elevated trains and subways help ease traffic jams. The chart below shows how crowded the country's roads have become.*

Background

The nation's first underground subway station was built in Boston, Massachusetts, in 1897. People in Boston no longer had to walk to work. The New York City subway trains began taking riders back and forth to work. In Los Angeles, trolleys—horse-drawn rail cars that ran above the ground—rumbled along with their bells clanging. Most people in the young city lived within four blocks of a trolley line.

For many years, public transportation, as it is called, was the way many people in big cities got to and from work. Then, around 1900, a new machine took to the roads—the automobile, or "horseless carriage." From the start, automobiles were wildly popular. Throughout the country, people began buying and driving cars.

Instead of putting money into more public transportation, cities began building new roads.

Crowded Highways

1970
28 cars per mile

1986
45 cars per mile

Highway construction boomed in the 1950s. As cities like Los Angeles got larger in size, people there built more and more miles of highway. Some cities continued to build new public transportation systems. But highways and cars quickly took over the city landscape.

▼ *In Boston, roads look like parking lots during rush hours.*

Conflict Over Transportation

By the 1970s, cars clogged the roads of major cities. Skies turned yellowish-gray, filled with smog from car fumes. There were traffic jams and accidents.

Some people began calling for better public transportation. They pointed out that trains are fast, safe, cause less smog, and allow riders to relax and read instead of fighting traffic. The supporters of public transportation are still working to get more of the money that is spent to build and fix roads.

But people are proud of their cars. They love them, they take care of them, and they enjoy being behind the wheel. Driving gives them a feeling of freedom. They can go where they want, whenever they want—while trains only stop in certain places at certain times. Many people say they won't switch to public transportation.

Decision Point

1. What are the advantages and disadvantages of driving cars?
2. What are the advantages and disadvantages of using public transportation?
3. What do people who want public transportation value most?
4. What do people who prefer car travel value most?
5. Can you think of any other solutions to the dispute over cars and trolleys? For example, are there better ways to use both forms of transportation? Be creative.

Should people drive cars or take public transportation?

Public Transportation:
- causes less smog
- reduces traffic jams
- uses less fuel

Cars:
- go when you want
- go where you want
- more comfortable

Build more public transportation systems.

Build more roads and highways.

Chapter Review

Reviewing Key Terms

communications (p. 311) interstate highway (p. 309)
commute (p. 310) network (p. 308)
economy (p. 318) satellite (p. 313)
interdependent (p. 318)

A. Choose the key term that best completes each sentence.
1. ____ far out in space transmit television pictures across great distances.
2. The invention of the telephone was a major improvement in our system of ____.
3. Each day, millions of people in the United States ____ to and from work by car.
4. Because each region of the country needs what the others have to offer, all the regions are ____.
5. The way a region produces and sells its resources, goods, and services is the ____ of that region.
6. Throughout the United States, a ____ of roadways crisscrosses the country.
7. A system of ____ links the East Coast with the West Coast.

B. Write the definition of each key term below. Then write one or two sentences that show how the terms are related.
1. network
2. interstate highways
3. commute

Exploring Concepts

A. Copy the timeline below on a separate piece of paper. First, add the following two events: Henry Ford builds the first Model T Ford in 1908, and NBC begins to broadcast shows for home use in 1939. Next, look in the chapter for three more events that have helped people in the United States build national networks and add them to your timeline. Which event on your timeline do you think has been most important in linking different regions of the United States?

B. Write a few sentences to answer each question below. Use details from this chapter to support your answers.
1. How did President Eisenhower help improve the country's roads?
2. What advances in telephone service have happened over the last 50 years?
3. Why are interstate highways important in the United States?
4. How has the invention of the telephone changed the lives of people in the United States?
5. What methods of communication do people of the United States use today?

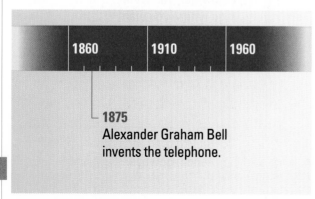

1875
Alexander Graham Bell
invents the telephone.

1860   1910   1960

Reviewing Skills

1. The chart at the right shows how much telephone wire was in use in the United States in four different years. Use this information to make a bar graph. Then answer these questions: What do the bars on your graph stand for? During what year was the most wire used?

2. Why do you think a bar graph is a good way to organize the information on this chart? Of the three types of graphs—bar, line, and circle—which is the best one to present this information? Which is the least effective? Why?

Telephone Wire	
Year	**Miles of Wire**
1950	1 hundred million
1960	3 hundred million
1970	6 hundred million
1980	11 hundred million

Using Critical Thinking

1. The interstate highways were built with money voted by Congress. Why do you think the U.S. government, rather than state governments, built the interstate highways?

2. If you had to give up the use of a telephone, a car, or a television, which one would you choose to do without? Give reasons for your choice.

3. In the past, barriers like mountains separated regions. How have changes in transportation and communications broken barriers down? What barriers still remain between regions?

Preparing for Citizenship

1. **GROUP ACTIVITY** Some people think that children should be limited in how much television they watch. Divide into two teams to debate this topic. One team will stress the advantages of watching television and the other the disadvantages. Each team should choose two members to present the team's arguments and respond to the arguments of the other team.

2. **WRITING ACTIVITY** Imagine that you are a newspaper reporter at the scene of the first telephone conversation between Alexander Graham Bell and Thomas Watson. Write a newspaper story about this historic event.

3. **COLLABORATIVE LEARNING** As a class, make a picture album that shows the transportation and communication links between regions of the United States. Using the lessons of this chapter, decide what pictures you want to include. Work in small groups to draw those pictures and write a few sentences explaining each one. Place the finished pictures in an album called "Linking the Regions of the United States."

4. **COLLABORATIVE LEARNING** The chapter tells about some positive effects of new advances in communication. Make a list of some of the negative effects. Share your list with the class and discuss them. Do the negative effects outweigh the positive ones? Explain.

Chapter 14
Global Connections

Travel, communications, and trade are bringing the people of the world closer together. Flip on your TV and watch a program from Australia. Fly a supersonic plane to Europe in just three hours. Or simply walk to a store and see everything that comes from faraway places. As our world becomes more connected, we must work with our global neighbors to solve the problems we all share.

Airplanes like the supersonic Concorde shown above are creating record travel times around the world.

Hong Kong, located on the coast of southern China, is one of the world's busiest trade centers. Goods from Hong Kong are sent to hundreds of different countries, including the United States.

From space, you cannot see that the world has many different countries. It is clear that we all share the same living space, and must take care of it together.

L E S S O N   1

People on the Move

How does travel link us to the rest of the world?

Key Term

- transatlantic

➤ *In the early 1900s, millions of immigrants entered the United States through Ellis Island in New York Harbor.*

The voyage on the ship was a long one, about three weeks, and we were probably in what was known as steerage—the lower deck—where the women and children slept together in one big section and the men in another. I have some faint memories of hundreds and thousands of people on this big ship. I remember being sick and sleepy and waiting, day by day.

Anthony Sorrentino was 6 years old when his family sailed 4,000 miles from Naples, Italy, to New York City in 1919. The Sorrentinos settled in Chicago, where he was surprised by "all the noises: the trucks, and even, in those days, the horse-drawn vehicles galloping through the streets."

Seventy-one years later, in 1980, Thu Banh's family traveled 11,000 miles to the United States from Vietnam. Thu's journey across the Pacific was much longer but also much faster and more comfortable than Anthony's voyage. The trip took Thu's family just three days.

Chapter 14

How People Travel

Improvements in transportation have brought our world closer together by letting people travel farther and faster. The trip that took Anthony Sorrentino's family three weeks in 1919 can now be made by ship in just a few days. However, people who travel such long distances today usually fly in airplanes.

In fact, jet travelers fly between Italy and New York in just eight hours. This is called a **transatlantic** flight because it crosses the Atlantic Ocean. Supersonic airplanes can make the trip in even less time—just three hours! These planes fly faster than the speed of sound.

Trace Anthony's and Thu's routes to the United States on the world map on page 400–401. Then look at the graph on this page. Compare the fastest way to travel when Anthony's family moved to this country with how fast we can travel today.

The future promises even speedier methods of travel. Some airplane makers are thinking about building an airplane that can go more than twice as fast as today's supersonic airplanes. Flying high over the earth's atmosphere, this plane would cut the flying time between Los Angeles and Tokyo from 12 hours to a lightning-fast 2 hours!

As travel times grow shorter traveling to distant places for business and pleasure will become even easier. Also, more people from distant places will be able to visit us. ■

■ *How has travel between continents improved since 1919?*

◄ *Through the years, traveling across the Atlantic Ocean has become faster and safer. Can you imagine how long the trip will take in the year 2050?*

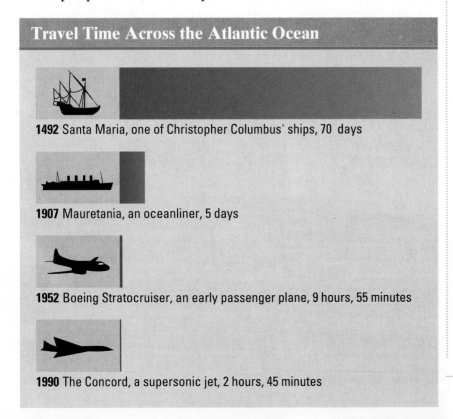

Travel Time Across the Atlantic Ocean

1492 Santa Maria, one of Christopher Columbus' ships, 70 days

1907 Mauretania, an oceanliner, 5 days

1952 Boeing Stratocruiser, an early passenger plane, 9 hours, 55 minutes

1990 The Concord, a supersonic jet, 2 hours, 45 minutes

Why People Travel

People travel to other countries for several reasons. Sometimes people travel to make a new home in another country. They may leave their own country to find better jobs, to escape hunger or war, or to join family members.

As you have learned, a person who enters a new country to live or work is called an immigrant. Our country welcomes more immigrants than any other country in the world. Some, like Anthony and Thu, come here to live. Others come for just a short time, to work. To read about another immigrant family, see *A Jar of Dreams* on pages 332–335.

Perhaps you are an immigrant to the United States or maybe you know someone else who is. One thing is for sure. At some time in the past, someone in your family was an immigrant. Even Native Americans moved here from Asia between 10,000 and 40,000 years ago.

▲ *The Eiffel Tower, shown above, is a popular tourist attraction for travelers from the United States.*

Business Travel

Today, people also travel for business. With the speed of today's transportation, businesspeople can work in several countries in just one day.

For example, in 1988 one American business traveler began her day in Dusseldorf, Germany. At 7:00 A.M. she

➤ *Countries as distant from one another as Greece and Japan are easily linked by airplane.*

Flights leave from the Tampa International Airport for countries all over the world.

flew to Paris, France, where she caught a supersonic plane that got her to New York in three hours. A jet flight took her to a lunch meeting in Houston, Texas, and from there she flew to an 8:00 P.M. dinner in Las Vegas, Nevada. Her working day included four airplane journeys, five cities, and more than 6,500 miles!

Travel for Pleasure

More than ever before, people are visiting other countries just to see a part of the world they've never been to before. Between 1970 and 1989, the number of American tourists visiting other countries almost tripled.

And each year more of our faraway friends come to visit us, too. In 1989 alone, almost 14 million tourists came to the United States from other countries. Did any of them come to your home town? ■

▲ *American travelers who want to visit foreign countries, such as China, need a United States passport like the one shown above.*

■ *Why do people travel to other countries?*

REVIEW

1. **FOCUS** How does travel link us to the rest of the world?
2. **CONNECT** What three cities in the United States would you recommend to a tourist from another country. Explain why you would recommend these cities.
3. **GEOGRAPHY** Using the map on page 410, tell how many times zones you would be in during a trip from Miami to Anchorage.
4. **CRITICAL THINKING** What are some problems you think an immigrant might face in a new country?
5. **ACTIVITY** On the world map on page 400, locate the country or countries from which you or your relatives came to the United States. How did they travel to the United States?

331

A Jar of Dreams

Yoshiko Uchida

Young Rinko and her family live in America now. When Aunt Waka comes to visit from Japan and brings a gift of a kimono, Rinko has mixed feelings about her Japanese family and her life in the United States. Her thoughts and actions tell of the difficulties many immigrants feel when they become part of a new culture. As you read this story, try to imagine how it would feel to be in Rinko's place.

As you read in Lesson I, new forms of travel have made it easier for people to move from one country to another. Many of these people borrow customs from their new countries while keeping others from their homelands, just like Rinko.

rice paper thin paper made from an Asian tree

brocade a heavy cloth with a rich design

peonies large flowers

A promise is a promise, so on Sunday after dinner, I got out the kimono Aunt Waka had brought me. It was in my bureau drawer still folded nice and flat inside its soft rice paper wrapping.

One good thing about kimonos is that they don't wrinkle if you fold them properly on the seams. Also almost anybody can wear the same size because there are no buttons or snaps. If you're short, you just pull up more to make a tuck and tie it in place with a silk cord. I thought that was pretty clever when Aunt Waka pointed it out to me.

She had to help me get dressed in the kimono because I certainly couldn't do it by myself. She made sure I overlapped the left side over the right (boys do the opposite), and she wound the wide brocade obi around and around my middle and tied an enormous knot in back.

I felt as if I was bound up in a silk cocoon and could hardly bend down to put the white tabi socks on my feet. It was hard to walk, too, with the thongs of the zori —the sandals—digging in between my toes, and I discovered why Aunt Waka took those small steps when she walked. You have to, with the long narrow kimono coming down to your ankles.

"There, you look beautiful," Aunt Waka said, when she'd finished. "Go look at yourself in the mirror."

I padded over in small steps to the bureau and looked at myself. I held out my arms to look at the white peonies blooming on the long blue silky sleeves. I turned around and twisted my head to look at the knot of the obi in back. I knew then exactly how Aunt Waka felt when we made her get into her western clothes.

"That's not me," I said.

Aunt Waka smiled. "I know how you feel, but it's you all right."

Then she hurried me out to the parlor to show Mama and Papa how I looked.

Mama's eyes really lit up when she saw me. "Why, Rinko, you look so pretty." And then she said, "Stand up straight now." But she didn't say it the way she usually does in order to improve my posture. She said it as though she wanted me to feel proud of myself.

I guess Papa was about as pleased as Mama. He stood back and studied me as though he was taking a picture of me.

"I suppose you wouldn't consider going to the hospital to show Uncle Kanda how you look, would you? That would really cheer him up, you know."

"Never in a million years," I said.

So Papa told Joji to get the box camera he got for Christmas and take my picture for Uncle Kanda. Aunt Waka got her camera too. We all trooped outside, and I stood beside the peach tree squinting at the sun.

"Stop squinting, Rinky Dink," Joji said.

"Don't you call me that, Joji Tsujimura," I said. I raised my arm to give him a whack and that's when he took my picture.

"Smile," Aunt Waka said, focusing her camera.

I blinked, and that's when she squeezed the shutter.

Mama wanted a picture with all of us in it, so I went over to get Mrs. Sugar. She looked exactly the way I thought she would when she saw me wearing a kimono. Her mouth made a big O, but no sound came out.

Then she said, "Why, it's my sweet little Japanese Rinko," and she gave me a hug. But it was hard to hug her back being wrapped up like a package in all that stiff brocade.

Mrs. Sugar lined us up in front of Papa's garage and made sure she got his big sign in the picture too.

"There," she said when she'd taken three pictures. "This will be a fine commemoration of your aunt's visit."

She sounded just like the people at church. They are always taking pictures to commemorate Easter or Memorial

shutter part of a camera that opens the lens to expose the film

circulation the
movement of blood
through the body

mothballs small
balls stored with
clothes to keep away
moths

Day or somebody's baptism or even somebody's funeral.

I could hardly wait to get out of the kimono when we were finished with all the picture-taking. Aunt Waka untied and unwound everything, and I shook my bones loose to get my circulation going again.

"Boy, am I glad to get out of that thing," I said.

Then I remembered the kimono was a present from Aunt Waka, and I tried to think of something nicer to say.

"I'll have Mama put it in her trunk and cover it with mothballs," I said.

I guess that wasn't exactly what Aunt Waka wanted to hear either. I thought she probably would've liked me to say I'd get it out and wear it once in a while.

But she didn't say that. She just smiled and said, "Ah, Rinko, you certainly are a child of America." Then she turned serious and said, "But don't ever forget, a part of you will always be Japanese too, even if you never wear a kimono again."

"I know," I said. "It's the part that makes me feel different and not as good as the others."

It was the strangest thing. Suddenly, it was as if I'd opened a faucet in my head and everything inside came pouring out. I told Aunt Waka all about how I felt at school—how the boys called me names and the girls made me feel left out. And I told her a terrible secret I'd kept to myself and never told anybody, ever.

Once when there was going to be a PTA meeting at school and we had notes to bring home, I tore up my note and never gave it to Mama. I did it because I didn't want Mama to go. I didn't want her bowing to all my teachers and talking to them in the funny English she sometimes uses. I didn't want Mama to be ignored by everybody and left sitting in a corner. I guess maybe I was a little bit ashamed of Mama. But mostly I was ashamed of myself.

"I hate always being different and left out," I told Aunt Waka.

Aunt Waka was folding my kimono and obi on top of my bed, smoothing them out carefully so there would be no wrinkles. She wrapped them up again in the soft rice paper and tied them up just the way they were when she'd brought them. Then she put them aside and sat down on my bed.

"I think I understand how you feel, Rinko," she said in a soft whispery voice. "When I was young and couldn't run or play with my friends, they used to tease me and call me a cripple. They often made me cry."

I thought of the old photograph of Aunt Waka standing with the crutch. "But you were smiling anyway," I said, as if she'd know what I was remembering.

"Just because you're different from other people doesn't mean you're not as good or that you have to dislike yourself," she said.

She looked straight into my eyes, as if she could see all the things that were muddling around inside my brain.

"Rinko, don't ever be ashamed of who you are," she said. "Just be the best person you can. Believe in your own worth. And someday I know you'll be able to feel proud of yourself, even the part of you that's different...the part that's Japanese.

I was still in my slip sitting next to Aunt Waka and wriggling my toes as I listened to her. And then it happened, like a light bulb had been switched on in my head. At that very minute I finally knew what made Aunt Waka seem so special. She was exactly the kind of person she was telling me to be. She believed in herself and she liked herself. But mostly, I guess she was proud of who she was.

cripple a person who is partly disabled or lame

wriggling turning and twisting

Further Reading

Dragonwings. Laurence Yep. This is the story of Moon Shadow, a Chinese immigrant boy who helps his father test their homemade airplane.

Sunday for Sona. Gladys Yessayan Cretan. Sona's work on a sailboat brings her into conflict with her strict Armenian grandmother.

Soy Chicano: I Am a Mexican-American. Bob Fitch and Lynne Fitch. This book tells about Guadalupe Maria Saludo and the Mexican-American farm laborers of California.

Journey Home. Yoshiko Uchida. Yuki and her family return to California after World War II.

LESSON 2

The Global Village

THINKING FOCUS

How do communications and trade link us to the rest of the world?

Key Terms

- telecommunication
- export
- import

Your jeep rumbles along through the Amboseli Game Reserve in Kenya, East Africa. Ahead of you towers Mount Kilimanjaro, topped with snow. The cool distant icecap looks out of place above the hot African plain.

Did you hear those monkeys chattering while their young ones leaped about in the vines? And there's a lion, taking a lazy afternoon nap. Your driver slows the jeep to a stop so you can watch giraffes nibble the leaves on the highest tree branches. Hoping to see an elephant, you look for the signs—flat grass, broken branches, and trees with their bark rubbed off. But instead of an elephant, you suddenly spot a cape buffalo. With huge curled horns and gleaming eyes, the animal is charging straight towards you!

As the jeep's wheels spin in the dirt road, you hear a familiar voice calling, "Turn off that safari video and go clean your room!"

➤ *Thanks to modern communication, you can visit places such as the African grasslands, where this female lion lives.*

Fast-Moving Ideas

By renting a videotape or simply by watching television, you can enjoy many adventures without ever leaving home. Just as people are traveling farther and faster, pictures from faraway places are also reaching us more quickly than ever before.

Today's world is circled by a giant information network that grows larger every year. In the past, we depended on books, newspapers, and letters, to share thoughts and ideas with people in faraway places. We still use these printed materials. But we also use **telecommunication**. This is any electronic system used to exchange information over huge distances. Telephones, televisions, computers, and radios are examples of telecommunication systems. These systems connect us almost instantly with people living thousands of miles away.

▼ Telephones that carry pictures and sound could be sold to households by the year 2000.

Messages from Space

Satellites make telecommunication possible. Today, hundreds of human-made satellites circle the Earth. The satellites relay telephone calls, computer images, television pictures, and information from books, to receivers anywhere in the world. It used to take a month of sea travel for a letter to reach Europe. Today students in The United States can communicate with European students in seconds.

Satellites also have cameras in them that take pictures of the Earth's surface. The pictures give scientists information such as the direction of a storm, or changes in the earth's surface that may signal an earthquake.

In 1969, telecommunication let 100 million viewers watch the first person land on the moon. By 1988, 30 times that number of people watched the Olympic Games. ■

■ Which objects in your home allow you to communicate with people on the other side of the world?

Our Plugged-In World

The fast movement of ideas connects people all over the world and affects almost every part of our lives. Telecommunication is changing the way we work, learn, play, and eat.

For example, telecommunication allows some workers to simply plug in their computers at home and do their

337

> *The Soviet Union launched the first satellite into space in 1957. Since then hundreds of satellites have been used to speed communication and gather important information about the Earth and other planets in the solar system.*

work without having to go to the office. A business in one country can now hire people from many countries to do jobs such as word processing, computer programming, and telephone sales.

Telecommunication will change school, too. Computers are now used to link students with faraway teachers and to send written messages between students on different continents. Try to imagine the electronic classroom of the future. Students in three or four classrooms in different parts of the country will be able to see and talk with one another as though they were all in the same room!

As we discover more about the people we share the world with, we can learn about other people and cultures. For example, a group of sixth grade students in Arizona sent a computer message to some Inuit students in Alaska, asking them what they liked to eat. One Inuit student answered, "whale fat mixed with seal oil."

At the same time, many other foods the Inuit listed sounded much more familiar. We are learning that while the world is still different, it is becoming more alike. Today, people all over the world listen to much of the same music and watch many of the same TV programs. In January 1990, a 12-year-old Russian boy in St. Petersburg wrote his pen-pal in Illinois about the video games he likes to play and the movie stars from the United States he admires.

We even eat many of the same foods as people who live far away. Italian food is a favorite. The pizza that people in the United States eat each day would cover 75 acres of land. And have you ever heard the expression "American as apple pie"? That's a food people in Moscow can't seem to get enough of in their newest fast-food restaurant. In a world where ideas travel so quickly, national borders are beginning to fade. ■

■ *In what ways are we becoming more like people who live in other parts of the world?*

One Big Marketplace

National borders begin to fade even more when we try to figure out where our belongings come from. Consider your family's car, for example. Even if your car was made in the United States, many of its parts are imports from all over the world. An **import** is a product that a country brings in from another country to buy. Look at the map below that shows all the places one United States car company gets parts, puts them together, and sells its cars.

For example, your car's transmission may have been imported from France, its electronic parts from Canada, its ball bearings from Puerto Rico, its engine from Brazil, and its radio from Japan. The car company may have bought the platinum used to make your car's anti-pollution system from the Soviet Union. The undercoating that protects your car from icy road salts started out as zinc. Perhaps this min-

▼ *How many different countries are involved in the car business?*

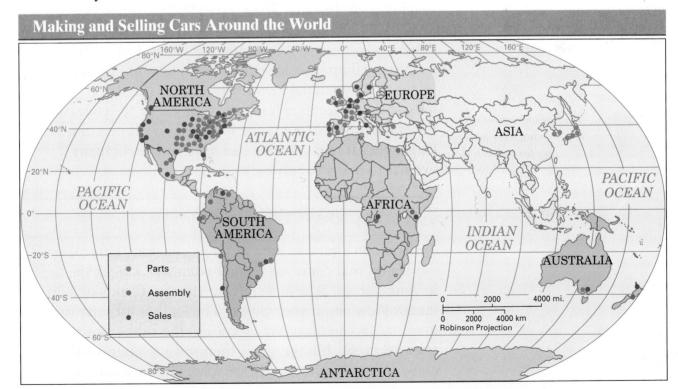

Making and Selling Cars Around the World

- Parts
- Assembly
- Sales

0   2000   4000 mi.

0   2000   4000 km
Robinson Projection

➤ *Millions of workers in countries all over the world helped make the cars you see in a parking lot.*

eral was mined in Australia. The cloth that makes up the seats may have been sewn by workers in Mexico, then shipped back to the United States to be put into your car. Finally, the rubber to make the tires was probably harvested from trees in Malaysia or Africa.

The rubber Malaysia ships to the United States is called an export. An **export** is a product one country sends to another country to be sold.

The United States sends many exports to other countries, including the wheat used in Italy to make spaghetti and lasagna. The United States also buys many imports from other countries, including coffee from South America.

■ *Name three countries on different continents that may have supplied the parts for an American car.*

Many companies have found that they are most successful when they sell their products all over the world. Take a look at the instruction book for your car or for your calculator or tape recorder. Are the instructions printed in several languages? If they are, you can tell that the company exports to many countries. ■

The Whole World's Business

You don't need to look as far as your car to find everyday things that come from other countries. Check the tags in your clothes. Where were your shirt and pants or skirt made? How about your shoes? The leather for your shoes may have come from Argentina and the rubber for the soles from Malaysia, but the shoes themselves were probably made somewhere in Southeast Asia. On the world map on pages 400–401 can you find the many places that supplied the clothes and belongings you used today?

As you saw with your car and shoes, it's not always possible to say where a product is "from." Today, more and more companies with partners from many countries are working together to make the cars we drive, the clothes and shoes we wear, the newspapers we read, and the foods we eat. To make a single product, an international company may use managers and machinery from one country, money and workers from another, and raw materials from other countries.

Improvements in transportation help these materials and finished products move more quickly among countries. And with telecommunication, computers can instantly send billions of dollars from one country to another. Since computers don't need to sleep, global trading goes on 24 hours a day.

Today we can no longer talk about any one country's business. The business of any one country affects many other countries as well. Along with the movement of people and ideas, the movement of products from country to country has also helped to bring our world closer together. ■

People from around the world exchange goods and money every day. The money pictured here comes from Australia, Japan, Italy, and France. How is the money similar to United States' money? How is it different?

■ *Why might it be difficult to say where a particular product is from?*

R E V I E W

1. **FOCUS** How do communication and trade link us to the rest of the world?

2. **CONNECT** Which region of the United States is best known for its car manufacturing? How do you think people in this region feel about more and more foreign cars being exported into the United States?

3. **CULTURE** Name three ways you could learn more about a child who lives on the other side of the world.

4. **CRITICAL THINKING** How has improved transportation allowed companies to use parts and laborers from so many different countries to make their products?

5. **ACTIVITY** Bring to class a newspaper article that discusses trade or communication between two different countries.

341

Sharing Our World

What kinds of action are needed to protect the earth?

Key Terms

- community
- recycling

➤ *The Great Barrier Reef is the biggest coral reef in the world. Thousands of sea animals make their home among the colorful coral.*

Zip yourself into your wetsuit. Get your goggles and mouthpiece in place. Now, dive!

You're going to the coast of Australia to visit the largest underwater apartment house in the world. It's called the Great Barrier Reef, and it's just under the surface of the Pacific Ocean. This "house" is home to billions of sea animals and plants. It's as large as the state of Kansas and as colorful as any garden on land.

The 1,250-mile reef is a structure made of limestone. The limestone is actually the shells of tiny animals, called coral, that have grown there and then died. Over millions of years, all those old shells have created a huge barrier under the water. Millions of coral animals still grow on the reef, so it keeps getting bigger and bigger. Some parts of the barrier have actually grown so high that they've become islands.

As you dive into the reef you see strange, beautiful sights. A 400-pound sea turtle glides slowly through coral that looks like a deer's antlers. Thousands of fish surround you, living and feeding among the coral. One has a blue face with yellow polka dots. Another fish seems to have blown itself up like a balloon.

You can only stay down here for a few hours while your air supply lasts. The fish are luckier, though. They get to stay here all the time.

Protecting Our Oceans

The creatures living along the reef need each other to survive. Damage to one life form can upset the delicate balance of life throughout the reef. For example, in recent times, fishermen have caught so many sharks that the shark population around the reef has gone way down. That can cause an increase in the population of the type of fish the shark usually eats. All those fish, in turn, gobble up too much of the food supply. The balance is upset.

Humans present many dangers to ocean life, not just near the Great Barrier Reef, but throughout the world. The huge oil tankers sometimes crash or leak, spilling sticky, poisonous oil into the ocean. This oil kills fish and birds.

Some countries and cities load tons of garbage onto ships and dump it far out to sea. Items like plastic garbage bags don't just disappear in the water. They stay there for hundreds of years. Whales and other fish can swallow them or get trapped in them. And the garbage just keeps coming.

Protecting the oceans is one of the largest environmental problems on Earth. Nearly three-fourths of the world is covered by water. The oceans touch each of the seven continents. So the problem can only be solved by the whole world community. **A community** is a group of people who live together or share ideas and problems. The people who share this planet and its problems are a community.

Saving all the Earth's oceans will require the cooperation of the world community. Australia, for example, is taking steps to protect the Great Barrier

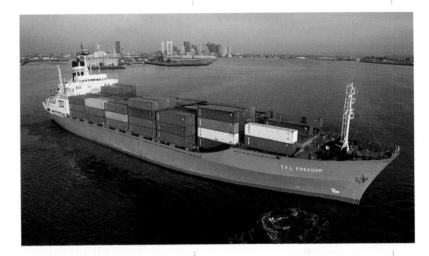

▼ *Huge container ships carry goods around the world. Increased ship traffic has increased the chance of collisions and oil spills.*

Across Time & Space

During the 1960s and 1970s, there was a major effort to clean up dirty lakes and rivers in the United States. One river, the Cuyahoga in Cleveland, Ohio, had so much oil and chemicals in it that it used to catch on fire. Today the river is much cleaner, and fish have started to return to it.

► *Shipping accidents harm wildlife in the water and on the land. A worker is shown here cleaning up oil that spilled from a tanker in Alaska.*

Reef. Most of the reef is now a national park. Fishing is limited or banned in some areas.

But many other countries will have to work to keep the oceans healthy and clean. They will need to find better ways to clean up oil spills and to prevent future spills. They will also need to find new ways to get rid of garbage. ■

■ *How can the world community help protect the oceans?*

UNDERSTANDING COMMUNITY

When Anthony Sorrentino and his family came to the United States, they settled in a community made up of Italian immigrants. Here they shared common tools, customs, and beliefs with other families that had come from Italy.

A community is a group of people who have similar concerns and who believe they belong to the group. But community is not just any group of people. For example, not all the people who have brown eyes are a community. To be a community, people must share the same customs and have some common purpose.

You belong to many different communities. You may be a member of a community of people who share the same race, culture, or religion. The group of people who make up your school, your neighborhood, your city or town, your state, your region, and your country are some of the communities you belong to.

In addition to these communities, you also belong to a much larger community, the world community. Each day advances in travel, communication, and trade bring you in closer touch with the rest of this community. You are learning how many interests and goals you share with your world neighbors. Donald Williams, a United States astronaut, put it this way: "The things that we share in our world are far more valuable than those which divide us."

344

You Can Help

Individuals like you can help too—even with a problem as big as the oceans. For example, think about what kinds of garbage you throw away. Today, many materials can be recycled. **Recycling** is the process of taking scrap materials and using them over again. Materials such as glass, tin, aluminum, paper, and plastic can be recycled instead of being thrown out. For example, most newspapers are made from recycled paper. Plastic bottles can be recycled by shredding them and using the shreds as packaging material. The more you reuse and recycle, the less garbage that will be thrown into dumps or into the oceans. This is one of many ways you can help save the environment.

The Earth needs your help. Russian astronaut Aleksandr Aleksandrov could tell you why. When he saw the planet from space, he wrote about what he saw. ■

▲ *By separating his trash for recycling, this boy is doing his part to make the Earth a cleaner place.*

■ *Why is recycling important?*

*O*ne morning I woke up and decided to look out the window, to see where we were. We were flying over America . . . . A few minutes later we were flying over the Atlantic, then Europe, and then Russia. . . . And then it struck me that we are all children of our Earth. It does not matter what country you look at. We are all Earth's children and we should treat her as our Mother.

R E V I E W

1. **FOCUS** What kinds of action are needed to protect the earth?
2. **CONECT** What does the Great Barrier Reef have in common with other national parks you've learned about?
3. **GEOGRAPHY** Why are the oceans important to the whole world?
4. **CRITICAL THINKING** Choose one enterprise in this book and explain how it affects the land or water. How do you think that industry could help protect the environment?
5. **ACTIVITY** Make a list of glass, paper, and plastic items that you throw away. If your family recycles any materials, make a list of those too.

345

Global Connections

Planning a Project

When you work in a group, you can do projects that one person cannot do alone. Suppose you and a group of your classmates are thinking, after reading Lesson 3, about doing a project that will help protect the environment. A group discussion is a good way both to choose a project to do together and to get started.

Here's How

To have a discussion, follow these guidelines.

1. Stick to the discussion topic.
2. Join in the discussion. Give your ideas, and ask questions about points that are not clear to you.
3. Listen carefully to the ideas of others. Wait quietly for your turn to speak. Do not interrupt when someone else is speaking.
4. Think before you speak. Speak so that everyone can understand you.

Some students in Mr. Nakamura's fourth-grade class had a discussion to decide on a project. As you read part of what they said, keep the discussion guidelines in mind.

> Jill: Let's tell people to recycle paper.
> Lee: That's a silly idea!
> Jo: I think—
> Sam: Did you read the comics today?
> Carlo: Jill's idea about recycling paper is really good. How could we tell people, Jill?

Which students were following the guidelines? Which ones weren't?

Try It

Have a discussion with four or five other students. Suppose you want to tell your neighbors and friends why it is important to recycle paper. How would you plan this project? Be sure to follow the guidelines for discussion.

Apply It

Meet with five classmates to discuss a service project that you can do for your community. Write a list of discussion topics similar to those below. When you have decided on a project, plan how to do it. Share your plan with the class, and then put your plan into action.

Recycling Project: Topics for Discussion
1. What do we know about recycling in our community?
2. What more do we need to find out?
3. Whom do we need to contact to get more information?
4. What jobs are there to do?
5. How many people do we need?
6. How do we let people know about our project?

Chapter Review

Reviewing Key Terms

community (p. 343)   recycling (p. 345)
export (p. 340)   telecommunication (p. 337)
import (p. 339)   transatlantic (p. 329)

A. Choose the key term that best completes each sentence.

1. We can help limit the amount of garbage that litters the Earth by ____ as many materials as we can.
2. Many businesses in the United States ____ their products to many countries around the world.
3. People in a ____ live together or share many of the same ideas and problems.
4. When we trade with other countries, we often ____ their goods and raw materials into our country.
5. Through ____, ideas and information travel quickly throughout the world.
6. A ____ airplane flight could take off from Philadelphia and land in London, England.

B. Write a sentence for each pair of words below.

1. recycling, garbage
2. community, people
3. export, nations
4. telecommunication, satellites
5. transatlantic, travelers

Exploring Concepts

A. Copy the cluster diagram below on a separate piece of paper. Use information from the chapter to add other words related to each "link with the world."

B. Write a paragraph telling how transportation, trade, and telecommunications link distant areas of the world.

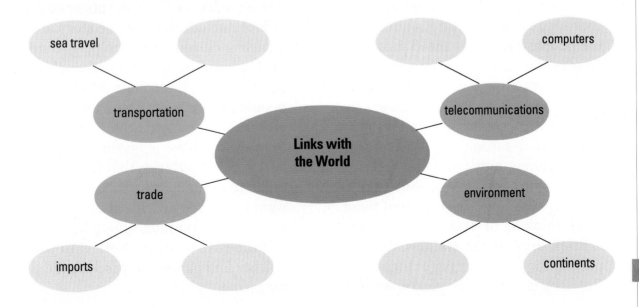

Reviewing Skills

1. Suppose your class is having a discussion to plan the yearly field trip. The class must first decide where it wants to go. Everyone has lots of ideas, and soon the whole class is talking excitedly. The classroom gets noisy. How can the class get the discussion under control so they can make a decision?

2. As the discussion continues, someone suggests a day trip to visit your state government representatives. You're not sure what the representatives do. Is knowing this information important to the decision you may make about where to go on the class trip?

3. Using the state information contained in the Minipedia on pages 350–399, make a bar graph showing the population of your state and two other states in your region.

Using Critical Thinking

1. Based on what you have learned about the Native Americans and their view of the land, explain what they might think of the statement made by the Soviet cosmonaut: "We are all Earth's children and we should treat her as our mother."

2. Some people call the United States a "melting pot" of different people. Other people have called the United States a "salad bowl" of people from other countries and cultures. Explain what you think these two terms mean. How do these two terms differ?

3. People often have mistaken views about citizens of other countries. How can traveling to other countries or meeting foreign travelers help people understand each other better?

Preparing for Citizenship

1. **ART ACTIVITY** Each year millions of tourists visit the United States. Design a poster welcoming visitors to your area of the country. Think about the tourist sites, the natural resources, or the people you may want to show on your poster. You may want to use the state information included in the Mini-pedia on pages 350–399 for ideas.

2. **COLLABORATIVE LEARNING** As a class project, put together a magazine about your school community. Everyone in the class should contribute to the project. Form groups to perform each of these tasks: thinking of story ideas, writing articles, drawing illustrations, and putting the magazine pages together. Begin by choosing one person from each group to lead that group's magazine staff.

    The magazine should contain articles about people and events in your school. Include at least one story about an active citizen who is helping to solve problems inside or outside the school community. Also include articles about people in your school who are immigrants to the United States. Or, you may want to have magazine staff members write about trips that they have taken to other countries. You may also want to include articles about projects your school community is doing to protect the environment. Work with your teacher and parents to produce the magazine.

Time/Space Databank

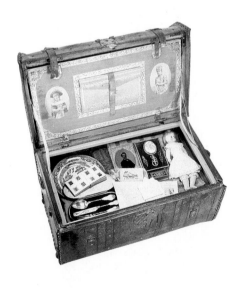

Alabama   Facts in brief

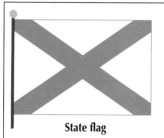

State flag

The state flag, adopted in 1895, bears a diagonal crimson cross on a white field. The cross is suggestive of the Confederate battle flag.

Government

Statehood: Dec. 14, 1819, the 22nd state.
State capital: Montgomery

State government
Governor: 4-year term
State senators: 35; 4-year terms
State representatives: 105; 4-year terms
Counties: 67

Federal government
United States senators: 2
United States representatives: 7
Electoral votes: 9

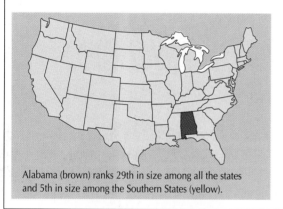

Alabama (brown) ranks 29th in size among all the states and 5th in size among the Southern States (yellow).

Land

Area: 51,705 sq. mi. (133,915 km²), including 938 sq. mi. (2,428 km²) of inland water but excluding 560 sq. mi. (1,450 km²) of Gulf of Mexico coastal water.
Elevation: *Highest*—Cheaha Mountain, 2,407 ft. (734 m) above sea level. *Lowest*—sea level along the Gulf of Mexico.

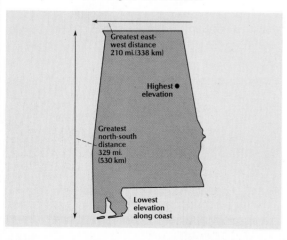

Greatest east-west distance 210 mi. (338 km)
Highest ● elevation
Greatest north-south distance 329 mi. (530 km)
Lowest elevation along coast

People

Population: 4,062,608 (1990 census)
Rank among the states: 22nd
Density: 79 persons per sq. mi. (30 per km²), U.S. average 69 per sq. mi. (27 per km²)
Distribution: 62 per cent urban, 38 per cent rural
Largest cities in Alabama

Birmingham	265,968	Huntsville	159,789
Mobile	196,278	Tuscaloosa	77,759
Montgomery	187,106	Dothan	53,589

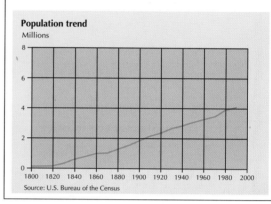

Population trend
Millions
Source: U.S. Bureau of the Census

Economy

Chief products

Agriculture: chickens, beef cattle, eggs, peanuts, cotton.
Manufacturing: paper products, chemicals, primary metals, textiles, clothing, machinery, rubber and plastics products.
Mining: coal, natural gas, petroleum, limestone.

Economic activities

Category	Per cent of gross state product*	Number of employed workers
Manufacturing	23	383,800
Wholesale & retail trade	16	349,100
Government	15	314,700
Community, social, & personal services	15	302,400
Finance, insurance, & real estate	12	70,900
Transportation, communication, & utilities	11	80,100
Construction	3	75,900
Mining	3	63,800
Agriculture	2	11,300
Total	100	1,652,000

*Gross state product = the total value of goods and services produced in a year.

Important dates

1519	Alonso Álvarez de Piñeda of Spain entered Mobile Bay.
1702	French Canadians founded Fort Louis on the Mobile River.
1783	Great Britain gave the United States much of present-day Alabama.
1819	Alabama became the 22nd state on December 14.
1861	Alabama seceded from the Union.
1868	Alabama was readmitted to the Union.
1880	The state's first blast furnace began operating in Birmingham.
1933	The Tennessee Valley Authority was created.
1940's	Huntsville became a center of rocket and spacecraft research.
1965	Martin Luther King, Jr., led a march from Selma to Montgomery to demonstrate the demands of blacks for an end to discrimination in voter registration.
1986	Guy Hunt became the first Republican to be elected governor of Alabama since Reconstruction.

Alaska   Facts in brief

On the state flag, adopted in 1927, the Big Dipper is formed by gold stars representing Alaska's gold resources. The North Star stands for the state's far-north location.

State flag

Government

Statehood: Jan. 3, 1959, the 49th state.
State capital: Juneau

State government
Governor: 4-year term
State senators: 20; 4-year terms
State representatives: 40; 2-year terms
Organized boroughs: 14

Federal government
United States senators: 2
United States representatives: 1
Electoral votes: 3

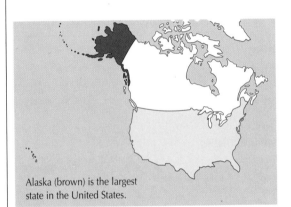

Alaska (brown) is the largest state in the United States.

Land

Area: 591,004 sq. mi. (1,530,700 km²), including 20,171 sq. mi. (52,243 km²) of inland water.
Elevation: *Highest*—Mount McKinley, 20,320 ft. (6,194 m) above sea level. *Lowest*—sea level.

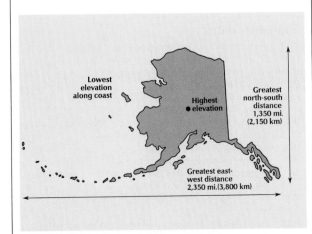

Lowest elevation along coast

Highest elevation

Greatest north-south distance 1,350 mi. (2,150 km)

Greatest east-west distance 2,350 mi.(3,800 km)

People

Population: 551,947 (1990 census)
Rank among the states: 49th
Density: 93 persons per 100 sq. mi. (36 per 100 km²), U.S. average 69 per sq. mi. (27 per km²)
Distribution: 64 per cent urban, 36 per cent rural
Largest cities in Alaska

Anchorage	226,338	College*	11,249
Fairbanks	30,843	Sitka	8,588
Juneau	26,751	Ketchikan	8,263

*Unincorporated place.

Population trend
Thousands

Source: U.S. Bureau of the Census

Economy

Chief products

Fishing industry: salmon.
Manufacturing: food products, petroleum products, wood products, paper products.
Mining: petroleum.

Economic activities

Category	Per cent of gross state product*	Number of employed workers
Mining	34	10,100
Government	16	68,900
Transportation, communication, & utilities	10	20,700
Community, social, & personal services	9	47,100
Wholesale & retail trade	8	44,200
Finance, insurance, & real estate	7	10,500
Manufacturing	7	16,000
Construction	7	9,800
Fishing and agriculture	2	13,200
Total	100	240,500

*Gross state product = the total value of goods and services produced in a year.

Important dates

1741	Captain Vitus Bering, a Danish navigator, landed on Alaskan islands.
1784	Russians established the first white settlement in Alaska on Kodiak Island.
1867	The United States purchased Alaska from Russia.
1897-1898	The Klondike and Alaska gold rush began.
1912	Congress established Alaska as a U.S. territory.
1942	The Japanese invaded the Aleutians.
1959	Alaska became the 49th state on January 3.
1964	A severe earthquake on March 27 caused widespread destruction in south-central Alaska.
1968	Large oil reserves were discovered near Prudhoe Bay.
1977	The Trans-Alaska Pipeline was completed.
1989	The Exxon *Valdez* ran aground in Prince William Sound, spilling over 10 million gallons (38 million liters) of oil.

Arizona   Facts in brief

On the state flag, adopted in 1917, rays represent a setting sun in the colors of Spain, which once controlled the region. A copper-colored star is for the chief mineral product.

State flag

Government

Statehood: Feb. 14, 1912, the 48th state.
State capital: Phoenix

State government
Governor: 4-year term
State senators: 30; 2-year terms
State representatives: 60; 2-year terms
Counties: 15

Federal government
United States senators: 2
United States representatives: 6
Electoral votes: 8

Arizona (brown) ranks sixth in size among all the states and third in size among the Southwestern States (yellow).

Land

Area: 114,000 sq. mi. (295,260 km²), including 492 sq. mi. (1,274 km²) of inland water.
Elevation: *Highest*—Humphreys Peak, 12,633 ft. (3,851 m) above sea level. *Lowest*—70 ft. (21 m) above sea level along the Colorado River in Yuma County.

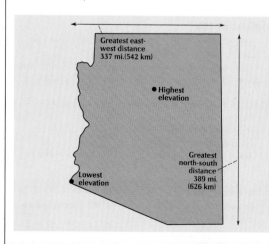

Greatest east-west distance 337 mi.(542 km)
●Highest elevation
Greatest north-south distance 389 mi. (626 km)
●Lowest elevation

People

Population: 3,677,985 (1990 census)
Rank among the states: 24th
Density: 32 persons per sq. mi. (12 per km²), U.S. average 69 per sq. mi. (27 per km²)
Distribution: 84 per cent urban, 16 per cent rural
Largest cities in Arizona

Phoenix	983,403	Glendale	148,134
Tucson	405,390	Tempe	141,865
Mesa	288,091	Scottsdale	130,069

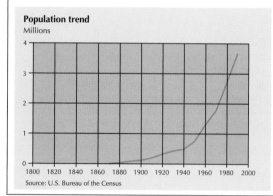

Population trend
Millions

Source: U.S. Bureau of the Census

Economy

Chief products

Agriculture: beef cattle, cotton, milk, lettuce.
Manufacturing: transportation equipment, electrical equipment, machinery.
Mining: copper, gold.

Economic activities

Category	Per cent of gross state product*	Number of employed workers
Community, social, & personal services	20	389,000
Wholesale & retail trade	17	366,700
Finance, insurance, & real estate	16	92,600
Government	15	246,100
Manufacturing	13	188,000
Transportation, communication, & utilities	9	76,700
Construction	7	85,900
Agriculture	2	38,700
Mining	1	12,200
Total	**100**	**1,495,900**

*Gross state product = the total value of goods and services produced in a year.

Important dates

1539	Marcos de Niza, a Franciscan priest, entered what is now Arizona.
1540	Coronado led a Spanish expedition into the region.
1776	Spaniards established a fort at Tucson.
1821	Arizona became part of Mexico.
1848	Mexico ceded most of present-day Arizona to the United States following the Mexican War.
1853	The Gadsden Purchase from Mexico added territory to Arizona.
1912	Arizona became the 48th state on February 14.
1936	The Hoover Dam was completed.
1948	Arizona Indians received the right to vote.
1974	Construction began on the Central Arizona Project, designed to bring water to needy areas of the state.
1975	Raul H. Castro became the first Mexican-American governor of Arizona.
1988	The Arizona Senate convicted Governor Evan Mecham on two misconduct charges and he was removed from office.

Arkansas Facts in brief

The state flag, adopted in 1913, has a diamond-shaped design. It represents Arkansas as a major diamond-producing state.

State flag

Government

Statehood: June 15, 1836, the 25th state.
State capital: Little Rock

State government
Governor: 4-year term
State senators: 35; 4-year terms
State representatives: 100; 2-year terms
Counties: 75

Federal government
United States senators: 2
United States representatives: 4
Electoral votes: 6

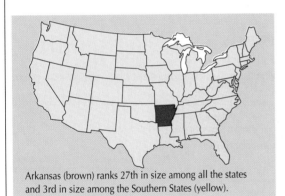

Arkansas (brown) ranks 27th in size among all the states and 3rd in size among the Southern States (yellow).

Land

Area: 53,187 sq. mi. (137,754 km²), including 1,109 sq. mi. (2,871 km²) of inland water.
Elevation: *Highest*—Magazine Mountain, 2,753 ft. (839 m) above sea level. *Lowest*—Ouachita River in Ashley and Union counties, 55 ft. (17 m) above sea level.

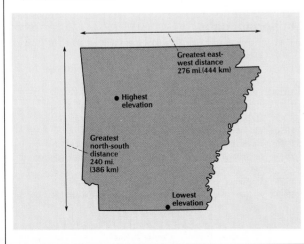

Greatest east-west distance 276 mi.(444 km)

● Highest elevation

Greatest north-south distance 240 mi. (386 km)

Lowest elevation

People

Population: 2,362,239 (1990 census)
Rank among the states: 33rd
Density: 44 persons per sq. mi. (17 per km²), U.S. average 69 per sq. mi. (27 per km²)
Distribution: 52 per cent urban, 48 per cent rural
Largest cities in Arkansas

Little Rock	175,795	Pine Bluff	57,140
Fort Smith	72,798	Jonesboro	46,535
North Little Rock	61,741	Fayetteville	42,099

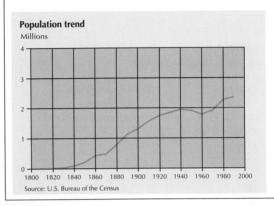

Population trend
Millions

Source: U.S. Bureau of the Census

Economy

Chief products

Agriculture: chickens, soybeans, rice, beef cattle, eggs, cotton.
Manufacturing: food products, electrical equipment, paper products, fabricated metal products, machinery.
Mining: natural gas, petroleum.

Economic activities

Category	Per cent of gross state product*	Number of employed workers
Manufacturing	25	230,000
Wholesale & retail trade	15	204,400
Finance, insurance, & real estate	13	38,300
Community, social, & personal services	13	173,700
Transportation, communication, & utilities	11	54,500
Government	10	154,000
Agriculture	7	63,400
Construction	4	32,500
Mining	2	4,100
Total	100	954,900

*Gross state product = the total value of goods and services produced in a year.

Important dates

1541	Hernando de Soto of Spain explored the region.
1682	René-Robert Cavelier, Sieur de la Salle, claimed the Mississippi Valley for France.
1686	Henri de Tonti of France established a camp at the mouth of the Arkansas River.
1803	The United States acquired Arkansas as part of the Louisiana Purchase.
1836	Arkansas became the 25th state on June 15th.
1921	The first oil well was drilled in the El Dorado field.
1957	National Guard units and federal troops helped enforce a court order to integrate Little Rock's Central High School.
1970	The Arkansas River Development Program opened the river to navigation from the Mississippi River to Oklahoma.
1980	The people of Arkansas voted against the adoption of a new constitution.

California   Facts in brief

The state flag, adopted in 1911, shows a grizzly bear and a single red star.

State flag

Government

Statehood: Sept. 9, 1850, the 31st state.
State capital: Sacramento

State government
Governor: 4-year term
State senators: 40; 4-year terms
Members of theAssembly: 80;
   2-year terms
Counties: 58

Federal government
United States senators: 2
United States representatives: 52
Electoral votes: 54

California (brown) ranks third in size among all the states and is the largest of the Pacific Coast States (yellow).

Land

Area: 158,706 sq. mi. (411,049 km²), including 2,407 sq. mi. (6,234 km²) of inland water but excluding 69 sq. mi. (179 km²) of Pacific coastal water.
Elevation: *Highest*—Mount Whitney, 14,495 ft. (4,418 m) above sea level. *Lowest*—282 ft. (86 m) below sea level in Death Valley.

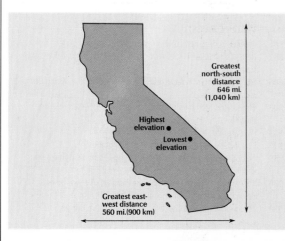

Greatest
north-south
distance
646 mi.
(1,040 km)

Highest
elevation ●

Lowest ●
elevation

Greatest east-
west distance
560 mi.(900 km)

People

Population: 29,839,250 (1990 census)
Rank among the states: 1st
Density: 188 persons per sq. mi. (73 per km²), U.S. average 69 per sq. mi. (27 per km²)
Distribution: 91 per cent urban, 9 per cent rural
Largest cities in California

Los Angeles	3,485,398	San Francisco	723,959
San Diego	1,110,549	Long Beach	429,433
San Jose	782,248	Oakland	372,242

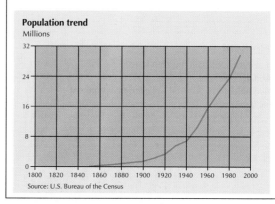

Population trend
Millions

Source: U.S. Bureau of the Census

Economy

Chief products

Agriculture: milk, beef cattle, greenhouse and nursery products, cotton, grapes, hay, tomatoes.
Manufacturing: transportation equipment, machinery, food products, electrical equipment.
Mining: petroleum, natural gas.

Economic activities

Category	Per cent of gross state product*	Number of employed workers
Community, social, & personal services	21	3,271,500
Finance, insurance, & real estate	18	836,300
Wholesale & retail trade	17	2,968,400
Manufacturing	17	2,158,600
Government	12	2,002,100
Transportation, communication, & utilities	7	599,500
Construction	5	643,600
Agriculture	2	454,200
Mining	1	41,600
Total	100	12,975,800

*Gross state product = the total value of goods and services produced in a year.

Important dates

1542   Juan Rodríguez Cabrillo, a Portuguese sailor employed by Spain, explored San Diego Bay.
1769   Junípero Serra established the first Franciscan mission, near the site of present-day San Diego.
1822   California became part of Mexico.
1848   James W. Marshall discovered gold at Sutter's Mill. Mexico gave California to the United States following the Mexican War.
1850   California became the 31st state on September 9.
1906   An earthquake and fire destroyed much of San Francisco.
1915   International expositions at San Diego and San Francisco marked the opening of the Panama Canal.
1963   California became the state with the largest population.
1989   A strong earthquake struck the San Francisco-Oakland-San Jose area.

Colorado   Facts in brief

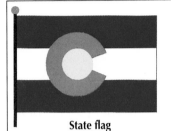

The state flag was adopted in 1911. It has a red C for *Colorado*—Spanish for *colored red*. The golden ball stands for gold production; the bars for blue skies and white snows.

State flag

Government

Statehood: Aug. 1, 1876, the 38th state.
State capital: Denver

State government
Governor: 4-year term
State senators: 35; 4-year terms
State representatives: 65; 2-year terms
Counties: 63

Federal government
United States senators: 2
United States representatives: 6
Electoral votes: 8

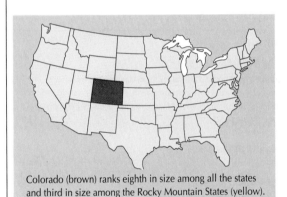

Colorado (brown) ranks eighth in size among all the states and third in size among the Rocky Mountain States (yellow).

Land

Area: 104,091 sq. mi. (269,595 km²), including 496 sq. mi. (1,285 km²) of inland water.
Elevation: *Highest*—Mount Elbert, 14,433 ft. (4,399 m) above sea level. *Lowest*—3,350 ft. (1,021 m) above sea level along the Arkansas River in Prowers County.

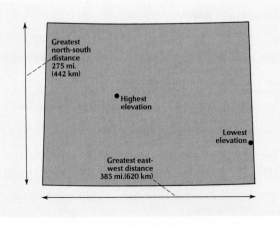

Greatest north-south distance 275 mi. (442 km)
Highest elevation
Lowest elevation
Greatest east-west distance 385 mi.(620 km)

People

Population: 3,307,912 (1990 census)
Rank among the states: 26th
Density: 32 persons per sq. mi. (12 per km²), U.S. average 69 per sq. mi. (27 per km²)
Distribution: 81 per cent urban, 19 per cent rural
Largest cities in Colorado

Denver	467,610	Lakewood	126,481
Colorado Springs	281,140	Pueblo	98,640
Aurora	222,103	Arvada	89,235

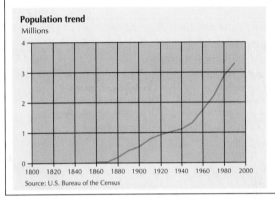

Population trend
Millions

Source: U.S. Bureau of the Census

Economy

Chief products

Agriculture: beef cattle, hay, wheat, milk, corn.
Manufacturing: scientific instruments, food products, machinery, fabricated metal products, electrical equipment, printed materials.
Mining: petroleum, coal, natural gas.

Economic activities

Category	Per cent of gross state product*	Number of employed workers
Community, social, & personal services	20	380,600
Wholesale & retail trade	17	360,400
Finance, insurance, & real estate	15	96,000
Government	14	270,800
Manufacturing	13	193,000
Transportation, communication, & utilities	12	92,700
Construction	4	58,500
Agriculture	3	48,400
Mining	2	19,700
Total	100	1,520,100

*Gross state product = the total value of goods and services produced in a year.

Important dates

1706	Juan de Ulibarri claimed the Colorado region for Spain.
1803	The United States acquired eastern Colorado as part of the Louisiana Purchase.
1848	The United States took western Colorado after the Mexican War.
1858	Gold was discovered at Cherry Creek, near the site of present-day Denver.
1870	The Denver Pacific Railroad was completed to Denver.
1876	Colorado became the 38th state on August 1.
1906	The U.S. Mint in Denver issued its first coins.
1958	The U.S. Air Force Academy's permanent campus opened near Colorado Springs.
1966	North American Air Defense Command—now North American Aerospace Defense Command—completed its operations center in Cheyenne Mountain.

Connecticut   Facts in brief

State flag

The state flag, adopted in 1897, bears a shield with three grapevines. The grapevines symbolize the colony brought from Europe and transplanted in the wilderness.

Government

Statehood: Jan. 9, 1788, the fifth state.
State capital: Hartford

State government
Governor: 4-year term
State senators: 36; 2-year terms
State representatives: 151; 2-year terms
Towns: 169 (no county government)

Federal government
United States senators: 2
United States representatives: 6
Electoral votes: 8

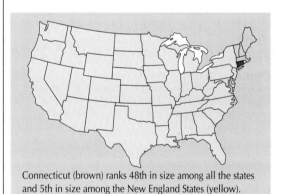

Connecticut (brown) ranks 48th in size among all the states and 5th in size among the New England States (yellow).

Land

Area: 5,018 sq. mi. (12,997 km²), including 147 sq. mi. (380 km²) of inland water and excluding 573 sq. mi. (1,484 km²) of Long Island Sound.
Elevation: *Highest*—2,380 ft. (725 m) above sea level, on the south slope of Mount Frissell. *Lowest*—sea level along the Long Island Sound shore.

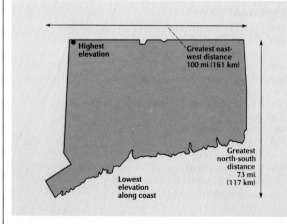

Highest elevation
Greatest east-west distance 100 mi.(161 km)
Greatest north-south distance 73 mi. (117 km)
Lowest elevation along coast

People

Population: 3,295,669 (1990 census)
Rank among the states: 27th
Density: 657 persons per sq. mi. (254 per km²), U.S. average 69 per sq. mi. (27 per km²)
Distribution: 79 per cent urban, 21 per cent rural
Largest cities in Connecticut

Bridgeport	141,686	Waterbury	108,961
Hartford	139,739	Stamford	108,056
New Haven	130,474	Norwalk	78,331

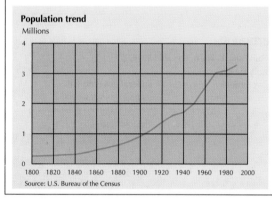

Population trend
Millions

Source: U.S. Bureau of the Census

Economy

Chief products

Agriculture: greenhouse and nursery products, eggs, milk.
Manufacturing: transportation equipment, machinery, fabricated metal products, scientific instruments, chemicals, electrical equipment, printed materials.
Mining: crushed stone.

Economic activities

Category	Per cent of gross state product*	Number of employed workers
Finance, insurance, & real estate	22	151,500
Manufacturing	20	360,200
Community, social, & personal services	18	425,400
Wholesale & retail trade	17	383,500
Government	10	209,200
Transportation, communication, & utilities	8	72,500
Construction	4	76,300
Agriculture	1	21,700
Mining	†	1,300
Total	**100**	**1,701,600**

*Gross state product = the total value of goods and services produced in a year.
†Less than one-half of 1 per cent.

Important dates

1614	Adriaen Block claimed Connecticut for the Dutch.
1633	The first English settlement was made in Windsor.
1636	The towns of Hartford, Wethersfield, and Windsor united to form the Connecticut Colony.
1638	A group of wealthy Puritans founded New Haven.
1639	The Connecticut Colony adopted the Fundamental Orders.
1662	The Connecticut Colony received a charter from England that served as a constitution until 1818.
1665	The Connecticut and New Haven colonies united.
1788	Connecticut became the fifth state on January 9.
1910	New London became the U.S. Coast Guard Academy's home.
1954	The *Nautilus*, the first nuclear-powered submarine, was built and launched in Groton.
1979	Connecticut passed a law banning construction of new nuclear power plants.

Delaware   Facts in brief

The state flag appeared in 1913. On it, a farmer and a soldier support a shield with symbols of agriculture. Dec. 7, 1787, is the date Delaware became the first state.

State flag

Government

Statehood: Dec. 7, 1787, the first state.
State capital: Dover

State government
Governor: 4-year term
State senators: 21; 4-year terms
State representatives: 41; 2-year terms
Counties: 3

Federal government
United States senators: 2
United States representatives: 1
Electoral votes: 3

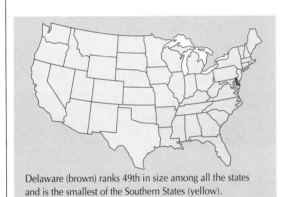

Delaware (brown) ranks 49th in size among all the states and is the smallest of the Southern States (yellow).

Land

Area: 2,044 sq. mi. (5,295 km²), including 112 sq. mi. (290 km²) of inland water but excluding 350 sq. mi. (906 km²) of Delaware Bay.
Elevation: *Highest*—442 ft. (135 m) above sea level on Ebright Road in New Castle County. *Lowest*—sea level along the coast.

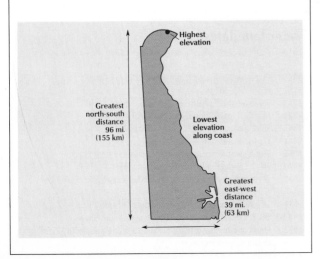

Highest elevation

Greatest north-south distance 96 mi. (155 km)

Lowest elevation along coast

Greatest east-west distance 39 mi. (63 km)

People

Population: 668,696 (1990 census)
Rank among the states: 46th
Density: 327 persons per sq. mi. (126 per km²), U.S. average 69 per sq. mi. (27 per km²)
Distribution: 71 per cent urban, 29 per cent rural
Largest cities in Delaware

Wilmington	71,529	Brookside*	15,307
Dover	27,630	Claymont*	9,800
Newark	25,098	Wilmington Manor*	8,568

*Unincorporated place.

Population trend
Thousands

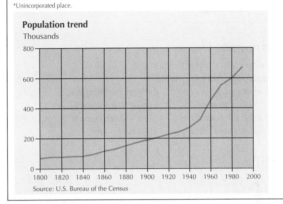

Source: U.S. Bureau of the Census

Economy

Chief products

Agriculture: chickens.
Manufacturing: chemicals, food products, transportation equipment.

Economic activities

Category	Per cent of gross state product*	Number of employed workers
Manufacturing	26	72,600
Finance, insurance, & real estate	21	30,200
Community, social, & personal services	15	82,600
Wholesale & retail trade	14	74,800
Government	10	47,900
Transportation, communication, & utilities	8	14,700
Construction	4	20,400
Agriculture	2	6,500
Mining	†	100
Total	100	349,800

*Gross state product - the total value of goods and services produced in a year.
†Less than one-half of 1 per cent.

Important dates

1609 The English explorer Henry Hudson, sailing for the Dutch, visited Delaware Bay.
1638 Swedish colonists founded New Sweden. They established Fort Christina, Delaware's first permanent white settlement, at present-day Wilmington.
1655 The Dutch captured New Sweden.
1664 The English seized Dutch territory on the Delaware River.
1682 William Penn of England gained control of the region.
1787 Delaware became the first state on December 7.
1802 Éleuthère Irénée du Pont founded a powder mill on the banks of Brandywine Creek.
1951 The Delaware Memorial Bridge opened, connecting Delaware with New Jersey.
1971 The Delaware Coastal Zone Act prohibited construction of industrial plants in coastal areas.

Florida   Facts in brief

The state flag, adopted in 1899, bears diagonal red bars and the state seal. The seal displays a native Florida Indian maiden; a Florida steamboat; and a sabal palm, the state tree.

State flag

Government

Statehood: March 3, 1845, the 27th state.
State capital: Tallahassee

State government

Governor: 4-year term
State senators: 40; 4-year terms
State representatives: 120; 2-year terms
Counties: 67

Federal government

United States senators: 2
United States representatives: 23
Electoral votes: 25

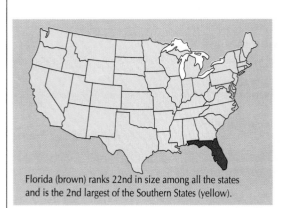

Florida (brown) ranks 22nd in size among all the states and is the 2nd largest of the Southern States (yellow).

Land

Area: 58,664 sq. mi. (151,939 km²), including 4,511 sq. mi. (11,683 km²) of inland water but excluding 1,735 sq. mi. (4,494 km²) of Atlantic and Gulf of Mexico coastal water.
Elevation: *Highest*—345 ft. (105 m) above sea level in Walton County. *Lowest*—sea level.

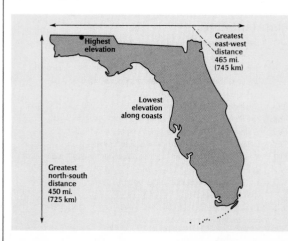

Highest elevation

Greatest east-west distance 465 mi. (745 km)

Lowest elevation along coasts

Greatest north-south distance 450 mi. (725 km)

People

Population: 13,003,362 (1990 census)
Rank among the states: 4th
Density: 222 persons per sq. mi. (86 per km²), U.S. average 69 per sq. mi. (27 per km²)
Distribution: 84 per cent urban, 16 per cent rural
Largest cities in Florida

Jacksonville	672,971	St. Petersburg	238,629
Miami	358,548	Hialeah	188,004
Tampa	280,015	Orlando	164,693

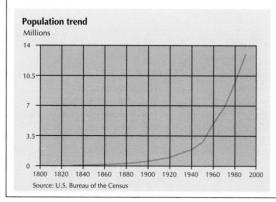

Population trend
Millions

Source: U.S. Bureau of the Census

Economy

Chief products

Agriculture: oranges, greenhouse and nursery products.
Manufacturing: food products, electrical equipment, printed materials, scientific instruments, machinery, chemicals.
Mining: phosphate rock.

Economic activities

Category	Per cent of gross state product*	Number of employed workers
Community, social, & personal services	20	1,502,000
Wholesale & retail trade	19	1,439,700
Finance, insurance, & real estate	19	371,500
Government	12	805,200
Manufacturing	10	541,400
Transportation, communication, & utilities	8	265,700
Construction	6	341,100
Agriculture	2	185,500
Mining	2	9,300
Total	100	5,461,400

*Gross state product = the total value of goods and services produced in a year.

Important dates

1513	Juan Ponce de León landed on the Florida coast and claimed the region for Spain.
1565	Pedro Menéndez de Avilés founded St. Augustine.
1763	Spain ceded Florida to England.
1783	Spain regained control of Florida.
1821	Florida formally came under U.S. control.
1845	Florida became the 27th state on March 3.
1861	Florida seceded from the Union.
1868	Florida was readmitted to the Union.
1920-1925	Land speculators flocked to the state.
1961	The first U.S. manned space flights were launched from Cape Canaveral.
1971	The Walt Disney World opened near Orlando.
1983-1985	Cold and disease destroyed many citrus groves.
1992	Hurricane Andrew caused at least 38 deaths and about $20 billion in damage in Flordia.

Georgia Facts in brief

State flag

The state flag, adopted in 1956, shows one side of the state seal and the Confederate battle flag. On the seal, a man with a sword represents aid in defending the Constitution.

Government

Statehood: Jan. 2, 1788, the fourth state.
State capital: Atlanta

State government
Governor: 4-year term
State senators: 56; 2-year terms
State representatives: 108; 2-year terms
Counties: 159

Federal government
United States senators: 2
United States representatives: 11
Electoral votes: 13

Georgia (brown) ranks 21st in size among all the states and is the largest of the Southern States (yellow).

Land

Area: 58,910 sq. mi. (152,576 km²), including 854 sq. mi. (2,211 km²) of inland water but excluding 48 sq. mi. (124 km²) of Atlantic coastal water.
Elevation: *Highest*—Brasstown Bald Mountain, 4,784 ft. (1,458 m) above sea level. *Lowest*—sea level along the Atlantic coast.

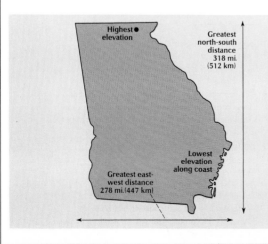

Highest● elevation
Greatest north-south distance 318 mi. (512 km)
Lowest elevation along coast
Greatest east-west distance 278 mi. (447 km)

People

Population: 6,508,419 (1990 census)
Rank among the states: 11th
Density: 110 persons per sq. mi. (43 per km²), U.S. average 69 per sq. mi. (27 per km²)
Distribution: 62 per cent urban, 38 per cent rural
Largest cities in Georgia

Atlanta	394,017	Macon	106,612
Columbus	179,278	Albany	78,122
Savannah	137,560	South Augusta*	55,998

*Unincorporated place

Population trend
Millions

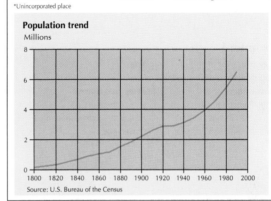

Source: U.S. Bureau of the Census

Economy

Chief products

Agriculture: chickens, peanuts, eggs, beef cattle, hogs, milk.
Manufacturing: transportation equipment, textiles, food products, paper products, chemicals, electrical equipment, clothing.
Mining: clays, crushed stone.

Economic activities

Category	Per cent of gross state product*	Number of employed workers
Wholesale & retail trade	20	752,300
Manufacturing	19	568,200
Community, social, & personal services	16	609,500
Finance, insurance, & real estate	14	163,500
Government	13	512,700
Transportation, communication, & utilities	11	183,900
Construction	4	146,500
Agriculture	2	85,000
Mining	1	8,700
Total	100	3,030,300

*Gross state product = the total value of goods and services produced in a year.

Important dates

1540	The Spanish explorer Hernando de Soto passed through what is now Georgia.
1733	English settlers led by James Oglethorpe established Georgia's first permanent white settlement at present-day Savannah.
1754	Georgia became a British royal province.
1788	Georgia became the fourth state on January 2.
1793	Eli Whitney invented the cotton gin near Savannah.
1861	Georgia seceded from the Union and joined the Confederacy.
1870	Georgia was permanently readmitted to the Union.
1943	Georgia became the first state to allow 18-year-olds to vote.
1973	Maynard H. Jackson, Jr., was elected mayor of Atlanta. He became the first black mayor of a large Southern city.
1983	A new state constitution went into effect.

Hawaii Facts in brief

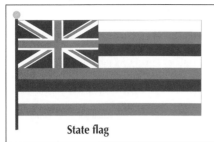

State flag

The state flag, adopted in 1959, bears eight alternating red, white, and blue stripes. They represent Hawaii's eight major islands.

Government

Statehood: Aug. 21, 1959, the 50th state.
State capital: Honolulu

State government
Governor: 4-year term
State senators: 25; 4-year terms
State representatives: 51; 2-year terms
Counties: 5

Federal government
United States senators: 2
United States representatives: 2
Electoral votes: 4

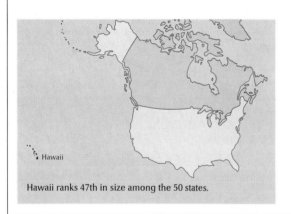

Hawaii ranks 47th in size among the 50 states.

Land

Area: 6,471 sq. mi. (16,759 km²), including 46 sq. mi. (118 km²) of inland water.
Elevation: *Highest*—Mauna Kea, 13,796 ft. (4,205 m) above sea level. *Lowest*—sea level along coast.

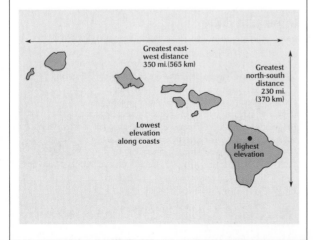

Greatest east-west distance 350 mi.(565 km)
Greatest north-south distance 230 mi. (370 km)
Lowest elevation along coasts
Highest elevation

People

Population: 1,115,274 (1990 census)
Rank among the states: 40th
Density: 172 persons per sq. mi. (67 per km²), U.S. average 69 per sq. mi. (27 per km²)
Distribution: 87 per cent urban, 13 per cent rural
Largest cities in Hawaii

Honolulu	365,272	Kaneohe*	35,448
Hilo*	37,808	Waipahu	31,435
Kailua*	36,818	Pearl City*	30,993

*Unincorporated place.

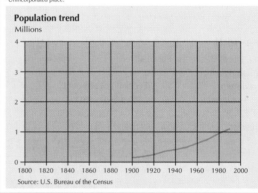

Population trend
Millions

Source: U.S. Bureau of the Census

Economy

Chief products

Agriculture: sugar cane, pineapples, flowers.
Manufacturing: food products, printed materials, petroleum products.
Mining: crushed stone.

Economic activities

Category	Per cent of gross state product*	Number of employed workers
Government	21	101,500
Community, social, & personal services	21	144,600
Finance, insurance, & real estate	18	35,100
Wholesale & retail trade	16	132,900
Transportation, communication, & utilities	10	40,200
Construction	8	29,200
Manufacturing	5	21,300
Agriculture	1	15,700
Mining	†	100
Total	100	520,600

*Gross state product = the total value of goods and services produced in a year.
†Less than one-half of 1 per cent.

Important dates

1778	Captain James Cook of Britain reached Hawaii.
1795	King Kamehameha I unified Hawaii.
1835	The first permanent sugar plantation in Hawaii was started on Kauai Island.
c. 1885	Hawaii's pineapple industry began with the importation of Jamaican pineapple plants.
1893	A revolution led by nine Americans and four Europeans removed Queen Liliuokalani from the throne.
1894	The Republic of Hawaii was established.
1898	The United States annexed Hawaii.
1900	Hawaii became a U.S. territory.
1941	The Japanese attacked Pearl Harbor on December 7, plunging the United States into World War II.
1959	Hawaii became the 50th state on August 21.
1992	Hurricane Iniki caused at least three deaths and much property damage in Hawaii.

Idaho Facts in brief

State flag

The state flag, adopted in 1907, bears the state seal. On the seal, justice is symbolized by a woman holding scales. A miner stands for Idaho's mineral resources.

Government

Statehood: July 3, 1890, the 43rd state.
State capital: Boise

State government
Governor: 4-year term
State senators: 42; 2-year terms
State representatives: 84; 2-year terms
Counties: 44

Federal government
United States senators: 2
United States representatives: 2
Electoral votes: 4

Idaho (brown) ranks 13th in size among all the states and is the smallest of the Rocky Mountain States (yellow).

Land

Area: 83,564 sq. mi. (216,432 km²), including 1,153 sq. mi. (2,985 km²) of inland water.
Elevation: *Highest*—Borah Peak, 12,662 ft. (3,859 m) above sea level. *Lowest*—Snake River at Lewiston in Nez Perce County, 710 ft. (216 m) above sea level.

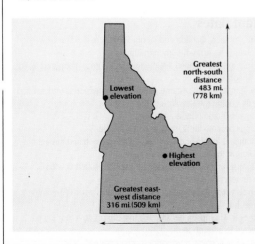

Greatest north-south distance 483 mi. (778 km)
Lowest elevation
Highest elevation
Greatest east-west distance 316 mi. (509 km)

People

Population: 1,011,986 (1990 census)
Rank among the states: 42nd
Density: 12 persons per sq. mi. (5 per km²), U.S. average 69 per sq. mi. (27 per km²)
Distribution: 54 per cent urban, 46 per cent rural

Largest cities in Idaho

Boise	125,738	Nampa	28,365
Pocatello	46,080	Lewiston	28,082
Idaho Falls	43,929	Twin Falls	27,591

Population trend
Millions

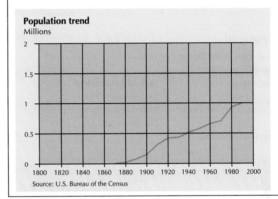

Source: U.S. Bureau of the Census

Economy

Chief products

Agriculture: beef cattle, potatoes, milk, hay, wheat, barley, sugar beets.
Manufacturing: food products, wood products, chemicals, electrical equipment, printed materials.
Mining: silver, phosphate rock, gold.

Economic activities

Category	Per cent of gross state product*	Number of employed workers
Manufacturing	17	60,600
Wholesale & retail trade	16	94,300
Community, social, & personal services	16	76,300
Finance, insurance, & real estate	14	19,300
Government	12	78,100
Agriculture	12	37,700
Transportation, communication, & utilities	9	19,100
Construction	3	16,000
Mining	1	3,600
Total	**100**	**405,000**

*Gross state product = the total value of goods and services produced in a year.

Important dates

1805	Lewis and Clark passed through the Idaho region.
1809	David Thompson, a British explorer, built the first fur-trading post in Idaho.
1860	Mormons founded Franklin, Idaho's first permanent white settlement. Gold was discovered on Orofino Creek.
1863	Congress established the Idaho Territory.
1874	The Utah Northern Railroad entered Idaho at Franklin.
1890	Idaho became the 43rd state on July 3.
1892-1899	Violence broke out between union miners and mine owners.
1951	Electricity was generated from nuclear energy for the first time at a reactor testing station near Idaho Falls.
1959-1968	Engineers completed the Brownlee, Oxbow, and Hells Canyon dams on the Snake River.
1988	Voters approved a state lottery.

Illinois Facts in brief

The state flag, adopted in 1915, bears the state seal. An eagle on the seal holds a shield representing the original 13 states. The sunrise over the prairie represents progress.

State flag

Government

Statehood: Dec. 3, 1818, the 21st state.
State capital: Springfield

State government
Governor: 4-year term
State senators: 59; 2- or 4-year terms
State representatives: 118; 2-year terms
Counties: 102

Federal government
United States senators: 2
United States representatives: 20
Electoral votes: 22

Illinois (brown) ranks 24th in size among all the states and 8th in size among the Midwestern States (yellow).

Land

Area: 56,345 sq. mi. (145,934 km²), including 700 sq. mi. (1,814 km²) of inland water, but excluding 1,526 sq. mi. (3,952 km²) of Lake Michigan.
Elevation: *Highest*—Charles Mound, 1,235 ft. (376 m) above sea level. *Lowest*—279 ft. (85 m) above sea level along the Mississippi River in Alexander County.

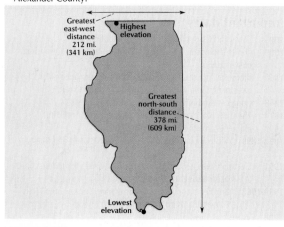

Greatest east-west distance 212 mi. (341 km)
Highest elevation
Greatest north-south distance 378 mi. (609 km)
Lowest elevation

People

Population: 11,466,682 (1990 census)
Rank among the states: 6th
Density: 204 persons per sq. mi. (79 per km²), U.S. average 69 per sq. mi. (27 per km²)
Distribution: 83 per cent urban, 17 per cent rural
Largest cities in Illinois

Chicago	2,783,726	Springfield	105,227
Rockford	139,426	Aurora	99,581
Peoria	113,504	Naperville	85,351

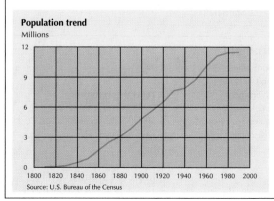

Population trend
Millions

Source: U.S. Bureau of the Census

Economy

Chief products

Agriculture: corn, soybeans, hogs, beef cattle, milk.
Manufacturing: machinery, food products, fabricated metal products, electrical equipment, chemicals, printed materials.
Mining: coal, petroleum, crushed stone, sand and gravel.

Economic activities

Category	Per cent of gross state product*	Number of employed workers
Manufacturing	19	981,500
Community, social, & personal services	19	1,278,800
Wholesale & retail trade	18	1,274,500
Finance, insurance, & real estate	18	372,400
Transportation, communication, & utilities	10	304,400
Government	9	738,000
Construction	4	209,500
Agriculture	2	126,700
Mining	1	19,800
Total	100	5,305,600

*Gross state product = the total value of goods and services produced in a year.

Important dates

1673	Louis Jolliet of Canada and Jacques Marquette of France were probably the first white men in Illinois.
1699	French priests founded a settlement in Cahokia, the oldest town in Illinois.
1783	The Illinois region became part of the United States under the treaty ending the Revolutionary War.
1809	Congress made Illinois a territory.
1818	Illinois became the 21st state on December 3.
1858	Abraham Lincoln and Stephen A. Douglas debated throughout Illinois in their senatorial campaigns.
1942	Scientists at the University of Chicago controlled an atomic chain reaction for the first time.
1970	Illinois voters approved a new constitution, which went into effect July 1, 1971.
1986	James R. Thompson became the first Illinois governor to be elected to a fourth term.

Indiana   Facts in brief

The state flag, adopted in 1917, has a torch that stands for liberty and enlightenment. The 19th and largest star above the torch represents Indiana as the 19th state.

State flag

Government

Statehood: Dec. 11, 1816, the 19th state.
State capital: Indianapolis

State government
Governor: 4-year term
State senators: 50; 4-year terms
State representatives: 100; 2-year terms
Counties: 92

Federal government
United States senators: 2
United States representatives: 10
Electoral votes: 12

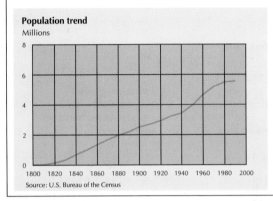

Indiana (brown) ranks 38th in size among all the states and 12th in size among the Midwestern States (yellow).

Land

Area: 36,185 sq. mi. (93,720 km²), including 253 sq. mi. (656 km²) of inland water but excluding 228 sq. mi. (591 km²) of Lake Michigan.
Elevation: *Highest*—1,257 ft. (383 m) above sea level in Wayne County. *Lowest*—320 ft. (98 m) above sea level in Posey County.

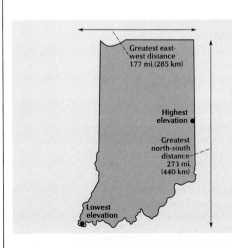

Greatest east-west distance 177 mi.(285 km)

Highest elevation

Greatest north-south distance 273 mi. (440 km)

Lowest elevation

People

Population: 5,564,228 (1990 census)
Rank among the states: 14th
Density: 154 persons per sq. mi. (59 per km²), U.S. average 69 per sq. mi. (27 per km²)
Distribution: 64 per cent urban, 36 per cent rural
Largest cities in Indiana

Indianapolis	731,327	Gary	116,646
Fort Wayne	173,072	South Bend	105,511
Evansville	126,272	Hammond	84,236

Population trend
Millions

Source: U.S. Bureau of the Census

Economy

Chief products

Agriculture: corn, hogs, soybeans.
Manufacturing: primary metals, transportation equipment, electrical equipment, chemicals, machinery, food products.
Mining: coal.

Economic activities

Category	Per cent of gross state product*	Number of employed workers
Manufacturing	28	642,200
Wholesale & retail trade	16	590,400
Finance, insurance, & real estate	15	122,100
Community, social, & personal services	14	503,200
Transportation, communication, & utilities	9	128,100
Government	9	358,500
Construction	5	115,000
Agriculture	3	92,600
Mining	1	7,800
Total	100	2,559,900

*Gross state product = the total value of goods and services produced in a year.

Important dates

1679	The French explorer René-Robert Cavelier, Sieur de La Salle, reached the Indiana region.
c.1732	The French founded Vincennes, Indiana's first permanent white settlement.
1763	France gave up the Indiana region to Great Britain after the French and Indian War.
1779	American soldiers led by George Rogers Clark captured Vincennes during the Revolutionary War.
1816	Indiana became the 19th state on December 11.
1886	The state's first gas well was drilled at Portland.
1889	The Standard Oil Company built one of the world's largest oil refineries in Whiting.
1906	The United States Steel Corporation began building Gary, and put up its largest steel plant there.
1911	The first Indianapolis 500 automobile race was held.
1963	The legislature established a retail sales tax.

Iowa Facts in brief

State flag

The state banner, adopted in 1921, bears the eagle from the state seal. The eagle carries the state motto: *Our Liberties We Prize and Our Rights We Will Maintain.*

Government

Statehood: Dec. 28, 1846, the 29th state.

State capital: Des Moines

State government

Governor: 4-year term

State senators: 50; 4-year terms

State representatives: 100; 2-year terms

Counties: 99

Federal government

United States senators: 2

United States representatives: 5

Electoral votes: 7

Iowa (brown) ranks 25th in size among all the states and 9th in size among the Midwestern States (yellow).

Land

Area: 56,275 sq. mi. (145,753 km²), including 310 sq. mi. (803 km²) of inland water.

Elevation: *Highest*—1,670 ft. (509 m) above sea level along the north boundary of Osceola County. *Lowest*—480 ft. (146 m) above sea level at the junction of the Mississippi and Des Moines rivers in Lee County.

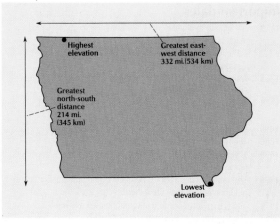

People

Population: 2,787,424 (1990 census)

Rank among the states: 30th

Density: 50 persons per sq. mi. (19 per km²), U.S. average 69 per sq. mi. (27 per km²)

Distribution: 59 per cent urban, 41 per cent rural

Largest cities in Iowa

Des Moines	193,187	Sioux City	80,505
Cedar Rapids	108,751	Waterloo	66,467
Davenport	95,333	Iowa City	59,738

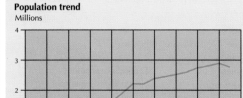

Population trend
Millions

Source: U.S. Bureau of the Census

Economy

Chief products

Agriculture: hogs, corn, soybeans, beef cattle.

Manufacturing: food products, farm machinery, electrical equipment, chemicals, printed materials, transportation equipment.

Mining: limestone, sand and gravel.

Economic activities

Category	Per cent of gross state product*	Number of employed workers
Manufacturing	22	234,000
Finance, insurance, & real estate	18	68,400
Wholesale & retail trade	16	306,400
Community, social, & personal services	15	276,100
Agriculture	9	124,700
Government	9	217,000
Transportation, communication, & utilities	8	55,700
Construction	3	40,500
Mining	†	2,000
Total	100	1,324,800

*Gross state product = the total value of goods and services produced in a year.
†Less than one-half of 1 per cent.

Important dates

1673 Louis Jolliet of Canada and Jacques Marquette of France became the first white people to see Iowa.

1762 France ceded part of its Louisiana colony, including Iowa, to Spain.

1788 Julien Dubuque, a French-Canadian, became Iowa's first white settler.

1800 Spain ceded the Louisiana region back to France.

1803 The United States acquired Iowa in the Louisiana Purchase.

1833 Permanent settlements began in the Iowa region.

1846 Iowa became the 29th state on December 28.

1867 The first railroad was completed across Iowa, from the Mississippi River to Council Bluffs.

1913 The Keokuk Dam was completed.

Mid-1970's Manufacturing overtook agriculture as a source of income in Iowa.

Kansas   Facts in brief

State flag

The state flag, adopted in 1927, has the state seal. On the seal, 34 stars represent Kansas as the 34th state. The farmer and cabin stand for future prosperity through agriculture.

Government

Statehood: Jan. 29, 1861, the 34th state.

State capital: Topeka

State government
Governor: 4-year term
State senators: 40; 4-year terms
State representatives: 125; 2-year terms
Counties: 105

Federal government
United States senators: 2
United States representatives: 4
Electoral votes: 6

Kansas (brown) ranks 14th in size among all the states, and 2nd in size among the Midwestern States (yellow).

Land

Area: 82,277 sq. mi. (213,098 km²), including 499 sq. mi. (1,293 km²) of inland water.

Elevation: *Highest*—Mount Sunflower, 4,039 ft. (1,231 m) above sea level. *Lowest*—680 ft. (207 m) above sea level along the Verdigris River in Montgomery County.

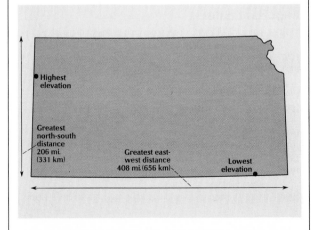

Highest elevation

Greatest north-south distance 206 mi. (331 km)

Greatest east-west distance 408 mi. (656 km)

Lowest elevation

People

Population: 2,485,600 (1990 census)

Rank among the states: 32nd

Density: 30 persons per sq. mi. (12 per km²), U.S. average 69 per sq. mi. (30 per km²)

Distribution: 67 per cent urban, 33 per cent rural

Largest cities in Kansas

Wichita	305,011	Overland Park	111,790
Kansas City	149,767	Lawrence	65,608
Topeka	119,883	Olathe	63,352

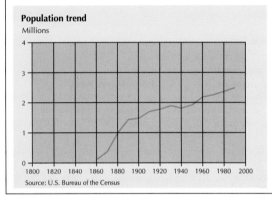

Population trend
Millions

Source: U.S. Bureau of the Census

Economy

Chief products

Agriculture: beef cattle, wheat, grain sorghum, hay, hogs, corn, soybeans.

Manufacturing: transportation equipment, food products, printed materials, chemicals, machinery.

Mining: petroleum, natural gas.

Economic activities

Category	Per cent of gross state product*	Number of employed workers
Manufacturing	19	184,600
Wholesale & retail trade	16	267,000
Finance, insurance, & real estate	16	58,100
Community, social, & personal services	15	231,000
Government	12	210,900
Transportation, communication, & utilities	12	66,000
Agriculture	4	77,100
Construction	4	40,500
Mining	2	9,400
Total	**100**	**1,144,600**

*Gross state product = the total value of goods and services produced in a year.

Important dates

1541	The Spanish explorer Francisco Vásquez de Coronado entered Kansas.
1803	The United States acquired Kansas as part of the Louisiana Purchase.
1821	William Becknell established the Santa Fe Trail.
1850's	Fighting over the slavery issue gave the region the nickname *Bleeding Kansas.*
1861	Kansas became the 34th state on January 29.
1870's	Mennonite immigrants from Russia planted and raised the first Turkey Red wheat in Kansas.
1894	Kansas oil and gas fields began producing.
1905	The country's first helium was discovered at Dexter.
1934-1935	Dust storms damaged great areas of Kansas farmland.
1962	The legislature authorized a statewide system of vocational schools to train workers for new jobs.
1986	Kansas voters approved a state lottery.

Kentucky   Facts in brief

The state flag was adopted in 1918. It bears the state seal, on which a frontiersman and a statesman embrace.

State flag

Government

Statehood: June 1, 1792, the 15th state.
State capital: Frankfort

State government
Governor: 4-year term
State senators: 38; 4-year terms
State representatives: 100; 2-year terms
Counties: 120

Federal government
United States senators: 2
United States representatives: 6
Electoral votes: 8

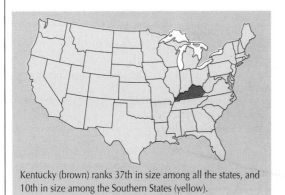

Kentucky (brown) ranks 37th in size among all the states, and 10th in size among the Southern States (yellow).

Land

Area: 40,409 sq. mi. (104,660 km²), including 740 sq. mi. (1,917 km²) of inland water.
Elevation: *Highest*—Black Mountain, 4,145 ft. (1,263 m) above sea level. *Lowest*—257 ft. (78 m) above sea level along the Mississippi River in Fulton County.

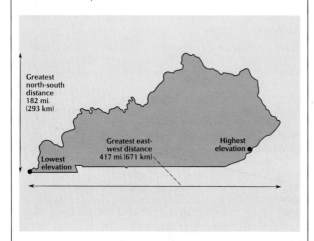

Greatest north-south distance 182 mi. (293 km)

Greatest east-west distance 417 mi.(671 km)

Highest elevation

Lowest elevation

People

Population: 3,698,969 (1990 census)
Rank among the states: 23rd
Density: 92 persons per sq. mi. (35 per km²), U.S. average 69 per sq. mi. (27 per km²)
Distribution: 51 per cent urban, 49 per cent rural
Largest cities in Kentucky

Louisville	269,063	Covington	43,264
Lexington	225,366	Bowling Green	40,641
Owensboro	53,549	Hopkinsville	29,809

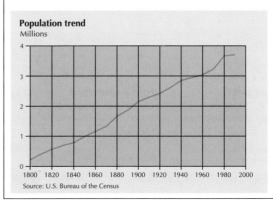

Population trend
Millions

Source: U.S. Bureau of the Census

Economy

Chief products

Agriculture: tobacco, beef cattle, horses, milk, corn, hay.
Manufacturing: transportation equipment, machinery, electrical equipment, food products, chemicals, tobacco products.
Mining: coal.

Economic activities

Category	Per cent of gross state product*	Number of employed workers
Manufacturing	24	238,000
Wholesale & retail trade	14	346,800
Finance, insurance, & real estate	14	60,500
Community, social, & personal services	14	312,900
Government	11	253,200
Transportation, communication, & utilities	9	76,700
Construction	5	66,100
Agriculture	5	119,400
Mining	4	34,100
Total	100	1,553,600

*Gross state product = the total value of goods and services produced in a year.

Important dates

1750	Thomas Walker, a pioneer scout, made the first thorough exploration of what is now Kentucky.
1767	Pioneer Daniel Boone made his first journey to Kentucky.
1774	Harrodsburg, Kentucky's first permanent white settlement, was founded.
1792	Kentucky became the 15th state on June 1.
1904-1909	Western Kentucky farmers broke a tobacco monopoly during the Black Patch War.
1914	The state legislature authorized a statewide system of roads.
1936	The U.S. Treasury established a gold vault at Fort Knox.
1955	Kentucky lowered its voting-age requirement to 18.
1969	The Tennessee Valley Authority completed its largest steam-generating plant, at Paradise.
1990	Kentucky began a statewide reform of its public school system.

Louisiana Facts in brief

The state flag, adopted in 1912, bears a mother pelican in a nest with three young pelicans. The design represents the state as the protector of its people and resources.

State flag

Government

Statehood: April 30, 1812, the 18th state.
State capital: Baton Rouge

State government
Governor: 4-year term
State senators: 39; 4-year terms
State representatives: 105; 4-year terms
Parishes: 64

Federal government
United States senators: 2
United States representatives: 7
Electoral votes: 9

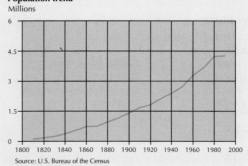

Louisiana (brown) ranks 31st in size among all the states and sixth in size among the Southern States (yellow).

Land

Area: 47,752 sq. mi. (123,677 km²), including 3,230 sq. mi. (8,366 km²) of inland water but excluding 1,016 sq. mi. (2,631 km²) of Gulf of Mexico coastal water.
Elevation: *Highest*—Driskill Mountain, 535 ft. (163 m) above sea level. *Lowest*—5 ft. (1.5 m) below sea level at New Orleans.

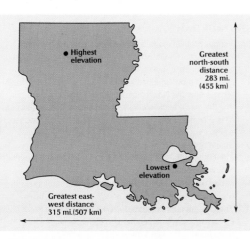

Highest elevation

Greatest north-south distance 283 mi. (455 km)

Lowest elevation

Greatest east-west distance 315 mi. (507 km)

People

Population: 4,238,216 (1990 census)
Rank among the states: 21st
Density: 89 persons per sq. mi. (34 per km²), U.S. average 69 per sq. mi. (27 per km²)
Distribution: 69 per cent urban, 31 per cent rural

Largest cities in Louisiana

New Orleans	496,938	Metairie*	149,428
Baton Rouge	219,531	Lafayette	94,440
Shreveport	198,525	Kenner	72,033

*Unincorporated place.

Population trend
Millions

Source: U.S. Bureau of the Census

Economy

Chief products

Agriculture: soybeans, beef cattle, cotton, milk, rice, sugar cane, corn.
Manufacturing: chemicals, petroleum products, transportation equipment, paper products, food products.
Mining: natural gas, petroleum.

Economic activities

Category	Per cent of gross state product*	Number of employed workers
Mining	15	54,500
Community, social, & personal services	15	344,900
Wholesale & retail trade	14	365,500
Finance, insurance, & real estate	14	78,700
Manufacturing	14	174,000
Transportation, communication, & utilities	11	106,100
Government	10	312,200
Construction	5	80,200
Agriculture	2	52,600
Total	**100**	**1,568,700**

*Gross state product = the total value of goods and services produced in a year.

Important dates

1541	Hernando de Soto led a Spanish expedition into the lower Mississippi River area.
1682	René-Robert Cavelier, Sieur de La Salle, claimed the Mississippi River Valley for France.
1699	The royal French colony of Louisiana was founded.
1803	The United States purchased Louisiana from France.
1812	Louisiana became the 18th state on April 30.
1861	Louisiana seceded from the Union.
1868	Louisiana was readmitted to the Union.
1879	The mouth of the Mississippi River was deepened so that large ocean ships could reach New Orleans.
1901	Oil was discovered near Jennings and White Castle.
1963	The Mississippi River-Gulf Outlet, a short-cut for shippers between New Orleans and the sea, opened.
1975	A new state constitution went into effect.

Maine   Facts in brief

State flag

The state flag, adopted in 1909, bears the state seal. On the seal, a farmer and a seaman hold a shield that symbolizes the state's forests and wildlife areas.

Government

Statehood: March 15, 1820, the 23rd state.
State capital: Augusta

State government
Governor: 4-year term
State senators: 35; 2-year terms
State representatives: 151; 2-year terms
Counties: 16

Federal government
United States senators: 2
United States representatives: 2
Electoral votes: 4

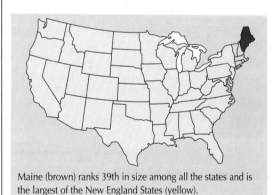

Maine (brown) ranks 39th in size among all the states and is the largest of the New England States (yellow).

Land

Area: 33,265 sq. mi. (86,156 km²), including 2,270 sq. mi. (5,879 km²) of inland water but excluding 1,102 sq. mi. (2,854 km²) of Atlantic coastal water.
Elevation: *Highest*—Mount Katahdin, 5,268 ft. (1,606 m) above sea level. *Lowest*—sea level along the coast.

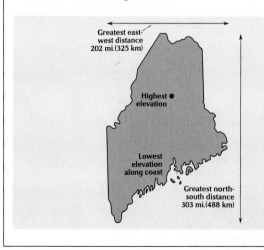

Greatest east-west distance 202 mi.(325 km)

Highest elevation

Lowest elevation along coast

Greatest north-south distance 303 mi.(488 km)

People

Population: 1,233,223 (1990 census)
Rank among the states: 38th
Density: 34 persons per sq. mi. (14 per km²), U.S. average 69 per sq. mi. (27 per km²)
Distribution: 52 per cent rural, 48 per cent urban
Largest cities in Maine

Portland	64,358	Auburn	24,309
Lewiston	39,757	South Portland	23,163
Bangor	33,181	Augusta	21,325

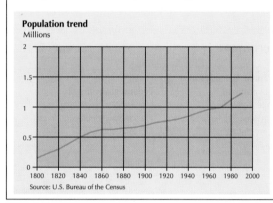

Population trend
Millions

Source: U.S. Bureau of the Census

Economy

Chief products

Agriculture: milk, potatoes, eggs.
Manufacturing: paper products, electrical equipment, transportation equipment, wood products, leather products, food products.
Mining: sand and gravel.

Economic activities

Category	Per cent of gross state product*	Number of employed workers
Manufacturing	19	106,300
Wholesale & retail trade	17	138,600
Finance, insurance, & real estate	17	25,500
Community, social, & personal services	16	123,600
Government	12	94,700
Transportation, communication, & utilities	8	21,900
Construction	7	33,100
Agriculture & fishing	3	21,000
Mining	1	100
Total	100	564,800

*Gross state product = the total value of goods and services produced in a year.

Important dates

1000? Vikings probably visited the Maine coast.
1607 English settlers established the Popham Colony near the mouth of the Kennebec River.
1641 Gorgeana (now York) became the first chartered English city in what is now the United States.
1775 The first naval battle of the Revolutionary War took place off the Maine coast. Patriots captured the British armed schooner *Margaretta*.
1820 Maine became the 23rd state on March 15.
1842 The Webster-Ashburton Treaty settled a long dispute over the Maine-Canada border.
1911 Maine adopted a direct-primary voting law.
1969 Maine adopted personal and corporate incoming taxes.
1980 The U.S. government agreed to pay $81½ million to the Passamaquoddy and Penobscot Indians of Maine for lands seized during the late 1700's and early 1800's.

Maryland Facts in brief

State flag

The state flag, adopted in 1904, has the coats of arms of two families related to Lord Baltimore. The black-and-gold arms are the Calverts'; the red-and-white, the Crosslands'.

Government

Statehood: April 28, 1788, the seventh state.
State capital: Annapolis

State government

Governor: 4-year term
State senators: 47; 4-year terms
State delegates: 141; 4-year terms
Counties: 23

Federal government

United States senators: 2
United States representatives: 8
Electoral votes: 10

Maryland (brown) ranks 42nd in size among all the states, and 13th in size among the Southern States (yellow).

Land

Area: 10,460 sq. mi. (27,092 km²), including 623 sq. mi. (1,614 km²) of inland water but excluding 1,726 sq. mi. (4,470 km²) of Chesapeake Bay.
Elevation: *Highest*—Backbone Mountain, 3,360 ft. (1,024 m) above sea level. *Lowest*—sea level along the coast.

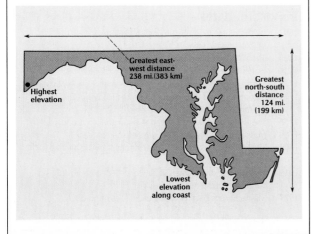

Greatest east-west distance 238 mi. (383 km)
Greatest north-south distance 124 mi. (199 km)
Highest elevation
Lowest elevation along coast

People

Population: 4,798,622 (1990 census)
Rank among the states: 19th
Density: 459 persons per sq. mi. (177 per km²), U.S. average 69 per sq. mi. (27 per km²)
Distribution: 80 per cent urban, 20 per cent rural

Largest cities in Maryland

Baltimore	736,014	Dundalk*	65,800
Silver Spring	76,046	Bethesda*	62,936
Columbia*	75,883		

*Unincorporated place.

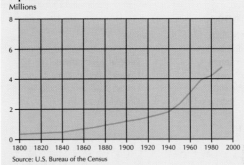

Population trend
Millions

Source: U.S. Bureau of the Census

Economy

Chief products

Agriculture: chickens, milk, greenhouse and nursery products.
Manufacturing: electrical equipment, food products, chemicals, printed materials.
Mining: crushed stone, coal, sand and gravel.

Economic activities

Category	Per cent of gross state product*	Number of employed workers
Community, social, & personal services	22	591,400
Wholesale & retail trade	18	540,500
Government	17	410,700
Finance, insurance, & real estate	17	131,300
Manufacturing	10	209,000
Transportation, communication, & utilities	9	100,800
Construction	6	162,300
Agriculture	1	39,500
Mining	†	1,700
Total	100	2,187,200

*Gross state product = the total value of goods and services produced in a year.
†Less than one-half of 1 per cent.

Important dates

1608	Capt. John Smith of Virginia explored Chesapeake Bay.
1631	William Claiborne of Virginia established a trading post on Kent Island.
1632	King Charles I of England granted the Maryland charter to Cecil Calvert, second Lord Baltimore.
1774	Marylanders burned the *Peggy Stewart* and its cargo of tea in protest against the Boston Port Bill.
1788	Maryland became the seventh state on April 28.
1791	Maryland gave land for the District of Columbia.
1814	Francis Scott Key wrote "The Star-Spangled Banner" during the British bombardment of Fort McHenry.
1828	Construction of the Baltimore & Ohio Railroad began.
1952	The Chesapeake Bay Bridge (now the William Preston Lane, Jr., Memorial Bridge) was opened to traffic.
1972	Maryland voters approved a state lottery to raise money for the state government.

Massachusetts   Facts in brief

The state flag, adopted in 1971, bears a shield on which an Indian—a Massachusetts symbol since 1629—is shown. A star represents Massachusetts as one of the original 13 colonies.

State flag

Government

Statehood: Feb. 6, 1788, the sixth state.
State capital: Boston

State government

Governor: 4-year term
State senators: 40; 2-year terms
State representatives: 160; 2-year terms
Counties: 14

Federal government

United States senators: 2
United States representatives: 10
Electoral votes: 12

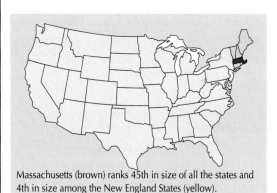

Massachusetts (brown) ranks 45th in size of all the states and 4th in size among the New England States (yellow).

Land

Area: 8,284 sq. mi. (21,456 km²), including 460 sq. mi. (1,191 km²) of inland water but excluding 959 sq mi. (2,484 km²) of Atlantic coastal water.
Elevation: *Highest*—Mount Greylock, 3,491 ft. (1,064 m) above sea level. *Lowest*—sea level along the Atlantic Ocean.

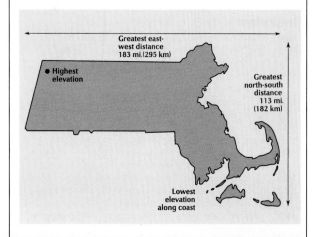

Greatest east-west distance 183 mi.(295 km)

● Highest elevation

Greatest north-south distance 113 mi. (182 km)

Lowest elevation along coast

People

Population: 6,029,051 (1990 census)
Rank among the states: 13th
Density: 728 persons per sq. mi. (281 per km²), U.S. average 69 per sq. mi. (27 per km²)
Distribution: 84 per cent urban, 16 per cent rural
Largest cities in Massachusetts

Boston	574,283	Lowell*	103,439
Worcester	169,759	New Bedford	99,922
Springfield	156,983	Cambridge	95,802

*Unincorporated place.

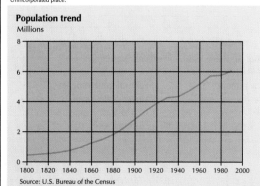

Population trend
Millions

Source: U.S. Bureau of the Census

Economy

Chief products

Agriculture: greenhouse and nursery products, cranberries, milk.
Fishing industry: flounder, scallops.
Manufacturing: machinery, scientific instruments, electrical equipment, printed materials, transportation equipment, fabricated metal products.
Mining: sand and gravel, crushed stone.

Economic activities

Category	Per cent of gross state product*	Number of employed workers
Community, social, & personal services	24	924,700
Manufacturing	19	563,300
Finance, insurance, & real estate	18	217,900
Wholesale & retail trade	17	746,000
Government	9	406,300
Transportation, communication, & utilities	7	128,000
Construction	5	127,700
Agriculture & fishing	1	36,400
Mining	†	1,500
Total	100	3,151,800

*Gross state product = the total value of goods and services produced in a year.
†Less than one-half of 1 per cent.

Important dates

1602	Bartholomew Gosnold, an English explorer, visited the Massachusetts region.
1620	The Pilgrims landed at Plymouth.
1636	Harvard became the first college in the colonies.
1770	British soldiers killed several colonists in the Boston Massacre.
1773	Patriots dumped British tea into Boston Harbor during the Boston Tea Party.
1775	The Revolutionary War began at Lexington and Concord.
1788	Massachusetts became the sixth state on February 6.
1807	The Embargo Act ruined Massachusetts shipping and led to the rise of manufacturing.
1912	A strike of textile workers at Lawrence led to improved conditions in the textile industry.
1971	Massachusetts began to reorganize its government.

Michigan   Facts in brief

State flag

The state flag, adopted in 1911, has a version of the state seal. The bald eagle is for the U.S. government; the elk and moose are for Michigan. *Tuebor* is Latin for *I Will Defend*.

Government

Statehood: Jan. 26, 1837, the 26th state.
State capital: Lansing

State government
Governor: 4-year term
State senators: 38; 4-year terms
State representatives: 110; 2-year terms
Counties: 83

Federal government
United States senators: 2
United States representatives: 16
Electoral votes: 18

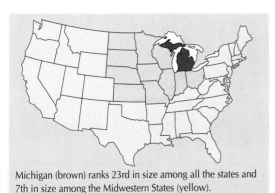

Michigan (brown) ranks 23rd in size among all the states and 7th in size among the Midwestern States (yellow).

Land

Area: 58,527 sq. mi. (151,586 km²), including 1,573 sq. mi. (4,075 km²) of inland water.
Elevation: *Highest*—Mount Curwood, 1,980 ft. (604 m) above sea level. *Lowest*—572 ft. (174 m) above sea level along Lake Erie.

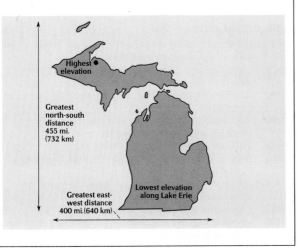

Highest elevation

Greatest north-south distance 455 mi. (732 km)

Greatest east-west distance 400 mi. (640 km)

Lowest elevation along Lake Erie

People

Population: 9,328,784 (1990 census)
Rank among the states: 8th
Density: 159 persons per sq. mi. (62 per km²), U.S. average 69 per sq. mi. (27 per km²)
Distribution: 71 per cent urban, 29 per cent rural
Largest cities in Michigan

Detroit	1,027,974	Flint	140,761
Grand Rapids	189,126	Lansing	127,321
Warren	144,864	Sterling Heights	117,810

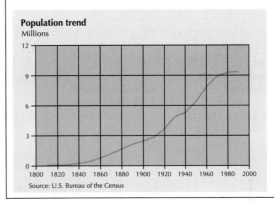

Population trend
Millions

Source: U.S. Bureau of the Census

Economy

Chief products

Agriculture: milk, corn, hay, beef cattle, hogs.
Manufacturing: transportation equipment, machinery, fabricated metal products, chemicals, food products.
Mining: natural gas, iron ore, petroleum.

Economic activities

Category	Per cent of gross state product*	Number of employed workers
Manufacturing	28	976,600
Finance, insurance, & real estate	17	188,600
Community, social, & personal services	17	900,200
Wholesale & retail trade	16	920,400
Government	10	627,300
Transportation, communication, & utilities	7	152,000
Construction	3	137,800
Agriculture	1	93,900
Mining	1	10,700
Total	100	3,998,500

*Gross state product = the total value of goods and services produced in a year.

Important dates

1620?	Étienne Brulé, a French explorer, visited what is now Michigan.
1668	Jacques Marquette of France founded Michigan's first permanent white settlement at Sault Ste. Marie.
1783	The United States gained Michigan from the British after the Revolutionary War.
1837	Michigan became the 26th state on January 26. Congress gave Michigan the entire Upper Peninsula.
1845	Michigan's iron-mining industry began at Negaunee.
1899	Ransom E. Olds established Michigan's first automobile factory in Detroit.
1935	Michigan's workers formed the United Automobile Workers union.
1957	Mackinac Bridge linked the Upper and Lower peninsulas.
1967	Michigan's legislature adopted a state income tax.
1972	Michigan established a state lottery.

Minnesota   Facts in brief

The state flag, adopted in 1957, has a version of the state seal. The dates indicate first settlement (1819); statehood (1858); and adoption of the original flag (1893).

State flag

Government

Statehood: May 11, 1858, the 32nd state.
State capital: St. Paul

State government
Governor: 4-year term
State senators: 67; 4-year terms
State representatives: 134; 2-year terms
Counties: 87

Federal government
United States senators: 2
United States representatives: 8
Electoral votes: 10

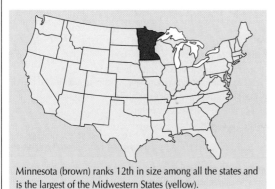

Minnesota (brown) ranks 12th in size among all the states and is the largest of the Midwestern States (yellow).

Land

Area: 84,402 sq. mi. (218,601 km²), including 4,854 sq. mi. (12,571 km²) of inland water but excluding 2,212 sq. mi. (5,729 km²) of Lake Superior.
Elevation: *Highest*—Eagle Mountain, 2,301 ft. (701 m) above sea level. *Lowest*—602 ft. (83 m) above sea level along Lake Superior.

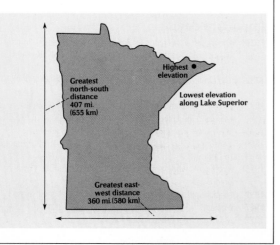

Highest elevation
Greatest north-south distance 407 mi. (655 km)
Lowest elevation along Lake Superior
Greatest east-west distance 360 mi. (580 km)

People

Population: 4,387,029 (1990 census)
Rank among the states: 20th
Density: 52 persons per sq. mi. (20 per km²), U.S. average 69 per sq. mi. (27 per km²)
Distribution: 67 per cent urban, 33 per cent rural
Largest cities in Minnesota

Minneapolis	368,383	Duluth	85,493
St. Paul	272,235	Rochester	70,745
Bloomington	86,335	Brooklyn Park	56,381

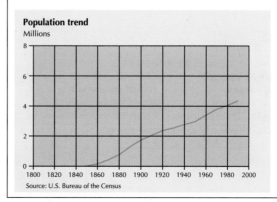

Population trend
Millions

Source: U.S. Bureau of the Census

Economy

Chief products

Agriculture: milk, corn, soybeans, beef cattle, hogs.
Manufacturing: machinery, food products, printed materials, fabricated metal products, scientific instruments, electrical equipment, paper products.
Mining: iron ore.

Economic activities

Category	Per cent of gross state product*	Number of employed workers
Manufacturing	20	399,100
Wholesale & retail trade	18	517,400
Finance, insurance, & real estate	18	120,500
Community, social, & personal services	17	534,400
Government	10	327,600
Transportation, communication, & utilities	9	105,400
Agriculture	4	116,100
Construction	3	79,300
Mining	1	7,500
Total	100	2,207,300

*Gross state product = the total value of goods and services produced in a year.

Important dates

c. 1660 Pierre Esprit Radisson and Médard Chouart, Sieur des Groseilliers, of France visited the Minnesota region.
1679 Daniel Greysolon, Sieur Duluth, of France explored the western shore of Lake Superior.
1783 Great Britain granted the land east of the Mississippi River to the United States.
1803 The United States acquired the Minnesota area west of the Mississippi as part of the Louisiana Purchase.
1858 Minnesota became the 32nd state on May 11.
1884 The first shipment of iron ore from the Vermilion Range left Minnesota.
1889 William W. Mayo and his two sons founded the Mayo Clinic in Rochester.
1955 A Silver Bay plant began processing taconite.
1982 Minnesota adopted a state constitutional amendment establishing a Court of Appeals.

Mississippi   Facts in brief

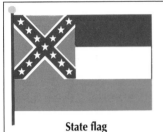

The state flag, adopted in 1894, shows Mississippi's ties to both the United States and the Confederacy. Bars in U.S. colors appear next to the Confederate battle flag.

State flag

Government

Statehood: Dec. 10, 1817, the 20th state.
State capital: Jackson

State government
Governor: 4-year term
State senators: 52; 4-year terms
State representatives: 122; 4-year terms
Counties: 82

Federal government
United States senators: 2
United States representatives: 5
Electoral votes: 7

Mississippi (brown) ranks 32nd in size among all the states and 7th in size among the Southern States (yellow).

Land

Area: 47,689 sq. mi. (123,515 km²), including 457 sq. mi. (1,183 km²) of inland water but excluding 556 sq. mi. (1,440 km²) of Gulf of Mexico coastal water.

Elevation: *Highest*—Woodall Mountain, 806 ft. (246 m) above sea level. *Lowest*—sea level along the coast.

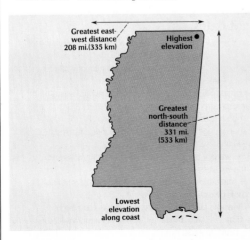

Greatest east-west distance 208 mi. (335 km)
Highest elevation
Greatest north-south distance 331 mi. (533 km)
Lowest elevation along coast

People

Population: 2,586,443 (1990 census)
Rank among the states: 31st
Density: 54 persons per sq. mi. (21 per km²), U.S. average 69 per sq. mi. (27 per km²)
Distribution: 53 per cent rural, 47 per cent urban
Largest cities in Mississippi

Jackson	196,637	Hattiesburg	41,882
Biloxi	46,319	Meridian	41,036
Greenville	45,226	Gulfport	40,775

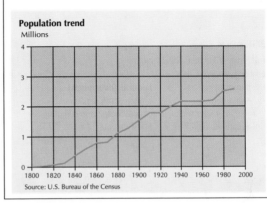

Population trend
Millions

Source: U.S. Bureau of the Census

Economy

Chief products

Agriculture: chickens, cotton, soybeans, beef cattle, milk.
Manufacturing: food products, transportation equipment, electrical equipment, wood products, paper products, clothing, furniture.
Mining: petroleum, natural gas.

Economic activities

Category	Per cent of gross state product*	Number of employed workers
Manufacturing	27	243,400
Wholesale & retail trade	15	197,500
Government	13	200,200
Finance, insurance, & real estate	13	38,900
Community, social, & personal services	12	153,400
Transportation, communication, & utilities	9	45,600
Agriculture	5	54,900
Construction	4	36,400
Mining	2	5,900
Total	100	976,200

*Gross state product = the total value of goods and services produced in a year.

Important dates

1540	Hernando de Soto of Spain entered the Mississippi region.
1699	Pierre le Moyne, Sieur d'Iberville, established Mississippi's first European settlement at Old Biloxi.
1763	England gained control of the region after the French and Indian War.
1817	Mississippi became the 20th state on December 10.
1858	A swamp drainage program began in the Delta.
1861	Mississippi seceded from the Union.
1870	Mississippi was readmitted to the Union.
1936	Mississippi adopted laws to encourage manufacturing.
1939	Petroleum was discovered at Tinsley.
1954	The state legislature passed a law banning required union membership.
1969	A federal court ordered the desegregation of Mississippi's public schools.

Missouri   Facts in brief

State flag

The state flag, adopted in 1913, bears red, white, and blue stripes symbolizing loyalty to the Union. The 24 stars around the coat of arms represent Missouri as the 24th state.

Government

Statehood: Aug. 10, 1821, the 24th state.
State capital: Jefferson City

State government
Governor: 4-year term
State senators: 34; 4-year terms
State representatives: 163; 2-year terms
Counties: 114

Federal government
United States senators: 2
United States representatives: 9
Electoral votes: 11

Missouri (brown) ranks 19th in size among all the states and 6th in size among the Midwestern States (yellow).

Land

Area: 69,697 sq. mi. (180,516 km²), including 752 sq. mi. (1,948 km²) of inland water.
Elevation: *Highest*—Taum Sauk Mountain, 1,772 ft. (540 m) above sea level. *Lowest*—230 ft. (70 m) above sea level, along the St. Francis River near Cardwell.

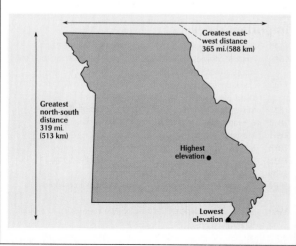

Greatest east-west distance 365 mi. (588 km)
Greatest north-south distance 319 mi. (513 km)
Highest elevation
Lowest elevation

People

Population: 5,137,804 (1990 census)
Rank among the states: 15th
Density: 74 persons per sq. mi. (28 per km²), U.S. average 69 per sq. mi. (27 per km²)
Distribution: 68 per cent urban, 32 per cent rural
Largest cities in Missouri

Kansas City	435,146	Independence	112,301
St. Louis	396,685	St. Joseph	71,852
Springfield	140,494	Columbia	69,101

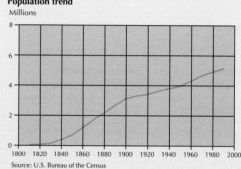

Population trend
Millions
Source: U.S. Bureau of the Census

Economy

Chief products
Agriculture: soybeans, beef cattle, hogs, corn, hay.
Manufacturing: transportation equipment, chemicals, food products, fabricated metal products, printed materials, electrical equipment, machinery.
Mining: limestone, lead, coal.

Economic activities

Category	Per cent of gross state product*	Number of employed workers
Manufacturing	21	438,900
Community, social, & personal services	18	552,800
Wholesale & retail trade	17	569,400
Finance, insurance, & real estate	16	135,100
Transportation, communication, & utilities	11	150,500
Government	10	358,600
Construction	4	97,500
Agriculture	3	124,900
Mining	†	5,200
Total	**100**	**2,432,900**

*Gross state product = the total value of goods and services produced in a year.
†Less than one-half of 1 per cent.

Important dates

1682	René-Robert Cavelier, Sieur de la Salle, claimed the Mississippi Valley, including Missouri, for France.
c. 1735	Settlers established Missouri's first permanent white settlement, at Ste. Genevieve.
1803	The United States acquired the Missouri region as part of the Louisiana Purchase.
1821	Missouri became the 24th state on August 10.
1837	Missouri gained its six northwestern counties as a result of the Platte Purchase.
1854	Border warfare began between antislavery Kansans and proslavery Missourians.
1861-1865	Missouri was a battleground of the Civil War.
1904	St. Louis held the Louisiana Purchase Exposition.
1931	The Bagnell Dam on the Osage River was completed.
1965	The Gateway Arch, the tallest U.S. monument, was completed in St. Louis. It is 630 feet (192 meters) high.

Montana   Facts in brief

The state flag, adopted in 1905, displays an adaptation of the state seal, which symbolizes Montana's vast natural resources. The word *MONTANA* was added to the flag in 1981.

State flag

Government

Statehood: Nov. 8, 1889, the 41st state.
State capital: Helena

State government
Governor: 4-year term
State senators: 50; 4-year terms
State representatives: 100; 2-year terms
Counties: 56

Federal government
United States senators: 2
United States representatives: 1
Electoral votes: 3

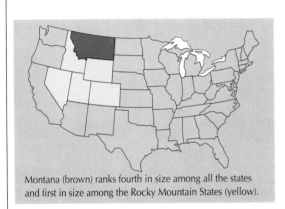

Montana (brown) ranks fourth in size among all the states and first in size among the Rocky Mountain States (yellow).

Land

Area: 147,046 sq. mi. (380,848 km²), including 1,657 sq. mi. (4,293 km²) of inland water.
Elevation: *Highest*—Granite Peak, 12,799 ft. (3,901 m) above sea level. *Lowest*—1,800 ft. (549 m) above sea level along the Kootenai River in Lincoln County.

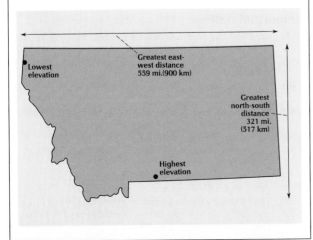

Lowest elevation
Greatest east-west distance 559 mi.(900 km)
Greatest north-south distance 321 mi. (517 km)
Highest elevation

People

Population: 803,655 (1990 census)
Rank among the states: 44th
Density: 5 persons per sq. mi. (2 per km²), U.S. average 69 per sq. mi. (27 per km²)
Distribution: 53 per cent urban, 47 per cent rural

Largest cities in Montana

Billings	81,151	Butte	33,941
Great Falls	55,097	Helena	24,569
Missoula	42,918	Bozeman	22,600

Population trend
Thousands

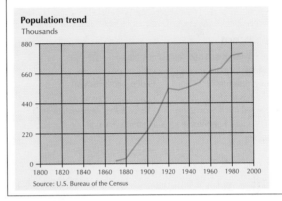

Source: U.S. Bureau of the Census

Economy

Chief products

Agriculture: beef cattle, wheat, hay, barley.
Manufacturing: wood products, food products.
Mining: coal, copper, gold, petroleum.

Economic activities

Category	Per cent of gross state product*	Number of employed workers
Finance, insurance, & real estate	16	13,200
Community, social, & personal services	15	71,600
Wholesale & retail trade	14	77,600
Government	12	70,100
Transportation, communication, & utilities	11	20,000
Agriculture	10	27,600
Mining	8	6,300
Manufacturing	7	22,000
Construction	7	9,700
Total	**100**	**318,100**

*Gross state product = the total value of goods and services produced in a year.

Important dates

1803	The United States acquired eastern Montana as part of the Louisiana Purchase.
1846	Northwestern Montana became U.S. territory as a result of the Oregon treaty with England.
1862	Gold was discovered on Grasshopper Creek.
1876	The Sioux and Cheyenne Indians defeated U.S. Cavalry troops at the Battle of the Little Bighorn.
1877	The Nez Percé Indians surrendered to federal troops.
1889	Montana became the 41st state on November 8.
1910	Congress established Glacier National Park.
1940	Fort Peck Dam was completed.
1951	The first oil wells in the Montana section of the Williston Basin started production.
1955	The Anaconda Aluminum Company dedicated a $65-million plant at Columbia Falls.
1984	The Libby Dam hydroelectric project was completed.

Nebraska   Facts in brief

The state flag, adopted in 1925, bears the state seal. On the seal, a smith with a hammer and an anvil stands for the mechanical arts. Corn and wheat symbolize agriculture.

State flag

Government

Statehood: March 1, 1867, the 37th state.
State capital: Lincoln

State government
Governor: 4-year term
State senators: 49; 4-year terms (Nebraska has a one-house legislature)
Counties: 93

Federal government
United States senators: 2
United States representatives: 3
Electoral votes: 5

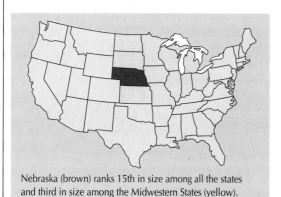

Nebraska (brown) ranks 15th in size among all the states and third in size among the Midwestern States (yellow).

Land

Area: 77,355 sq. mi. (200,350 km²), including 744 sq. mi. (1,927 km²) of inland water.
Elevation: *Highest*—5,426 ft. (1,654 m) above sea level in southwestern Kimball County. *Lowest*—840 ft. (256 m) above sea level in Richardson County.

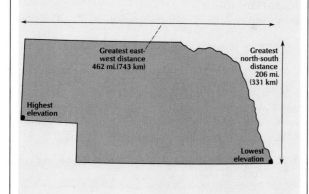

Greatest east-west distance 462 mi.(743 km)
Greatest north-south distance 206 mi. (331 km)
Highest elevation
Lowest elevation

People

Population: 1,584,617 (1990 census)
Rank among the states: 36th
Density: 20 persons per sq. mi. (8 per km²), U.S. average 69 per sq. mi. (27 per km²)
Distribution: 63 per cent urban, 37 per cent rural
Largest cities in Nebraska

Omaha	335,795	Bellevue	30,982
Lincoln	191,972	Kearney	24,396
Grand Island	39,386	Fremont	23,680

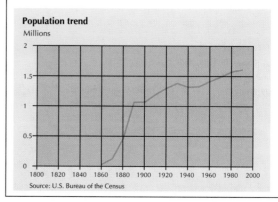

Population trend
Millions
Source: U.S. Bureau of the Census

Economy

Chief products

Agriculture: beef cattle, corn, hogs, soybeans.
Manufacturing: food products, electrical equipment, machinery.
Mining: petroleum.

Economic activities

Category	Per cent of gross state product*	Number of employed workers
Finance, insurance, & real estate	17	48,300
Wholesale & retail trade	17	183,700
Community, social, & personal services	16	167,200
Manufacturing	14	94,800
Government	12	140,500
Transportation, communication, & utilities	11	45,800
Agriculture	10	65,100
Construction	3	23,900
Mining	†	1,500
Total	100	770,800

*Gross state product = the total value of goods and services produced in a year.
†Less than one-half of 1 per cent

Important dates

1682   René-Robert Cavelier, Sieur de la Salle, claimed the region drained by the Mississippi River for France.
1714   Étienne Veniard de Bourgmont of France traveled up the Missouri River to the mouth of the Platte River.
1803   The United States acquired Nebraska as part of the Louisiana Purchase.
1863   One of the first free U.S. homesteads was claimed by Daniel Freeman near Beatrice.
1867   Nebraska became the 37th state on March 1.
1905   The North Platte River Project was begun to irrigate 165,000 acres (66,770 hectares) in western Nebraska.
1934   Nebraskans voted to adopt a one-house legislature.
1939   Petroleum was discovered in southeastern Nebraska.
1967   Nebraska adopted both a sales and an income tax.
1982   Nebraska adopted Initiative 300, which prohibits corporations from buying farms or ranches in Nebraska.

Nevada   Facts in brief

State flag

The state flag, adopted in 1929, bears a silver star. The words *Battle Born* signify Nevada's admission to the Union during the Civil War.

Government

Statehood: Oct. 31, 1864, the 36th state.
State capital: Carson City

State government
Governor: 4-year term
State senators: 21; 4-year terms
Assembly members: 42; 2-year terms
Counties: 17

Federal government
United States senators: 2
United States representatives: 2
Electoral votes: 4

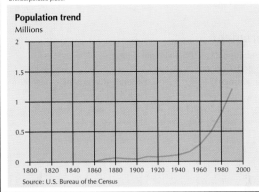

Nevada (brown) ranks seventh in size among all the states and second among the Rocky Mountain States (yellow).

Land

Area: 110,561 sq. mi. (286,352 km²), including 667 sq. mi. (1,728 km²) of inland water.
Elevation: *Highest*—Boundary Peak, 13,140 ft. (4,005 m) above sea level. *Lowest*—470 ft. (143 m) above sea level along the Colorado River in Clark County.

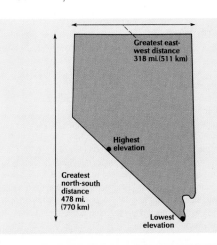

Greatest east-west distance 318 mi. (511 km)
Highest elevation
Greatest north-south distance 478 mi. (770 km)
Lowest elevation

People

Population: 1,206,152 (1990 census)
Rank among the states: 39th
Density: 11 persons per sq. mi. (4 per km²), U.S. average 69 per sq. mi. (27 per km²)
Distribution: 85 per cent urban, 15 per cent rural
Largest cities in Nevada

Las Vegas	258,295	Sunrise Manor*	95,362
Reno	133,850	Henderson	64,942
Paradise*	124,682	Sparks	53,367

*Unincorporated place.

Population trend
Millions

Source: U.S. Bureau of the Census

Economy

Chief products

Agriculture: hay, beef cattle.
Manufacturing: machinery, printed materials, food products.
Mining: gold.

Economic activities

Category	Per cent of gross state product*	Number of employed workers
Community, social, & personal services	35	251,100
Wholesale & retail trade	14	119,700
Finance, insurance, & real estate	13	25,500
Government	10	70,800
Transportation, communication, & utilities	9	30,600
Construction	9	45,600
Mining	5	13,600
Manufacturing	4	25,400
Agriculture	1	8,500
Total	100	590,800

*Gross state product = the total value of goods and services produced in a year.

Important dates

1825-1830	Peter S. Ogden discovered the Humboldt River. Jedediah S. Smith crossed southern Nevada. Both men traveled with fur trappers.
1848	The United States gained Nevada from Mexico after the Mexican War.
1859	Silver was discovered near Virginia City.
1864	Nevada became the 36th state on October 31.
1931	The legislature reduced the divorce residence requirement to six weeks and also legalized gambling.
1936	Boulder (now Hoover) Dam was completed.
1951	The Atomic Energy Commission began testing nuclear weapons in southern Nevada.
1980	The legislature passed conservation laws to protect Lake Tahoe from pollution.
1983	The Water Project (now the Robert B. Griffith Water Project) brought more water to the Las Vegas area.

New Hampshire   Facts in brief

The state flag, adopted in 1909, has the state seal. It shows the Revolutionary War frigate *Raleigh*, which was built in Portsmouth. A granite boulder is for the state's rugged terrain.

State flag

People

Population: 1,113,915 (1990 census)
Rank among the states: 41st
Density: 119 persons per sq. mi. (46 per km²), U.S. average 69 per sq. mi. (27 per km²)
Distribution: 52 per cent urban, 48 per cent rural
Largest cities in New Hampshire

Manchester	99,567	Rochester	26,630
Nashua	79,662	Portsmouth	25,925
Concord	36,006	Dover	25,042

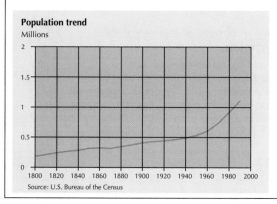

Population trend
Millions

Source: U.S. Bureau of the Census

Government

Statehood: June 21, 1788, the ninth state.
State capital: Concord

State government
Governor: 2-year term
State senators: 24; 2-year terms
State representatives: 400; 2-year terms
Counties: 10

Federal government
United States senators: 2
United States representatives: 2
Electoral votes: 4

New Hampshire (brown) ranks 44th in size among the states and is the 3rd largest of the New England States (yellow).

Economy

Chief products

Agriculture: milk.
Manufacturing: machinery, scientific instruments, electrical equipment, plastic products, printed materials, paper products.
Mining: sand and gravel.

Economic activities

Category	Per cent of gross state product*	Number of employed workers
Manufacturing	23	113,900
Finance, insurance, & real estate	21	32,700
Community, social, & personal services	18	124,300
Wholesale & retail trade	16	136,500
Government	9	69,900
Construction	6	31,100
Transportation, communication, & utilities	6	17,600
Agriculture	1	8,600
Mining	†	400
Total	100	535,000

*Gross state product = the total value of goods and services produced in a year.
†Less than one-half of 1 per cent.

Land

Area: 9,351 sq. mi. (24,219 km²), including 382 sq. mi. (988 km²) of inland water.
Elevation: *Highest*—Mount Washington, 6,288 ft. (1,917 m) above sea level. *Lowest*—sea level along the Atlantic coast.

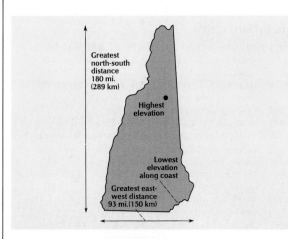

Greatest north-south distance 180 mi. (289 km)

Highest elevation

Lowest elevation along coast

Greatest east-west distance 93 mi.(150 km)

Important dates

1603	Martin Pring of England explored the mouth of the Piscataqua River.
1614	The English Captain John Smith landed on the Isles of Shoals.
1620's	David Thomson and Edward Hilton of England established the area's first permanent white settlements.
1641	Massachusetts Colony took control of New Hampshire.
1680	New Hampshire became a separate royal colony.
1776	New Hampshire broke away from Great Britain.
1784	New Hampshire adopted its present constitution.
1788	New Hampshire became the ninth state on June 21.
1838	The first railroad in New Hampshire was completed.
1944	The International Monetary Conference was held at Bretton Woods.
1964	The New Hampshire sweepstakes lottery began. It was the first legal U.S. lottery since the 1890's.
1986	Christa McAuliffe, a Concord teacher, died in the space shuttle Challenger explosion.

New Jersey   Facts in brief

State flag

The state flag, adopted in 1896, has a version of the state seal, on which three plows represent agriculture. The two figures are Liberty (*at left*) and Ceres, goddess of agriculture.

Government

Statehood: Dec. 18, 1787, the third state.
State capital: Trenton

State government
Governor: 4-year term
State senators: 40; 2- or 4-year terms
Members of the general assembly: 80; 2-year terms
Counties: 21

Federal government
United States senators: 2
United States representatives: 13
Electoral votes: 15

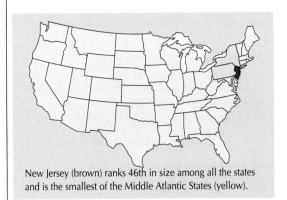

New Jersey (brown) ranks 46th in size among all the states and is the smallest of the Middle Atlantic States (yellow).

Land

Area: 7,787 sq. mi. (20,169 km²), including 319 sq. mi. (827 km²) of inland water but excluding 384 sq. mi. (995 km²) of Delaware Bay and New York Harbor.
Elevation: *Highest*—High Point, 1,803 ft. (550 m) above sea level. *Lowest*—sea level along the Atlantic Ocean.

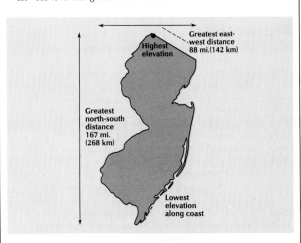

Greatest east-west distance 88 mi.(142 km)
Highest elevation
Greatest north-south distance 167 mi. (268 km)
Lowest elevation along coast

People

Population: 7,748,634 (1990 census)
Rank among the states: 9th
Density: 995 persons per sq. mi. (384 per km²), U.S. average 69 per sq. mi. (27 per km²)
Distribution: 89 per cent urban, 11 per cent rural
Largest cities in New Jersey

Newark	275,221	Elizabeth	110,002
Jersey City	228,537	Edison	88,680
Paterson	140,891	Camden	87,492

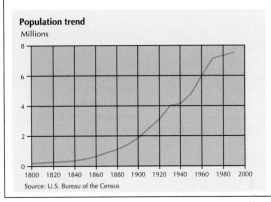

Population trend
Millions

Source: U.S. Bureau of the Census

Economy

Chief products

Agriculture: greenhouse and nursery products, milk.
Manufacturing: chemicals, food products, printed materials, transportation equipment, electrical equipment.
Mining: crushed stone, sand and gravel.

Economic activities

Category	Per cent of gross state product*	Number of employed workers
Finance, insurance, & real estate	21	242,700
Community, social, & personal services	20	951,700
Manufacturing	17	653,500
Wholesale & retail trade	17	891,200
Government	10	558,800
Transportation, communication, & utilities	9	241,900
Construction	5	167,500
Agriculture	1	41,000
Mining	†	2,500
Total	100	3,750,800

*Gross state product = the total value of goods and services produced in a year.
†Less than one-half of 1 per cent.

Important dates

1524	Giovanni da Verrazano, an Italian navigator sailing for France, explored the New Jersey coast.
1609	Henry Hudson, an Englishman sailing for the Dutch, explored Sandy Hook Bay and sailed up the Hudson River.
1660	The Dutch established the area's first permanent white settlement, in Bergen.
1664	The Dutch surrendered New Jersey to England.
1787	New Jersey became the third state on December 18.
1858	The first dinosaur skeleton discovered in North America was found buried in Haddonfield.
1879	Thomas A. Edison invented the electric light in Menlo Park.
1952	The New Jersey Turnpike opened.
1976	New Jersey adopted an individual income tax.
1977	The state legislature voted to allow gambling casinos in Atlantic City.

New Mexico Facts in brief

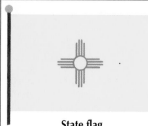

The state flag, adopted in 1925, bears the ancient sun symbol of the Zia Pueblo Indians. The flag's colors are those of Queen Isabella I of Spain. Spain once controlled the region.

State flag

Government

Statehood: Jan. 6, 1912, the 47th state.
State capital: Santa Fe

State government
Governor: 4-year term
State senators: 42; 4-year terms
State representatives: 70; 2-year terms
Counties: 33

Federal government
United States senators: 2
United States representatives: 3
Electoral votes: 5

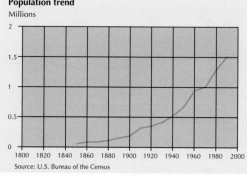

New Mexico (brown) ranks 5th in size among all the states and 2nd in size among the Southwestern States (yellow).

Land

Area: 121,593 sq. mi. (314,295 km²), including 258 sq. mi. (667 km²) of inland water.
Elevation: *Highest*—Wheeler Peak, 13,161 ft. (4,011 m) above sea level. *Lowest*—2,817 ft. (859 m) above sea level at Red Bluff Reservoir in Eddy County.

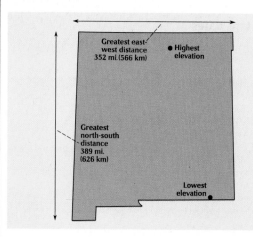

Greatest east-west distance 352 mi. (566 km)
Highest elevation
Greatest north-south distance 389 mi. (626 km)
Lowest elevation

People

Population: 1,521,779 (1990 census)
Rank among the states: 37th
Density: 13 persons per sq. mi. (5 per km²), U.S. average 69 per sq. mi. (27 per km²)
Distribution: 72 per cent urban, 28 per cent rural
Largest cities in New Mexico

Albuquerque	384,736	Roswell	44,654
Las Cruces	62,126	Farmington	33,997
Santa Fe	55,859	Rio Rancho	32,505

Population trend
Millions

Source: U.S. Bureau of the Census

Economy

Chief products
Agriculture: beef cattle, milk, hay.
Manufacturing: electrical equipment, food products, printed materials.
Mining: natural gas, petroleum.

Economic activities

Category	Per cent of gross state product*	Number of employed workers
Government	17	144,600
Community, social, & personal services	17	139,100
Finance, insurance, & real estate	14	26,500
Wholesale & retail trade	13	134,200
Mining	12	14,500
Transportation, communication, & utilities	10	28,900
Manufacturing	9	42,100
Construction	6	30,600
Agriculture	2	19,600
Total	100	580,100

*Gross state product = the total value of goods and services produced in a year.

Important dates

1540-1542	Francisco Vásquez de Coronado of Spain explored New Mexico.
1598	Juan de Oñate founded the region's first permanent Spanish colony, at San Juan.
1821	New Mexico became a province of Mexico. The Santa Fe Trail was established.
1848	Mexico ceded New Mexico to the United States.
1853	New Mexico acquired part of the Gila Valley.
1912	New Mexico became the 47th state on January 6.
1922	Geologists discovered oil in the southeastern and northwestern regions of New Mexico.
1945	The world's first atomic bomb was exploded at Trinity Site near Alamogordo.
1950	Uranium was discovered in the northwest region.
1970's	Completion of the San Juan-Chama project brought water to north-central New Mexico.

New York   Facts in brief

State flag

The state flag, adopted in 1909, bears the New York coat of arms. The arms shows a landscape and two figures—Liberty on the left and Justice on the right.

Government

Statehood: July 26, 1788, the 11th state.
State capital: Albany

State government
Governor: 4-year term
State senators: 61; 2-year terms
State representatives: 150; 2-year terms
Counties: 62

Federal government
United States senators: 2
United States representatives: 31
Electoral votes: 33

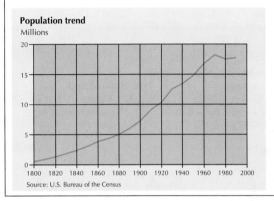

New York (brown) ranks 30th in size among all the states and is the largest of the Middle Atlantic States (yellow).

Land

Area: 49,108 sq. mi. (127,189 km²), including 1,731 sq. mi. (4,483 km²) of inland water, but excluding 4,376 sq. mi. (11,334 km²) of Lakes Erie and Ontario, New York Harbor, and Long Island Sound.
Elevation: *Highest*—Mount Marcy, 5,344 ft. (1,629 m) above sea level. *Lowest*—sea level along the Atlantic Ocean.

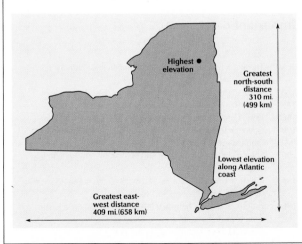

Highest elevation

Greatest north-south distance 310 mi. (499 km)

Lowest elevation along Atlantic coast

Greatest east-west distance 409 mi. (658 km)

People

Population: 18,044,505 (1990 census)
Rank among the states: 2nd
Density: 367 persons per sq. mi. (142 per km²), U.S. average 69 per sq. mi. (27 per km²)
Distribution: 85 per cent urban, 15 per cent rural
Largest cities in New York

New York City	7,322,564	Yonkers	188,082
Buffalo	328,123	Syracuse	163,860
Rochester	231,636	Albany	101,082

Population trend
Millions

```
20
15
10
 5
 0
  1800 1820 1840 1860 1880 1900 1920 1940 1960 1980 2000
```
Source: U.S. Bureau of the Census

Economy

Chief products

Agriculture: milk.
Manufacturing: printed materials, scientific instruments, machinery, chemicals, electrical equipment.
Mining: crushed stone.

Economic activities

Category	Per cent of gross state product*	Number of employed workers
Finance, insurance, & real estate	24	794,500
Community, social, & personal services	22	2,346,800
Wholesale & retail trade	16	1,736,000
Manufacturing	14	1,192,400
Government	11	1,446,900
Transportation, communication, & utilities	8	406,500
Construction	4	336,100
Agriculture	1	105,400
Mining	†	5,700
Total	100	8,370,300

*Gross state product = the total value of goods and services produced in a year.
†Less than one-half of 1 per cent.

Important dates

1609	Henry Hudson, an Englishman sailing for the Dutch, explored the Hudson River.
1624	The Dutch established Fort Orange (now Albany), the area's first permanent white settlement.
1664	The Dutch surrendered New Amsterdam (now New York City) to England.
1788	New York became the 11th state on July 26.
1825	The Erie Canal was opened.
1901	President William McKinley was assassinated at the Pan American Exposition in Buffalo.
1959	The St. Lawrence Seaway opened.
1960	The New York State Thruway (now the Governor Thomas E. Dewey Thruway) was completed.
1986	A bond act to finance environmental projects, especially the cleaning up of hazardous waste sites, was approved by voters.

North Carolina   Facts in brief

The state flag, adopted in 1885, bears a red, white, and blue field with the state's initials. Dates indicate when North Carolina moved toward independence from Britain.

State flag

Government

Statehood: Nov. 21, 1789, the 12th state.
State capital: Raleigh

State government
Governor: 4-year term
State senators: 50; 2-year terms
State representatives: 120; 2-year terms
Counties: 100

Federal government
United States senators: 2
United States representatives: 12
Electoral votes: 14

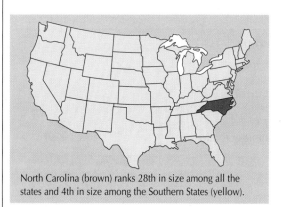

North Carolina (brown) ranks 28th in size among all the states and 4th in size among the Southern States (yellow).

Land

Area: 52,669 sq. mi. (136,413 km²), including 3,826 sq. mi. (9,909 km²) of inland water.
Elevation: *Highest*—Mount Mitchell, 6,684 ft. (2,037 m) above sea level. *Lowest*—sea level along the Atlantic Ocean.

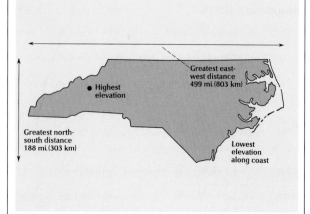

Greatest east-west distance 499 mi.(803 km)

Highest elevation

Greatest north-south distance 188 mi.(303 km)

Lowest elevation along coast

People

Population: 6,657,630 (1990 census)
Rank among the states: 10th
Density: 126 persons per sq. mi. (49 per km²), U.S. average 69 per sq. mi. (27 per km²)
Distribution: 52 per cent rural, 48 per cent urban
Largest cities in North Carolina

Charlotte	395,934	Winston-Salem	143,485
Raleigh	207,951	Durham	136,611
Greensboro	183,521	Fayetteville	75,695

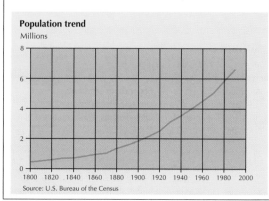

Population trend
Millions

Source: U.S. Bureau of the Census

Economy

Chief products

Agriculture: tobacco, chickens, hogs, turkeys.
Manufacturing: tobacco products, textiles, chemicals, electrical equipment, machinery, food products.
Mining: crushed stone, phosphate rock.

Economic activities

Category	Per cent of gross state product*	Number of employed workers
Manufacturing	30	867,800
Wholesale & retail trade	16	713,200
Finance, insurance, & real estate	13	132,300
Community, social, & personal services	13	560,300
Government	12	473,400
Transportation, communication, & utilities	9	152,300
Construction	4	163,700
Agriculture	3	106,900
Mining	†	4,900
Total	100	3,174,800

*Gross state product = the total value of goods and services produced in a year.
†Less than one-half of 1 per cent.

Important dates

1585	The English established their first colony in what is now the United States, at Roanoke Island.
1650?	The area's first permanent settlers came to the Albemarle region from Virginia.
1789	North Carolina became the 12th state on Nov. 21.
1861	North Carolina seceded from the Union.
1868	North Carolina was readmitted to the Union.
1901	Governor Charles B. Aycock began a campaign to improve North Carolina public schools.
1903	The Wright brothers made the first successful powered-airplane flight near Kitty Hawk.
1959	Research Triangle Park, operated by three universities to serve industry, was opened near Durham.
1960	Four black students launched the sit-in movement at a lunch counter in Greensboro.
1971	A new state constitution went into effect.

North Dakota   Facts in brief

The state flag, adopted in 1911, bears a modified version of the U.S. coat of arms on a blue field. The state's name is under the arms.

State flag

Government

Statehood: Nov. 2, 1889, the 39th state.
State capital: Bismarck

State government
Governor: 4-year term
State senators: 53; 4-year terms
State representatives: 106; 2-year terms
Counties: 53

Federal government
United States senators: 2
United States representatives: 1
Electoral votes: 3

North Dakota (brown) ranks 17th in size among all the states and 5th in size among the Midwestern States (yellow).

Land

Area: 70,702 sq. mi. (183,119 km²), including 1,403 sq. mi. (3,633 km²) of inland water.
Elevation: *Highest*—White Butte, 3,506 ft. (1,069 m) above sea level. *Lowest*—750 ft. (229 m) above sea level in Pembina County.

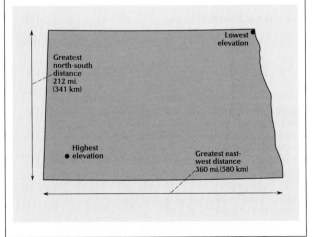

Lowest elevation

Greatest north-south distance 212 mi. (341 km)

Highest elevation

Greatest east-west distance 360 mi. (580 km)

People

Population: 641,364 (1990 census)
Rank among the states: 47th
Density: 9 persons per sq. mi. (4 per km²), U.S. average 69 per sq. mi. (27 per km²)
Distribution: 51 per cent rural, 49 per cent urban
Largest cities in North Dakota

Fargo	74,111	Minot	34,544
Grand Forks	49,425	Dickinson	16,097
Bismarck	49,256	Jamestown	15,571

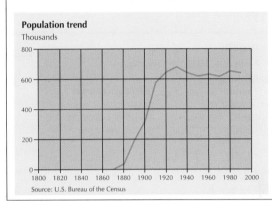

Population trend
Thousands

Source: U.S. Bureau of the Census

Economy

Chief products

Agriculture: wheat, beef cattle, barley, hay, sunflower seeds, milk, sugar beets.
Manufacturing: food products, machinery.
Mining: petroleum, coal.

Economic activities

Category	Per cent of gross state product*	Number of employed workers
Finance, insurance, & real estate	17	12,200
Wholesale & retail trade	17	69,400
Community, social, & personal services	15	65,900
Government	12	65,600
Transportation, communication, & utilities	11	17,000
Agriculture	11	36,800
Manufacturing	6	16,400
Mining	6	4,000
Construction	5	9,800
Total	**100**	**297,000**

*Gross state product = the total value of goods and services produced in a year.

Important dates

1682	René-Robert Cavelier, Sieur de la Salle, claimed all the land drained by the Mississippi River for France.
1738	Pierre Gaultier de Varennes, Sieur de la Vérendrye, a French-Canadian, explored the North Dakota region.
1803	The United States acquired southwestern North Dakota as part of the Louisiana Purchase.
1818	The United States acquired northeastern North Dakota by a treaty with Great Britain.
1863	The Dakota territory was opened for homesteading.
1889	North Dakota became the 39th state on November 2.
1951	Oil was discovered near Tioga.
1956	The first generator at Garrison Dam began to produce electric power. The dam was completed in 1960.
1986	Congress approved a modified version of the Garrison Diversion Project. Construction on the project had begun in 1968 to increase the state's water supply.

Ohio Facts in brief

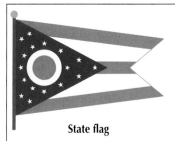

The state flag, adopted in 1902, has triangles representing Ohio's hills and valleys, and stripes symbolizing its roads and waterways. The 17 stars represent Ohio as the 17th state.

State flag

Government

Statehood: March 1, 1803, the 17th state.
State capital: Columbus

State government	Federal government
Governor: 4-year term	United States senators: 2
State senators: 33; 4-year terms	United States representatives: 19
State representatives: 99; 2-year terms	Electoral votes: 21
Counties: 88	

Ohio (brown) ranks 35th in size among all the states and 11th in size among the Midwestern States (yellow).

Land

Area: 41,330 sq. mi. (107,044 km²), including 325 sq. mi. (843 km²) of inland water but excluding 3,457 sq. mi. (8,954 km²) of Lake Erie.
Elevation: *Highest*—Campbell Hill in Logan County, 1,550 ft. (472 m) above sea level. *Lowest*—433 ft. (132 m) above sea level along the Ohio River in Hamilton County.

Greatest east-west distance 227 mi.(365 km)

● Highest elevation

Lowest elevation

Greatest north-south distance 245 mi. (394 km)

People

Population: 10,887,325 (1990 census)
Rank among the states: 7th
Density: 263 persons per sq. mi. (102 per km²), U.S. average 69 per sq. mi. (27 per km²)
Distribution: 73 per cent urban, 27 per cent rural
Largest cities in Ohio

Columbus	632,910	Toledo	332,943
Cleveland	505,616	Akron	223,019
Cincinnati	364,040	Dayton	182,044

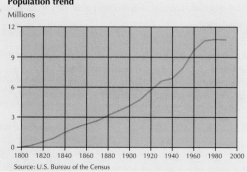

Population trend
Millions

Source: U.S. Bureau of the Census

Economy

Chief products

Agriculture: corn, soybeans, milk, hogs, beef cattle, hay.
Manufacturing: transportation equipment, machinery, fabricated metal products, chemicals, primary metals, processed foods, electrical equipment.
Mining: coal, natural gas.

Economic activities

Category	Per cent of gross state product*	Number of employed workers
Manufacturing	27	1,123,000
Community, social, & personal services	17	1,140,800
Wholesale & retail trade	16	1,168,300
Finance, insurance, & real estate	16	252,600
Government	10	705,700
Transportation, communication, & utilities	9	215,900
Construction	3	193,900
Agriculture	1	126,100
Mining	1	17,800
Total	100	4,943,300

*Gross state product = the total value of goods and services produced in a year.

Important dates

c. 1670 French explorer René-Robert Cavelier, Sieur de la Salle, probably was the first white man in the region.
1763 France surrendered its Ohio claim to Great Britain.
1788 The first permanent white settlement in Ohio was established in Marietta.
1803 Ohio became the 17th state on March 1.
1832 The Ohio and Erie Canal was completed.
1836 The Ohio-Michigan boundary dispute was settled.
1845 The Miami and Erie Canal was completed.
1914 Ohio passed the Conservancy Act after floods in 1913.
1922 The Miami River Valley flood-control project was finished.
1938 The Muskingum River Valley flood-control project was completed.
1955 The Ohio Turnpike was opened to traffic.
1971 Ohio adopted an income tax.

Oklahoma   Facts in brief

The state flag, adopted in 1925, bears an Osage Indian warrior's shield decorated with eagle feathers. Two symbols of peace, an olive branch and a peace pipe, cross the shield.

State flag

Government

Statehood: Nov. 6, 1907, the 46th state.
State capital: Oklahoma City

State government
Governor: 4-year term
State senators: 48; 4-year terms
State representatives: 101; 2-year terms
Counties: 77

Federal government
United States senators: 2
United States representatives: 6
Electoral votes: 8

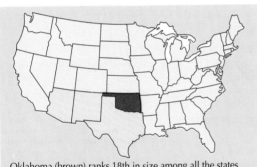

Oklahoma (brown) ranks 18th in size among all the states and is the smallest of the Southwestern States (yellow).

Land

Area: 69,956 sq. mi (181,186 km²), including 1,301 sq. mi. (3,369 km²) of inland water.
Elevation: *Highest*—Black Mesa, 4,973 ft. (1,516 m) above sea level. *Lowest*—287 ft. (87 m) above sea level along the Little River in McCurtain County.

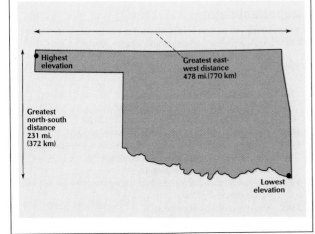

Highest elevation

Greatest east-west distance 478 mi.(770 km)

Greatest north-south distance 231 mi. (372 km)

Lowest elevation

People

Population: 3,157,604 (1990 census)
Rank among the states: 28th
Density: 45 persons per sq. mi. (17 per km²), U.S. average 69 per sq. mi. (27 per km²)
Distribution: 67 per cent urban, 33 per cent rural
Largest cities in Oklahoma

Oklahoma City	444,719	Norman	80,071
Tulsa	367,302	Broken Arrow	58,043
Lawton	80,561	Edmond	52,315

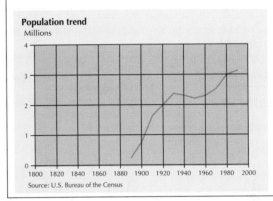

Population trend
Millions

Source: U.S. Bureau of the Census

Economy

Chief products

Agriculture: beef cattle, wheat, hay.
Manufacturing: transportation equipment, machinery, electrical equipment, rubber products.
Mining: natural gas, petroleum.

Economic activities

Category	Per cent of gross state product*	Number of employed workers
Wholesale & retail trade	16	275,900
Government	15	254,100
Community, social, & personal services	15	259,200
Manufacturing	14	163,000
Finance, insurance, & real estate	12	58,500
Transportation, communication, & utilities	11	65,000
Mining	9	43,200
Agriculture	4	70,600
Construction	4	35,000
Total	**100**	**1,224,500**

*Gross state product = the total value of goods and services produced in a year.

Important dates

1541	Francisco Vásquez de Coronado, a Spanish explorer, crossed western Oklahoma in search of gold.
1682	René-Robert Cavelier, Sieur de la Salle, claimed Oklahoma as part of French Louisiana.
1803	The United States acquired the Oklahoma region, except for the Panhandle, as part of the Louisiana Purchase.
1830-1842	The Five Civilized Tribes moved to Oklahoma.
1889	Part of Oklahoma was opened to white settlement. A producing oil well was drilled near Chelsea.
1890	Congress added the Panhandle to Oklahoma.
1893	The Dawes Commission was established to manage the affairs of the Five Civilized Tribes. The Cherokee Outlet was opened to white settlement.
1907	Oklahoma became the 46th state on November 16.
1984	Oklahoma counties received the right to decide whether to make alcohol sales legal within their borders.

Oregon   Facts in brief

State flag

The state flag, adopted in 1925, bears the state seal. On the seal, 33 stars represent Oregon as the 33rd state. An ox-drawn wagon symbolizes the settling of the region.

Government

Statehood: Feb. 14, 1859, the 33rd state.
State capital: Salem

State government

Governor: 4-year term
State senators: 30; 4-year terms
State representatives: 60; 2-year terms
Counties: 36

Federal government

United States senators: 2
United States representatives: 5
Electoral votes: 7

Oregon (brown) ranks 10th in size among all the states and 2nd in size among the Pacific Coast States (yellow).

Land

Area: 97,073 sq. mi. (251,416 km²), including 889 sq. mi. (2,302 km²) of inland water but excluding 48 sq. mi. (124 km²) of Pacific coastal water.
Elevation: *Highest*—Mount Hood, 11,239 ft. (3,426 m) above sea level. *Lowest*—sea level.

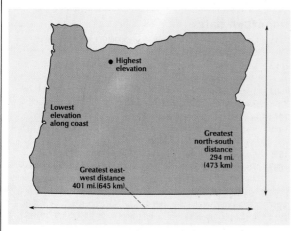

- Highest elevation
- Lowest elevation along coast
- Greatest north-south distance 294 mi. (473 km)
- Greatest east-west distance 401 mi.(645 km)

People

Population: 2,853,733 (1990 census)
Rank among the states: 29th
Density: 29 persons per sq. mi. (11 per km²), U.S. average 69 per sq. mi. (27 per km²)
Distribution: 68 per cent urban, 32 per cent rural
Largest cities in Oregon

Portland	437,319	Gresham	68,235
Eugene	112,669	Beaverton	53,310
Salem	107,786	Medford	46,951

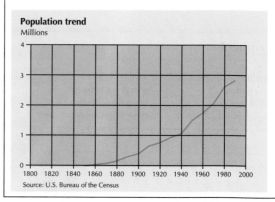

Population trend
Millions

Source: U.S. Bureau of the Census

Economy

Chief products

Agriculture: timber, beef cattle, milk, greenhouse and nursery products, wheat, hay.
Manufacturing: wood products, food products, paper products, machinery, scientific instruments, electrical equipment.

Economic activities

Category	Per cent of gross state product*	Number of employed workers
Manufacturing	19	217,200
Finance, insurance, & real estate	18	75,300
Wholesale & retail trade	17	309,600
Community, social, & personal services	17	279,900
Government	12	215,200
Transportation, communication, & utilities	10	62,900
Agriculture	4	74,900
Construction	3	45,200
Mining	†	1,400
Total	100	1,281,600

*Gross state product = the total value of goods and services produced in a year.
†Less than one-half of 1 per cent.

Important dates

1792	American Captain Robert Gray sailed into the Columbia River.
1811	John Jacob Astor, an American fur trader, founded Astoria, the area's first white settlement.
1819	A treaty between the United States and Spain fixed the present southern border of Oregon.
1846	A treaty made the 49th parallel the chief boundary between British and U.S. territory in the Oregon region.
1850	Congress passed the Oregon Donation Land Law.
1859	Oregon became the 33rd state on February 14.
1902	Oregon adopted the *initiative* and *referendum,* procedures that permit voters to take a direct part in lawmaking.
1937	Bonneville Dam was completed.
1982	Construction was completed on enlarging the powerhouse facilities of Bonneville Dam.
1985	Oregon adopted a state lottery.

Pennsylvania   Facts in brief

State flag

The state flag, adopted in 1907, bears the state seal, which is supported by two horses. The seal shows a shield with a sailing ship, a plow, and sheaves of wheat.

Government

Statehood: Dec. 12, 1787, the second state.
State capital: Harrisburg

State government
Governor: 4-year term
State senators: 50; 4-year terms
State representatives: 203; 2-year terms
Counties: 67

Federal government
United States senators: 2
United States representatives: 21
Electoral votes: 23

Pennsylvania (brown) ranks 33rd in size among all the states and 2nd in size among the Middle Atlantic States (yellow).

Land

Area: 45,308 sq. mi. (117,348 km²), including 420 sq. mi. (1,088 km²) of inland water but excluding 735 sq. mi. (1,904 km²) of Lake Erie.
Elevation: *Highest*—Mount Davis, 3,213 ft. (979 m) above sea level. *Lowest*—sea level along the Delaware River.

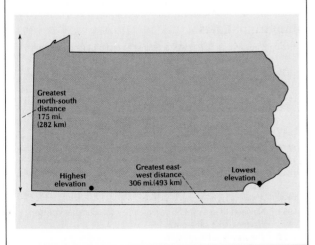

Greatest north-south distance 175 mi. (282 km)
Highest elevation
Greatest east-west distance 306 mi.(493 km)
Lowest elevation

People

Population: 11,924,710 (1990 census)
Rank among the states: 5th
Density: 263 persons per sq. mi. (102 per km²), U.S. average 69 per sq. mi. (27 per km²)
Distribution: 69 per cent urban, 31 per cent rural
Largest cities in Pennsylvania

Philadelphia	1,585,577	Allentown	105,090
Pittsburgh	369,879	Scranton	81,805
Erie	108,718	Reading	78,380

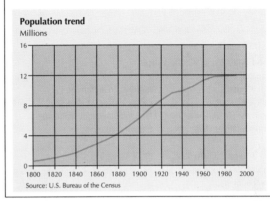

Population trend
Millions

Source: U.S. Bureau of the Census

Economy

Chief products

Agriculture: milk, greenhouse and nursery products, hay, beef cattle, eggs, corn.
Manufacturing: food products, chemicals, machinery, printed materials, fabricated metal products, electrical equipment, transportation equipment.
Mining: coal, natural gas, limestone.

Economic activities

Category	Per cent of gross state product*	Number of employed workers
Community, social, & personal services	21	1,379,200
Manufacturing	20	1,049,800
Finance, insurance, & real estate	17	296,300
Wholesale & retail trade	16	1,176,400
Transportation, communication, & utilities	10	253,800
Government	10	697,100
Construction	4	235,300
Agriculture	1	103,200
Mining	1	27,000
Total	100	5,218,100

*Gross state product = the total value of goods and services produced in a year.

Important dates

1643	Swedish settlers established a capital in Tinicum Island, near present-day Philadelphia.
1655	Dutch troops captured New Sweden from the Swedes.
1664	England took control of the Pennsylvania region.
1681	King Charles II granted the region to William Penn.
1776	The Declaration of Independence was adopted in Philadelphia.
1787	Pennsylvania became the second state on Dec. 12.
1859	Edwin Drake drilled the nation's first commercially successful oil well, near Titusville.
1940	The first section of the Pensylvania Turnpike opened.
1979	An accident at the Three Mile Island nuclear power plant threatened the release of deadly levels of radiation, but workers prevented a major disaster.
1985	Tornadoes caused 65 deaths and about $375 million in damage in Pennsylvania.

Rhode Island   Facts in brief

State flag

The state flag, adopted in 1897, bears 13 gold stars representing the original 13 colonies. The state motto, *Hope,* appears on a ribbon below an anchor, a symbol of hope.

Government

Statehood: May 29, 1790, the 13th state.
State capital: Providence

State government
Governor: 2-year term
State senators: 50; 2-year terms
State representatives: 100; 2-year terms
Cities and towns: 39 with local governments (Rhode Island has no counties)

Federal government
United States senators: 2
United States representatives: 2
Electoral votes: 4

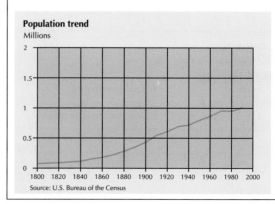

Rhode Island (brown) ranks as the smallest of all the states. It is one of the New England States (yellow).

Land

Area: 1,212 sq. mi. (3,140 km²), including 158 sq. mi. (408 km²) of inland water but excluding 14 sq. mi. (36 km²) of coastal water.
Elevation: *Highest*—Jerimoth Hill, 812 ft. (247 m) above sea level. *Lowest*—sea level along the Atlantic coast.

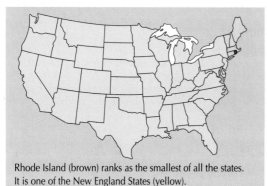

Greatest east-west distance 40 mi. (65 km)
Highest elevation
Greatest north-south distance 59 mi. (95 km)
Lowest elevation along coast

People

Population: 1,005,984 (1990 census)
Rank among the states: 43rd
Density: 830 persons per sq. mi. (320 per km²), U.S. average 69 per sq. mi. (27 per km²)
Distribution: 87 per cent urban, 13 per cent rural
Largest cities in Rhode Island

Providence	160,728	Pawtucket	72,644
Warwick	85,427	East Providence	50,380
Cranston	76,060	Woonsocket	43,877

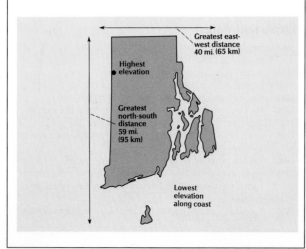

Population trend
Millions

Source: U.S. Bureau of the Census

Economy

Chief products

Agriculture: greenhouse and nursery products.
Fishing industry: clams, flounder, lobster.
Manufacturing: jewelry and silverware, fabricated metal products, electrical equipment, primary metals.

Economic activities

Category	Per cent of gross state product*	Number of employed workers
Manufacturing	21	108,500
Community, social, & personal services	20	123,700
Finance, insurance, & real estate	19	27,000
Wholesale & retail trade	17	107,300
Government	12	58,900
Transportation, communication, & utilities	6	15,400
Construction	3	20,100
Agriculture	1	6,000
Mining	1	100
Total	100	467,000

*Gross state product = the total value of goods and services produced in a year.

Important dates

1524	Giovanni da Verrazano, an Italian navigator sailing for France, entered Narragansett Bay.
1636	Providence, the region's first permanent white settlement, was founded by the minister Roger Williams.
1647	The settlements of Providence, Portsmouth, Newport, and Warwick were united after England granted Roger Williams a charter in 1644.
1774	Rhode Island prohibited the importation of slaves.
1776	Rhode Island declared its independence from England.
1790	Rhode Island became the 13th state on May 29.
1842	The Dorr Rebellion helped bring about a more liberal state constitution.
1938	A disastrous hurricane struck Rhode Island.
1969	Newport Bridge over Narragansett Bay was completed, linking Newport with Jamestown.
1971	The state legislature approved a personal income tax.

388

South Carolina   Facts in brief

The state flag, adopted in 1861, bears a palmetto, the state tree. The crescent is an emblem that the state's soldiers wore on their caps in the Revolutionary War.

State flag

Government

Statehood: May 23, 1788, the eighth state.
State capital: Columbia

State government
Governor: 4-year term
State senators: 46; 4-year terms
State representatives: 124; 2-year terms
Counties: 46

Federal government
United States senators: 2
United States representatives: 6
Electoral votes: 8

South Carolina (brown) ranks 40th in size among all the states and 11th in size among the Southern States (yellow).

Land

Area: 31,113 sq. mi. (80,582 km²), including 909 sq. mi. (2,355 km²) of inland water but excluding 138 sq. mi. (357 km²) of Atlantic coastal water.
Elevation: *Highest*—Sassafras Mountain, 3,560 ft. (1,805 m) above sea level. *Lowest*—sea level along the coast.

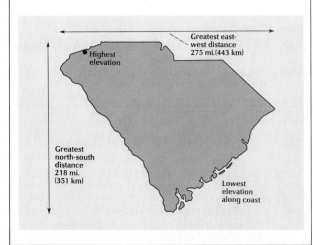

Greatest east-west distance 275 mi.(443 km)

• Highest elevation

Greatest north-south distance 218 mi. (351 km)

Lowest elevation along coast

People

Population: 3,505,707 (1990 census)
Rank among the states: 25th
Density: 113 persons per sq. mi. (44 per km²), U.S. average 69 per sq. mi. (27 per km²)
Distribution: 54 per cent urban, 46 per cent rural
Largest cities in South Carolina

Columbia	98,052	Greenville	58,282
Charleston	80,414	Spartanburg	43,467
North Charleston	70,218	Sumter	41,943

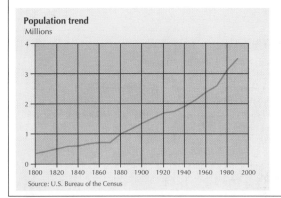

Population trend
Millions

Source: U.S. Bureau of the Census

Economy

Chief products

Agriculture: tobacco, beef cattle, milk, chickens, eggs, soybeans.
Manufacturing: textiles, chemicals, paper products, machinery, electrical equipment, rubber and plastics products.
Mining: granite, limestone.

Economic activities

Category	Per cent of gross state product*	Number of employed workers
Manufacturing	26	390,700
Wholesale & retail trade	17	339,000
Government	16	270,800
Community, social, & personal services	14	275,200
Finance, insurance, & real estate	13	68,200
Transportation, communication, & utilities	8	63,600
Construction	4	93,000
Agriculture	2	45,000
Mining	†	1,800
Total	100	1,547,300

*Gross state product = the total value of goods and services produced in a year.
†Less than one-half of 1 per cent.

Important dates

1521 Francisco Gordillo of Spain explored the Carolina coast.
1670 Englishmen established the first permanent white settlement in South Carolina, at Albemarle Point.
1719 South Carolina became a separate royal province.
1788 South Carolina became the eighth state on May 23.
1860 South Carolina seceded from the Union.
1861 The Civil War began on April 12 when Confederate forces fired on Fort Sumter.
1868 South Carolina was readmitted to the Union.
1941 The Santee-Cooper navigational project and hydroelectric dam was completed.
1953 Operations began at the Savannah River Atomic Energy Plant near Aiken.
1989 Hurricane Hugo struck South Carolina, killing 18 people and causing $5 billion in property damage.

South Dakota   Facts in brief

State flag

The state flag, adopted in 1963, has the state seal. It bears symbols of agriculture, mining, transportation, and commerce. Golden rays—for the blazing sun—surround the seal.

Government

Statehood: Nov. 2, 1889, the 40th state.
State capital: Pierre

State government
Governor: 4-year term
State senators: 35; 2-year terms
State representatives: 70; 2-year terms
Counties: 66

Federal government
United States senators: 2
United States representatives: 1
Electoral votes: 3

South Dakota (brown) ranks 16th in size among all the states and 4th among the Midwestern States (yellow).

Land

Area: 77,116 sq. mi. (199,730 km²), including 1,164 sq. mi. (3,041 km²) of inland water.
Elevation: *Highest*—Harney Peak, 7,242 ft. (2,207 m) above sea level. *Lowest*—Big Stone Lake, 962 ft. (293 m) above sea level.

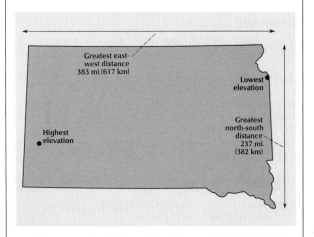

Greatest east-west distance 383 mi.(617 km)
Lowest elevation
Greatest north-south distance 237 mi. (382 km)
Highest elevation

People

Population: 699,999 (1990 census)
Rank among the states: 45th
Density: 9 persons per sq. mi. (4 per km²), U.S. average 69 per sq. mi. (27 per km²)
Distribution: 54 per cent rural, 46 per cent urban
Largest cities in South Dakota

Sioux Falls	100,814	Watertown	17,592
Rapid City	54,523	Brookings	16,270
Aberdeen	24,927	Mitchell	13,798

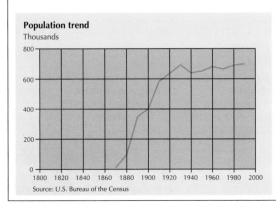

Population trend
Thousands
Source: U.S. Bureau of the Census

Economy

Chief products

Agriculture: beef cattle, hogs, corn, hay, wheat, milk, sunflowers.
Manufacturing: food products, machinery, scientific instruments.
Mining: gold.

Economic activities

Category	Per cent of gross state product*	Number of employed workers
Finance, insurance, & real estate	18	15,700
Wholesale & retail trade	17	72,900
Community, social, & personal services	15	67,100
Agriculture	14	37,000
Government	12	61,300
Manufacturing	10	31,700
Transportation, communication, & utilities	9	13,400
Construction	4	10,100
Mining	1	2,700
Total	100	311,900

*Gross state product = the total value of goods and services produced in a year.

Important dates

1682	René-Robert Cavelier, Sieur de La Salle, claimed the area drained by the Mississippi River for France.
1743	François and Louis-Joseph La Vérendrye, French-Canadian explorers, reached the South Dakota region.
1803	The United States acquired South Dakota as part of the Louisiana Purchase.
1817	The region's first permanent white settlement was founded at what is now Fort Pierre.
1874	Gold was discovered in the Black Hills.
1889	South Dakota became the 40th state on November 2.
1930's	South Dakota suffered its worst drought.
1944	Congress authorized construction of Fort Randall, Oahe, Gavins Point, and Big Bend dams.
1980	The U.S. Supreme Court ordered the federal government to pay $122½ million to eight Sioux tribes for land seized by the government in 1877.

Tennessee   Facts in brief

The state flag, adopted in 1905, has three stars. They represent East, Middle, and West Tennessee.

State flag

Government

Statehood: June 1, 1796, the 16th state.
State capital: Nashville

State government
Governor: 4-year term
State senators: 33; 4-year terms
State representatives: 99; 2-year terms
Counties: 95

Federal government
United States senators: 2
United States representatives: 9
Electoral votes: 11

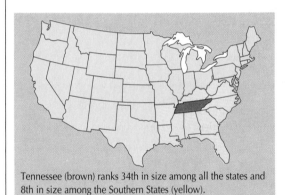

Tennessee (brown) ranks 34th in size among all the states and 8th in size among the Southern States (yellow).

Land

Area: 42,114 sq. mi. (109,152 km²), including 989 sq. mi. (2,561 km²) of inland water.
Elevation: *Highest*—Clingmans Dome, 6,643 ft. (2,025 m) above sea level. *Lowest*—182 ft. (55 m) above sea level in Shelby County.

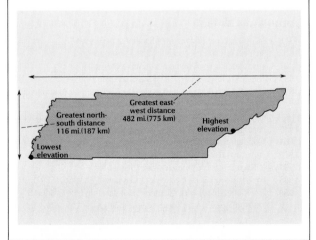

Greatest east-west distance 482 mi.(775 km)
Greatest north-south distance 116 mi.(187 km)
Highest elevation
Lowest elevation

People

Population: 4,896,641 (1990 census)
Rank among the states: 17th
Density: 116 persons per sq. mi. (45 per km²), U.S. average 69 per sq. mi. (27 per km²)
Distribution: 60 per cent urban, 40 per cent rural
Largest cities in Tennessee

Memphis	610,337	Chattanooga	152,466
Nashville	510,784	Clarksville	75,494
Knoxville	165,121	Johnson City	49,381

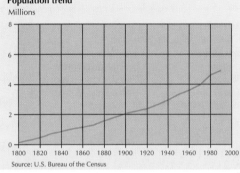

Population trend
Millions

Source: U.S. Bureau of the Census

Economy

Chief products

Agriculture: beef cattle, milk, soybeans, hogs, tobacco, hay.
Manufacturing: chemicals, food products, transportation equipment, machinery, electrical equipment, fabricated metal products, rubber products.
Mining: coal, crushed stone, zinc.

Economic activities

Category	Per cent of gross state product*	Number of employed workers
Manufacturing	24	523,700
Wholesale & retail trade	18	507,600
Community, social, & personal services	17	465,200
Finance, insurance, & real estate	14	103,600
Government	12	334,300
Transportation, communication, & utilities	8	115,100
Construction	4	97,400
Agriculture	3	110,300
Mining	†	6,300
Total	100	2,263,500

*Gross state product = the total value of goods and services produced in a year.
†Less than one-half of 1 per cent.

Important dates

1540	Hernando de Soto of Spain led the first white expedition into the Tennessee region.
1682	René-Robert Cavelier, Sieur de La Salle, claimed the Mississippi River Valley for France.
1714	A French trading post was established near the present site of Nashville.
1796	Tennessee became the 16th state on June 1.
1818	The Chickasaw Indians sold all their land east of the Mississippi River to the U.S. government.
1861	Tennessee seceded from the Union.
1866	Tennessee was readmitted to the Union.
1878	Yellow fever killed about 5,200 people in Memphis.
1933	Congress created the Tennessee Valley Authority.
1942	The federal government began building an atomic energy center at Oak Ridge.
1982	A world's fair was held at Knoxville.

Texas   Facts in brief

The state flag, known as the *Lone Star Flag*, was adopted in 1839. The red stands for bravery, the white represents purity, and the blue is for loyalty.

State flag

Government

Statehood: Dec. 29, 1845, the 28th state.
State capital: Austin

State government
Governor: 4-year term
State senators: 31; 4-year terms
State representatives: 150; 2-year terms
Counties: 254

Federal government
United States senators: 2
United States representatives: 30
Electoral votes: 32

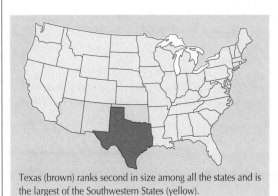

Texas (brown) ranks second in size among all the states and is the largest of the Southwestern States (yellow).

Land

Area: 266,807 sq. mi. (691,030 km²), including 4,790 sq. mi. (12,407 km²) of inland water but excluding 7 sq. mi. (18 km²) of Gulf of Mexico coastal water.

Elevation: *Highest*—Guadalupe Peak, 8,751 ft. (2,667 m) above sea level. *Lowest*—sea level, along the Gulf of Mexico.

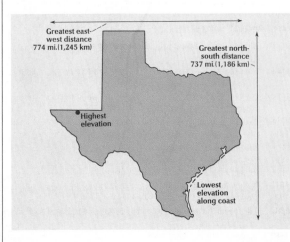

Greatest east-west distance 774 mi.(1,245 km)
Greatest north-south distance 737 mi.(1,186 km)
Highest elevation
Lowest elevation along coast

People

Population: 17,059,805 (1990 census)
Rank among the states: 3rd
Density: 64 persons per sq. mi. (25 per km²), U.S. average 69 per sq. mi. (27 per km²)
Distribution: 80 per cent urban, 20 per cent rural
Largest cities in Texas

Houston	1,630,553	El Paso	515,342
Dallas	1,006,877	Austin	465,622
San Antonio	935,933	Fort Worth	447,619

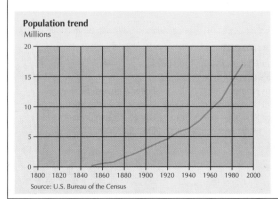

Population trend
Millions

Source: U.S. Bureau of the Census

Economy

Chief products

Agriculture: beef cattle, cotton.
Manufacturing: chemicals, food products, electrical equipment, petroleum products, machinery, transportation equipment.
Mining: petroleum, natural gas.

Economic activities

Category	Per cent of gross state product*	Number of employed workers
Manufacturing	17	969,500
Community, social, & personal services	16	1,610,000
Wholesale & retail trade	16	1,685,500
Finance, insurance, & real estate	13	432,500
Government	11	1,222,200
Transportation, communication, & utilities	11	400,700
Mining	9	174,000
Construction	4	315,200
Agriculture	2	237,000
Total	100	7,046,600

*Gross state product = the total value of goods and services produced in a year.

Important dates

1519	Alonso Àlvarez de Piñeda of Spain reached Texas.
1682	Spanish missionaries built the area's first missions.
1821	Texas became part of the new Empire of Mexico.
1835	The Texas Revolution against Mexico began.
1836	Texas declared its independence from Mexico. The Alamo fell to Mexican forces. Sam Houston defeated the Mexicans in the Battle of San Jacinto. Texas became the independent Republic of Texas.
1845	Texas became the 28th state on December 29.
1861	Texas seceded from the Union.
1870	Texas was readmitted to the Union.
1901	Oilmen discovered the great Spindletop field.
1963	President John F. Kennedy was assassinated in Dallas.
1964	The Manned Spacecraft Center in Houston (now the Lyndon B. Johnson Space Center) became headquarters for U.S. astronauts.

Utah   Facts in brief

The state flag, adopted in 1913, has the state seal. On the seal, a beehive on a shield stands for hard work and industry. The date 1847 is the year the Mormons came to Utah.

State flag

Government

Statehood: Jan. 4, 1896, the 45th state.
State capital: Salt Lake City

State government
Governor: 4-year term
State senators: 29; 4-year terms
State representatives: 75; 2-year terms
Counties: 29

Federal government
United States senators: 2
United States representatives: 3
Electoral votes: 5

Utah (brown) ranks 11th in size among all the states and 5th in size among the Rocky Mountain States (yellow).

Land

Area: 84,899 sq. mi. (219,889 km²), including 2,826 sq. mi. (7,320 km²) of inland water.
Elevation: *Highest*—Kings Peak, 13,528 ft. (4,123 m) above sea level. *Lowest*—Beaverdam Creek in Washington County, 2,000 ft. (610 m) above sea level.

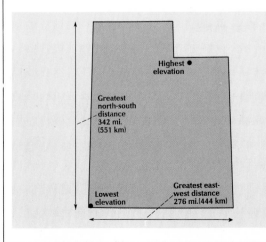

Highest elevation
Greatest north-south distance 342 mi. (551 km)
Lowest elevation
Greatest east-west distance 276 mi.(444 km)

People

Population: 1,727,784 (1990 census)
Rank among the states: 35th
Density: 20 persons per sq. mi. (8 per km²), U.S. average 69 per sq. mi. (27 per km²)
Distribution: 84 per cent urban, 16 per cent rural
Largest cities in Utah

Salt Lake City	159,963	Sandy	75,058
West Valley City	86,976	Orem	67,561
Provo	86,835	Ogden	63,909

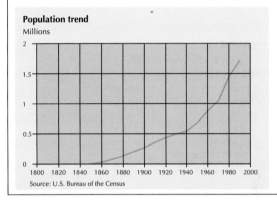

Population trend
Millions

Source: U.S. Bureau of the Census

Economy

Chief products

Agriculture: beef cattle, milk.
Manufacturing: transportation equipment, food products, scientific instruments, printed materials, machinery.
Mining: petroleum, coal, natural gas.

Economic activities

Category	Per cent of gross state product*	Number of employed workers
Community, social, & personal services	17	167,100
Manufacturing	17	102,600
Wholesale & retail trade	16	166,200
Finance, insurance, & real estate	15	33,300
Government	14	146,000
Transportation, communication, & utilities	13	41,300
Construction	4	26,200
Mining	2	8,100
Agriculture	2	19,700
Total	100	710,500

*Gross state product = the total value of goods and services produced in a year.

Important dates

1776	Silvestre Velez de Escalante and Francisco Atanasio Domínguez, Franciscan friars, explored the Utah area.
1824-1825	Jim Bridger, a famous scout, was probably the first white person to see the Great Salt Lake.
1847	Brigham Young and the first Mormon pioneers arrived in the Great Salt Lake region.
1848	The United States won the Utah area from Mexico.
1896	Utah became the 45th state on January 4.
1913	The Strawberry River reservoir was completed.
1952	Rich uranium deposits were found near Moab.
1964	Flaming Gorge and Glen Canyon dams were completed.
1967	Construction began on the Central Utah Project, a program to provide water for Utah's major growth areas.
1974	Oil companies invested millions of dollars to lease federally owned oil-shale land in Utah.

Vermont   Facts in brief

The state flag, adopted in 1923, bears the Vermont coat of arms. It shows a large pine tree, three sheaves of grain, and a cow. Mountains rise in the background.

State flag

Government

Statehood: March 4, 1791, the 14th state.
State capital: Montpelier

State government
Governor: 2-year term
State senators: 30; 2-year terms
State representatives: 150; 2-year terms
Towns: 237 (towns are the main units of local government in Vermont)

Federal government
United States senators: 2
United States representatives: 1
Electoral votes: 3

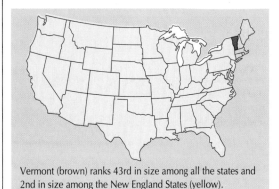

Vermont (brown) ranks 43rd in size among all the states and 2nd in size among the New England States (yellow).

Land

Area: 9,614 sq. mi. (24,900 km²), including 341 sq. mi. (883 km²) of inland water.
Elevation: *Highest*—Mount Mansfield, 4,393 ft. (1,339 m) above sea level. *Lowest*—Lake Champlain in Franklin County, 95 ft. (29 m) above sea level.

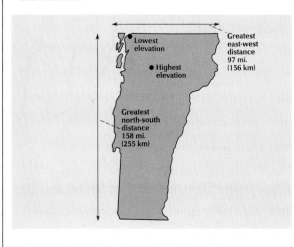

Lowest elevation

Highest elevation

Greatest east-west distance 97 mi. (156 km)

Greatest north-south distance 158 mi. (255 km)

People

Population: 564,964 (1990 census)
Rank among the states: 48th
Density: 59 persons per sq. mi. (23 per km²), U.S. average 69 per sq. mi. (27 per km²)
Distribution: 66 per cent rural, 34 per cent urban
Largest cities in Vermont

Burlington	39,127	Bennington*	9,532
Rutland	18,230	Barre	9,482
South Burlington	12,809	Brattleboro*	8,612

*Unincorporated place.

Population trend
Thousands

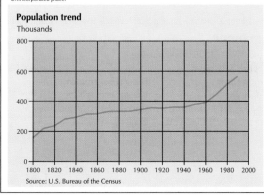

Source: U.S. Bureau of the Census

Economy

Chief products
Agriculture: milk.
Manufacturing: electrical equipment, fabricated metal products, printed materials, paper products, machinery, food products, transportation equipment.
Mining: granite.

Economic activities

Category	Per cent of gross state product*	Number of employed workers
Manufacturing	20	48,200
Finance, insurance, & real estate	19	12,900
Community, social, & personal services	18	66,900
Wholesale & retail trade	16	62,000
Government	10	42,400
Transportation, communication, & utilities	7	10,200
Construction	7	18,200
Agriculture	3	10,800
Mining	†	500
Total	**100**	**272,100**

*Gross state product = the total value of goods and services produced in a year.
†Less than one-half of 1 per cent.

Important dates

1609	Samuel de Champlain claimed the Vermont region for France.
1724	Massachusetts established Fort Dummer, the first permanent white settlement in the Vermont region.
1763	England gained control of Vermont.
1775	Ethan Allen and the Green Mountain Boys captured Fort Ticonderoga from the British in the Revolutionary War.
1777	Vermont declared itself an independent republic.
1791	Vermont became the 14th state on March 4.
1823	The opening of the Champlain Canal created a water route from Vermont to New York City.
1970	The state legislature passed the Environmental Control Law, permitting Vermont to limit major developments that could harm the state's environment.
1984	Madeleine M. Kunin became the first woman to be elected governor of Vermont.

Virginia   Facts in brief

The state flag, adopted in 1931, bears one side of the state seal. It shows Virtue, dressed as an Amazon, triumphant over Tyranny. The design is based on one created in 1776.

State flag

Government

Statehood: June 25, 1788, the 10th state.
State capital: Richmond

State government
Governor: 4-year term
State senators: 40; 4-year terms
State representatives: 100; 2-year terms
Counties: 95

Federal government
United States senators: 2
United States representatives: 11
Electoral votes: 13

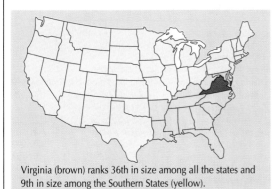

Virginia (brown) ranks 36th in size among all the states and 9th in size among the Southern States (yellow).

Land

Area: 40,767 sq. mi. (105,586 km²), including 1,063 sq. mi. (2,753 km²) of inland water but excluding 1,511 sq. mi. (3,913 km²) of Chesapeake Bay.
Elevation: *Highest*—Mount Rogers, 5,729 ft. (1,746 m) above sea level. *Lowest*—sea level.

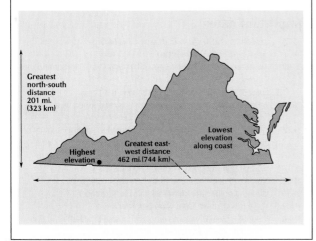

Greatest north-south distance 201 mi. (323 km)

Highest elevation

Greatest east-west distance 462 mi.(744 km)

Lowest elevation along coast

People

Population: 6,216,568 (1990 census)
Rank among the states: 12th
Density: 152 persons per sq. mi. (59 per km²), U.S. average 69 per sq. mi. (27 per km²)
Distribution: 66 per cent urban, 34 per cent rural
Largest cities in Virginia

Virginia Beach	393,069	Arlington*	170,936
Norfolk	261,229	Newport News	170,045
Richmond	203,056	Chesapeake	151,976

*Unincorporated place.

Population trend
Millions

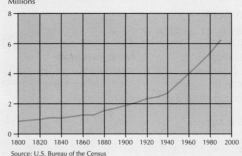

Source: U.S. Bureau of the Census

Economy

Chief products

Agriculture: tobacco, beef cattle, milk, chickens.
Manufacturing: chemicals, tobacco products, transportation equipment, food products, electrical equipment.
Mining: coal.

Economic activities

Category	Per cent of gross state product*	Number of employed workers
Government	18	563,300
Community, social, & personal services	18	703,300
Manufacturing	16	428,100
Finance, insurance, & real estate	16	152,200
Wholesale & retail trade	15	656,900
Transportation, communication, & utilities	9	149,100
Construction	6	195,900
Agriculture	1	71,900
Mining	1	15,000
Total	**100**	**2,935,700**

*Gross state product = the total value of goods and services produced in a year.

Important dates

1607	The Virginia Company of London established Jamestown.
1612	Colonist John Rolfe helped save the colony by introducing tobacco growing and exporting.
1619	America's first representative legislature, the House of Burgesses, met in Jamestown.
1776	Virginia declared its independence and adopted its first constitution, including a declaration of rights.
1788	Virginia became the 10th state on June 25.
1831	Nat Turner led a famous slave revolt.
1861-1865	Virginia seceded from the Union and became the major battleground of the Civil War.
1863	West Virginia was formed from northwestern Virginia.
1870	Virginia was readmitted to the Union.
1940-1945	New industries opened during World War II.
1971	A new state constitution went into effect.
1987	Voters approved a state lottery.

Washington   Facts in brief

The state flag, first adopted in 1923, bears the state seal. It has a likeness of George Washington, for whom the state was named. The green field is for the state's forests.

State flag

Government

Statehood: Nov. 11, 1889, the 42nd state.
State capital: Olympia

State government
Governor: 4-year term
State senators: 49; 4-year terms
State representatives: 98; 2-year terms
Counties: 39

Federal government
United States senators: 2
United States representatives: 9
Electoral votes: 11

Washington (brown) ranks 20th in size among all the states and is the smallest of the Pacific Coast States (yellow).

Land

Area: 68,139 sq. mi. (176,479 km²), including 1,627 sq. mi. (4,215 km²) of inland water but excluding 2,397 sq. mi. (6,208 km²) of Pacific coastal water, Puget Sound, and the Straits of Georgia and Juan de Fuca.

Elevation: *Highest*—Mount Rainier, 14,410 ft. (4,392 m) above sea level. *Lowest*—sea level along the coast.

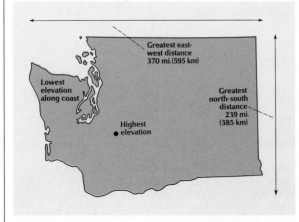

Greatest east-west distance 370 mi. (595 km)

Lowest elevation along coast

Greatest north-south distance 239 mi. (385 km)

Highest elevation

People

Population: 4,887,941 (1990 census)
Rank among the states: 18th
Density: 72 persons per sq. mi. (28 per km²), U.S. average 69 per sq. mi. (27 per km²)
Distribution: 74 per cent urban, 26 per cent rural
Largest cities in Washington

Seattle	516,259	Bellevue	86,874
Spokane	177,196	Federal Way*	69,961
Tacoma	176,664	Everett	54,827

*Unincorporated place.

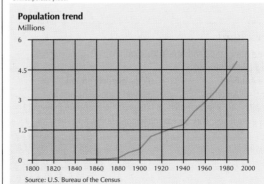

Population trend
Millions

Source: U.S. Bureau of the Census

Economy

Chief products

Agriculture: timber, milk, beef cattle, wheat, apples.
Manufacturing: transportation equipment, food products, paper products, chemicals.

Economic activities

Category	Per cent of gross state product*	Number of employed workers
Wholesale & retail trade	19	500,900
Manufacturing	17	361,300
Community, social, & personal services	16	473,400
Finance, insurance, & real estate	15	112,300
Government	15	379,400
Transportation, communication, & utilities	8	107,900
Construction	6	106,600
Agriculture	4	103,000
Mining	†	3,600
Total	**100**	**2,148,400**

*Gross state product = the total value of goods and services produced in a year.
†Less than one-half of 1 per cent.

Important dates

1775	Bruno Heceta and Juan Francisco de la Bodega y Quadra of Spain landed in Washington.
1792	American Captain Robert Gray sailed into Grays Harbor and the Columbia River. George Vancouver of England surveyed the coast of Washington and Puget Sound.
1810	A British-Canadian fur-trading post was established near present-day Spokane.
1818	Great Britain and the United States agreed to joint occupancy of the Oregon region, including Washington.
1846	United States and Great Britain agreed to a treaty establishing Washington's boundary at the 49th parallel.
1883	Northern Pacific Railroad linked the area to the East.
1889	Washington became the 42nd state on November 11.
1942	The Grand Coulee Dam was completed.
1980	Mount St. Helens volcano erupted, causing 57 deaths and enormous damage in southwestern Washington.

West Virginia Facts in brief

State flag

The state flag, adopted in 1929, bears one side of the state seal. It shows a miner, a farmer, and the date of statehood.

Government

Statehood: June 20, 1863, the 35th state.
State capital: Charleston

State government	Federal government
Governor: 4-year term	United States senators: 2
State senators: 34; 4-year terms	United States representatives: 3
State delegates: 100; 2-year terms	Electoral votes: 5
Counties: 55	

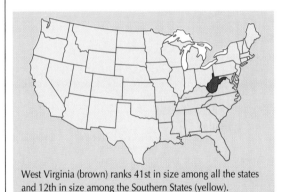

West Virginia (brown) ranks 41st in size among all the states and 12th in size among the Southern States (yellow).

Land

Area: 24,231 sq. mi. (62,759 km²), including 112 sq. mi. (291 km²) of inland water.
Elevation: *Highest*—Spruce Knob, 4,863 ft. (1,482 m) above sea level. *Lowest*—240 ft. (73 m) above sea level along the Potomac River in Jefferson County.

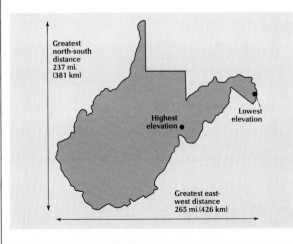

Greatest north-south distance 237 mi. (381 km)

Highest elevation

Lowest elevation

Greatest east-west distance 265 mi. (426 km)

People

Population: 1,801,625 (1990 census)
Rank among the states: 34th
Density: 74 persons per sq. mi. (29 per km²), U.S. average 69 per sq. mi. (27 per km²)
Distribution: 64 per cent rural, 36 per cent urban
Largest cities in West Virginia

Charleston	57,287	Parkersburg	33,862
Huntington	54,844	Morgantown	25,879
Wheeling	34,882	Weirton	22,124

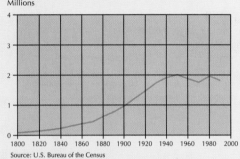

Population trend
Millions

Source: U.S. Bureau of the Census

Economy

Chief products

Agriculture: beef cattle, milk, hay, chickens.
Manufacturing: chemicals; primary metals; stone, clay, and glass products.
Mining: coal, natural gas.

Economic activities

Category	Per cent of gross state product*	Number of employed workers
Finance, insurance, & real estate	15	24,000
Wholesale & retail trade	15	145,200
Manufacturing	15	87,600
Community, social, & personal services	14	137,500
Transportation, communication, & utilities	13	36,400
Mining	11	33,500
Government	11	125,100
Construction	5	23,400
Agriculture	1	23,700
Total	100	636,400

*Gross state product = the total value of goods and services produced in a year.

Important dates

1669	John Lederer and his companions became the first Virginians to see the West Virginia region.
1727	Germans from Pennsylvania established a settlement at New Mecklenburg (now Shepherdstown).
1742	Coal was discovered on the Coal River.
1815	Gas was discovered near Charleston.
1859	John Brown and his followers raided the arsenal at Harpers Ferry in an attempt to start a slave revolt.
1861	The counties of western Virginia refused to secede from the Union with Virginia.
1863	West Virginia became the 35th state on June 20.
1920-1921	Miners fought with mine guards, police, and federal troops in a dispute over organizing unions.
1946	Chemical industries settled in the Ohio River Valley.
1968	A coal mine disaster led to new mine safety laws.
1985	The legislature established a state lottery.

Wisconsin   Facts in brief

WISCONSIN

1848

State flag

The state flag, first adopted in 1913, bears the state seal. It has symbols of agriculture, mining, navigation, and manufacturing. The year 1848 is when Wisconsin became a state.

Government

Statehood: May 29, 1848, the 30th state.
State capital: Madison

State government

Governor: 4-year term
State senators: 33; 4-year terms
State representatives: 99; 2-year terms
Counties: 72

Federal government

United States senators: 2
United States representatives: 9
Electoral votes: 11

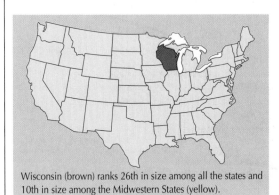

Wisconsin (brown) ranks 26th in size among all the states and 10th in size among the Midwestern States (yellow).

Land

Area: 56,153 sq. mi. (145,436 km²), including 1,727 sq. mi. (4,472 km²) of inland water but excluding 10,062 sq. mi. (26,060 km²) of Lake Michigan and Lake Superior.
Elevation: *Highest*—Timms Hill, 1,952 ft. (595 m) above sea level. *Lowest*—581 ft. (177 m) above sea level along Lake Michigan.

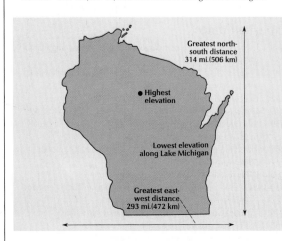

Greatest north-south distance 314 mi.(506 km)

● Highest elevation

Lowest elevation along Lake Michigan

Greatest east-west distance 293 mi.(472 km)

People

Population: 4,906,745 (1990 census)
Rank among the states: 16th
Density: 87 persons per. sq. mi. (34 per km²), U.S. average 69 per sq. mi. (27 per km²)
Distribution: 64 per cent urban, 36 per cent rural
Largest cities in Wisconsin

Milwaukee	628,088	Racine	84,298
Madison	191,262	Kenosha	80,352
Green Bay	96,466	Appleton	65,695

Population trend
Millions

Source: U.S. Bureau of the Census

Economy

Chief products

Agriculture: milk.
Manufacturing: machinery, food products, paper products, fabricated metal products, electrical equipment.
Mining: crushed stone, sand and gravel.

Economic activities

Category	Per cent of gross state product*	Number of employed workers
Manufacturing	27	556,200
Finance, insurance, & real estate	18	118,100
Wholesale & retail trade	15	529,900
Community, social, & personal services	15	508,500
Government	10	334,000
Transportation, communication, & utilities	7	99,900
Agriculture	5	117,900
Construction	3	80,800
Mining	†	2,300
Total	100	2,347,600

*Gross state product = the total value of goods and services produced in a year.
†Less than one-half of 1 per cent.

Important dates

1634	Jean Nicolet, a French explorer, landed on Green Bay shore.
c. 1670	Fathers Claude Jean Allouez and Louis André founded a misisonary center at De Pere.
1763	England gained the Wisconsin region from France.
1783	Wisconsin became a U.S. territory as part of the treaty ending the Revolutionary War.
1848	Wisconsin became the 30th state on May 29.
1901	Robert M. La Follette, Sr., became Wisconsin's governor, and the Progressive era began.
1911	The state legislature set up a teachers' pension, established a commission to settle labor disputes, and passed other progressive legislation.
1932	Wisconsin passed the first state unemployment-compensation act.
1971	The state created the University of Wisconsin System.
1987	Wisconsin adopted a state lottery.

Wyoming Facts in brief

The state flag was adopted in 1917. It shows the state seal on a buffalo representing the branding of livestock. On the seal, a woman symbolizes equal rights in Wyoming.

State flag

Government

Statehood: July 10, 1890, the 44th state.
State capital: Cheyenne

State government
Governor: 4-year term
State senators: 30; 4-year terms
State representatives: 64; 2-year terms
Counties: 23

Federal government
United States senators: 2
United States representatives: 1
Electoral votes: 3

Wyoming (brown) ranks ninth in size among all the states and fourth among the Rocky Mountain States (yellow).

Land

Area: 97,809 sq. mi. (253,326 km²), including 820 sq. mi. (2,125 km²) of inland water.
Elevation: *Highest*—Gannett Peak, 13,804 ft. (4,207 m) above sea level. *Lowest*—Belle Fourche River in Crook County, 3,100 ft. (945 m) above sea level.

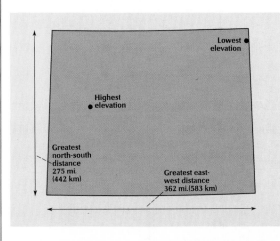

Lowest elevation

Highest elevation

Greatest north-south distance 275 mi. (442 km)

Greatest east-west distance 362 mi.(583 km)

People

Population: 455,975 (1990 census)
Rank among the states: 50th
Density: 5 persons per sq. mi. (2 per km²), U.S. average 69 per sq. mi. (27 per km²)
Distribution: 63 per cent urban, 37 per cent rural
Largest cities in Wyoming

Cheyenne	50,008	Rock Springs	19,050
Casper	46,742	Gillette	17,635
Laramie	26,687	Sheridan	13,900

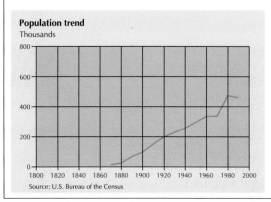

Population trend
Thousands

Source: U.S. Bureau of the Census

Economy

Chief products

Agriculture: beef cattle.
Manufacturing: chemicals, petroleum products.
Mining: petroleum, coal, natural gas.

Economic activities

Category	Per cent of gross state product*	Number of employed workers
Mining	25	17,100
Transportation, communication, & utilities	15	14,400
Finance, insurance, & real estate	14	7,300
Government	13	54,900
Wholesale & retail trade	10	44,400
Community, social, & personal services	9	36,500
Construction	8	10,100
Manufacturing	4	8,800
Agriculture	2	12,100
Total	**100**	**205,600**

*Gross state product = the total value of goods and services produced in a year.

Important dates

1803	The United States acquired most of the Wyoming region as part of the Louisiana Purchase.
1812	Oregon fur traders, led by Robert Stuart, discovered South Pass across the Rocky Mountains.
1833	Oil was discovered east of the Wind River Mountains.
1834	Fort William (later Fort Laramie), the area's first permanent trading post, was established.
1867	The Union Pacific Railroad entered Wyoming.
1872	Yellowstone became the first U.S. national park.
1883	The area's first oil well was drilled in Dallas Field.
1890	Wyoming became the 44th state on July 10.
1925	Nellie Tayloe Ross became the first woman governor in the United States.
1951-1952	Major uranium deposits were found in the state.
1960	The first U.S. operational intercontinental ballistic missile base opened near Cheyenne.

WORLD: *Political*

ABBREVIATIONS

BOS. AND HERZ.
    Bosnia and Herzegovina
CEN. AFR. REP.
    Central African Republic
DEN. Denmark
FR. France
GR. Greece
IT. Italy
N. North, Northern
NETH. Netherlands
N.Z. New Zealand
PORT. Portugal
S. South
SP. Spain
U.A.E. United Arab
    Emirates
U.K. United Kingdom
U.S. United States
W. Western

—— National boundary

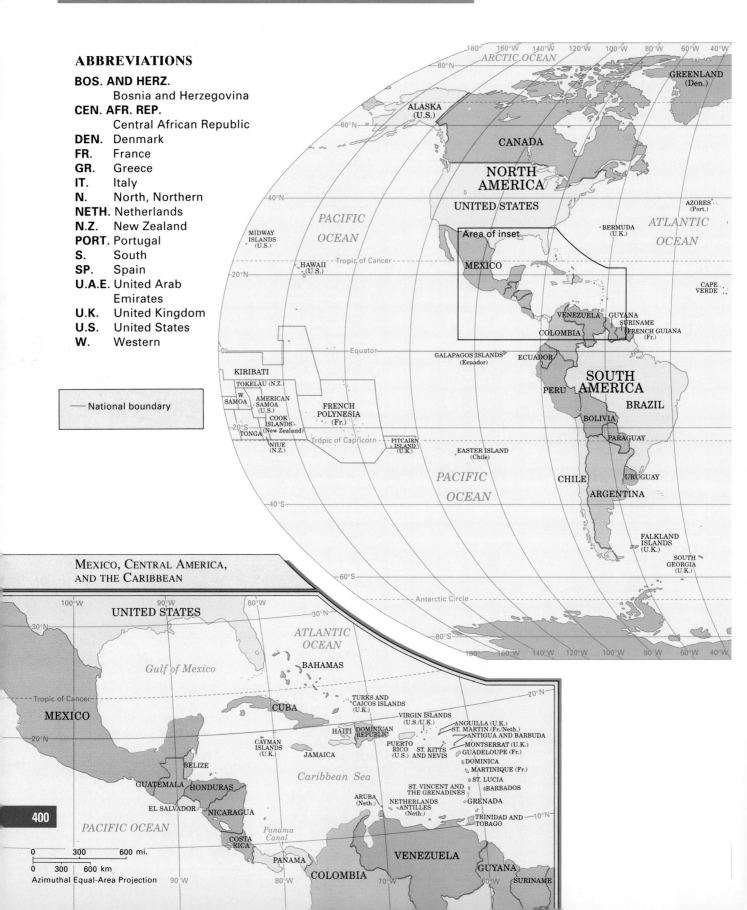

MEXICO, CENTRAL AMERICA, AND THE CARIBBEAN

0   300   600 mi.
0   300   600 km
Azimuthal Equal-Area Projection

ARCTIC OCEAN

80°N

RUSSIA

60°N

ASIA

40°N

Arctic Circle

ICELAND

Area of inset

EUROPE

KAZAKHSTAN

MONGOLIA

N. KOREA

GEORGIA
ARMENIA
TURKEY
AZERBAIJAN
TURKMENISTAN
UZBEKISTAN
KYRGYZSTAN
TAJIKISTAN

S.
KOREA

JAPAN

CYPRUS
LEBANON
ISRAEL
SYRIA
IRAQ
IRAN
AFGHANISTAN

PEOPLE'S REPUBLIC OF
CHINA

PACIFIC
OCEAN

MOROCCO

TUNISIA

JORDAN
KUWAIT
QATAR
PAKISTAN
NEPAL
BHUTAN
TAIWAN

20°N

CANARY IS.
(Sp.)

ALGERIA

LIBYA

EGYPT

BAHRAIN
SAUDI
ARABIA
U.A.E.
OMAN

INDIA

BANGLADESH
MYANMAR
(BURMA)
THAILAND
LAOS
HONG
KONG
(U.K.)

N. MARIANA
ISLANDS
(U.S.)

WESTERN
SAHARA
(Morocco)

VIETNAM
CAMBODIA

PHILIPPINES

GUAM (U.S.)

MARSHALL
ISLANDS

MAURITANIA

MALI

NIGER

YEMEN

FEDERATED
STATES OF
MICRONESIA

SENEGAL
GAMBIA
GUINEA
BISSAU
GUINEA
SIERRA
LEONE
LIBERIA
BURKINA
FASO
CÔTE
D'IVOIRE
GHANA
TOGO
BENIN

AFRICA

CHAD

SUDAN

DJIBOUTI

PALAU (U.S.)

NIGERIA

CEN. AFR. REP.

ETHIOPIA

SRI
LANKA

BRUNEI
MALAYSIA
SINGAPORE

EQUATORIAL GUINEA

CAMEROON

UGANDA

SOMALIA

MALDIVES

SÃO TOMÉ AND
PRINCIPE

GABON

KENYA

INDONESIA

PAPUA
NEW GUINEA

NAURU

KIRIBATI

RWANDA

CABINDA
(Angola)

CONGO

ZAIRE

BURUNDI

TANZANIA

SEYCHELLES

INDIAN OCEAN

SOLOMON
ISLANDS

TUVALU

ATLANTIC

OCEAN

ANGOLA

ZAMBIA

MALAWI

MOZAMBIQUE

COMOROS

VANUATU

FIJI

20°S

WALVIS BAY
(S. Africa)

ZIMBABWE

MADAGASCAR

MAURITIUS

NEW
CALEDONIA
(Fr.)

NAMIBIA

BOTSWANA

Prime Meridian

SWAZILAND

SOUTH
AFRICA

LESOTHO

AUSTRALIA

NEW
ZEALAND

40°S

N

W   E

S

Scale at Equator

0   1000   2000 mi.

0   1000   2000 km.

Robinson Projection

60°S

80°S

ANTARCTICA

20°W   0°   20°E   40°E   60°E   80°E   100°E   120°E   140°E   160°E   180°

EUROPE

20°E
30°E
40°E

10°E

NORWAY

SWEDEN

FINLAND

60°N

North
Sea

DENMARK

ESTONIA

Baltic Sea

LATVIA

RUSSIA

IRELAND

UNITED
KINGDOM

LITHUANIA
(Russia)

0   300   600 mi.

NETHERLANDS

BELARUS

0   300   600 km

Azimuthal Equal-Area Projection

BELGIUM

GERMANY

POLAND

UKRAINE

LUXEMBOURG

CZECHOSLOVAKIA

60°N

ATLANTIC

FRANCE

LIECHTENSTEIN
SWITZERLAND
AUSTRIA

HUNGARY

MOLDOVA

OCEAN

SLOVENIA

ROMANIA

Black
Sea

40°N

MONACO
ANDORRA

SAN
MARINO

CROATIA
BOS.
AND
HERZ.

YUGOSLAVIA

PORTUGAL

SPAIN

CORSICA
(Fr.)

ITALY

VATICAN
CITY

Adriatic Sea

BULGARIA

MACEDONIA

20°W

BALEARIC IS.
(Sp.)

SARDINIA
(It.)

ALBANIA

GREECE

TURKEY

GIBRALTAR
(U.K.)

Prime Meridian

Mediterranean Sea

SICILY
(It.)

CRETE
(Gr.)

MOROCCO

ALGERIA

MALTA

20°E

30°E

10°W

0°

10°E

401

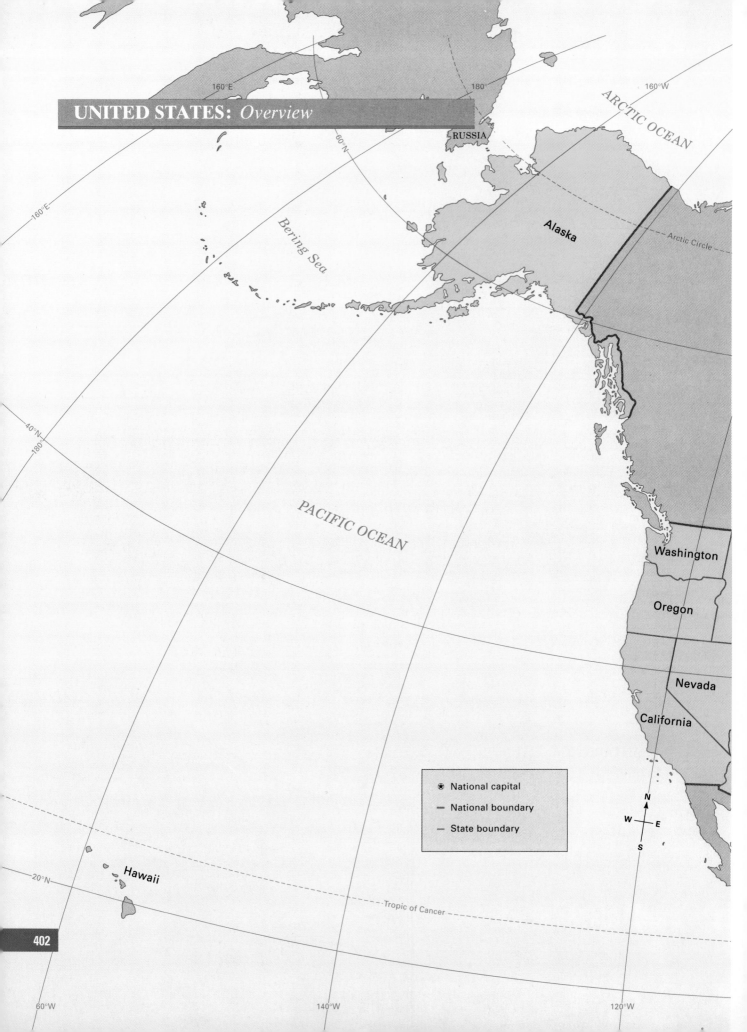

ARCTIC OCEAN

160°E

180

160°W

RUSSIA

Alaska

Arctic Circle

60°N

Bering Sea

160°E

40°N

180

PACIFIC OCEAN

Washington

Oregon

Nevada

California

National capital

National boundary

State boundary

N
W   E
S

20°N

Hawaii

Tropic of Cancer

60°W

140°W

120°W

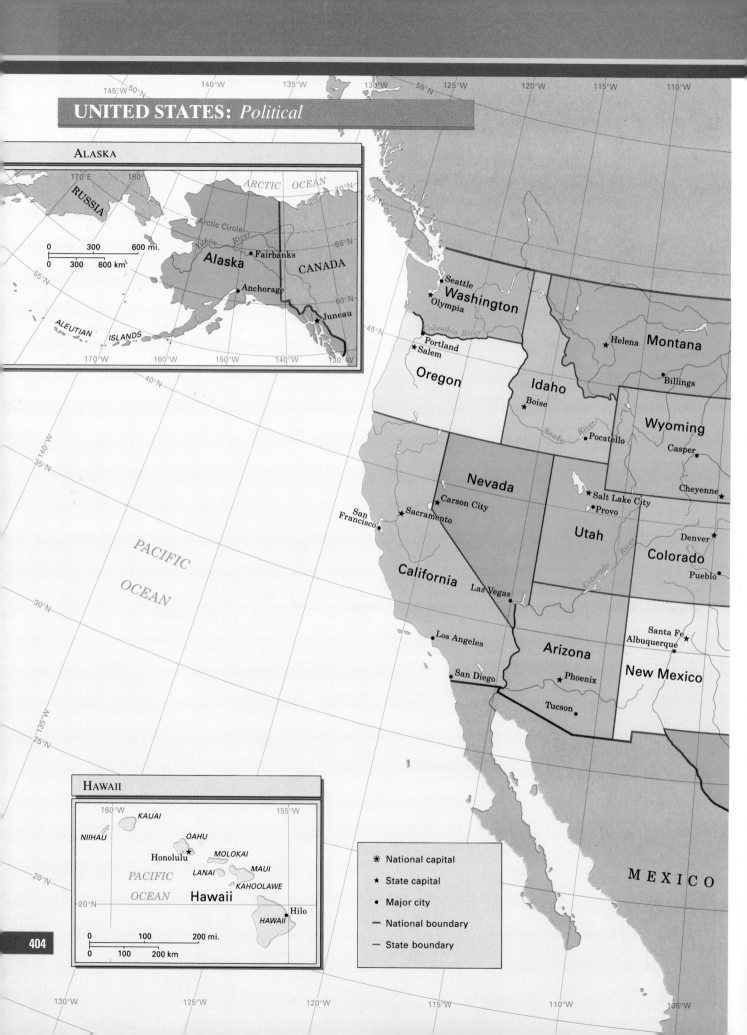

UNITED STATES: *Political*

CANADA

Lake Superior

North Dakota
Bismarck ★   Fargo •

Minnesota

Lake Huron

Michigan

Lake Ontario

Maine
Augusta ★

Vermont
Burlington •   Montpelier ★   **New**   Portland •
Hampshire   Concord ★

St. Paul ★
Minneapolis •

Wisconsin
Milwaukee •

Lansing ★

Lake Erie

Albany ★
New York   **Massachusetts**
Hartford ★   Providence ★
New Haven •   **Rhode Island**
Connecticut

Boston ★

South Dakota
Pierre ★

Sioux Falls •

Madison ★

Chicago •

Detroit •

Cleveland •

Pennsylvania
Harrisburg ★   **New**   New York •
Pittsburgh •   **Jersey**
Wilmington •   Trenton ★
Iowa
Sioux City •
Des Moines •

Nebraska
Omaha •

Ohio
Columbus ★

Philadelphia •

Missouri River
Platte River

Lincoln ★

Illinois
Springfield ★   **Indiana**
Indianapolis •

Baltimore •   **Delaware**
Dover ★
Washington •   Annapolis ★
Maryland

Kansas
Topeka ★
Wichita •

Kansas City •

St. Louis •   Louisville •   Frankfort ★

West
Virginia
Charleston ★

Virginia

Richmond •   Norfolk •

Arkansas River

Jefferson City ★

Evansville •

Kentucky

Missouri

Ohio River

Tulsa •

Oklahoma City ★

Oklahoma

Fort Smith •

Little Rock ★

Arkansas
Memphis •

Nashville ★
Tennessee

Raleigh •

North Carolina
Charlotte •

South
Columbia ★
Carolina

Charleston •

ATLANTIC

OCEAN

Red River

Dallas •

Greenville •

Birmingham •

Georgia

Atlanta ★

Savannah •

Texas

Austin ★
Houston •

Louisiana
Jackson ★

Mississippi

Baton Rouge ★
New Orleans •

Mississippi River

Alabama
Montgomery ★

Tallahassee ★

Florida
Tampa •

Rio Grande

Gulf of Mexico

N
W   E
S

Miami •

BAHAMAS

CUBA

0   200   400 mi.
0   200   400 km
Albers Equal-Area Projection

UNITED STATES: *Physical*

ALASKA

RUSSIA

ARCTIC OCEAN

BROOKS RANGE

Arctic Circle

SEWARD PEN.

Bering Strait

CANADA

Mt. McKinley
20,320 ft.
6,194 m

ALASKA RANGE

ALEUTIAN ISLANDS

KODIAK

170°E 180 170°W 160°W 150°W 140°W 130°W

70°N 65°N 60°N 55°N

0 300 600 mi.
0 300 600 km

PACIFIC OCEAN

COASTAL RANGES

CASCADE RANGE

Puget Sound

Mt. Rainier
14,410 ft.
4,392 m

Mt. St. Helens
8,364 ft.
2,549 m

Mt. Hood
11,239 ft.
3,426 m

COLUMBIA PLATEAU

Columbia River

Snake River

BITTERROOT RANGE

ROCKY MOUNTAINS

Missouri River

Yellowstone River

BIG HORN MTS.

CONTINENTAL

Mt. Shasta
14,162 ft.
4,317 m

SIERRA NEVADA

CENTRAL VALLEY

San Joaquin River

Sacramento River

San Francisco Bay

GREAT BASIN

Great Salt Lake

WASATCH RANGE

UINTA MTS.

DIVIDE

Pikes Peak
14,110 ft.
4,310 m

Mt. Whitney
14,494 ft.
4,418 m

DEATH VALLEY

MOJAVE DESERT

CHANNEL ISLANDS

GRAND CANYON

Colorado River

PAINTED DESERT

Salton Sea

Gila River

Colorado River

Rio Grande

SANGRE DE CRISTO MTS.

SACRAMENTO MTS.

Pecos River

MEXICO

HAWAIIAN ISLANDS

KAUAI

NIIHAU

OAHU

MOLOKAI

LANAI MAUI

KAHOOLAWE

PACIFIC OCEAN

HAWAII

160°W 155°W

20°N

0 100 200 mi.
0 100 200 km

Land Elevation

Feet	Meters
13,120	4,000
6,560	2,000
1,640	500
656	200
0	0
Below sea level	Below sea level

Ice-covered land

▲ Mountain Peak

130°W 125°W 120°W 115°W 110°W 105°W

105°W 100°W 95°W 90°W 85°W 80°W 75°W 70°W 55°N 65°W 60°W

50°N

CANADA

45°N

Lake of
the Woods

MESABI
RANGE   Lake Superior

G   WHITE
R   MTS.
E   BLACK   Lake   ▲ Mt. Washington
A   HILLS   Huron   6,288 ft.
T   BADLANDS   Lake   1,917 m
                                      Michigan
                                                ADIRONDACK
                                                MTS.
            SAND HILLS   CATSKILL   NANTUCKET
                                                       MTS.   MARTHA'S
            Platte   River   Lake Ontario   VINEYARD
P   Des   LONG ISLAND   40°N
L   Moines   Lake Erie   Susquehanna
A   Arkansas River   River   River   Delaware
I   Missouri   Bay
N   River   CENTRAL   PLAINS   ALLEGHENY
S   Mississippi   PLATEAU   Chesapeake Bay
                    River   Wabash   River   Ohio   River   35°N
                    OZARK   River   A   ATLANTIC
CRISTO MTS.   PLATEAU   CUMBERLAND P P
Peak   PLATEAU   A   BLUE   OCEAN   70°W
ft.   OUACHITA   Arkansas   L   RIDGE ▲ Mt. Mitchell
▲   MOUNTAINS   River   A   MTS.   6,684 ft.
                             Mississippi   C   2,037 m   FALL LINE
            LLANO   River   Tennessee H   ATLANTIC
            ESTACADO   Red River   River   I   COASTAL
                            Red   Sabine   A   PLAIN   30°N
                            Colorado River   Tombigbee   N   Savannah River
            EDWARDS   Brazos   River   River   River Chattahoochee
Pecos   PLATEAU   River   Alabama   M   River
River   Colorado   Pearl   River River   T   Altamaha
                   River   GULF   COASTAL   PLAIN   S   R.
Rio   Galveston   Pensacola
Grande   Bay   Mobile   Bay
                                     Bay
                                                   N
                                             Tampa
O   Bay   Lake
                                          W E Okeechobee   BAHAMAS   25°N
                            Gulf of Mexico   EVERGLADES
                                          S

                            0   200   400 mi.
                            0   200   400 km   FLORIDA KEYS
                            Albers Equal-Area Projection   CUBA   20°N

100°W   95°W   90°W   85°W   80°W   75°W

407

UNITED STATES: *Climate*

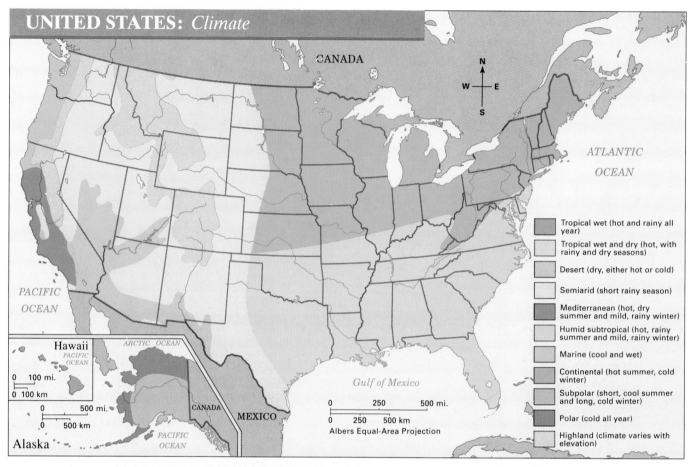

CANADA

ATLANTIC OCEAN

PACIFIC OCEAN

Gulf of Mexico

MEXICO

Hawaii
PACIFIC OCEAN
ARCTIC OCEAN

0 100 mi.
0 100 km

0 500 mi.
0 500 km

CANADA

Alaska
PACIFIC OCEAN

0   250   500 mi.
0   250   500 km
Albers Equal-Area Projection

- Tropical wet (hot and rainy all year)
- Tropical wet and dry (hot, with rainy and dry seasons)
- Desert (dry, either hot or cold)
- Semiarid (short rainy season)
- Mediterranean (hot, dry summer and mild, rainy winter)
- Humid subtropical (hot, rainy summer and mild, rainy winter)
- Marine (cool and wet)
- Continental (hot summer, cold winter)
- Subpolar (short, cool summer and long, cold winter)
- Polar (cold all year)
- Highland (climate varies with elevation)

UNITED STATES: *Vegetation*

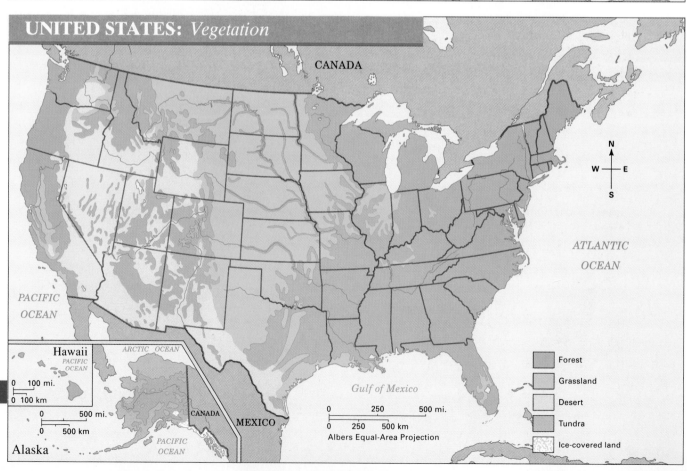

CANADA

ATLANTIC OCEAN

PACIFIC OCEAN

Gulf of Mexico

MEXICO

Hawaii
PACIFIC OCEAN
ARCTIC OCEAN

0 100 mi.
0 100 km

0 500 mi.
0 500 km

CANADA

Alaska
PACIFIC OCEAN

0   250   500 mi.
0   250   500 km
Albers Equal-Area Projection

- Forest
- Grassland
- Desert
- Tundra
- Ice-covered land

408

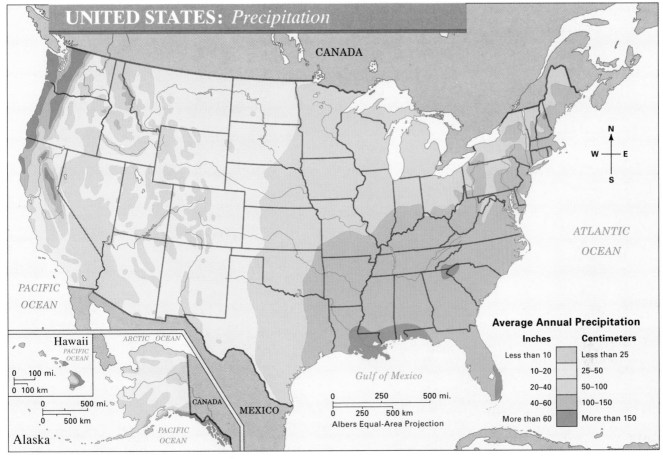

UNITED STATES: *Precipitation*

CANADA

PACIFIC
OCEAN

ATLANTIC
OCEAN

Gulf of Mexico

Average Annual Precipitation

Inches	Centimeters
Less than 10	Less than 25
10–20	25–50
20–40	50–100
40–60	100–150
More than 60	More than 150

Hawaii
PACIFIC
OCEAN
0 100 mi.
0 100 km

ARCTIC OCEAN

CANADA

MEXICO

0 500 mi.
0 500 km
Alaska
PACIFIC
OCEAN

0   250   500 mi.
0   250   500 km
Albers Equal-Area Projection

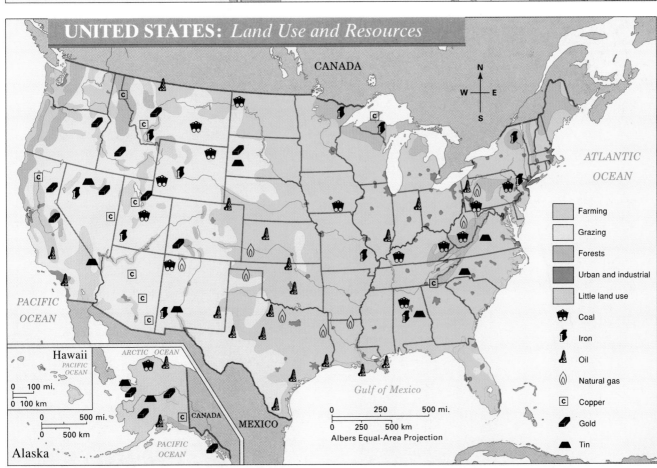

UNITED STATES: *Land Use and Resources*

CANADA

PACIFIC
OCEAN

ATLANTIC
OCEAN

Gulf of Mexico

	Farming
	Grazing
	Forests
	Urban and industrial
	Little land use
	Coal
	Iron
	Oil
	Natural gas
C	Copper
	Gold
	Tin

Hawaii
PACIFIC
OCEAN
0 100 mi.
0 100 km

ARCTIC OCEAN

CANADA

MEXICO

0 500 mi.
0 500 km
Alaska
PACIFIC
OCEAN

0   250   500 mi.
0   250   500 km
Albers Equal-Area Projection

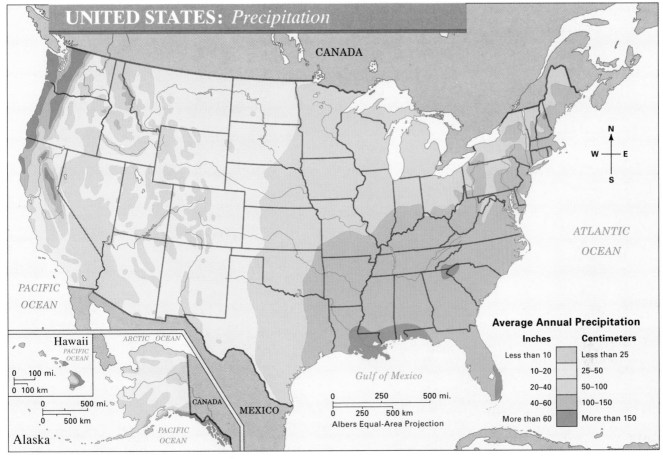

409

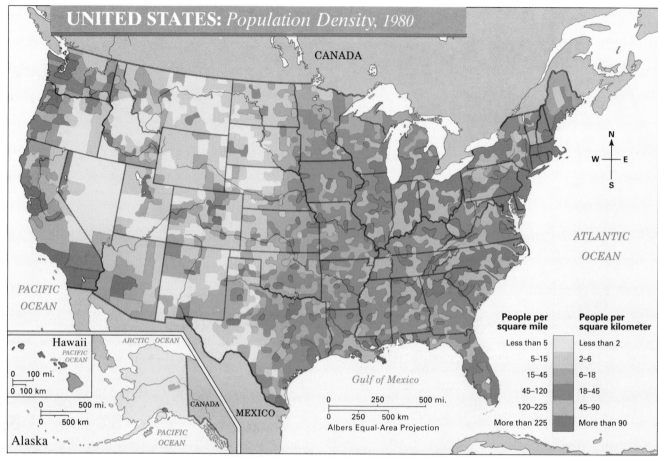

UNITED STATES: *Population Density, 1980*

CANADA

ATLANTIC OCEAN

PACIFIC OCEAN

N
W · E
S

Gulf of Mexico

ARCTIC OCEAN

Hawaii
PACIFIC OCEAN
0 100 mi.
0 100 km

CANADA

MEXICO

Alaska
PACIFIC OCEAN

0   250   500 mi.
0   250   500 km
Albers Equal-Area Projection

People per square mile	People per square kilometer
Less than 5	Less than 2
5–15	2–6
15–45	6–18
45–120	18–45
120–225	45–90
More than 225	More than 90

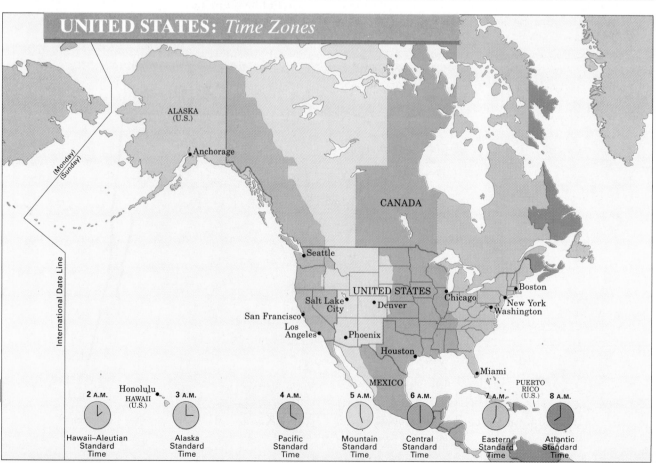

UNITED STATES: *Time Zones*

ALASKA (U.S.)
Anchorage

(Monday)
(Sunday)

International Date Line

CANADA

Seattle

UNITED STATES

Salt Lake City
Denver
Chicago
Boston
New York
Washington

San Francisco
Los Angeles
Phoenix

Houston

Miami

MEXICO

PUERTO RICO (U.S.)

2 A.M.
Honolulu
HAWAII (U.S.)
Hawaii–Aleutian Standard Time

3 A.M.
Alaska Standard Time

4 A.M.
Pacific Standard Time

5 A.M.
Mountain Standard Time

6 A.M.
Central Standard Time

7 A.M.
Eastern Standard Time

8 A.M.
Atlantic Standard Time

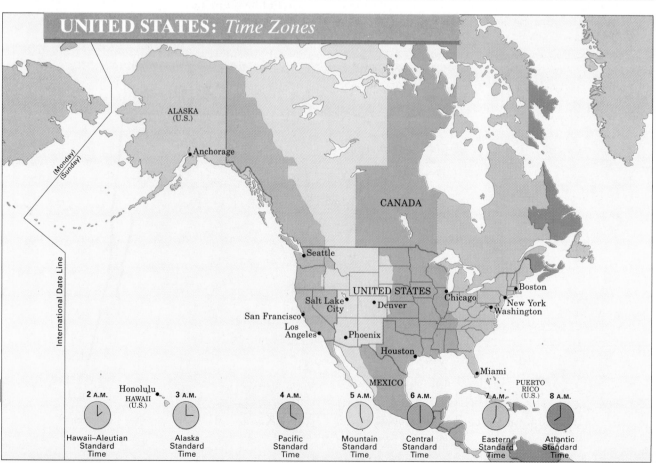

This Gazetteer will help you locate many of the places discussed in this book. Latitude and longitude given for large areas of land and water refer to the centermost point of the area; latitude and longitude of rivers refer to the river mouth. The page number tells you where to find each place on a map.

PLACE	LAT.	LONG.	PAGE
A			
Africa (continent)			**G6**
Alabama (state)	32°N	87°W	**403**
Alaska (state)	64°N	150°W	**402**
Albany (capital of New York)	43°N	74°W	**145**
Annapolis (capital of Maryland)	39°N	76°W	**145**
Appalachian Mountains (range in Eastern U.S.)	37°N	82°W	**14**
Arizona (state)	34°N	113°W	**403**
Arkansas (state)	34°N	93°W	**403**
Atlanta (capital of Georgia)	33°N	84°W	**97**
Augusta (capital of Maine)	44°N	70°W	**145**
Austin (capital of Texas)	30°N	98°W	**249**
Australia (continent)			**G4**
B			
Baton Rouge (capital of Louisiana)	30°N	91°W	**97**
Beijing (capital of the country of China)	40°N	117°E	**G7**
Bismarck (capital of North Dakota)	47°N	101°W	**199**
Boise (capital of Idaho)	44°N	116°W	**299**
Boston (capital of Massachusetts)	42°N	71°W	**145**
Brazil (country in South America)			**G13**
C			
Calcutta (city, in the country of India)	22°N	88°E	**G8**
California (state)	38°N	121°W	**402**
Canada (country in North America)	50°N	100°W	**400**
Cape Canaveral (Florida launch site)	28°N	81°W	**97**
Caribbean (Sea and islands southeast of U.S.)			**G12**
Carson City (capital of Nevada)	39°N	120°W	**299**
Cascade Range (mountains in Western U.S.)	42°N	122°W	**14**
Central Plains (eastern part of the Interior Plains)			**14**

PLACE	LAT.	LONG.	PAGE
Central Valley (valley in central California)	38°N	122°W	**255**
Chicago (Illinois, third largest city in U.S.)	42°N	88°W	**199**
China (country in Asia)			**G7**
Coastal Plain borders Atlantic coast of U.S.)			**14**
Charleston (capital of West Virginia)	38°N	82°W	**97**
Cheyenne (capital of Wyoming)	41°N	105°W	**299**
Colorado (state)	39°N	106°W	**403**
Colorado River (river in the Southwest U.S.)	32°N	115°W	**205**
Columbia (capital of South Carolina)	34°N	81°W	**97**
Columbia River (river in the Western U.S.)	46°N	123°W	**255**
Columbus (capital of Ohio)	40°N	83°W	**199**
Concord (capital of New Hampshire)	43°N	72°W	**145**
Connecticut (state)	41°N	73°W	**403**
Continental Divide (imaginary line in the Rocky Mountains that separates rivers that flow east from those that flow west)			**406**
D			
Death Valley (California desert; lowest point in U.S.)	36°N	117°W	**255**
Delaware (state)	38°N	75°W	**403**
Denver (capital of Colorado)	40°N	105°W	**299**
Des Moines (capital of Iowa)	42°N	94°W	**199**
Dover (capital of Delaware)	39°N	75°W	**145**
E			
Everglades (swamp in Florida)	26°N	81°W	**51**
F			
Florida (state)	28°N	82°W	**403**
Frankfort (capital of Kentucky)	38°N	85°W	**97**

PLACE	LAT.	LONG.	PAGE

G

Georgia (state)	32°N	83°W	**403**
Grand Canyon (Arizona, largest canyon in U.S)	36°N	113°W	**406**
Great Basin desert area in Western U.S.)	40°N	117°W	**14**
Great Lakes lakes between U.S. and Canada)			**G1**
Great Plains (western part of the Interior Plains)	45°N	104°W	**14**
Great Salt Lake (saltwater lake in Utah)	41°N	112°W	**255**
Gulf of Mexico (part of Atlantic Ocean, east of Mexico, south of U.S.)	25°N	93°W	**14**

H

Harrisburg (capital of Pennsylvania)	40°N	77°W	**145**
Hartford (capital of Connecticut)	42°N	73°W	**145**
Hawaii (state)	20°N	157°W	**402**
Helena (capital of Montana)	47°N	112°W	**299**
Honolulu (capital of Hawaii)	21°N	158°W	**299**
Hudson River (river in northeastern U.S.)	41°N	73°W	**103**

I

Idaho (state)	44°N	115°W	**403**
Illinois (state)	40°N	90°W	**403**
Indiana (state)	39°N	86°W	**403**
Indianapolis (capital of Indiana)	40°N	86°W	**199**
Iowa (state)	42°N	94°W	**403**

J

Jackson (capital of Mississippi)	32°N	90°W	**97**
Jamestown (first permanent English settlement in U.S.)	38°N	78°W	**55**
Jefferson City (capital of Missouri)	38°N	92°W	**199**
Juneau (capital of Alaska)	58°N	134°W	**299**

PLACE	LAT.	LONG.	PAGE

K

| Kansas (state) | 38°N | 99°W | **403** |
| Kentucky (state) | 37°N | 87°W | **403** |

L

Lansing (capital of Michigan)	43°N	85°W	**199**
Lincoln (capital of Nebraska)	41°N	97°W	**199**
Little Rock (capital of Arkansas)	35°N	92°W	**97**
Los Angeles (second largest city in U.S.)	34°N	118°W	**299**
Louisiana (state)	30°N	92°W	**403**

M

Madison (capital of Wisconsin)	43°N	89°W	**199**
Maine (state)	45°N	69°W	**403**
Maryland (state)	39°N	76°W	**403**
Massachusetts (state)	42°N	72°W	**403**
Mesabi Range (low hills in northern Minnesota where iron ore is mined)	47°N	93°W	**151**
Mexico (country in North America)	23°N	104°W	**400**
Michigan (state)	45°N	87°W	**403**
Minnesota (state)	46°N	90°W	**403**
Mississippi (state)	32°N	89°W	**403**
Mississippi River (river in midwestern U.S.)	31°N	91°W	**14**
Missouri (state)	38°N	94°W	**403**
Missouri River (river in midwestern U.S.)	40°N	96°W	**151**
Montana (state)	47°N	111°W	**403**
Montgomery (capital of Alabama)	32°N	86°W	**97**
Montpelier (capital of Vermont)	44°N	73°W	**145**
Mount McKinley (North America's highest mountain; located in Alaska)	64°N	150°W	**255**

N

| Nashville (capital of Tennessee) | 36°N | 87°W | **97** |
| Nebraska (state) | 41°N | 101°W | **403** |

Nevada (state)	39°N	117°W	**402**
New Hampshire (state)	43°N	71°W	**403**
New Jersey (state)	40°N	74°W	**403**
New Mexico (state)	34°N	107°W	**403**
New York (state)	42°N	78°W	**403**
New York City (largest city in the U.S.)	41°N	74°W	**145**
North America (one of the Earth's seven continents; U.S. located there)			**400**
North Carolina (state)	35°N	81°W	**403**
North Dakota (state)	47°N	101°W	**403**

O

Ohio (state)	40°N	83°W	**403**
Ohio River (river in midwestern U.S.)	37°N	89°W	**407**
Oklahoma (state)	36°N	98°W	**403**
Oklahoma City (capital of Oklahoma)	35°N	98°W	**249**
Olympia (capital of Washington)	47°N	123°W	**299**
Oregon (state)	43°N	121°W	**402**

P

Painted Desert (desert in Arizona)	36°N	112°W	**205**
Pennsylvania (state)	41°N	78°W	**403**
Phoenix (capital of Arizona)	33°N	112°W	**249**
Piedmont (an area of low hills east of the Appalachian Mountains)	39°N	75°W	**51**
Pierre (capital of South Dakota)	44°N	100°W	**199**
Providence (capital of Rhode Island)	42°N	71°W	**145**

R

Raleigh (capital of North Carolina)	36°N	79°W	**97**
Rhode Island (state)	42°N	72°W	**403**
Richmond (capital of Virginia)	38°N	77°W	**97**
Rio Grande (river in the southwestern U.S.)	29°N	100°W	**205**
Rocky Mountains (range in Western North America)	50°N	114°W	**14**

S

Sacramento (capital of California)	39°N	121°W	**299**

St. Lawrence River (river in the northeastern U.S. and southeastern Canada)	48°N	70°W	**103**
St. Paul (capital of Minnesota)	45°N	93°W	**199**
Salem (capital of Oregon)	45°N	123°W	**299**
Salt Lake City (capital of Utah)	41°N	112°W	**299**
Santa Fe (capital of New Mexico)	36°N	106°W	**249**
Sierra Nevada (mountain range in California)	39°N	120°W	**14**
South Carolina (state)	34°N	81°W	**403**
South Dakota (state)	44°N	101°W	**403**
Southeast Asia (part of the continent of Asia)			**G10**
Springfield (capital of Illinois)	40°N	90°W	**199**

T

Tallahassee (capital of Florida)	30°N	84°W	**97**
Tennessee (state)	35°N	88°W	**403**
Texas (state)	31°N	101°W	**403**
Topeka (capital of Kansas)	39°N	96°W	**199**
Trenton (capital of New Jersey)	40°N	75°W	**145**

U

United States (country in North America)	38°N	110°W	**400**
Utah (state)	39°N	112°W	**403**

V

Vermont (state)	43°N	72°W	**403**
Virginia (state)	37°N	80°W	**403**

W

Washington (state)	47°N	121°W	**402**
Washington, D.C. (capital of the U.S.)	38°N	77°W	**403**
West Virginia (state)	39°N	80°W	**403**
Wisconsin (state)	44°N	91°W	**403**
Wyoming (state)	42°N	108°W	**403**

GLOSSARY OF GEOGRAPHIC TERMS

glacier
a large ice mass that moves slowly down a mountain or over land

mountain
a steeply raised mass of land, much higher than the surrounding country

ocean or **sea**
a salty body of water covering a large area of the earth

mountain range
a row of mountains

tree line
on a mountain, the area above which no trees grow

mountain pass
a gap between mountains

valley
low land between hills or mountains

basin
a bowl-shaped area of land surrounded by higher land

hill
a raised mass of land, smaller than a mountain

mesa
a wide, flat-topped mountain with steep sides, found mostly in dry areas

prairie
a large, level area of grassland without trees

desert
a dry area where few plants grow

cliff
the steep, almost vertical, edge of a hill, mountain, or plain

plain
a broad, flat area of land

sea level
the level of the surface of the ocean

volcano
an opening in the earth, often raised, through which lava and gasses from the earth's interior escape

harbor
a sheltered body of water where ships can safely dock

strait
a narrow channel of water connecting two large bodies of water

coast
the land next to an ocean

bay
part of a lake or ocean extending into the land

peninsula
land mostly surrounded by water but connected to the mainland

island
a body of land completely surrounded by water

isthmus
a narrow strip of land connecting two large bodies of land

river
a large stream that runs into a lake, ocean, or another river

lake
a body of water completely surrounded by land

Pronunciation Key

This chart presents the system of phonetic respellings used to indicate pronunciation in the Biographical Dictionary and in the chapters of this book.

Spellings	Symbol	Spellings	Symbol	Spellings	Symbol
pat	a	kick, cat, pique	k	thin, this	th
pay	ay	lid, needle	l	cut	uh
care	air	mum	m	urge, term, firm, word, heard	ur
father	ah	no, sudden	n		
bib	b	thing	ng	valve	v
church	ch	pot, horrid	ah	with	w
deed, milled	d	toe	oh	yes	y
pet	eh	caught, paw, for	aw	zebra, xylem	z
bee	ee	noise	oy	vision, pleasure, garage	zh
life, phase, rough	f	took	u		
gag	g	boot	oo	about, item, edible, gallop, circus	uh
hat	h	out	ow		
which	hw	pop	p	butter	ur
pit	ih	roar	r		
pie, by	eye, y	sauce	s	Capital letters indicate stressed syllables.	
pier	ihr	ship, dish	sh		
judge	j	tight, stopped	t		

A

Arkwright, Sir Richard 1732–1792, inventor from England who developed the water frame for spinning thread (p. 128).

B

Bell, Alexander Graham 1847–1922, inventor of the telephone (p. 311).

C

Catlin, George 1796–1872, painter of many pictures of North American Indians and their cultures (p. 154).

Carter, Jessie Lee b. 1901, member of a family that left its farm in Tennessee to work in a textile mill in North Carolina in 1905 (p. 91).

Carver, George Washington 1864(?)–1943, scientist who helped farmers to use better farming methods like crop rotation (p. 76).

Clinton, DeWitt 1769–1828, governor of New York who helped build the Erie Canal (p. 133).

Cochran, Jacqueline 1910–1980, pilot who became the first woman to fly faster than the speed of sound (p. 291).

Coronado, Francisco Vasquez *(vas KWEHZ)* **de** 1510–1554, Spanish explorer who led an expedition into the Southwest in 1540 (p. 213).

D

Deere, John 1804–1886, inventor who developed a steel plow; helped advance corn farming on the midwestern prairie (p. 161).

E

Eisenhower, Dwight David 1890–1969, 34th President of the United States; supported the building of the interstate highway system (p. 309).

Estéban d. 1539, slave who was sent by Marcos de Niza to find the legendary cities of Cibola; became first person from beyond the Atlantic Ocean to meet Pueblo Indians (p. 212).

Evans, Oliver 1755–1819, inventor who developed new ways to mill wheat; later worked at developing steam engines for use in industry (p. 121).

F

Ford, Henry 1863–1947, automaker who developed the assembly line; helped make cars that people in the United States could afford (p. 188).

Frémont, Jessie Benton 1824–1902, writer who worked with her husband John to write about his western explorations (p. 262).

Frémont, John C. 1813–1890, explorer who, along with his wife Jessie, wrote books about his expeditions in the western region (p. 262).

G

Gary, Elbert Henry 1846–1927, head of U. S. Steel; founded the city of Gary, Indiana (p. 183).

Gillespie, Henry, founder of Aspen, Colorado (p. 267).

Goodnight, Charles 1836–1929, rancher who was one of the earliest and most successful of the settlers from the United States in the Southwest; helped break the Goodnight-Loving cattle trail (p. 219).

Greene, Catharine Littlefield 1755–1814, financial backer and supporter of Eli Whitney, inventor of the cotton gin (p. 62).

Guthrie, Woodrow Wilson 1912–1967, folk singer and composer (p. 8).

H

Hazen, Chester 1800s, businessman who opened Wisconsin's first cheese factory using modern machinery in 1864 (p. 182).

Higgins, Pattillo 1863–1955, Texas oilman; helped promote the discovery of oil at Spindletop (p. 236).

Hoard, William Dempster 1836–1919, newspaper editor who promoted dairy farming as an alternative to wheat farming (p. 172).

J

Jones, Mary Harris 1830–1930, known as "Mother Jones"; coal mine labor organizer who led many strikes (p. 88).

Judah, Anna 1828–1895, wife of Theodore Judah and strong supporter of her husband's plans for a transcontinental railroad (p. 274).

Judah, Theodore Dehone 1826–1863, engineer; planned the route for the first transcontinental railroad; founder of the Central Pacific Railroad Company (p. 273).

K

Kellogg, Will Keith 1860–1951, inventor and manufacturer who developed the corn flake and other foods (p. 178).

Kennedy, John Fitzgerald 1917–1963, 35th President of the United States; supported the exploration of space (p. 293).

King, Martin Luther, Jr. 1929–1968, church leader who fought for civil rights in the 1950s–1960s (p. 99).

Kino *(KEE noh)*, **Eusebio** *(ay oo ZA byoh)* **Francisco** 1645–1711, padre who founded several missions in the Southwest; helped introduce ranching to the region (p. 215).

Kipling, Rudyard 1865–1936, English author who wrote *Captains Courageous* and other books (p. 115).

L

Lewis, John L. 1880–1969, coal mine labor organizer who helped set up the United Mine Workers labor union and the Committee for Industrial Organization, the CIO (p. 87).

Lowell, Francis Cabot 1775–1817, built the first mill in the United States for manufacturing cloth (p. 129).

M

Marshall, James W. 1810–1885, person who discovered gold at sawmill owned by John Sutter; helped start California's gold rush (p. 264).

McCormick, Cyrus Hall 1809–1884, inventor of a machine, the reaper, used to harvest wheat (p. 162).

Muir, John 1838–1914, naturalist who studied and wrote about the West's wilderness areas; founded the Sierra Club (p. 301).

N

Nelson, Klondy 1900s, writer who recorded events of her childhood as the daughter of an Alaskan gold miner (p. 263).

Niza *(NEE suh)*, **Marcos de** 1500s, explorer sent by the King of Spain to find the mythical Cibola, thought to be in the Southwest region (p. 212).

O

Oñate *(aw NYAH tee)*, **Juan de** 1549(?)–1628(?), Spanish explorer who helped found the first Spanish settlement in New Mexico (p. 214).

Olds, Ransom Eli 1864–1950, built one of the first cars in the United States in Michigan (p. 189).

P

Parks, Rosa b. 1913, woman whose actions helped inspire major civil rights activities in the Southeast (p. 98).

Penn, William 1644–1718, Englishman who founded the state of Pennsylvania (p. 119).

Pillsbury, Charles Alfred 1842–1899, flour miller who introduced European rolling equipment to the United States (p. 179).

Pope, Albert Augustus 1843–1909, manufacturer of bicycles (p. 307).

Powell, John Wesley 1834–1902, geologist and explorer; became first person from the United States to explore the Grand Canyon (p. 233).

Pynchon, William 1590–1662, English settler who founded Springfield, Massachusetts (p. 110).

R

Ride, **Sally Kristen** b. 1951, astronaut; became first American woman to travel in space (p. 294).

Rolfe, John 1585–1622, European settler who helped develop the tobacco crop in Virginia. Married the Native American Pocahontas and helped improve settler-Indian relations (p. 55).

Roosevelt, Theodore 1858–1919, 26th President of the United States; set up an agency in the United States government to organize the building of dams (p. 233).

S

Slater, Samuel 1768–1835, Built the first textile mill in the United States on the Blackstone River, Pawtucket, Rhode Island (p. 126).

Smith, Jedediah Strong 1799(?)–1831, fur trapper and explorer; was one of the first settlers to cross the Sierra Nevada (p. 261).

Smedes, Susan Dabney 1840–1913, writer who recorded events of her life on a Mississippi plantation (p. 64).

Standing Bear, Luther 1868(?)–1939, Sioux Indian leader (p. 156).

Stratton, Joanna, writer who found the material for her book *Pioneer Women* while searching through her grandmother's attic (p. 160).

Strong, Harriet Russell 1844–1926, California farmer who designed a new type of irrigation system and introduced new crop varieties (p. 283).

Sutter, John Augustus 1803–1880 pioneer who started a trading post in California. Discovery of gold at his sawmill led to the gold rush (p. 264).

Swift, Gustavus Franklin 1839–1903, meatpacker from Chicago, Illinois; developed a refrigerated car that advanced the meat industry (p. 181).

Swilling, Jack d. 1879, prospector who helped settle Phoenix, Arizona; formed a canal company to bring water to the city (p. 232).

T

Thomson, J. Edgar 1808–1874, president of the Pennsylvania Railroad; helped introduce a kind of organization widely used in corporations today (p. 139).

Twain, Mark (pen name of Samuel L. Clemens) 1835–1910, author; wrote about life in California during the 1860s. (p. 200).

W

Watson, Thomas Augustus 1854–1934, inventor who helped Alexander Graham Bell invent the telephone (p. 311).

Whitney (*HWIHT nee*), **Eli** 1765–1825, inventor and manufacturer. Invented the cotton gin, which greatly advanced the Southeast cotton industry (p. 62).

Wilder, Laura Ingalls 1867–1957, author who wrote about farm life on the Midwestern prairie (p. 171).

Willard, Simon 1600s, English settler who founded the town of Concord, Massachusetts (p. 110).

Pronunciation Key

This chart presents the pronunciation key used in the Glossary. For a key to the phonetic respellings used to indicate pronunciation in the text of the chapters, see page 337.

Spellings	Symbol	Spellings	Symbol	Spellings	Symbol
pat	ă	**kick**, **c**at, pi**que**	k	**th**in	th
pay	ā	lid, need**l**e	l	**th**is	*th*
care	âr	**mum**	m	**c**ut	ŭ
father	ä	**no**, sudde**n**	n	**ur**ge, t**er**m, f**ir**m,	ûr
bib	b	thi**ng**	ng	w**or**d, h**ear**d	
church	ch	pot, horrid	ŏ	**v**al**ve**	v
deed, mi**ll**ed	d	**toe**	ō	**w**ith	w
pet	ĕ	**caught**, **paw**, **for**	ô	**y**es	y
bee	ē	n**oi**se	oi	**z**ebra, **x**ylem	z
li**fe**, **ph**ase, rou**gh**	f	t**oo**k	ŏŏ	vi**s**ion, plea**s**ure,	zh
gag	g	b**oo**t	ōō	gara**g**e	
hat	h	**out**	ou	**a**bout, it**e**m, edibl**e**,	ə
which	hw	**pop**	p	gall**o**p, circ**u**s	
pit	ĭ	**roar**	r	butt**er**	ər
pie, by	ī	sauce	s		
pier	îr	**ship**, di**sh**	sh	Primary stress ´	
judge	j	**t**igh**t**, stopp**ed**	t	Secondary stress ´	

A

adobe (ə-dō´bē) a type of brick that is made from clay and straw and then dried in the sun (p. 209).

aerospace (âr´ō-spās´) the technology used to design, build, and fly aircraft and spacecraft (p. 293).

agriculture (ăg´rĭ-kŭl´chər) the science and business of growing crops and raising livestock (p. 74).

aqueduct (ăk´wĭ-dŭkt´) a large pipe that carries water from a faraway source to a dry region (p. 234).

assembly line (ə-sĕm´blē līn) a line of workers and machines that a product passes by on a moving belt; each worker or machine in turn adds something or performs a task until the product is finished (p. 189).

aviation (ā´vē-ā´shən) the production and flying of aircraft (p. 291).

B

barrier (băr´ē-ər) something such as a desert or a mountain range that makes passage difficult or impossible (p. 261).

border (bôr´dər) the line separating two areas that may be agreed upon by people or made by nature, or both (p. 35).

broadleaf tree (brôd´lēf´trē) a tree whose leaves are fairly broad and flat, such as an oak, maple, or birch tree (p. 37).

C

canal (kə-năl´) a waterway built by humans and used for shipping, travel, or irrigation (p. 132).

cash crop (kăsh krŏp) a crop that farmers raise to sell for money rather than for their own use (p. 55).

cattle drive (kăt´l drīv) moving a herd of cattle from open land to a faraway market or railroad (p. 220).

claim (klām)the piece of land on which a miner finds gold or silver and marks off as his or her own to mine (p. 265).

climate (klī´mĭt) the weather, including the degree of coldness and hotness and the amount of rain, snow, and wind, that occurs in an area over time (p. 12).

colony (kŏl´ə-nē) an area of land settled by people from a faraway country and ruled by that home country (p. 55).

communications (kə-myōō´nĭ-kā´shənz) a means of sending or receiving information or ideas, such as a telephone, a television, or a computer (p. 311).

community (kə-myōō´nǐ-tē) a group of people who live together or who have common interests or ideas (p. 343).

commute (kə-myōōt´) to travel regularly to or from the place where one works, especially over a long distance (p. 310).

conservation (kŏn´sûr-vā´shən) the careful use and protection of the environment and natural resources (p. 244).

continent (kŏn´tə-nənt) one of the seven large landmasses of the Earth—Africa, Antarctica, Asia, Australia, Europe, North America, and South America (p. 10).

corporation (kôr pə rā´shən) a company that has certain legal rights, including the right to raise money from the public (p. 139).

craftsman (krăfts´mən) a worker who has a certain skill, such as a blacksmith, a carpenter, or a mechanic (p. 113).

crop rotation (krŏp rō tā´shən) the practice of planting a different crop in one field from year to year in order to keep the soil from wearing out (p. 76).

culture (kŭl´chər) the beliefs and way of life of a group of people (p. 155).

D

dairy farming (dâr´ē färm´ing) the business of raising cows to produce milk and milk products (p. 172).

dam (dăm) a barrier built in a waterway to slow or stop the flow of water (p. 233).

E

economy (ǐ kŏn´ə mē) the system of producing or selling natural resources, goods, and services (p. 318).

environment (ĕn-vī´rən-mənt) the natural surroundings, including the soil, plants, animals, water, and air (p. 259).

ethnic group (ĕth´nĭk grōōp) a group of people who share a common culture, religion, race, or nationality (p. 5).

export (ĕk´-spôrt´) a product that is sent to another country to be sold (p. 340).

F

forty-niner (fôr´tē-nī´nər) the name given to a person mining for gold during California's 1849 gold rush (p. 264).

frontier (frŭn-tîr´) the part of a country that people have not yet settled (p. 160).

fuel (fyōō´əl) a substance such as coal or gas that is burned to make heat or to produce power (p. 84).

G

geography (jē-ŏg´rə-fē) the study of the land, water, plants, animal life, and climate of a region; the study of how people use the land and its resources (p. 41).

growing season (grō´ĭng sē´zən) the part of the year when there are no frosts and the weather is warm enough for crops to grow (p. 64).

H

human resources (hyōō´mən rē´sôr´səz) the energy, ideas, skills, and effort people use in their work (p. 25).

I

immigrant (ĭm´ĭ grənt) a person who moves to another country, usually in search of a better life (p. 128).

import (ĭm´-pôrt´) a product that is bought from another country (p. 339).

industry (ĭn´də-strē) the making and selling of a product or service (p. 91).

interdependent (ĭn´tər dĭ pĕn´dənt) a condition in which two or more nations or states need one another for goods, services, or natural resources (p. 318).

interstate highway (ĭn´tər stat´ hī´wā´) a highway that runs through and connects two or more states (p. 309).

invention (ĭn vĕn´shən) a new tool, idea, process, or material that has been produced or put together through study and experimentation (p. 63).

invest (ĭn-vĕst´) to give money, such as to a business, in hopes of making more money in return (p. 139).

iron ore (ī´ərn ôr) rock or earth containing large amounts of iron, a strong, useful kind of metal (p. 184).

irrigation (ĭr´ĭ-gā´shən) the use of ditches and canals to bring water to a dry area (p. 209).

L

labor union (lā´bər yōōn´yən) a group of workers who join together to protect their interests concerning wages and working conditions (p. 87).

livestock (līv´stŏk´) animals such as cattle, pigs, or sheep that are raised for home use or to be sold (p. 180).

lumber (lŭm´bər) wood that has been sawed into boards, planks, or beams (p. 288).

M

manufactured goods (măn´yə făk´chərd gōōdz) products that are made by a mechanical or industrial method, usually to be sold (p. 107).

market (mär´kĭt) a town, country, or region where goods can be bought and sold (p. 179).

mesa (mā´sə) a flat-topped hill or mountain that has steep sides that rise from a plain (p. 209).

migrant worker (mī´grənt wər´kər) a worker who moves from one farm to another, picking ripe crops (p. 284).

mineral (mĭn´ər əl) a substance such as gold, silver, coal, or copper that is found in nature, usually by digging for it in the ground (p. 18).

mission (mĭsh´ən) a settlement formed by Catholic priests in order to bring their religious beliefs to the local people (p. 215).

N

natural gas (năch´ər əl găs) a colorless, odorless gas, often found underground with oil, that is used as a fuel (p. 240).

natural resource (năch´ər əl rē´sôrs´) a useful material found in nature, such as water, forests, or minerals (p. 18).

needleleaf tree (nēd´l lēf trē) a tree with thin, narrow leaves resembling needles, such as a pine, fir, or spruce tree (p. 38).

network (nĕt´wûrk´) a system of routes or lines, as in highway routes or railroad lines, that cross and that are often connected (p. 308).

P

padre (pä´drā) a priest of the Spanish missions in the Southwest and West (p. 214).

pasture (pas´chər) a large field or piece of land where animals such as cattle or sheep graze (p. 170).

petrochemical (pĕt´rō kĕm´ĭ kəl) a chemical obtained by breaking down petroleum or natural gas (p. 243).

petroleum (pə trō´lē əm) a dark, oily liquid that is usually found under the ground and from which gasoline, plastic, and other materials are made (p. 237).

pioneer (pī´ə-nîr´) a person who first explores or settles a new region, leading the way for others to follow (p. 160).

plantation (plăn tā´shən) a large estate or farm where one main crop is raised, usually by workers who live on the grounds (p. 60).

population (pŏp´yə lā´shən) all of the people who live in a certain area (p. 7).

port (pôrt) a place on a river, lake, or ocean, usually near a city or town, where ships can load and unload goods (p. 120).

prairie (prâr´ē) a large, open plain that is covered with grass (p. 161).

precipitation (prĭ sĭp´ĭ tā´shən) any form of water that falls to the earth, such as rain or snow (p. 64).

produce (prŏd´ōōs) farm products, especially fresh fruit and vegetables (p. 283).

pueblo (pwĕb´lō) a Southwest Indian village made up of adobe houses that are grouped together (p. 209).

R

rancho (răn´chō) the livestock farm or ranch of the Spanish settlers (p. 217).

raw material (rô mə tîr´ē əl) a natural substance such as wood or iron ore that is processed in some way to make a finished product (p. 116).

recycling (rē sī´kəl ĭng) the practice of reusing or preparing for reuse waste materials such as glass, paper, or plastic (p. 345).

refinery (rē fī´nə rē) a place where petroleum is broken down into separate products, such as gasoline, kerosene, and petrochemicals (p. 242).

refrigeration (rĭ frĭj´ə rā´shən) the use of ice or cold air to keep food fresh (p. 181).

region (rē´jən) an area of land that shares one or many of the same features, including geography, climate, people, and industries (p. 33).

reservoir (rĕz´ər vwär´) a natural or human-made lake that is used to store water for a town or region (p. 234).

river valley (rĭv´ər văl´ē) an area of land beside a river that often has rich soil as a result of repeated flooding of the river (p. 119).

roundup (round´ŭp) the herding together of cattle for branding, counting, or guiding to a far-away market or railroad (p. 220).

S

satellite (săt´ə līt´) an object made by people that circles the Earth or another planet and relays and records information (p. 313).

sharecropper (shâr´krŏp´ər) a farmer who raises crops on land owned by another person, and who gives part of the harvest to the landowner as rent (p. 75).

slave (slāv) a person who is owned as property by another person, usually as a source of labor (p. 59).

smelting (smĕlt´ĭng) the process of melting ore in order to separate the metals from it (p. 184).

stampede (stăm-pēd´) a sudden rush of a herd of frightened animals such as cattle, buffalo, or horses (p. 220).

T

technology (tĕk nŏl´ə jē) the scientific methods and ideas used in industry, agriculture, and trade (p. 274).

telecommunication (tĕl´ə kə myo͞o´nĭ-kā´shən) the technology of sending information by means of an electronic instrument such as a telephone, television, computer, or fax machine (p. 337).

textile mill (tĕks´tīl´mĭl) a place where fibers such as cotton and wool are woven or knitted into different kinds of cloth (p. 90).

timber (tĭm´bər) trees, when they are spoken of as a source of wood (p. 288).

trade (trād) the exchange of one product or service for another product or service (p. 107).

transatlantic (trăns´ət lăn´tĭk) crossing the Atlantic Ocean, as do airplanes, ships, and cables (p. 329).

transcontinental (trăns´kŏn tə nĕn´tl) stretching from one side of a continent to the other side (p. 273).

transportation (trăns´pər tā´shən) the means by which people and goods are moved from one place to another, such as cars, trains, or airplanes (p. 132).

V

vaquero (vä-kâr´ō) a cowboy who works on a rancho (p. 217).

vegetation (vĕj´ĭ-tā´shən) plant life, especially that of a certain region (p. 18).

W

wage (wāj) money paid to a person for the work done or services given in a certain period of time, often an hour, week, or month (p. 128).

Italic numbers refer to pages on which illustrations or maps appear.

Text *(continued from page iv)*

Frontispiece from "This Is My Country" by Don Raye and Al Jacobs. Copyright © 1940 (Renewed) Shawnee Press, Inc. International Copyright Secured. Used by permission. **xiii, 171** From *Little House in the Big Woods* by Laura Ingalls Wilder. Text copyright © 1932 by Laura Ingalls Wilder. Copyright renewed 1960 by Roger L. MacBride. Reprinted by permission of Harper & Row, Publishers, Inc. **xv, 113** From *Frame Up!* by Dana Story. Copyright © 1963 by Dana Story. Published by Barre Publishers. **xv, 244** From "Throwing It All Away" by Lonnie Williamson. Copyright © 1988 by *Outdoor Life* magazine. Reprinted by permission of *Outdoor Life*. **xvi–xvii** From *The Life and Legend of George McJunkin: Black Cowboy* by Franklin Folsom. Copyright © 1973 by Franklin Folsom. Used by permission of the author's agent, Evelyn Singer Agency, Inc. **8** From *This Land is Your Land*, Words and Music by Woody Guthrie. TRO – © Copyright 1956 (Renewed), 1958 (Renewed), and 1970. Ludlow Music, Inc., New York, N.Y. Used by permission. **9** "Orbiter 5 Shows How Earth Looks from the Moon" from *New & Selected Things Taking Place* by May Swenson. Copyright © 1969 by May Swenson. Reprinted by permission of the Literary Estate of May Swenson. **11** From *Mojave* by Diane Siebert. Text copyright © 1988 by Diane Siebert. Reprinted by permission of Harper & Row, Publishers, Inc. **13** From *The WPA Guide to America*, edited by Bernard A. Weisberger. Copyright © 1985 by Bernard A. Weisberger. Reprinted by permission of Pantheon Books, a division of Random House, Inc. **57** "Poor, Unhappy Transported Felon" by James Revel. From *Old Dominion in the Seventeenth-Century* edited by Warren Billings. Copyright © 1975. Published by University of North Carolina Press. **64** From *Gone Are the Days: An Illustrated History of the Old South* by Harnett Kane. Copy-right © 1960 by Harnett Kane. Reprinted by permission of E. P. Dutton, a division of Penguin USA, Inc. **80** From *George Washington Carver: The Story of a Great American* by Anne Terry White. Copyright © 1953 by Anne Terry White. Reprinted by permission of Random House, Inc. **84** From *Journey to Jericho* by Scott O'Dell. Copyright © 1969 by Scott O'Dell. Reprinted by permission of McIntosh and Otis, Inc. **86** From *Growing Up Hard in Harlan County* by G. C. Jones. Copyright © 1985 by the University Press of Kentucky. Reprinted by permission of the University Press of Kentucky. **108** Quote from a Montagnais Indian, 1634. **127** From Charles Cist, *Cincinnati in 1841: Its Early Annals and Future Prospects*. Cincinnati, 1841, page 237. **131** From *The History of the First Locomotives in America*, from Original Documents and the Testimony of Living Witnesses, by William H. Brown, pp. 150-151. New York: D. Appleton and Company. 1874. **134** Quote from John Pendleton Kennedy, *Letters of a Man of the Times* (Sands and Nielson, 1836), originally a letter to the "American." **137** "The Erie Canal" by William S. Allen. From *A Treasury of American Song* edited by Olin Downes and Elie Siegmeister. Copyright © 1940 by Olin Downes and Elie Siegmeister. Reprinted by permission of Jerry Vogel Music Co., Inc. **141** From *A Great Place to Work: What Makes Employees So Good and Most So Bad* by Robert Levering and Milton Moskowitz. Copyright © 1988 by Robert Levering. Reprinted by permission of Random House, Inc. **141** Quote from Rene McPherson in *In Search of Excellence: Lessons from America's Best-Run Companies* by Thomas J. Peters and Robert H. Waterman, Jr. Copyright © 1982 by Thomas J. Peters and Robert H. Waterman, Jr. **156** From *Land of the Spotted Eagle* by Chief Luther Standing Bear. Copyright © 1933 by Chief Luther Standing Bear. Published by Houghton Mifflin Co. **164** From *Sarah, Plain and Tall* by Patricia MacLachlan. Copyright © 1985 by Patricia MacLachlan. Reprinted by permission of HarperCollins Publishers. **185** From *No Star Nights* by Anna Egan Smucker. Copyright © 1989 by Anna Egan Smucker. Reprinted by permission of Alfred A. Knopf, Inc. **188** From *My Life and Work* by Henry Ford with Samuel Crowther. Copyright © 1922 by Doubleday, a division of Bantam, Doubleday, Dell, renewed by the widow of the author. **194** From *The Story of the American Roads* by Val Hart. Copyright © 1950 by Val Hart **208** Quote told to Alice Marriott by informants who prefer their names withheld from *American Indian Mythology* by Alice Marriott and Carol K. Rachlin. Copyright © 1968 by Alice Marriott and Carol K. Rachlin. **212** From *The Westerners* by Dee Brown. Copyright © 1974 George Rainbird, Ltd. **215** From *Aztlan: The Southwest and Its Peoples* by Luis F. Hernandez. Copyright © 1975 by Hayden Book Co. Reprinted by permission of Hayden

Books. **218** "I'm Bound to Follow the Longhorn Cows" from *Cowboy Songs*, Lomax (Macmillan, N.Y., 1910, 1938). **221** From *Cowboy — The Man and the Myth* by Robin May and Joseph G. Rosa. NEL, an imprint of The New English Library. Copyright © 1980. **224** From *The Life and Legend of George McJunkin: Black Cowboy* by Franklin Folsom. Copyright © 1973 by Franklin Folsom. Used by permission of the author's agent, Evelyn Singer Agency, Inc. **240** From *Oil Notes* by Rick Bass. Copyright © 1989 by Rick Bass. Reprinted by permission of Houghton Mifflin Co./Seymour Lawrence. **263** From *Daughter of the Gold Rush* by Klondy Nelson with Corey Ford. Copyright © 1955, 1956 by The Curtis Publishing Company, © 1958 by Klondy Nelson and Corey Ford. Reprinted by permission of Harold Ober Associates, Inc. **268** From *By The Great Horn Spoon!* by Sid Fleischman. Copyright © 1963 by Albert S. Fleischman. By permission of Little, Brown and Company. **282** From "The Horticulturist," xii: 314, 1857. **286** From *Tall Timber Tales: More Paul Bunyan Stories* by Dell J. McCormick. Copyright © 1939 by The Caxton Printers, Ltd., renewed © 1966 by Mrs. Dell J. McCormick. Reprinted by permission of The Caxton Printers, Ltd. **291** From *Jackie Cochran: An Autobiography* by Jacqueline Cochran and Maryann Bucknum Brinley. Copyright © 1987 by Rufus Publications, Inc. **306** "Southbound on the Freeway" from *To Mix With Time* by May Swenson. Copyright © 1963 by May Swenson. First appeared in The New Yorker. Reprinted by permission of the Literary Estate of May Swenson. **328** From T*ales of the Elders: A Memory Book of Men and Women Who Came To America as Immigrants, 1900-1930* by Carol Ann Bales. Copyright © 1977 by Carol Ann Bales. Reprinted by permission of Allyn and Bacon. **332** Reprinted with permission of Margaret K. McElderry Books, an imprint of Macmillan Publishing Company from *A Jar of Dreams* by Yoshiko Uchida. Copyright © 1981 by Yoshiko Uchida. **345** Quote by Aleksandr Aleksandrov from Kevin W. Kelley, *The Home Planet*, © 1988 by Kevin W. Kelley. Reprinted with permission of Addison-Wesley Publishing Co., Inc., Reading, Massachusetts.

Illustrations

Ligature 28, 46, 56, 63, 70, 79, 91, 94, 95, 102–103, 106–107b, 116, 117, 122, 130, 132, 142, 150, 151, 172, 174, 186, 187, 192, 196, 204, 205, 221c, 223, 228, 229, 237, 241, 246, 254, 255, 278, 287, 290, 292, 296, 297, 309, 321, 323, 324, 325, 329, 346, 347, **Precision Graphics** 15, 16, 39, 42-43, 78, 121, 128–129, 141, 143, 179, 189, 197, 220b, 264–265, 277, 314–315, 322, **Linda Bladholm** 36 **John Burgoyne** 161 **Susan Johnston Carlson** 74,76 **Pat & Robin Dewitt** 91 (inset), 107 (inset), 116 (inset), 161, 172 (inset), 287 (inset), **Dale Glascow** 56 (inset), 318 **Hank Iken** 238, 240 **Joe LeMonnier** 12–13, 233 **Al Lorenz** 274 **Yoshi Miyake** 157, 216, **Rick Porter** 20, 92, 114, 218, 266

Maps

Mapping Specialists G1-G14, 14, 19, 33, 37 Adapted by permission of the publisher from *American Regional Dialects: A Word Geography* by Craig A. Carver (Ann Arbor: University of Michigan Press, 1987), map 8.1., 38, 42, 43, 45, 47, 51, 55, 65, 68, 69, 77, 85, 97, 103, 109, 112, 132, 140, 145, 151, 163, 168, 169, 173, 181, 184, 199, 205, 213, 221, 235, 245, 249, 255, 259, 273, 284, 289, 299, 307, 339

Photographs

AL—Allan Landau; **BA**—The Bettmann Archive; **BC**—Bruce Coleman, Inc.; **DRF**—David R. Frazier Photolibrary; **DM**—David Muench 1990; **GH**—Grant Heilman Photography, Inc.; **JCBL**—Courtesy of the John Carter Brown Library at Brown University; **JJ**—Jerry Jacka Photography; **LOC**—Library of Congress; **NYPL**—The New York Public Library; **OMH**— Courtesy the Oakland Museum History Department, Oakland, CA; **OP**—Odyssey Produc-tions; **PMHU**—Peabody Museum of Archaeology and Ethnology, Harvard University, photo by Hillel Burger; **PR**—Photographic Resources, Inc.; **RJB**—Ralph J. Brunke; **SB**—Stock Boston, Inc.; **SS**—SuperStock; **TIB**—The Image Bank; **VA**—Viesti Associates, Inc.

Front cover Peter Bosy; **Back cover** detail, OMH; **G2** © Earth Satellite Corporation; **G5** © SS; **G12** © AL; **G13** J. Messerschmidt/H. Armstrong Roberts; **G14** © Owen Franken/SB; **G15** AL; **1** © DM; **2** © Joe Viesti, VA (r); RJB (l); **3** © Keith Gunnar, BC (t); © Walter Hodges,